PRAISE FOR
Pets in America

A *New York Times Book Review* Editors' Choice

"This work explores the history of animal-human bonding in the context of a growing country with a diverse population. The narrative is entwined with the development of veterinary medicine, animal humane movements, and pet products. If the well-written prose is not enough, the illustrations provide a telling accent."
—*Bloomsbury Review*

"An encyclopedic history . . . Scholarly, thorough, informative and animal friendly."
—*Publishers Weekly*

"Fascinating. Grier shows her devotion to animals. [A] wealth of . . . information any pet lover would appreciate."
—*Choice* magazine

"The first comprehensive history of pet-keeping in the United States . . . Grier treats readers to many intriguing details."
—*Princeton Alumni Weekly* magazine

"*Pets in America* is a labor of love and a delight to read."
—James A. Serpell, University of Pennsylvania

Pets
IN AMERICA

Pets
IN AMERICA

→ A History ←

KATHERINE C. GRIER

A Harvest Book
Harcourt, Inc.
Orlando   Austin   New York   San Diego   Toronto   London

Requests for permission to make copies of any part of the work
should be submitted online at www.harcourt.com/contact or mailed
to the following address: Permissions Department, Harcourt, Inc.,
6277 Sea Harbor Drive, Orlando, Florida 32887-6777.

www.HarcourtBooks.com

First U.S. edition published by University of North Carolina Press in 2006.

Chapter 3 appeared earlier, in somewhat different form, as
"'The Eden of Home': Changing Understandings of Cruelty
and Kindness to Animals in Middle-Class American Households,
1820–1900," in *Animals in Human Histories: The Mirror of Nature and
Culture,* ed. Mary Henninger-Voss (Rochester, N.Y.: University of
Rochester Press, 2002). It is reprinted here with permission. Chapter 5
appeared earlier, in somewhat different form, as "Buying Your Friends:
The Pet Business and American Consumer Culture," in *Commodifying
Everything: Relationships of the Market,* ed. Susan Strasser (New York:
Routledge, 2003), 43–71. It is reproduced here by permission
of Routledge/Taylor & Francis Books, Inc.

Library of Congress Cataloging-in-Publication Data
Grier, Katherine C., 1953–
Pets in America: a history/Katherine C. Grier.—1st Harvest ed.
p.   cm.—(A harvest book)
Originally published: Chapel Hill, NC:
University of North Carolina Press, c2006.
Includes index.
1. Pets—United States—History.   2. Human-animal relationships—
United States—History.   I. Title.
SF411.36.U6G75   2007
636.088'790973—dc22   2006032698
ISBN 978-0-15-603176-9

Text set in Fairfield Light
Designed by Lydia D'moch

Printed in the United States of America
First Harvest edition 2007
A C E G I K J H F D B

❧ Contents ❧

Pets

IN AMERICA

A MODERN PET OWNER

My mother, who has the most reliable memory of anyone in the family, informs me that my first word was "kitty." This fact alone is probably sufficient as an explanation for the existence of this book.

Relationships with animals have been a big part of my life since that first recognizable word. I grew up in the suburbs and spent my years from age six to thirteen in a new housing development outside an industrial city in upstate New York. Across the street from my house was a vacant lot with a shallow creek, and on the other end of the large cul-de-sac, which was ringed with split-level and ranch houses, was what we children called "The Woods," which featured a marshy area dubbed "The Swamp." The fields that covered most of our township were still part of working farms, home to herds of dairy cows. Our housing development was populated by a large number of school-age children and by family cats and dogs who were allowed to roam freely and were identified by both first and last names (Moose Pryor, Tipper

Mitchell). Our basset hound Gussie liked to sleep on the warm blacktop road in front of our house, and our neighbors knew to drive slowly and honk their horns to urge her up and out of the way. She also knew how to beg treats from the neighbors and made regular rounds in search of leftovers and dog biscuits.

In this setting, I grew up observing, collecting, playing with, and caring for a variety of small animals. In fact, I grew up in a family of pet keepers. Animals, both wild and tame, were cherished by my parents, by their parents before them, and by several generations before them. Their stories were part of family lore, and several are part of this book. But let me share one I particularly like that didn't fit anywhere else. My great-grandfather had a wooden leg—not a peg leg like a pirate, which I would have regarded as glamorous, but a slightly scary carved calf and foot that strapped on and was covered with a sock and shoe. When I was very small, he and Great Grandma had a big white cat named Snowball. When Snowball was a kitten, Great Grandpa got a laugh out of encouraging him to jump out from under the furniture and attack the wooden leg, which of course did not feel anything. However, Snowball soon learned to hide and attack everyone's legs. Visiting their house was suspenseful; when and whom would Snowball attack? No one considered getting rid of the cat, of course. Visitors simply had to be prepared in case of feline assault.

So I grew up in an indulgent environment for a child with an interest in animals. My brother and I collected pollywogs from The Swamp and were allowed to keep them until they metamorphosed into frogs, when they had to be returned to the setting of their nativity. We caught toads at a nearby quarry and transplanted them to my mother's rock gardens, where they seemed to thrive catching bugs. My dad knew a man who owned a pet store in an old building in downtown Utica, and he used to bring home surprises like a horned toad (it did not live long, I fear) and African diving frogs for the fish tank that sat on the breakfast bar between the kitchen and the dining room in our ranch house. The tank contained a huge goldfish named Ralph who was exceedingly tame and would take food from a hand.

I now realize that my parents were quite progressive pet owners for the 1950s and 1960s. Unlike the pets of many of our neighbors, our cats and dogs were always "fixed" (that is, spayed or neutered) before they could procreate, and we always took them to the veterinarian when they were sick. My mother also worked to instill other kinds of responsible behavior toward animals. She understood that asking children to be the primary caregivers and trainers for kittens and puppies was tantamount to sanctioning neglect and anarchy, so she assumed those responsibilities herself. However, my brother and I could have other, smaller animals if we cared for them. We complained, but we cleaned the hamster cages and guinea pig hutches built by my great-grandfather, although he did not care much for our "rats." One rule was always very clear, however: deliberately hurting an animal was never allowed. Nor was animal suffering. The message of our special responsibility was most profoundly apparent when an animal had to be "put to sleep," as we called it. (We used a Victorian euphemism for death without realizing it.) We all felt awful when that happened, but in my family there was no question that sometimes it was the right thing to do.

My connection to livestock was less constant, but I now recognize how fortunate I was to have some firsthand experience with large animals. As a child, I don't think that I ever considered the connection between hamburgers and cows, or bacon and pigs. The presentation of meat in paper trays covered with plastic in the markets where my mother shopped did not help clarify the relationship. Still, I had some exposure to life with livestock on a small farm. When my brother and I visited my great-aunt and -uncle in southwestern Virginia, a pair of resolutely old-fashioned people who had electricity but still used an outhouse, we drove their handful of cows from pasture to barn and helped (or tried to help) Uncle Norwood with the milking. I remember that the barn cats would sit around him while he milked, waiting for him to shoot milk directly from the cow's teats into their mouths. I fed my great-aunt's chickens and gathered the eggs—and got a case of bird lice while I was at it—but I never actually saw one killed for dinner, although those were the chickens we ate. Even if I had, I am not sure that it would have bothered me much; small children are pragmatic and often quite bloody-minded.

The greatest joy of my young life, and my most profound contact with large stock animals, occurred when I got my own horse at the age of fourteen. I had wanted and dreamed about horses for years. It's a good thing that Buck was a hardy animal of no particular breed because, in retrospect, he should have suffered both laminitus ("founder") and colic because of the way I fed him, and he probably had some kind of intestinal parasite most of the time. But he seemed to thrive despite my somewhat scattered ministrations. I even nursed him back to health after he suffered a deep wound in a trailer accident, and I was proud of my skill at caring for him. He was, in fact, my pet, although he kicked me a couple of times and tried to rub me off under trees periodically. I was sorry to have to give him away in college, but I could not afford to keep him. I hope that he had a good end at the hands of a kind owner, but I have learned that this is often not the case. Buck might have been sold for killing, and that thought still haunts me.

In my college years and during my twenties, even though my somewhat nomadic existence (group rental houses, graduate school, and a move across the country for my first professional job) should have precluded keeping pets, I am sorry to report that I continued to acquire cats and dogs, several of whom I deposited on the doorstep of my tolerant parents. I look back with shame on the story of one particular dog I took in, a Great Pyrenees who was beautiful but peculiar, the victim of a divorce in which no one wanted custody of the dog. She should have been guarding a flock of sheep somewhere, for she really did not like life indoors. Amanda escaped from every fence behind which she was confined, and she took the screens out of windows and doors so that she could go "walkabout." She suffered from strange rashes and, in retrospect, probably had undiagnosed food allergies. She was terrified of thunderstorms, moreover, which I suppose would have limited her sheep-guarding career, and she had to be tranquilized every time she heard a clap of thunder. I had to euthanize her after she was hit by a car.

I never thought much about our familial habit until one day in 1984 when one of my graduate school mentors, George Basalla, and I started talking about pets. Professor Basalla, now retired from the University of Delaware, is a historian of science and technology, curious about everything, and more widely read than just about anyone I know. The subject came up because the cultural geographer Yi Fu Tuan, whose work we liked, had recently published *Dominance and Affection: The Making of Pets*. Tuan explored the interplay of dominance and affection in the human desire to control and reshape the natural world, including gardens and domestic animals.

As a pet keeper, I remember that I had trouble acknowledging the role that my ability to dominate played in an activity that I loved. I still struggle with it, although I now think that accepting my own power to control or at least partly direct animal behavior is an inevitable part of choosing to share space with creatures whose wishes and natural behaviors are not always compatible with my routines. Ultimately, the issue becomes how much control is too much, how much has bad consequences for the animal, and how much coercion, no matter how well-intentioned, makes me a bully, too. Pet owners draw their lines in different places. For example, I spay and neuter my cats, a profound surgical intervention on their behavior and natural life courses, but I would never declaw them, another profound surgical intervention on behavior. I can offer a long explanation for why I accept one and reject the other, and some of the reasons make me what my community calls a "responsible pet owner." But in the end, I have set the line based on what I am comfortable with, the particular circumstances of my life, and what I judge is good for *them*.

At any rate, George Basalla and I agreed that someone should write a history of pet keeping. I was already well into my dissertation research on a less interesting topic, but I filed the thought away. Every time I found something about pets in nineteenth-century magazines and books, I photocopied the item and stuffed it into a file drawer. Although this is not a recommended research strategy, eventually I realized that there might be a project in that drawer. I also discovered that my hunch was supported by several important books. British historian Keith Thomas laid crucial groundwork for me with his wonderful *Man and the Natural World: A History of the Modern Sensibility* (1983), and Harriet Ritvo published her provocative study *The Animal Estate: The English and Other Creatures in the Victorian Age* in 1987. I knew quite a bit about pets from my own experience, and after reading these two books and shuffling through the contents of that file drawer, I was certain that there was more to be said.

This history, which is only a first look at a complicated subject, grew out of my own experience. That's what makes working on, or even simply reading, the history of everyday life a source of so much pleasure. Not only does this kind of history make the ordinary things that we do part of the permanent record of human activity, but it gives us an opportunity to think about what those ordinary things mean as part of the grand narrative of changing times. I pored over old magazines, scraps of paper written by people a century ago, weathered little books offering well-intentioned advice, brittle photograph albums, and artifacts that no one bothered to discard, and I listened to hundreds of stories. In the process, I realized how much pet keeping reveals about this society's complicated and not fully congruous or even fully acknowledged ideas about animals. It also addresses even more general questions about how we define the characteristics of a good society.

I have never been without at least one animal. The most notable, a nondescript tabby cat named Margaret, helped me write my dissertation and revise it into a book and helped with the early stages of this project. She sat on my desk every day, sometimes directly on my notes and drafts, and I still miss her loud purr and comforting presence. It has been interesting to be an active pet keeper while writing a history about Americans and their pets. I believe that it has made me more sympathetic to pet keeping than some other authors on the subject have been. I also think that my own experience has helped me to understand better the day-to-day texture of pet keeping in the past. I wanted to understand the story behind the daily routines I know so well: feeding, grooming, training, doctoring, cleaning up, and playing. I knew that the animals I enjoyed so much in my own life were sometimes the subjects of my intense attention; at other times, they were part of the background of daily living. But regardless of the level of my attention, my pets themselves lived out every day with their own established rhythms and routines. It is the interplay of these two kinds of agency, theirs and mine, that makes my relationship with the animals in my household so compelling. I hoped that I could capture a bit of that interplay in past relations between people and animals.

Working on this book over the years has also made me more thoughtful about my own relationships to animals—the ones I take care of, the ones that cross my path, and the invisible animal workers whose lives support my own. No historian is ever truly neutral about what he or she chooses as the subject for years of research and writing. We owe our chosen material due care and candor, not a pretend neutrality. My own ideas about my responsibilities as a steward to both domestic and wild creatures continue to evolve. This project has left me more self-conscious about the difficult questions of human responsibilities toward animals, and it has changed some of my own behavior. I hope that my work will provide historical context for some of the issues with which my readers grapple, whether in their personal lives with animals or in their volunteer or professional work on behalf of animals.

What Is a Pet?

Before summarizing the contents and arguments of *Pets in America,* a definition of the word is in order. "Pet" has a complex history and obscure origins; its age suggests when people became self-conscious enough about the idea to wish to label it concisely. The *Oxford English Dictionary* suggests that it may simply come from the root that gave us the French word "petit," meaning "little." First applied to people, "pet" was used by the early 1500s to describe "an indulged or spoiled child; any person indulged or treated as a favorite." By the mid-sixteenth century, "pet" included animals "domesticated or tamed and kept for pleasure or companionship." The term was especially applied to orphan lambs that required raising by hand. It morphed into a verb, meaning to fondle an animal, by the early 1600s, although it did not become slang for sexual foreplay until the early 1900s. Noah Webster's *American Dictionary of the English Language* of 1828 also defined "pet" as a "lamb brought up by hand," or "any little animal fondled and indulged"; as a verb it meant "to treat as a pet; to fondle; to indulge."

These definitions are based on human perception: no people, no pets. They also call attention to proximity and the importance of touch, and to ongoing care of the animal. In the eighteenth century, writing about pet animals still almost always used the word "favorite" instead of "pet." This usage suggests the most fundamental characteristic of pet keeping, the act of choosing a particular animal, differentiating it from all other animals. I know people who insist that their pet selected them first—and if you know dogs and cats, there is some reason to believe that this is true—but in the end, we choose to become their stewards. And it is not an equal relationship, although pet animals are capable of truly awe-inspiring displays of their own ideas about the way things should run.

There is some discomfort about the word "pet" nowadays. Uncomfortable with the ideas that pet animals are defined as sentient personal property under the law, animal welfare organizations and writers on the status of animals are trying to find alternatives that suggest the integrity of the animals as beings and de-emphasize some of the traditional rights of ownership. The Humane Society of the United States, which I consider a good measure on these issues, preferred "companion animal" until recently, when it bowed to popular usage and returned to "pet." Throughout my own work, I have chosen to use the word "pet" because it was, by the early nineteenth century, both in wide use and a word for which people had a practical understanding of its meaning.

Keith Thomas, who authored the first history to take pet keeping seriously as a historical subject, identified three characteristics of the pet in England between 1400 and 1800: (1) the animal was allowed into the house, (2) it was given an individual name, and (3) it was never eaten.[1] This was a good start because it recognized that a pet was defined by a set of behaviors, what I call a "lived definition." However, a close look at the behaviors associated with pet keeping, especially since the late nineteenth century, suggests that the definition has become considerably more complex. Even adding the idea of the "companion animal" does not do it justice. Not all pets are true companions, although some animals are indeed excellent company. Companionship suggests recognition on the part of the animal, and some pets, while they have come to understand that the shadows outside the tank deliver food, do not seem to recognize the human feeding them as a distinctive individual. This is not to suggest that the simplest creature cannot be a comforting presence or a welcome distraction; think of the fish tank in your dentist's office. Caring for any pet can add welcome routine to our days. But pets are kept for many reasons. Some are regarded primarily for the beauty of their bodies or their movements; others make beautiful sounds. Some are living toys; others are symbols of our desires for social status. Many pets combine more than one of these characteristics; high-status show dogs may also be their owners' "best friends."

Many pet animals do recognize us, and I mean that in a more profound sense than the simple learned behavior associating a human with food. That recognition, or the hope of it, across the species barrier is what keeps some people involved with pets. This is one reason I like living with pets so much, and why I am willing to tolerate the poop, tumbleweeds of shed hair in every corner, occasional decapitated mouse carcasses, and stinky food. I like looking into the eyes of my big old cat Ed and seeing him very clearly looking back at me. In 1894, Olive Thorne Miller, a now obscure author who wrote a number of books on pets, recognized well that pets could furnish "an every-fresh source of happiness to those who love them."[2] She was right.

Revising Thomas's simple definition, the most important quality pets share is that they have been singled out by human beings. Not all pets live indoors; large pets may not even live in the same location as their owners. Some pets do not, in fact, have names. And a few pets do eventually get eaten, which simply reflects the contingent status of the designation. Pets receive special attention intended to promote their well-being, at least as people understand that condition. Or we intend that they receive this attention; sometimes we fail miserably as pet keepers, as I myself have done.

Why Pets Matter

What I have discovered, in the years I worked on this project, is that the history of pet keeping is an integral part of the history of everyday life in the United States. It is connected to changing ideas about human nature, emotional life, individual responsibility, and our society's obligations to all kinds of dependent others, including people. Pet keeping is an important part of the history of childhood in America, and it speaks to evolving ideas about the proper roles of men and women and to the historical characteristics of the modern American middle classes. It is part of the industrial and commercial development of the United States, especially its evolution into a nation of consumers. It is part of the environmental history of the United States. It is even part of the story of municipal government, public health, and philanthropy. But the history of pet keeping also has its own integrity as part of a developing field that studies the history of animal-human inter-action. The stories I relate here are worth telling for their own sake, as one part of the larger narrative of our relations with other sentient beings generally. Social historians have been concerned with recovering the stories of the "voiceless" members of our so-ciety for decades. Animals are indeed part of our communities, and they are profoundly voiceless, something that Victorian advo-cates for animals emphasized repeatedly. Still they are, in their own small ways, the agents of their own lives. Their agency is often weak, especially when they face the power of human soci-eties, but it is there nonetheless. Where I could demonstrate this agency, I have.

Even if I did not know these things, I would still think that pet keeping is worth long, careful study simply because of its ubiquity today. Since the 1980s, the American Veterinary Medical Associ-ation (AVMA), the American Animal Hospital Association, the American Pet Products Manufacturers Association (APPMA), and the Pet Food Institute have all collected data on pet keeping.[3] While the information is based on modern statistical sampling, and even allowing for the inevitable variations from source to source, statistics on the pet population of the United States demonstrate that we are, indeed, a nation of pet keepers. A sur-vey done by the AVMA in 2001 estimated that 58.3 percent of households contain at least one pet; the APPMA 2003–4 pet own-ers survey upped that figure to 62 percent, estimating 77.7 million cats, 65 million dogs, 16.8 million small animals, 17.3 million birds, 8.8 million reptiles, 7 million saltwater fish, and 185 million freshwater fish.[4] Visit any gift shop or stop at a greeting-card rack and count how many images of pet animals you find there. Watch cable television or surf the World Wide Web and see how many programs and sites are devoted to them. Anything that Americans spend so much time thinking about is worth a closer look.

The most detailed surveys of pet-keeping practices and owner attitudes in America today come from the APPMA, which devotes a great deal of time to figuring out what will make owners spend more money on their pets. For example, the APPMA has found that American pet owners now routinely describe their animals as their best friends or as family members. (Even 20 percent of reptile owners describe their pets as being "like a child/family member.") Owners feel that their pets enhance daily life and their own health. They report that the greatest drawback of pet keeping is not the veterinary bills, the ruined carpets, the clawed upholstery, or that vaguely zoolike smell some children's rooms get from the cages of their pals; rather, the most noted disadvantage is the inevitability of a pet's death.[5]

Not everyone feels this way, of course. Some Americans do not like pets and the mess they almost inevitably cause; some think that animals should live outdoors; some do not have strong feelings either for or against; some have allergies to furry animals; some do not have any experience of pets or a history of pet ownership in their families. Americans who were uninvolved, indifferent, or even hostile to having pets in their households do turn up occasionally in this book, but they are not my subject. The fact is, increasing numbers of Americans liked pets over the course of the nineteenth and twentieth centuries, and I am interested in telling their stories.

Social and cultural change is usually gradual and uneven, and people experience change at different paces. Eventually, changes in the individual decisions people make accumulate into trends. Further, practices and ideas are often not completely in sync with one another. In the case of pet keeping, routines often did not change for many decades, even as more intense emotional involvement with pet animals became more common during the 1800s. Take, for example, how people dealt with the fertility of pet animals. Even fond pet owners dealt with litters of kittens and puppies by drowning all but one of the newborns, which the mother would be allowed to keep and nurse. As Americans became more self-conscious about the treatment of animals, people continued to drown kittens—they had little other recourse—but some of them clearly felt deep regret at what they were compelled to do. In 1805, Philadelphia diarist Elizabeth Drinker was appalled at having to drown kittens. But she did it nonetheless, and her feelings about it are recounted in Chapter 2. By the 1860s, advocates of kindness to animals even had to articulate an argument that drowning newborn animals was a positive kindness, apparently because so many people felt awful about it and were inclined to let kittens and puppies take their chances in the world. Owners made private ethical calculations based on their understanding of the sentience of newborn kittens and their future prospects for ownership, their own economic means, and what people had done before.

Class identity plays an important part in the story of pet keeping in America, too. The new American middle class set more demanding standards for pet keeping beginning in the nineteenth century, and it made kindness to animals an important subject for discussion and social action. However, class identity alone does not explain pet keeping, although it explicates some of its important features, such as increasing consumer interest in commercial pet supplies. People who simply liked animals and enjoyed the company of pets appeared in all classes, regions, and ethnic groups. My own evidence for this rests on the accumulated weight of all the stories I gathered. I anticipate that smaller-scale historical studies will add greater nuance to this assertion, although sources on the lives of some groups, particularly the poor, are hard to come by in any form. Even in the present day, this is a level of detail unavailable in current statistics on pet keeping, although it is information that would be extremely useful to animal welfare organizations and the thousands of shelters run by local governments.

Because change has occurred at such an uneven pace and the interplay between ideas and practices is so complex, figuring out a narrative structure for a first history of pet keeping in America has been a challenge. I soon realized that a strictly chronological account would be repetitive and would make the book difficult for readers to use as they sought information on specific subjects. So I decided on a topical approach: each chapter is dedicated to a particular theme (evolving attitudes toward kindness to animals or the role of the pet in the growth of the United States as a consumer society), and I treat that theme chronologically. While the chapters build one upon the other, this book's structure is intended to allow readers to read them individually, as topical essays.

I must also note that the majority of my examples throughout are from the northeastern and mid-Atlantic states. This fact is partly a matter of logistics, but it also reflects the fact that modern American pet-keeping practice—emotionally intensive, fully commercialized, and integrated into local government and other community institutions—originated in these states. My emphasis does not mean that pet keeping did not take place elsewhere, and I offer examples throughout the text. Having an established framework for studying pet keeping in America will make it easier to develop regional comparisons in the future.

Pets in America: A Synopsis

European settlers carried cats and dogs as workers and companions to the North American colonies, where indigenous people already enjoyed complex relations with their own dogs. Settlers also carried certain habits of pet keeping, such as caging songbirds. By the mid-eighteenth century, some American households already cared for a variety of animals, including dogs, cats, birds, and even rabbits, simply for pleasure. Some animals were companions to their owners, but others were present because of their looks or the sounds they made, the status they represented, or the novelty they provided.

Several examples I offer—the families of Elizabeth Drinker in Philadelphia, Samuel and Olivia Clemens in Hartford, Connecticut, and the extended Van Rensselaer-Elmendorf-Rankin family of Albany, New York—show that pet keeping did seem to run in families. However, pet keeping was also a typical behavior for many families when there were children in the house. Pet keeping was strongly associated with childhood by the nineteenth century. For both children and adults, caring for pets was one avenue for the cultivation of the self through expressive behavior during moments of leisure. At its best, the practice fostered gentle emotions, curiosity about the world, and even aesthetic appreciation.

In Chapter 1, I show that, by around 1870, the array of pets in American households was a pretty close approximation of the range of species found in the present day, with the notable exception of exotic creatures such as reptiles or tropical fish. Some animals, such as white mice and guinea pigs, were specifically regarded as children's pets. The "balanced" aquarium had been invented, but until the 1920s, its residents were either goldfish or freshwater creatures caught in local ponds and streams. While dogs and cats were still important workers in households, people also enjoyed their company, and many were no longer required to earn their livings. Most dogs were not purebreds in the modern sense, although they represented recognizable types such as spaniels, hounds, or terriers. By the 1870s, some Americans had become interested in purebred dogs. A smaller number favored pedigreed cats, and new breeds were introduced to the United States. However, registered purebred dogs did not become truly popular until the 1940s, and they are still a minority of the dogs in American households.

Little data enumerating the pet population of nineteenth-century America survives, if it ever existed, but the spread of pet keeping can be measured through the sheer proliferation of information sources. Instructional books and essays on pet keeping were published in numbers beginning in the 1840s; by the 1860s, a good bit of this literature was directed to children, reflecting the assumption that all children kept, or should keep, pets. Children's books and stories using pet animals as protagonists were published in increasing numbers. Printed pictures of pet animals were available in enormous quantity and variety, and Americans collected printed trade cards with images of pet animals doing the things pets do: getting into trouble, begging for food, hunting for mice, and caring for their young. While painted portraits of pets were rare, Americans brought dogs and, later, cats by the thousands into photographers' studios as soon as the technology arrived in America in the 1840s. As amateur photography grew simpler and more affordable, people started to make their own pictures of their pets. Trade catalogs and advertisements show that, by the 1870s, an expanded array of products for the care of birds, dogs, and cats were available, from tonics to prepared foods. These sources allowed me to reconstruct the routine behavior of pet keepers, including training practices, play, and the inclusion of pet animals in important family rituals such as portraiture and mourning, the subject of Chapter 2.

In Chapter 2, I also discuss important differences in the conditions of life for pets and the tough decisions American pet keepers sometimes made about their animals. Until quite recently, according to the historical record, pet keepers had to accept the biological realities of life and death that we now avoid through regular trips to the veterinarian. Small-animal veterinary practices were rare in many communities until the 1930s, and veterinarian friends of mine tell me that choosing small-animal practice over working for the livestock industry and in research was still somewhat stigmatized in veterinary schools until the 1960s. The people I discuss in this book accepted the inevitable and frequent mortality of their pets even as they regretted their early demises. (Let me suggest that this philosophical attitude still survives in relation to aquarium fish and rodent pets such as hamsters, whose life spans are quite short.) As I suggested above, people took direct responsibility for ending animal lives.

In the half-century before the Civil War, the era when a self-conscious and energetic middle class developed in the United States, many Americans began to rethink their relationships with the animals living in and around their households. The timing of these two phenomena is no coincidence. The new domestic ethic of kindness to animals was one product of a constellation of ideas and cultural ideals, including gentility, liberal evangelical Protestant religion, and domesticity, which I discuss in Chapter 3. Kindness to animals was linked to general ideas about socializing children to be citizens of the American republic. It was particularly associated with ideas about care for dependent beings—children, the elderly, the chronically ill, the enslaved, and others—who could not care for themselves alone in a rapidly changing society. The model for the good society was family life itself. Promoters of kindness relied on ways of talking about animals that conceptualized them as servants, the oldest way of speaking about animals, but also as children, parents, and friends. These metaphors appeared in both popular literature and the inexpensive prints that decorated American households in the nineteenth century. The latter suggested in literal terms what good relations with animals looked like. Drawing on popular media, which grew from what publishers saw going on around them, a new language of regard became part of the way ordinary Americans talked about animals, particularly pets. Increasingly, the domestic ethic of kindness promoted pet keeping as both a crucial part of childhood and a form of self-expression for adults.

By the last quarter of the nineteenth century, the domestic ethic had changed the baseline of acceptable behavior toward animals and had created a large population of respectable people who were self-consciously kind to animals and distinguished among other people on that basis. The domestic ethic underlay the expansion of pet keeping and of the creation of new animal welfare groups following the Civil War, and it became the basis of organized humane education activities beginning in the 1880s. Because of its focus on the heart of each individual and on the private household, however, the ethic had distinctive limits that impeded discussion of the structural character of cruelty in a large-scale, industrializing society. In cities in particular, large populations of animals lived on the fringes of pet keeping, part of a complex urban ecology.

In Chapter 4, I point out that pet keeping developed as an emotionally rich and complex practice at a time when most pet-keeping families still participated in the traditional animal-human interactions associated with farming and transportation. The separation of Americans from livestock and working animals was gradual; horses, cows, pigs, and chickens were part of daily life even in large cities through the 1920s. American families relied for their comfort and convenience on the direct labor of animal workers and on the products derived from their bodies (simply put, they knew where meat came from). Some livestock animals lived on the margins of pet keeping, and tenderhearted youngsters suffered when they tried to rationalize the differences between kinds of animals, especially since some animals could occupy more than one category. But other children seem to have absorbed the dissonances with little trouble, and most adults and children apparently were not troubled about the implications of loving some animals and eating others.

Case studies of other animals on the edges of pet keeping—tramps and strays, pet stock, and community and honorary pets—demonstrate both the cultural and historical character of what I call animal kinds. They also demonstrate how animals on the fringes of the practice, such as tramp dogs and urban cats, could be crucial participants in the ecology of American cities until the era of municipal housekeeping in the early twentieth century led to greater efforts to control them. Pet stock, the small animals who could be beloved pets, cosseted aesthetic objects, or dinner depending on the needs and goals of the owner, is an animal kind that we do not see much of nowadays, unless one has contact with the small-animal fanciers who still exhibit at county and state fairs.

Community or honorary pets, from celebrity dogs to the wild birds many people feed in the winter, show how Americans still use animals as a public way to express community and to represent our love for a natural world fewer and fewer of us know well.

Pet keeping in America is also characterized by its commercial nature. In Chapters 5 and 6, I explore this by examining the trade in live animals and the development of the modern pet store and its supplies and equipment. Between 1840 and 1930, all the elements of a modern "pet industry"—a term that reflects perfectly the tension between sentiment and commodification that still resonates throughout the business—gradually developed. By the 1840s, bird stores dotted larger American cities, gradually supplanting the informal trade in native songbirds that occurred in city markets. By the 1890s, the modern pet shop had come along, supplying both animals and an expanded array of specialized supplies and equipment to facilitate care and display. By the 1920s, pet supplies and sometimes the animals themselves were offered for sale in department stores and five-and-tens.

Like any retail business, pet shops had to have reliable access to fresh inventory. Local trade in small animals sometimes capitalized on the owner's skill at breeding his or her own stock, and small, hobbyist breeders sometimes sold animals to stores. But shopkeepers also traded with a new group of middlemen who bought and sold animals. The wholesale trade in cage birds, especially German-bred canaries, was already highly organized, if small, by the mid-nineteenth century. By the early twentieth century, canaries, budgerigars (parakeets), and other exotic birds were farm-raised in the warm weather of California and Florida. These operations, along with the goldfish farms dotting Long Island, Indiana, and Maryland by the turn of the century and the southern tropical fish breeders in place by the 1920s, were a unique branch of commercial livestock raising. The wholesale animal business was subject not only to the natural vagaries of husbandry—disease, feeding problems, failure to breed, and so on—but also to fads, as interest in particular kinds of animals waxed and waned. An increasingly controversial part of the trade is found in the rise of the "puppy mill," as demand for unregistered purebred puppies has led to operations that breed and rear dogs as livestock. Some of these are run by true large-scale breeders who meet Department of Agriculture standards of care; others are operated by the infamous "backyard breeders" whose dogs suffer from poor care. In both cases, many Americans are ambivalent about puppies produced this way, because dogs are not supposed to be "livestock."

Pet supplies and equipment, the subject of Chapter 6, were the most profitable aspect of the pet trade; they still are. By the late nineteenth century, purchasing or receiving an animal as a gift could set off years of transactions at the local pet store, the drug store, and eventually the local five-and-ten or grocery. It is one small sign of changing times that supplies for cage birds were the first commercial foods and medicines; Americans in the past cherished their caged birds. Dog and cat food, now a common feature on grocery lists, was a product that people had to be convinced to buy. The first makers, including Spratt's, the company that literally invented dry dog food in the 1860s, used methods that are still in place today to create demand: free samples, premiums, commercial sponsorships of dog and cat shows, and mass-media advertising. Their ads are windows into the concerns of owners for the health and happiness of their pets. Because the pet products business cost so little to get into, myriad small companies packaged or canned food and made objects for pet owners to buy. Cages, collars, coats, furniture, dishes, and toys all tell the story of owner attitudes and the place of the small entrepreneur in American consumer goods innovation.

I close with a brief epilogue that considers some of the most recent changes in American pet keeping. It seems to me that, since the 1970s in particular, the practice of pet keeping has evolved at an accelerated rate. This indicates prosperity and demographic change, as more American households are small and without children, but it also reflects something less tangible. I am especially interested in speculating about the tension between the apparent desire of American pet owners to experience the "animal" in our pets—through such trends as the biologically appropriate raw-food movement (which bears the unfortunate but memorable acronym BARF), "natural" training, and the provision of "enriched" environments for animals—and our simultaneous and increasing desire to regulate and control the lives of our pets. I am not against training or spaying and neutering, but I argue that we need to be thoughtful about our stewardship, including how much we control pets' abilities to move through the world outside our dwellings unimpeded, their opportunities to interact socially, and their expression of natural behaviors, especially those we regard as embarrassing or destructive. These contrasting impulses, toward the "natural" animal and the civilized pet, are augmented by increasing convictions that pet animals are distinctive individuals whose uniqueness should be celebrated. Pet keeping is the only one-on-one relationship with animals left to most of us, and I wonder what the long-term impact of this enhanced recognition of animals as individuals will eventually be on our treatment of the millions of invisible animals whose lives support our own.

⇒ *1* ⇐

A Natural History of Pets

$\mathcal{I}$n the late 1700s and 1800s, Americans were enthusiastic readers of popular natural history books. Evolving from a centuries-old tradition of scientific writing about minerals, plants, and animals, these texts mingled more or less scientific description and storytelling. While some natural histories for common readers represented the developing science of the age, others were little more than collections of thirdhand information, entertaining anecdotes, and thinly veiled moral lessons. This latter emphasis is particularly apparent in natural histories of animals. Directed to both children and adults, natural histories of animals enchanted readers with stories of the exotic wild beasts of the world (they were the wildlife documentaries of their day), but a surprising number emphasized common creatures—cows, sheep, horses, chickens, songbirds, cats, and dogs—and small incidents set in ordinary places.

Since the first questions in any history of pet keeping are "When did people actually have pets?" and "What kinds of animals did they have?" it seems right to begin this account of pet keeping in America with a chapter in the tradition of natural history. While animals were their subjects, many natural histories also shared stories of the interactions of animals and people, and the books were as much about human actions, ideas, and values as they were about the lives of other creatures. This chapter, too, is necessarily full of stories of the interactions of pets and the people who owned them, from the mid-eighteenth to the mid-twentieth centuries. After all, people create pets, a truism that has had important implications for the animals regarded this way. I follow the model of Mrs. R. Lee, the author of a popular natural history who explained the character of her work this way: "Dry details of science and classification have been laid aside" in an effort "to throw as much interest as possible over these recorded habits and actions of the brute creation."[1] In other words, scientific description was not the point then, and it is not mine now. Like readers of natural histories, I, too, am interested in stories.

Beginnings

Before the arrival of European migrants as permanent settlers, the indigenous people of North America had complex relationships with a wide variety of animals; animals were sources of food, raw materials, and muscle power. Animals occupied important positions in the cosmologies of cultural groups as well. Occasionally young wild animals lived in villages as casual pets and children's playthings. Native Americans' dogs occupied the most complex position of any animal in indigenous cultures. Depending on the tribe, Native American dogs were sources of muscle power pulling travois and sleds, representatives of cosmic forces that were sometimes sacrificed in religious ceremonies, fellow hunters, livestock herders, sources of protein, playmates for children, and beloved companions. In many Native American groups, dogs occupied multiple and, to modern eyes, contradictory roles simultaneously.[2]

Pet keeping in North America, in a form that we recognize as the antecedent of our modern practice, arrived with European settlers. The Spanish first carried European dogs to both North and South America as tools of war and conquest; in later colonization, settlers brought them as hunters, guardians, workers, and companions. Europeans also disembarked with long traditions of relationships with other small animals, and they either brought the animals to the New World, as in the case of the domestic cat, or they found comparable substitutes among local species. One of these relationships involved keeping animals simply for the purposes of delight; some people just liked animals. By the second half of the eighteenth century, caring for birds, squirrels, and small dogs was routine in some American households. Caged native songbirds—mockingbirds, cardinals, and goldfinches were among the most popular—may have been the most common pure pet, available to both rich and poor. However, continuing customs well established in England and northern Europe, families with the means and desire also succored "house" or "lap" dogs and other creatures who were not expected to be useful in the strictest sense. Then, as now, the edges of the category "pet" were flexible. Some Americans also grew very fond of animal workers—the mousing cats and watchful dogs essential to the good order and protection of the household or a docile, responsive milch cow or ox—to the extent that they were called "favorites," the term many people in the eighteenth century used instead of "pet." Mrs. Fobes, the subject of a large, three-quarter-length portrait with her pets painted by the provincial portraitist Rufus Hathaway in 1790, must have been quite fond of her cat, whose grumpy expression probably reflects young Hathaway's limited skill rather than the animal's temper (fig. 1.1).

Documents shedding light on everyday life in the early United States are much scarcer than those for the 1800s and later, but evidence of pet keeping in the eighteenth century can be pieced together using artifacts as evidence along with the written materials that do survive. Some museums have preserved birdcages and engraved brass dog collars from the 1700s as examples of folk art, fine woodworking, or metal founding and engraving (see fig. 1.2). These objects suggest that, in some early households, pets were

FIGURE 1.1. *Rufus Hathaway (American, 1770–1822),* Lady with Her Pets *(Molly Wales Fobes), oil on canvas, 1790. The Metropolitan Museum of Art, Gift of Edgar and Bernice Chrysler Garbisch, 1963. Some eighteenth-century portraits include animals, but they are often emblems, animal symbols that comment on the character of the sitter. Mrs. Fobes, however, chose to have herself painted with her pets—a parrot on his hanging perch, another bird on the back of her chair, and a rather awkward-looking cat at her side.*

already provided with housing or equipment that reflected the prosperity of their owners as well as the pleasure owners took in their animals. Newspapers provide other clues. While the majority of "lost dog" ads in newspapers of the time concern hunting or guard dogs whose economic value was clear, some notices for pet dogs—and the occasional cat or parrot—do appear: "Lost or stolen on Sunday morning last . . . a small Lap Dog, called Juliet. She is all white, except about her eyes which are brown—she was very round by the great care taken of her by her owner—who will be much obliged to any person that will give information where she may be got, or will deliver her at No. 101 Church street. A reasonable reward will be given if required."[3]

Eighteenth-century diaries like that of Elizabeth Sandwith Drinker of Philadelphia (kept from 1759 to 1807) are unusual in any case. Hers, however, is particularly notable for its observations on the behavior of the family's cats, dogs, and other small animals. During the 1760s and 1770s, when Drinker was a young wife and mother, occasional brief entries noted without comment

FIGURE 1.2. *Birdcage in the shape of a church with a two-tiered tower, white pine, tulip, glass, and wire (American). Courtesy, Winterthur Museum (65.2150). Originally painted in shades of black, white, green, and red-orange, this cage survived not because it was a particularly good environment for birds but as a craftsman's tour de force.*

such events as the death of the old watchdog and his replacement by another. Later, however, it becomes clear that this brevity was associated with the busy nature of Drinker's household rather than her feelings. (For years, her daily diary entries are little more than a record of the ailments of family members and her efforts at doctoring them.) As her age permitted more leisure, Drinker's notes about animals became more frequent and included more detail as she reminisced about pets kept by the family in the past: "a large mastiff dog" named Ranger, "a black cat—which we had for many years, and a white cock" called Chanticleer (named after one of the characters in *Reynard the Fox*, the most important "beast epic" of late medieval Europe), who was "a favorite of our sons." When her small house dog Tartar woke her with his barking during the night, she commented that "something there was to set him agoing [*sic*], as he is too fat and lazy to exert himself for nothing." She noted with pleasure that Tartar and the cat were the "first to welcome us" when the family returned from the country, and she commented on her grandchildren's pets, including unusual "English rabbits," chickens kept as "favorites," and an orphan kitten that had been suckled by a dog.

Drinker's diary also suggests that pet keeping was not confined to wealthy Philadelphians and that even working animals could become favorites. She noted when her son William "gave our little squirrel to a Negro lad over the way[,] a barber who has several petts and appears fond of them"; she was glad to be rid of the creature but worried about the quality of care it would receive. Drinker also shared moments in the life story of an animal worker, her cat Puss, who had been elevated to a special status. When the Drinkers fled to Germantown to escape the yellow fever epidemic in 1797, Puss was transported in a basket; most animals in the city had been left behind. The next year, Drinker noted with humor that "Our Cats progeny are much in demand[;] whether it is her real merit, or the value her mistress sits on her, that gives her such consequence I cant say."[4]

Drinker's life list of pets reflected the basic range of creatures kept by early American households, with the exception of cage birds. In the 1800s, pet-keeping households expanded on this basic catalog (see fig. 1.3). Although only fragmentary statistics survive until the mid-twentieth century, all evidence suggests that

FIGURE 1.3. *Eastman Johnson (American, 1824–1906),* The Pets, *oil on academy board, 1856 (25 × 28¾ in.). In the Collection of The Corcoran Gallery of Art, Washington, D.C. Gift of William Wilson Corcoran (69.44). Noted for his observation of everyday life, Johnson posed this little girl with a parrot, a kitten, a globe of goldfish, and a hutch containing either rabbits or guinea pigs.*

the trend over time was for more people to keep multiple animals as pets, and for more species to enter the category of "pet." Cage birds, dogs, and cats (a poor third but with their passionate advocates) continued as the most important species. By the mid-nineteenth century, however, both adults and children dabbled in the specialized husbandry of "pet stock," chickens, pigeons, and rabbits that were bred for their looks and sometimes shown competitively. By midcentury, some sturdy, relatively undemanding animals, including the recently introduced guinea pig and the white mouse, had become known as children's pets, and some families experimented with keeping a fish globe or the more complex "balanced" aquarium.

In turn, the list of pets in nineteenth-century America is roughly comparable to that of contemporary households, consisting of dogs and cats, small rodents, birds, fish, and occasional exotic animals. The differences lie in the relative popularity of one kind of animal over another; for example, cage birds are now much less popular as pets than they were 100 years ago. Another change is in the growing importance of novel small animals. Modern pet stores are full of "exotic" creatures that never would have been found in the suburban household of 1900: tropical fish, small animals such as the Syrian Golden Hamster or the African pygmy hedgehog, and reptiles. Even if a nineteenth-century family had wanted to keep a pet lizard (and I have yet to find one), most dwellings of the time lacked central heat or even a way to heat more than one or two rooms consistently. Such tender creatures could not have survived. The pets we know best, cats and dogs, also differ from their predecessors in interesting ways. Modern pets are larger and healthier, for one thing; so, for that matter, are today's people. Many of the most popular dog breeds of today were unknown or were recent introductions to America. Some, like the golden retriever or the Boston terrier, had not even existed until the late nineteenth century. Purebred cats were almost unheard of, and the very concept would have stunned most of the people who kept cats as household workers.

The Family Dog

Dogs were, as they still are, the most written-about and depicted pet animals in America. The images of dogs throughout this book suggest that well-loved dogs could be found in all sorts of households and that they were ubiquitous in both city and countryside. Dogs were also first-generation pioneers on the trek west. Whatever their function as hunters or guardians, even these dogs were often clearly regarded as companions. The Shores family of Custer Country, Nebraska, took care to include their small dog, seated in a chair, in the portrait that itinerant photographer Solomon Butcher made in front of their sod house in 1887 (see fig. 1.4).

The large and varied dog population of George Washington's plantation, which was almost a town in miniature, demonstrates the roles played by dogs in the eighteenth century, and the differences in status and care dogs experienced in all kinds of American communities. The canine inhabitants of Mount Vernon acted as watchdogs, hunting dogs, herders, coach dogs to ornament the general's livery, household workers, companions, and vagrants and thieves. Nowadays, George Washington the dog lover is most famous for his hunting pack, and he is credited as owner of one of the originating kennels for the (now rare) American foxhound. He imported seven "French hounds," obtained through the efforts of

FIGURE 1.4. *Jerry Shores Family near Westerville, Nebraska, 1887. Photograph by Solomon Butcher. Nebraska State Historical Society.*

his good friend the Marquis de Lafayette, in 1785, and over the years he kept records of the various matings and offspring of these dogs. Like the Dalmatians (including one named Madame Moose) that accompanied Washington's carriage, these hunting dogs were status symbols used for the gentlemanly pursuit of fox hunting. Gunner the Newfoundland, on the other hand, accompanied Washington's enslaved worker Tom Davis on his hunts to provide wildfowl for dining. The spaniels Pilot, Tipsy, and Old Harry were probably used for this same purpose. There is evidence of other working dogs at Mount Vernon: two "tarriers" used to catch mice and rats on the estate and at least one "Shepard's dog." The mansion itself housed companion dogs including the "Little hound bitch" Chloe and the small spaniels Pompey and Frish. Other dogs also ran on the plantation's acreage. Washington's personal dogs must have had some contact with the ragtag dogs that belonged to the plantation's enslaved people; sometimes these curs were able to mate with the master's purebred dogs. Slaves' dogs may have been companions, but they were also used to help their owners augment their diet by hunting wild animals—and by stealing Washington's own sheep and hogs. The predations of the slave cur-dog population grew so extensive that the general periodically felt compelled to kill them in numbers and to forbid new dogs from showing up in the quarters. However, it seems that campaigns to prevent slaves from keeping dogs were never successful.[5]

What Washington's hounds and coach dogs and the other canines of Mount Vernon looked like is not known, but as a community of dogs, their appearance was probably quite different from that of the group of canines that meets in your neighborhood dog park every evening. Even 100 years after Washington, family dogs did not look like the ubiquitous Labrador or golden retrievers who pull their owners up the street, tails wagging, every evening in my neighborhood. From the colonial era until the early 1900s, most family dogs were the progeny of a relatively narrow range of common types: spaniels, hounds, setters and pointers, rough- and short-coated terriers, large mastiff or "Newfoundland" dogs, and bulldogs (the only kind that seems to have been missing from George Washington's inventory of dogs). The differences in characteristics among these types resulted from their historical functions as hunters, guardians, workers, fighters, or companions.[6]

An explanation of what a breed is may be useful here. Breeds of animals occur within a particular species where mating within a closed population leads to the development of a particular set of appearances and behaviors. At first, most breeds of all domesticated animals, including dogs, were probably the result of local populations where a combination of natural fitness and human interventions gradually shaped both their bodies and behaviors. Over time, enthusiasts for purebred animals developed stud books, or registries, where the population of a breed was controlled even more closely by limiting the designation "pure" to animals resulting from matings only within the registered population.

Having a purebred dog in 1850 meant something different from what it means today. Until the American Kennel Club (AKC) was founded in 1884, there were few written breed standards (the set of specifications for the ideal physical specimen) or registry books in the United States. When Deborah Norris Logan of Germantown, Pennsylvania, referred in her diary to her family's "old breed of dog" (a medium-to-large white dog with brown spots, used for hunting) in 1837, she was probably referring to a characteristic-looking animal that had developed over a number of generations on the family farm.[7] Well-bred dogs were prized, just as highly bred horses were, but they were relatively uncommon except among the brotherhood of sport hunters, where some dog owners worked to maintain bloodlines of good pointers, setters, and hounds like Washington's foxhounds.

Until after the Civil War, an exotic specimen such as a poodle or an Italian greyhound was often the souvenir of a trip abroad or a companion for a sea captain. Families sometimes purchased or received a purebred animal as a special treat. One memoir writer recalled her parents bringing a St. Bernard puppy home from New York City as a gift for the children, while another recalled that her sister received a "lovely snow white Spitz dog" as a wedding gift in the 1880s.[8] Since we lack the aid of photography, the exact nature of some special "purebred" dogs will remain forever mysterious. In 1855, for example, the Van Rensselaer-Elmendorf-Rankin family of Cherry Hill in Albany, New York, took in a "beautiful West India dog" (named Bevis) of a "dark spotted colour" but having "no hair on the top of his 'back where the hair ought to grow.'"[9] Its true identity remains a mystery. Most family dogs were either mixed breeds, with a heavy representation of terrier and bulldog blood, or homegrown, unregistered "purebreds" picked up at city markets from local farmers, adopted from neighbors, or purchased from city dog dealers. Cities and towns were burdened with many tramp dogs, and sometimes one got lucky. In the summer of 1896, the Rankins adopted a wandering black puppy of unknown parentage and dubbed him "Stray." He immediately distinguished himself by eating two of the children's pet turtles.[10]

The first American shows devoted exclusively to dogs took place in the early 1860s. One, the International Dog Show held in Washington, D.C., in 1863, may have been a charity event for the United States Sanitary Commission, which raised funds for military hospitals. P. T. Barnum hosted the other, the Great National Dog Show, which offered "upwards of $2,200" in prizes for "whatever is most rare and beautiful among the canine species."[11] Livestock shows had been around for decades, and some groups began to include dogs as a sidebar to their main business in the 1860s. The 1869 exhibition of the New-York Poultry Society included cats, "lap-ear" rabbits, and dogs.[12] In the 1870s, an American dog fancy developed fully in imitation of the English model.[13] The first bench show (the form of dog show where dogs compete against their ideal breed standard and are exhibited in a "benching area") to receive widespread popular attention was held at the Centennial Exposition in Philadelphia, 4–8 September 1876. There the nation's "choicest specimens" were presented to the public.[14] The largest dog shows nowadays offer classes for 156 breeds officially recognized by the AKC. The AKC's most important competitor, the United Kennel Club, Inc., founded in 1889, represents an even larger array of breeds, 300. This club defines the concept of breed differently than does the AKC and emphasizes working dogs over companion breeds. Its shows tend to be smaller, specialty competitions.

The class list for the Centennial show is worth reproducing in its entirety because the categories summarize the purebred dog population of its era: Fox Hounds, Harriers, Beagles, Dachshunds, Greyhounds, Bloodhounds, Imported English Setters, Native English Setters, Imported Irish Setters, Native Irish Setters, Imported Gordon Setters, Native Gordon Setters, Pointer Dogs over 50 Lbs. Weight, Pointer Dogs under 50 Lbs. Weight, Retrievers and Chesapeake Bay Dogs, Irish Water Spaniels, Retrieving Spaniels Other than Pure Irish, Cocker Spaniels, Springer Dogs, Mastiffs, St. Bernards, Newfoundland Dogs, Siberian or Ulm Dogs, Dalmatian or Coach Dogs, Sheep Dogs, Bull Dogs, Bull Terriers, Fox Terriers, Black and Tan Terrier Dogs Not Exceeding Eleven Pounds Weight, Sky Terriers, Scotch Terriers, Broken Haired Terriers, Dandie Dinmont Terriers, Toy Terriers Not Exceeding Five Pounds Weight, Pomeranian or Spitz Dogs, Poodle Dogs, and Miscellaneous. The last category included a handful of distinctive-looking crossbreeds, Pugs, Italian Greyhounds, and a Chinese Hairless Dog owned by Thomas Manby of the Philadelphia Zoological Gardens. Of the 557 dogs shown, 273 were setters, demonstrating the predominance of interest in dogs with a traceable genealogy among sport hunters. One class, the Chesapeake Bay Dog (a curly-coated retriever), was already a recognizable American breed, and some of the other hunting dogs may have been proto-breeds now lost. Many of the dogs were listed as having been imported from Europe, making them ambulatory status symbols, and breeds that would soon be quite popular were just being introduced. Only three pugs were shown, all owned by Mr. J. C. Bailey of Philadelphia. Seven of the nine dachshunds were German imports, or their immediate descendants, owned by local doctor L. H. Twaddell.[15]

By the 1880s, some distinctive, recently imported dog breeds had even become the object of fads (just as the newly arrived, wrinkly Chinese sharpei dogs were in the United States in the 1980s). Two of the most popular were the pug and the St. Bernard. The likenesses of these animals turned up on commercial trade cards, greeting cards, calendars, children's books, inexpensive prints, and ceramic figurines.[16] By the 1880s, the "Scotch collie" had become the new fashionable suburban family dog, and around 1900, the favorite was the Boston terrier (see fig. 1.5). A deliberate hybrid of the English bulldog, the bull terrier, and other related types, the Boston terrier was probably first bred for the stigmatized but widespread entertainment of fighting. It gradually gained a club and registry, it was bred down in size, and its color was standardized. The result was a spiffy little black and white fellow in a tuxedo who seemed the epitome of a "modern" dog. Called "the American dog" by its fanciers, who were allowed to join the AKC in 1893, the Boston terrier was one of the top five registered purebred dogs in America through the 1940s.[17] Other fads also became long-standing preferences. German shepherds were rare in the United States until their service in World War I attracted attention to their utility as police dogs, and the subsequent movie stardom of Rin-Tin-Tin sealed their fame and desirability.

Importing pedigreed canine breeding stock from Europe and occasionally from Asia was principally a pastime for the well-to-do, and it was not without its critics. By the 1880s, some American

FIGURE 1.5. *Mary Harrod Northend (American, 1850–1926), unidentified woman with Boston terrier, date unknown (ca. 1900). Courtesy of Historic New England/ SPNEA. This dapper fellow, going for a walk in his turtleneck sweater, is a Boston terrier from the early decades of the breed.*

dog lovers were already complaining, using an old-fashioned rhetoric borrowed from political debates in the young republic about
"public virtue" and about the increasing wealth and "luxurious
self-gratification" that demanded the animal world be "ransacked
to pander to its bizarre and eccentric longing for novelty." As dogs
became part of the fashion system and were treated as if they were
luxury consumer goods (which some certainly were), they were
physically reshaped by the demands of fashion. "The points of the
same breed of dog are subject to modification and change," one
writer complained in 1885. "The jaw of the bull-dog, the curve of
his forelegs, the width of his skull; the head of the mastiff, the
snake-like cranium of the greyhound, the length of ears of the
King Charles spaniel, the nose of the pug, the coloring, markings
of the hair,—all these by skillful breeding may be modified to con-
form to the caprice of the moment."[18]

In the creation of a national kennel club, many of America's
serious dog breeders and showers followed closely their English
predecessors. Several decades earlier, the English dog fancy had
husbanded into existence an elaborate set of organizations and rituals that were heavily inflected by the social aspirations of its
largely middle-class participants.[19] This particular element of the
British model seems to have been less the case in the United
States. The pioneering sociologist and social critic Thorstein Veblen, however, pointed out that the value of the "canine monstrosi-
ties" that were the "prevailing styles of pet dogs" among the very
well-to-do in America were yet another example of "conspicuous
consumption," the term he coined to describe the ways people
spent money in social competition.[20]

Even if dog breeders complained that working animals were
being bred "too fine" at the sacrifice of "stamina, grit, go, and real

field worth," the purebred dogs of the 1880s and 1890s did not look like their pedigreed descendants.[21] Dogs are unusually malleable genetically. Thus not only have many different breeds of dogs appeared over the thousands of years that dogs have kept company with humans, but in the past 125 years, the catalogs of physical features by which show dogs are judged have evolved considerably. Portraits of prize-winning dogs and prints such as *House, Kennel and Field* (fig. 1.6), which represents the kinds of purebred dogs typically found in the 1890s, suggest that their muzzles were not as long and pointy or as squashed, their skulls were not as domelike, and their eyes were not as large and prominent as those of their descendants. Their legs and bodies were sturdier, and their coats were not as long or as thick. A good ex-

FIGURE 1.6. House, Kennel and Field, *chromolithograph, published by Currier and Ives, New York, 1892. Library of Congress, Division of Prints and Photographs.*

ample of the transformation of a traditional working dog into a canine aristocrat is the evolution of the collie, documented in a series of photographs published in 1912 in an article debating the relative merits of the "old-fashioned" versus the "modern type" of dog.[22] Although inbreeding clearly took place as fanciers tried to establish ever more distinctive features in their lines, the genetic problems that have surfaced in purebreds today, from "canine rage syndrome" to epilepsy and hip dysplasia, either had not yet appeared or were not recognized as such. That said, breeders did acknowledge that purebred puppies, particularly from the smallest breeds, seemed unusually fragile and disease prone.[23]

The debate over breeding in the early twentieth century signaled acceptance of the purebred dog as the beau ideal, at least in middle- and upper-class families. The authors of articles on the subject almost uniformly assumed that their readers would willingly spend good money to purchase a registered dog.[24] Even if they purchased a purebred animal, however, ordinary families had little contact with the dog fancy. Registration of individual dogs in the AKC did not break 10,000 per year until 1906. There is also evidence that regional preferences in purebred dogs and some regional hunting types, such as the coonhound and the feist (a small dog used for squirrel hunting) in the South, continued to thrive even as introduced breeds of dogs became known nationally.[25]

Along with beauty, the purebred animal was supposed to promise predictability in both looks and temperament. Some misguided promoters of purebred dogs described the advantages of the blooded animal over the mixed breed with language that echoed strikingly the early twentieth-century interest in eugenics and racial purity. According to one prominent veterinarian in 1928,

Many ill-bred "mutts," like so many human waifs, actually
develop by their own natural abilities into remarkably
bright, attractive, and worthy beings. But, and this is also
characteristic of the human breed, it is the well-bred dog
which is commonly looked to for natural development
along reliable lines—the ones from which something can be
expected. . . . Cross bred dogs may frequently be most ad-
mirable creatures. But as a class they can never hope to
equal the true, pure-blooded animals with their generations
of unmixed blood. In the mongrel one never knows what he
may depend on—what he may ultimately get in joy and
sorrow.[26]

Despite efforts to promote the purebred dog as the ideal family pet, growth in dog registrations was slow until the 1940s. Between 1960 and 1970, the decade of greatest growth, the number
of new AKC registrations jumped from 442,875 to 1,129,200. During this same decade, dog fanciers, veterinary organizations, and
private foundations jointly created the Orthopedic Foundation for
Animals, with a mandate to study and work to reduce the inci-
dence of canine hip dysplasia, the inherited malformation of the
hips that especially affects larger breeds. There is no doubt that
breeding in tightly closed populations leads to clusters of inherited problems in dogs. The orthopedic foundation currently main-
tains databases for breeders relating to disorders of the thyroid,
congenital heart problems, orthopedic defects, and other maladies. AKC registrations have been in decline since their peak in
1992 (1,528,392), although current advertising by the club and its
annual broadcast of the finals of the Westminster Kennel Club
show in New York City may have begun to reverse the trend.

However, the combined annual registrations of the AKC and the United Kennel Club total only about 1.5 million.[27] An estimated 65 million pet dogs live in America.

Just Plain Cats

Much less celebrated than dogs, although as ubiquitous, many pet cats were still household workers until the 1950s. Few felines are required to perform that function these days, however, when a cat presenting its owner with a chewed mouse carcass is more likely to provoke consternation than gratitude. Proven mousers were so prized that city folk could rent them from exterminators and animal dealers. Cats were crucial to urban rat control, especially around markets and stables. Their absence in early books of advice such as *The Book of Household Pets* (1866), the first general book of reference on pet keeping published in the United States, may simply reflect their ubiquity. The fact that cats are not mentioned, however, might also have something to do with their ambiguous position in the household as somehow less tame than dogs—independent contractors, really—and as unrepentant predators. Where households kept poultry, for example, neighborhood cats could be a nuisance because they found chicks such easy pickings. In May 1872, Alice Stone Blackwell, a cat lover who also cared for a small flock of fowl at her family's suburban house, found herself confronting her next-door neighbor to "tell him if he did not keep the cat shut up we should have to kill it."[28]

Families typically had what Samuel Canby Rumford called "just plain cats," acquired from friends or neighbors or adopted as strays. In places like the Rumfords' Wilmington, Delaware, barn, cats that lived on their own ingenuity "multiplied in great

FIGURE 1.7. A Happy Family in Chicopee Falls *[Massachusetts], postcard, photographer unknown, 1907–15. Author's collection. This card, produced by the photographer to demonstrate the capabilities of the "instantaneous flash-light," is a rare early image of a "just plain cat" nursing her new kittens.*

numbers" and were the subject of boyhood cat hunts with home-made crossbows and slingshots.[29] The 1881 journal of a curmudgeon named Gotham Bradbury of Farmington, Maine, suggests the casual way that some folks regarded even their house cats. On 26 January, a "professional magnetizer" named Dr. Douglas carried an "electrical machine" to the house and gave therapeutic shocks to the Bradbury family in their sitting room. Then, for the fun of it, he "gave the cats electricity which caused them to jump smartly." In February Bradbury complained about the "yawling concerts" of his neighbor's cats around the house, and in July he noted in passing in a list of chores that he had "killed a couple of our useless cats."[30] Advocates of animal welfare complained about the common practice among city folk of turning out cats for the summer when the family went on vacation, or of "keeping cats during the summer at the seaside or country house and leaving them behind when the family returns to the city for the winter."[31]

Still, then as now, some people were serious cat lovers. Lydia Jackson Emerson, Ralph Waldo Emerson's second wife, was one of these. Her stepdaughter Ellen complained in an 1859 letter to her sister that the family not only tolerated a black kitten and a large black cat, the barn cat, two others named Violet and Kitty Minot, and "Aunty's cat and all mother's pensioners," but they recently had been "much afflicted by the arrival of another cat."

Mother was waked by mewing, and looking out of the window saw a white cat standing on the piazza. Mother spoke to it and it bounded up the closet-roofs and into her arms. "A pretty, purring creature" said Mother. Since that time she frequents the house night and day, though full grown and an entire stranger. Father says that when she came into the window she told Mother that she was an Acton cat and wanted a home, and one day in Acton she met a cat who said "Why, haven't you heard? There's a Mis' Emerson down Concord-way what's kind to cats."[32]

While conventional wisdom considered cats to be pets for women and little girls, and although popular prints and advertisements usually depicted only women with cats, cat lovers were, in fact, both female and male. In the mid-1890s, the two young boys of the Rankin family in Albany, New York, were devoted to a cat named Grahame. Thirty years earlier, Hartford, Connecticut, newspaper editor and author Charles Dudley Warner had admired his Maltese cat Calvin, who could open doors with old-fashioned latches, took tidbits of food from a fork, and "insisted upon his meals in the dining-room." "He could do almost everything but speak," Warner recalled in an essay published after Calvin's death, "and you would declare sometimes that you could see a pathetic longing to do that in his intelligent face."[33] Warner's friend Samuel Clemens, better known as Mark Twain, was a passionate cat lover (which may surprise readers of *The Adventures of Tom Sawyer*, wherein Clemens discussed the trading and play value of a dead cat among small boys at some length). Clemens shared his love of cats with his mother, who, he recalled, succored scores of strays in the 1830s and 1840s.[34] Once he established his own family, Clemens indulged his passion for cats freely, and his daughters allowed him to name them all because he was so very good at it. This resulted in felines with names such as Abner, Apollonaris (after the French bottled mineral water), Motley, Fraulein, Famine, Cleveland, Buffalo Bill, and Sour Mash. His daughter recalled Clemens walking around with a cat named Lazy draped around his neck like a stole. Toward the end of the author's life, his cats were photographed, and the images were subsequently published as "Mark Twain's Cats" in the *Pictorial Review*.[35]

A handful of distinctive cat breeds were recognized by the late nineteenth century, particularly the Maltese (which had tiger-striped or tortoise-shell markings) and the long-haired Angora. According to their 1899 catalog, Johnson and Stokes, seedsmen, offered to ship anywhere in the United States "Thoroughbred Angora Cats" with "wonderfully Long" hair for $4.00 to $7.00.[36] The first truly exotic house cat breed, the Siamese, arrived in the United States by way of England in the early 1900s. Siamese were also the objects of what can be called the first real fad for a cat breed in the mid-twentieth century, when their exotic coloring and sleek bodies (and perhaps their featured role in Walt Disney's 1955 animated feature *Lady and the Tramp*) made them seem peculiarly modern. But the ready availability—even abundance—

of cats meant that most people would have scoffed at the idea of paying for such a beast. Cats are not as genetically variable as dogs, and there have never been as many distinctive regional types; nor have they proved able to perform a comparably wide range of tasks.

Thus it was difficult to create a parallel establishment for breeding and showing cats in Victorian America, a problem that was evident in the catalog of the first National Cat Show, held at the Music Hall, Boston, 21–26 January 1878. Classes included Short-Haired Cats of Any or No Sex and Any Color; their long-haired equivalents; Curiosities of Any Variety, which included a Maine coon cat, two cats born with only three legs, and two "Rabbit Cats," perhaps the dwarf cats now called Munchkins; Maltese cats; Manxes; Tabbies; Tigers; Tortoise-Shells; and cats of "Unusual Color." One class was devoted to specimens of large size and weight; the winner seems to have been Major, an eighteen-pounder.[37] Eleven-year-old Margaret Tileston of Concord attended the show with her family and was impressed by "a pure white cat weighing fifteen pounds, and named Flag of Truce," and "a tremendously large pure-yellow long furred big-headed beautiful cat." Her favorite, however, was a small gray kitty who "kept rolling over when I patted her, she upset her water."[38]

Thirty-eight different cat breeds are recognized by the Cat Fanciers of America, the oldest registry organization. On a small scale, debates similar to those surrounding purebred dogs have entered the cat fancy. One example of this is associated with the Siamese. In 1987, a group of breeders founded the Traditional Siamese Cat Association as a response to changes in the looks of the breed. By the 1960s, breeders and judges had remade the show-quality Siamese into an animal with an elongated body, a wedge-shaped head, and long, thin legs and tail. The old style, called appleheads, could no longer win at shows. The Traditional Cat Association, as it is now called, includes breeders of old-fashioned lines of Burmese, Persian, Balinese, and Siamese cats. The group argues that the show lines recognized in current standards have produced animals that are less healthy, and it operates a parallel show establishment.

Small Animals and Pet Stock

Households with children often contained a miscellany of other tame or semitame creatures considered good pets for children. No one knows when domesticated breeds of bunnies arrived in this country, but as mentioned earlier, Elizabeth Drinker's granddaughters had "English rabbits" at the turn of the eighteenth century. By the 1860s, American bird stores also sold cavies (guinea pigs), rodents indigenous to Central America, where they were long domesticated as a food source. Cavies were easy to care for and relatively hardy. Authors of pet-keeping advice split on their virtues—"stupid little things," sniffed one—but all agreed that they were gentle yet hardy enough for lives in the care of young children (see fig. 1.8).[39] In 1871, guinea pigs were still rare enough in Concord, Massachusetts, that they created a minor crisis of categorization at the town's annual cattle show. Prized guinea pigs were first displayed with the swine; they were later moved to the poultry department.[40]

The notion of the rodent pet reinforces the idea that all pets are made when people choose them and undertake to control their lives. While mice and rats were pursued relentlessly by conscientious housewives as vermin (the ambulatory equivalent of dirt), some children raised white mice and rats. Their whiteness, a recessive genetic trait that could be selected, suggested that the creatures were fundamentally different from their wild cousins. White mice even have a distinguished genealogy. According to a 1787 treatise on mouse breeding found in the Tokyo Imperial Library, a Chinese Buddhist priest carried a pair of tame "white mice with black eyes" to Japan in 1654. The descendants of this pair were considered to bring good fortune to the priest's followers and may have triggered a fancy for breeding mice that paralleled the Japanese interest in breeding and appreciating ornamental goldfish.[41] Albino mice were kept as pets in England before 1837, when Thomas Bell's *British Quadrupeds* noted the practice. Whether these were simply the descendants of unusual-looking house mice that had been scooped up and caged or the extended family of some fancy mice who were souvenirs of trade

FIGURE 1.8. *James S. Baillie (fl. 1838–55),* Guinea Pigs, *hand-colored lithograph, New York, undated. Harry T. Peters, "America on Stone" Lithography Collection (60.2340), National Museum of American History, Behring Center, Smithsonian Institution.*

with Asia is unknown.[42] However, Catherine (Kittie) B. Putnam of Albany, New York, recorded buying two white mice on a trip to New York City in 1871, when she was fourteen, and a wall-hung mouse cage (they were sometimes called mouse theaters) survives in the collection of the family's homestead, Cherry Hill.[43] White mice and rats were also called pocket pets, creatures that an enterprising boy could carry around and, because they were so prolific, use in trade with other boys.[44]

The most common pocket pet today, the hamster, is a relatively recent arrival. It appeared in pet stores for the first time in the late 1940s. By the early 1960s, an estimated 6 million hamsters were sold as pets each year.[45] What makes the introduction of the hamster so different from those of other small animals as pets is the hamster's origin in America as a modern laboratory animal. The Syrian Golden Hamster, a small desert rodent, had been described in 1839. Rediscovered in 1930, the species was soon chosen as a promising laboratory animal at a time when scientific experimentation using animals was becoming more important. In 1938, some specimens from England were shipped to the United States Public Health Service in Louisiana, where the hamster, an easy and prolific breeder, soon proved useful for research into human diseases. Laboratory demand made alert commercial rodent breeders, who were already producing guinea pigs, rabbits, and mice for use in labs and hospitals, aware of the hamster's commercial potential. At some point, some breeders or pet shop owners realized that hamsters were docile, hardy, and relatively clean. A new pet shop novelty—and in time a staple of childhood pet keeping—was born.

Well into the twentieth century, both boys and girls often took up a kind of "toy" animal husbandry, keeping small flocks of chickens or pigeons or hutches of rabbits. The child who wrote on the back of the snapshot postcard reproduced in figure 1.9 admired Alice Madsen, the little girl depicted, because her bunnies were "pretty well trained." Pet chickens, pigeons, and rabbits often were representatives of so-called fancy breeds—floppy-eared "lop" rabbits, Jacobin pigeons, or bantam chickens whose small size and gentle nature made them easy for children to hold and manage. The term "fancy," which had been applied to breeding animals for aesthetic purposes since at least the early nineteenth century, built upon an earlier sense that a fancy was a whimsical act of imagination and caprice that gave pleasure precisely because it was not useful. However, the name given to these sorts of animals by pet dealers, "pet stock," suggested that the understanding about where they belonged in the scheme of human-animal relationships was ambiguous. Indeed, enterprising and practical-minded children raised chickens and rabbits as

FIGURE 1.9. *Alice Madsen with her pet rabbits, 1911, postcard, photographer unknown; postmarked Corley, Iowa, 4 May 1911. Author's collection.*

both pets and a way to earn money by selling eggs or the animals for meat. In 1886, a young correspondent to *Harper's Young People* noted that her "chicken money" over five years had allowed her to purchase a "hand-sled," a rocking chair, books, and other furnishings for her room.[46] A case study of this kind of play husbandry undertaken by three siblings in the late 1890s appears in "The Bunnie States of America," following Chapter 2.

Wild Creatures

As opportunities presented themselves, people sometimes made wild animals into pets. Squirrels were the most popular. They were pretty and lively and, if caught young enough, grew quite tame.[47] Squirrel nests were raided systematically for their babies, and the young were sold in city markets (as in the case of the squirrel Elizabeth Drinker's adult son purchased as a pet) and in bird stores until the early twentieth century. Squirrels could chew their way through wood, so tinsmiths sold special cages for them with sturdy metal bars. When someone realized that squirrels would run on an exercise wheel, tinsmiths sometimes made amusing cages in the forms of mills with waterwheels. *The Book of Household Pets* rejected this kind of novelty cage as too small and dark and urged its readers to make their own cages "at least six feet long, and four feet high . . . with perches like the branch of a tree . . . and a sleeping box."[48] Sometimes squirrels were allowed out to play. Philadelphian Helen Kate Rogers kept a squirrel named Chickey in a cage in her room. In an 1846 letter she described him "cutting about all day[.] He would run and jump on Anne's bed and then on the chair by the window then on the window sill then he would jump on the floor and lick the mat then he would jump on the bed again."[49]

Squirrels were the most common wild animal pet, but many young animals proved susceptible to at least gentling if not training. In the early nineteenth century, young deer were popular pets among well-to-do families. Because deer had been so systematically overhunted, they were rare in the eastern United States, which made them desirable as living lawn ornaments in a small-scale version of the European country house "deer park." In the 1820s, the du Pont family of Delaware had deer named Azore, Zelia, Hector, Zamor, and Fanny.[50] The animals had their own house but were allowed to wander; they sometimes walked up onto the front porch to explore. In 1858, Aaron Greenwood, a surveyor from Gardner, Massachusetts, reported in his diary that his parents had raised and tamed a pair of young crows and that a tenant on their property had a fox chained in his backyard and a "tame woodchuck . . . permitted to go at large . . . [that] played with his fingers like a kitten."[51] My great-grandfather Howard "Hop" Yearick, the Pennsylvania German boss carpenter for a sawmill village in southeastern Virginia in the early twentieth century, also tamed a woodchuck that my grandmother had found and believed to be an orphan. It lived under the woodshed behind the house but was allowed to visit indoors—at least until it ripped off chunks of wallpaper from the front hall to line its burrow. Grandpa's woodchuck came when he called it and ate corn and other treats out of his hand. Someone took its picture, which was cut down later to be pasted into an album (fig. 1.10). Like many wildlife pets, however, the woodchuck met a bad end. When it disappeared, Great-Grandpa was sure it had been shot and eaten by a mountaineer neighbor, easy pickings because it was not afraid of people and toothsome because it had been well fed.

Captured wild creatures were often what may be termed casual pets, obtained as chance permitted and not mourned when they succumbed to unintentional mishandling, the wrong food, or the injuries or diseases that had made them easy to catch in the first place. Samuel Canby Rumford reported that, around 1890, his childhood "play room" had been home to a generally short-lived group including "a flying squirrel, caught after many efforts in its nest in a crack in the eaves of the attic . . . a young Screech Owl, injured pigeons, young robins and other birds, who apparently had no parents."[52] Small, harmless snakes were one of boy-

FIGURE 1.10. *Howard Yearick's groundhog, Konnarock, Virginia, ca. 1915, snapshot, trimmed for album. Author's collection.*

hood's casual pets, picked up, pocketed, and traded with other small boys until they escaped or expired. Mark Twain's autobiography includes a passage in which the author recalls that, while his band of boyhood friends killed rattlers and "fled without shame" from "the fabled 'hoop' breed" of snakes, "when they were 'house snakes' or 'garters' we carried them home and put them in Aunt Patsy's work basket for a surprise; for she was prejudiced against snakes, and always when she took the basket in her lap and they began to climb out of it, it disordered her mind."[53]

Wild creatures living free occasionally became semitame or honorary pets when people fed them regularly. Ralph Waldo Emerson's family fed corn to a pair of blue jays, Atrocious and Peter, each morning.[54] In the 1870s, Pliny Jewell, an elderly member of a prominent Connecticut family, amused himself by feeding the frogs in the pond on his grounds. He did not simply stand on the bank and fling bits of food into the water. Rather, each evening he sat in an armchair and rang a dinner bell. An observer recalled, "As the mellow tones filled the air, the frogs would emerge from the water and group themselves expectantly yet respectfully about Mr. Jewell, who fed them with bits of bread, which they received courteously. . . . To this gentleman every one of those frogs was an individual, and he had named them all. The largest was called Laura Matilda, and was his favorite. I have seen Laura draw near his armchair, take a bit of bread delicately from his fingers, eat it and then wipe her mouth daintily, like the Prioress in Chaucer."[55]

Port cities from Salem, Massachusetts, to Charleston, South Carolina, received a steady trickle of exotic animals that had been purchased by seamen and either given as gifts to family members or sold at the docks for extra cash. Large exotics, from orangutans to leopards, lived miserable lives as exhibits in commercial museums or traveling menageries. Small exotic animals often became pets. Lucy Larcom called them "living reminders of strange lands across the sea" and described escaped monkeys hiding behind chimney pots and "green parrots . . . scolding and laughing down the thimbleberry hedges that bordered the cornfields" around her hometown of Salem in the 1810s and 1820s.[56] She recalled that parrots were often passengers on the return voyages of Salem packets. That was how George Washington obtained a parrot for his wife in 1773; he purchased it from the captain of a West India trading ship that had stopped at the Potomac River docks of Mount Vernon.[57]

The rise of a more organized trade in exotic animals between Europe and America by the 1870s, and between Asia, South America, and the United States by the 1890s, meant that pet stores in big cities were increasingly able to stock wild-caught animals. As the death rate from the illegal trade in wild primates today suggests, the mortality rates from monkey importation alone must have been dreadful. Hence the marmosets, "straight-tailed Java monkeys," and "ring-tail" monkeys (perhaps lemurs) sold by turn-of-the-century pet stores were their most expensive stock. Not only were they expensive, but they were troublesome and delicate. The drafts and cold air common in ordinary houses made them prone to fatal respiratory infections.[58] While some progressive pet stores like Schmid's Pet Emporium in Washington, D.C., promoted reptiles as pets around 1900, few Americans were interested in keeping snakes or lizards as pets until the 1970s. Animal dealers did offer wholesale anolis lizards (the small, color-shifting "chameleons" of my childhood) from the southeastern United States and "horned toads" from the western deserts in *Pet Dealer* magazine by the late 1920s. Even when a reptile such as a large snake appeared in a pet store, it was more likely to be a shop pet, kept for the amusement of customers, than merchandise.

Cage Birds

Pet-keeping households of the nineteenth and early twentieth centuries cared for an extraordinary number and variety of caged birds. In fact, birds may have been the most favored "indoor pets," with a popularity that crossed lines of class, ethnicity, and race, although they were rarely documented by photographers (see fig. 1.11). Tidbits of information suggesting the popularity of bird keeping turn up in surprising places. In early twentieth-century Pittsburgh, while analyzing the budget for "sundries" (the expenses for "community life" and "recreation") of "one colored family where the man earns $2.10 a day," pioneering social worker Margaret F. Byington noted the weekly expenditure of two cents for "bird seed."[59] Birds of all kinds occupied a special place in popular sentiments toward animals because of their apparent monogamy and devoted parenting. These qualities meant that birds were natural models for middle-class family life, and some people may have kept pet birds as living examples for their children.

The ethereal songs of birds motivated most owners to undertake the work and expense associated with their care, however. When the author of one book on canary keeping misappropriated Thomas Carlyle's phrase "little dewdrops of celestial melody" to describe birds, he captured the popular sense that there was something otherworldly about the physical nature of birds and that the songs they offered recalled the Divine.[60] We live in a world where recorded music, radios, and television sets bathe us

FIGURE 1.11. *Unidentified women and a girl with birdcage and dog, tintype, photographer unknown, 1870s. Author's collection. In the 1870s, it was not unusual for pet owners to include their dogs in their portraits. Bringing the canary's cage into the photographer's studio was rare, however, and suggests how much the bird was prized by its owners.*

in constant chatter and music. The silence of rooms in the past is now largely unknown.[61] Until the 1910s, when gramophones became inexpensive enough for many families to purchase, having music required actively making it (even if just by pumping the pedals of a player piano)—unless one possessed singing cage birds. Thus thirteen-year-old Ellen Emerson called her canary "who sings ever so much" Benedict, "for he is a real blessing."[62]

Bird keeping was a very old practice transported to North America with European immigrants in the seventeenth century, and a number of indigenous American species soon proved tolerant of life behind bars. We know, for example that Norborne, Baron de Botetourt, royal governor of Virginia from 1768 to 1770, kept twenty-eight "red birds" (probably cardinals) with cages, and that cardinals, mockingbirds, and the now-extinct Carolina parakeet were all in demand in Georgian England.[63] Goldfinches, mockingbirds, and cardinals were relatively hardy creatures, and they seem to have been the most common American birds kept in cages. With good care, they were long lived. Deborah Norris Logan reported on the occasion of the death of her cardinal Reddy in 1838 that she believed he had lived "a full fifteen years."[64]

While working-class men and children trapped wild birds for sale in city markets, middle-class children sometimes played at it for fun, keeping some as pets and letting the rest go.[65] Until comprehensive federal laws were passed in the early twentieth century that prohibited killing, capturing, and interstate commerce in American songbirds, bird sellers commonly stocked mockingbirds, cardinals, Baltimore orioles, bobolinks, rose-breasted grosbeaks, goldfinches, eastern bluebirds, indigo buntings, catbirds, blue jays, and redwing blackbirds, all captured rather than cage-bred. More expensive indigenous European birds, including bullfinches from Germany trained to whistle one or two tunes, gray linnets, siskins, chaffinches, starlings, and English robins, among others, were also imported throughout the nineteenth century. By the 1880s, finches from Asia had been added to the list, and by the early twentieth century, bird dealers offered exotic birds from Asia, Australia, and South America in place of the forbidden indigenous species. By then, shell parakeets (also called budgerigars or budgies), small members of the parrot family that had arrived in England as a by-product of the colonization of Australia, and other "lovebirds" could also be had for about the same price as imported German canaries.[66]

But the most popular cage bird through the 1930s was the canary, the "Universal Parlor Bird."[67] Canaries had been domesticated by the seventeenth century and selectively bred for color until their original greenish-yellow plumage became bright yellow. While the date of their arrival in the United States is unknown, canaries were the object of an organized international trade between German breeders and American bird stores by the 1840s. They also thrived and bred in warm kitchens and parlor bay windows. Even children raised canaries and gave some of the progeny as gifts or earned a little pocket money by selling them.[68] Home breeders could build or purchase special divided cages that hung on a wall, providing the parent birds a bit more privacy, and that contained shelves designed to hold wire nesting pans (see fig. 1.12). The avian immigrants also made their way west with extraordinary rapidity, evidence of both their robust constitutions and the value people put on their songs. There are accounts of cages full of canaries in the small cabin of German American settlers in 1840s Missouri, of an enterprising farm woman in 1880s Iowa selling the offspring of her Birdie and

FIGURE 1.12. *Canary breeding cage, early twentieth century (American), wood and galvanized tin. Author's collection.*

making her own cages, and of the prized canaries owned by the wife of a hardscrabble miner in 1880s Colorado.[69] The photographs of Nebraska homesteads made in the 1880s and 1890s by Solomon Butcher, pioneer photographer and historian, sometimes show canary cages hanging in doorways or on the exterior walls of sod houses, where the birds received daily doses of sunlight and fresh air. Carrying the Universal Parlor Bird to the frontier represented the domestic ideals that families dreamed of attaining, and canaries were valued company for women who worked all day in prairie isolation.[70]

While single cages of birds were common even in working-class households, more prosperous families had the means to tend larger avian collections. In 1840, Philip Hone wrote in his diary about a conservatory he had seen in a New York City mansion. It contained an aviary occupied by an imported bullfinch, canaries, and a mockingbird (which he praised as "the great leader of the feathered orchestra").[71] Harriet Maria Elmendorf of Albany, New York, gathered an "extensive collection" of birds into an aviary in the mid-1870s.[72] By the 1890s, freestanding aviary cages housing colorful troops of small European or Asian finches were popular. Some enthusiasts even maintained "bird rooms" where birds could fly freely or built large screened enclosures indoors.[73]

Store-bought parrots were expensive and far less common than smaller caged birds, and they loomed large in the lives of the families that owned them. With care and luck, they lived for many years, although the author of one small book of pet-keeping advice noted that "from the number of these birds that find their way into the hands of the taxidermist, we may be sure that a good per cent of them do not live the allotted years of Parrot-life."[74] Edie and Ellen Emerson shared a small green parrot named Polly for at least eleven years. A letter written in 1857, when Ellen was eighteen, contains a lively observation of parrot behavior:

The other day came a thunderstorm and Polly came in absurdly frightened. She amused herself by going upstairs like a little child, hanging herself by her beak on the edge of the next stair and then clawing up. Presently Father came down stairs and Polly creaked with dignity to warn him of her presence. Father, looking about, beheld this dear animal patiently coming upstairs, her colours matching the carpet so beautifully that he called to Edie to come and "take away her green cat for no one would see her on the carpet." We said we would but forgot, and by and bye came Mother down. Dear Poll! Mother didn't see her and, catching her in her skirts, whisked the alarmed and indignant beauty down several stairs "Squacking" as loud as she could, Mother equally surprised at the fluttering and noise under her skirts. Released from her entanglement, Poll, with ruffled feathers and wounded dignity continued her ascent but was met at the top of the stairs by Edie and the Cage and carried into my room to sleep.[75]

Then, as now, parrots were demanding pets. They required strong, expensive cages and stands because they chewed them with their powerful beaks; their wings required clipping if they were to be let from their cages. They threw their food around (including expensive, out-of-season fruits and vegetables), screamed when they were bored, and fell ill when they were exposed to drafts. Although they were promoted as superb company, not everyone liked living with them. The case of another Polly, a sulfur-crested cockatoo who resided with the extended family at Cherry Hill in Albany, New York, is instructive.

The spoiled pet of Harriet Elmendorf, Polly was living at Cherry Hill by 1874. Polly was smart; she was also bad-tempered and noisy. A memoir of daily life at Cherry Hill recalled that the cockatoo "would shout 'whoa' & 'get up' to horses going up steep McCarty Ave & pray O'Lordy Lordy in imitation of the Gospel Tent next door (our lawn)."[76] When Harriet's daughter Hattie and her husband, John W. Gould, moved to northern New Jersey in 1884, Polly was often shuttled back and forth with her owner

between there and Cherry Hill.[77] Sometimes Harriet left Polly
with Hattie and John. A letter from Hattie suggests the trials of
living with the bird while her mother visited a cousin in Philadelphia: "Polly is well & behaves better. She has a good deal to say
during the day, but goes to sleep exhausted at night, which is all I
care for. Minnie [the housekeeper] does take good care of her,
but . . . sometimes when Minnie scolds her, she screams for me,
'Hattie' at the top of her lungs. . . . [Minnie] says Polly won't be as
glad to see you as she will."[78]

By 1895, John Gould, ordinarily a pet-lover, detested Polly
and no longer wanted her in his house. On 25 November, he
wrote a letter from his New York City office to the housekeeper
at Cherry Hill, making a desperate offer. "Ma [Harriet Maria El-
mendorf] is coming to us this week for the Winter and is worried
about that 'Bird of ill Omen' Polly that I decline to have in the
House where I am. . . . I would give $5.00 gladly [if] the D-/
beast would die or be found so by any means. A bunch of Pars-
ley a pin in her back or a Brick or flat Iron droped on her. If you
can accomplish this I will send you the above amount only keep
it to yourself and I shall. . . . Dont let Ma. or Mr Rankin know I
have written you."

On first reading, the letter seems to be in jest, but there is a
postscript under Gould's signature: "Be careful what you say best
say nothing, as I am writing to Mr Rankin today & he will tell you
the news."[79] The assassination plot apparently died aborning, for
Polly outlived Harriet by more than a year, finally expiring in
1899. According to one of the Rankin children, she was "70 more
or less year of age," had "very few fethers on her," and was blind
in one eye. A family friend agreed that Polly was no longer "a
thing of beauty."[80]

FIGURE 1.13. Fishing, *colored lithograph, E. B. and E. C. Kellogg, Hartford, Connecticut, publisher, between 1842 and 1848. Library of Congress, Division of Prints and Photographs. This print is evidence that cats were just as fascinated with captive fish in the nineteenth century as they are today. The printmaker chose to depict a very unusual, long-haired white cat.*

Beneath the Waters

Some pets were, of course, highly ephemeral and were little mourned when they passed on. The sentience of goldfish seems to have been much less important than their looks as living art objects, and no one argued on behalf of their moral character. An 1855 article in *Godey's Lady's Book* pointed out that "few objects can be more ornamental or amusing than a glass globe containing gold fish. The double refractions of the glass and water represent them, when in motion, in a most beautiful variety of sizes, shades, and colors, while the two mediums, glass and water, assisted by the concave-convex form of the vessel, magnify and distort them;

besides, we have the gratification of introducing another element and its beautiful inhabitants into our very own parlors and drawing-rooms."[81]

The concept behind the Victorian balanced aquarium was a good bit different from the living-jewel approach to the parlor goldfish. The insight leading to the aquarium was first articulated by an English surgeon and amateur entomologist named Nathaniel Bagshaw Ward. Ward discovered in 1829 that a chrysalis he had stored for the winter in a closed jar had not hatched but that two seedlings had sprouted and were thriving in the damp dirt in the bottom of the bottle. The almost airtight glass case seemed to sustain itself as a closed system indefinitely. Ward began to experiment with growing ferns in what came to be known, appropriately, as Wardian cases; these became prominent ornaments in well-to-do houses on both sides of the Atlantic in the late 1840s. Soon after his initial observations, Ward successfully introduced a miniature pool of fish, a small lizard, and a toad to closed environments, but the "aquarium principle" was not fully developed until 1850, and then by a chemist named Robert Warington. He explained that plants added to water in a container would give off enough oxygen to support animals, as long as their numbers did not grow too large; he himself had kept "two small goldfish and a *Valisneria spiralis* plant together in a twelve-gallon tank for almost a year without changing the water." The English aquarium craze was then launched by a naturalist named Philip Peter Gosse, who helped to create and stock an aquarium at the London zoo in 1853 and published the first manual, *The Aquarium,* in 1854. It was he who coined the term after flirting with the alternatives "vivarium" and "aqua-vivarium."[82]

The typical aquarium collection of pond flora and fauna or the contents of tidal pools was intended to serve the purposes of nat-

FRESH WATER AQUARIUM.

FIGURE 1.14. *Frontispiece, Henry D. Butler,* The Family Aquarium; or Aqua Vivarium, *1855.*

ural history more than the aesthetics of parlor life.[83] American-published aquarium books appeared by 1858, with Arthur M. Edwards's *Life Beneath the Waters; or the Aquarium in America* and Henry D. Butler's *The Family Aquarium; or Aqua Vivarium.* The latter suggested that an aquarium could be fitted up in almost any kind of glass container, which was important since the book's description for making a rectangular tank of expensive plate glass with a slate base failed to include a recipe for a viable cement. The next year, Ellen Tucker Emerson reported in a letter that "our great interest here for the past forenight has been Eddy's aquarium," made from a recycled goldfish globe. It contained "a minute copper-colored salamander, a few snails, and some remarkable and interesting creatures who swam on their backs by waving light green fringes, also a skater, and a great many very little bugs and worms."[84] This kind of miniature community probably required constant infusions of new creatures, since amateur aquarists often tried to maintain predators and their prey in the same container, and juvenile animals like tadpoles eventually grew legs and escaped if they were not returned to their natal waters.

Popular interest in aquariums was given a boost by the availability of warm-water tropical fish in the early twentieth century. Because of the expense of importing and caring for such fragile creatures, tropical fish were for adult men with deep pockets until the late 1920s. At that time, hardy "livebearers" such as guppies became available from American fish farms and were priced low enough to be carried routinely by neighborhood pet stores. The rearing of goldfish and tropical fish, a kind of aquafarming that involved scores of operations in the mid-Atlantic, lower Midwest, and Deep South, is discussed as part of the expanding commercialization of the live-animal trade in Chapter 6.

The creators and observers of household aquariums were not always amateur naturalists. Rather, they simply were entranced by the idea of possessing a hitherto mysterious world in miniature of their own creation. In 1871, Catherine (Kittie) B. Putnam, who had begun her adventures in fish keeping with goldfish purchased in Brooklyn earlier that year, was so fascinated by the aquatic realm she created and decorated that she filled several pages of her composition book with a meditation on its charms. She described her elaborate aquarium decor and offered a useful account of the realities of feeding fish.

One would think with seven fish and six snails I ought to be satisfied but the more I get the more I seem to want. I have been looking at the distant line of blue and brown hills and thinking so hard I forgot what I was writing about but as soon as I saw the globe in front of me and the seven lively little fish swimming through the caves and around my wonderful statue of Memnon [an Ethiopian king slain by Achilles in the Trojan War] I remembered what I was writing. To morrow will be Saturday and O! what bliss no composition, no lessons. I think if it is pleasant to morrow and if nothing happens to prevent I will go on one of my much loved fishing excursions as I would like to catch just two more fish and a few snails to crawl about my statue. My fish are very fond of fleas which we catch of of [sic] Ned [the family dog] and when they were plenty, we fed them three times a day, but it has become too cold for fleas to flourish so they have disappeared much to our comfort also our dog's, for parts unknown. We try to imagine that our fish grow but it is rather hard to believe sometimes they look so small beside the large gold fish that it seems almost incredible to think so. I do believe my fish know me for when ever I come to the globe they all come out from their hiding places in the caves and some times they will take things out of my fingers they are so tame.[85]

Kittie Putnam's musings on the mysterious small world she had created and was able to maintain in her aquarium bring to a close this natural history of pets and introduce the next chapter, which considers the routines and realities of pet keeping in the nineteenth and early twentieth centuries and what these practices can tell us about attitudes toward animals. Noting the pleasure Kittie obviously found in the idea that her fish recognized her and in decorating the small world she made suggests that keeping pets was an avenue for self-cultivation, one of the guiding preoccupations of Victorian culture in America. The cultivated person not only enjoyed an enriched interior life but had the capacity for engagement and delight in a rich web of relationships with other people and with other things in the world, including nonhuman beings.

This kind of engagement can also be found in Nathaniel Hawthorne's published journal of a three-week stay alone with his four-year-old son, Julian, in 1851. The entries include a running account of the life of Julian's rabbit, Bunny, who was also called Spring and Hindleg. At first, Hawthorne regarded the rabbit as dull, exhibiting "no playfulness, silent as a fish," and he even wished that the housekeeper would drown it. A few days, later, however, Hawthorne wrote, "It makes me smile to see how invariably he comes galloping to meet me, whenever I open the door, making sure that there is something in store for him." Eventually the author praised Bunny's "pleasant little ways" and "character well worth observing": "He has, I think, a great deal of curiosity, and an investigating disposition, and is very observant of what is going on around him."[86]

Few of the voices of pet owners that survive in the historical record are as exquisitely self-conscious as Hawthorne's or even as young Kittie Putnam's seems to have been. Throughout these chapters, however, the feelings of ordinary people about their pets can be glimpsed through fragments of text—brief messages on postcards, letters, and published observations—and through reconstructing the ordinary routines associated with having pet animals. The skills associated with caring for fish; the thrill of exhibiting pigeons at a fancier's show; the routine pleasures of observing, training, playing with, caring for, and being loved by a dog; and even the simple company of a singing bird in a world without recorded music—all of these were expressive activities, resonant with both personal and socially approved meanings just as were accomplishments such as playing a musical instrument or doing fine needlework. To my mind, it is no coincidence that pet keeping expanded dramatically in the nineteenth century at the same time that popular access to many other kinds of personal cultivation increased in nineteenth-century America.

❧ 2 ❧

AT HOME
WITH ANIMALS

People do not often write about them, but the routines of daily life are expressive behaviors, rich with meanings. In the practice of pet keeping, the acts of providing an animal with special food, allowing it to sit on a lap or shoulder, playing with it, and caring for it when it is sick all suggest something about the attitudes and feelings of the owner. So do the most momentous occasions, when pet animals are brought into the rituals of family life: having a portrait made, celebrating a holiday, or mourning a death.

The role of pet animals in the routines and rituals of family life can be recovered in surviving artifacts and images that are the traces of behavior that is unrecorded in written records. The snapshot by Boston amateur photographer Horace Parker Chandler in figure 2.1, for example, documents the act of playing ball with the dog. It also shows the dog's close attention to a game it clearly knows, the man's facial expression, and his familiar gesture of holding the dog's paw in his hand. Thousands of objects— cages and aquariums, dog muzzles and licenses, old catnip mice, and packages of patent medicine—also survive. Whether spared the trip to the dump by sentiment, thrift, or simple inertia, these artifacts not only document the practice of pet keeping but suggest a great deal about the range of relationships between people and pet animals in the past. An astonishing number of formal studio portraits of pets survive. Pets were carried to photographic studios beginning in the 1840s. The resulting images record moments when animals participated in a social ritual that was important to people. Sometimes artifacts are actually relics that help preserve the memory of a deceased pet. When my parents carefully preserved objects associated with our dog Jenny (1973–85), her collar and a favorite squeaky toy that she played with her entire life, they were doing something that pet keepers did 150 years before them.

Printed pictures, including inexpensive popular prints and illustrated advertisements, also offer glimpses of ordinary behavior with pets. When the small printed pictures called trade cards came along in the 1870s, they put into circulation images that were considered attractive to potential customers. (Trade cards were meant to be kept, and they were often collected and pasted into albums.) Images of people and pets and of pet animals engaged in play, hunting mice, getting into trouble, or simply posing for the viewer were among the most popular printed advertisements, reflecting both how common pets were and how they behaved in the world of humans.

Both artifacts and the traditional written documents that do survive demonstrate how the thousands of tiny decisions that make up daily behavior and the more weighty decisions of special occasions constitute a constantly evolving "lived definition" of the pet. However, reconstructing the practice of pet keeping also shows that there were significant practical differences between 1890 and 1990, differences that this chapter will begin to explore. While not every person who kept pets in the past was, as my grandmother would say, "foolish" over them, some felt as much affection for their animals as any doting owner today, and many of the habits of modern pet owners were well established by the late nineteenth century. However, the lives of pets, especially city animals and young ones, were more likely to be cut off too soon, since animals suffered and died from a variety of infectious diseases for which there were no effective medicines—just as their owners did. Other circumstances of pet ownership were different, too. For example, all pet owners today will agree that modern flea control is a wonderful thing. The people discussed here struggled with limited success to control the pests on their favorites and on themselves, and their inability to control fleas, bird

FIGURE 2.1. *Horace Parker Chandler (1842–1919), unidentified man throwing a ball for a dog, 1880s. Courtesy of Historic New England/SPNEA.*

lice, and other vermin meant that pets were often forced to live outdoors, at least during the warm months. There were striking differences in attitudes toward the fertility of pet animals, too, and in public acceptance of the idea that wandering animals were a nuisance but an inevitable feature of town life. Some routine practices from the past—cropping dogs' ears closely or capturing wild birds and confining them to cages—are now controversial or even against the law.

However, these differences do not mean that pet owners in the past were not fond of their animals. Even when we look back on past behaviors and label them ill advised or even cruel, it is important to understand what was possible and what was usual in a specific time and place. It is clear that when people engaged in the practices of pet keeping, they not only changed the trajectory and quality of animals' lives, but they often changed their own. By including animals in rituals of everyday life such as writing a social letter in a dog's voice or including a pet in a holiday celebration, pet owners—whether children or adults—acted out their feelings and attitudes, enriching their senses of themselves.

Having lots of pets ran in some families, just as it does now. While enthusiastic, pet-loving families were not the majority of American households, they represent one end of what we might think of as a spectrum of emotional attachment to nonhuman animals. Some Americans viewed animals generally as instruments for their purposes and would not think of keeping any creature that could not pay for itself or of cuddling an animal or of expending family resources on special food or medicine. At the other end of the spectrum were folks who clearly preferred animals to people. But most pet-keeping families operated somewhere in between these two poles—as most do today.

Closeness

One of the most important yet unremarked behaviors of pet keeping is how close people allow their pets to come and whether they pick them up, stroke them, or handle them gently (see fig. 2.2). Touching an animal or keeping it in close proximity does not require emotional closeness, but it can encourage it. In the past, Americans living in both town and country were used to working close to animals. Helping a cow deliver a calf stuck in her birth canal, gutting a freshly killed pig, shoveling small mountains of manure out of the barn, or sticking a hand under a hen to check her eggs were tasks requiring familiarity with handling living animals and the products of their bodies. The proximity and contact associated with pet keeping shares some characteristics of work with animals. Administering medicine to either a carriage horse or the family cat requires deft coercion. The proxemics of pet keeping also has distinctive characteristics. Pets have often shared the living spaces of the people who own them, and many pet animals enjoy—and some actively solicit—the holding, cuddling, and patting our society otherwise permits only between adults and young children, close relatives, or lovers.

In the past, allowing animals into the living space of a family and holding or stroking them were behaviors that generated little self-conscious commentary. After all, people did not write much about how close they let other people come to them, either.

FIGURE 2.2. *Unidentified man holding cat, photographer unknown, postcard, 1907–15 (American). Author's collection. This scene, captured in this instance by an amateur photographer, undoubtedly took place in tens of thousands of households. The man's hands are relaxed; this cat is happy being in his lap.*

Evidence of welcoming pets into family rooms to keep company with the people there, allowing animals to lie on beds or sit on furniture, encouraging them to come near, and stroking or cuddling does occasionally turn up in written sources, however. Closeness is particularly well documented in popular prints and photography. Even occasional complaints about cuddling and indulging animals can tell us what some people did routinely.

Photographs throughout this book provide ample documentation of people holding their animals in their laps or posing with their heads close to the animals'. Information on where animals lived, however, has to be gleaned from a variety of sources. These days, most family dogs spend much of their time inside enjoying the central heat and air conditioning, and many cat owners have chosen to make their pets strictly "indoor kitties." Family dogs and cats in the nineteenth and early twentieth centuries lived more of their lives outdoors. Well into the twentieth century, many city and suburban houses had outbuildings that were often pets' primary shelters, especially if the animals were large or still worked for their owners. For example, owners needed cats to prowl attics and sheds and hunt the rodents that lived off the goods of the pantry, spilled livestock feed, and family trash. Rabbits, bantam chickens, and fancy pigeons usually lived in outbuildings or outdoor hutches because of their numbers and the mess they made, although their distance from the family parlor should not be taken as an indication that they were not loved by their juvenile owners. Doghouses, ranging from elaborate miniature versions of human dwellings to a large wooden barrel laid on its side with a hole cut in one end as a door, also were common features of house yards (see fig. 2.3). To keep them from wandering, dogs were often chained to their houses at least part of the time, so they were important as real shelters. During the warm months in the northern states, and in warmer climates generally, dogs and cats were more likely to live outside because of the fleas they harbored.

Many family dogs and cats, however, were allowed to spend at least some time indoors. If housekeepers were fastidious, pets might be confined to the kitchen or have a nighttime bed near the banked fire in cold weather. In January 1833, Deborah Norris Logan called the dining room she heated with a stove "dog paradise." She also shared her retreat with a "black buck cat" and two cage birds; all but the birds were ejected for the night, however.[1] A letter written by Hattie Stowe, one of Harriet Beecher and Calvin Ellis Stowe's twin daughters, to her father in February 1852 described "what everyone in the dining room in the large yellow Titcomb house on top of the hill is doing" on an evening. Nine people were gathered together in that single heated room, including Harriet Beecher Stowe, who was working on the manuscript for *Uncle Tom's Cabin* (her powers of concentration were prodigious). Rover was there, too, "lying under the table on his back in a very interesting manner with his four legs . . . strait up as the mast of a ship fast asleep" while two kittens frolicked around.[2]

Letters and diaries sometimes offer glimpses of cats and dogs indoors behaving in ways that we recognize: "Spot sleeps on the Blue room bed and had a thrashing therefor this morning which he took without a growl. I have not had any trouble with him as to the chairs lately as I have given him a blow or two for that already."[3] In 1848, New Yorker Philip Hone commented that his dog Brandt was "fond of being caressed" but repaid the honor by jumping "to the injury of silk gowns and white pantaloons."[4] Samuel Canby Rumford recalled that his mother's black-and-tan terrier "was deathly afraid of thunderstorms and would spend the

FIGURE 2.3. *George E. Brown, Portland, Maine, family of pugs outside its doghouse, cabinet card photograph,* © *1886. Library of Congress, Division of Prints and Photographs.*

whole of each Fourth of July under a bureau in the bathroom."[5] Tidbits of information about animals indoors also appear in surprising places. When *Hill's Manual of Social and Business Forms,* a popular one-volume "cyclopedia" with articles as wide ranging as "How to Collect a Debt" and "Rules for Writing Poetry," included a list titled "Bad Manners at the Table" for its aspiring readers, it mentioned "Feeding a dog at the table."[6] Popular prints and advertising trade cards often featured images depicting a child trying to eat while household pets beg for or even steal his or her dinner (see fig. 2.4). Documenting the physical closeness of people and pets is easier once home photography became common in the 1880s. Camera owners took thousands of snapshots of friends and family posing, playing with, or holding animals on the front porch or in a family sitting room, everyday behavior that is largely missing from studio portraits.

Allowing a pet to sleep in bed with humans seems to have been more rare in the past than it is today. More than one-third of dog owners sampled in a recent survey admitted that their dogs sleep on their beds at night.[7] By the late nineteenth century, training advice for pet dogs did point out that a house dog needed a spot all its own and included the command "Go to bed."[8] Most family dogs probably retreated to a corner or a strip of old carpet or blanket, but wicker dog beds were available in pet stores by the turn of the century. Very privileged animals sometimes even enjoyed custom-upholstered quarters, as evidenced in figure 2.5 by the "oriental" pet bed of pink velveteen from the Back Bay home of the Gibson family of Boston. While two-thirds of cats stay indoors at night these days, only about 10 percent of owners report that their cats sleep on their beds, which is probably a function of cat behavior rather than human preference. However, in 1873, Samuel Clemens wrote to his wife, Olivia, who was away visiting family, that he allowed their cat and all its kittens to sleep with him and "have the run of the house. I wouldn't take thousands of dollars for them. Next to a wife I idolise, give me cat." The Clemens family cats generally seem to have lived indoors but were unceremoniously banished to the cellar at night (another common practice), at least when Mrs. Clemens was home.[9]

Proximity had its limits with large animals and small, cage-bound creatures. When family horses became special favorites, for example, affection had to be expressed outdoors, with rubs,

"Dere aint go'n'er be no leavin's"

FIGURE 2.4. *"Dere aint go'n'er be no leavin's,"* postcard for Egg-O-See Cereal, 1907. Author's collection. *The company used this postcard, depicting what was apparently a common scene of pets begging at the breakfast table, as a giveaway at the Jamestown Exposition of 1907.*

pats, hugs, and treats. Small pets were difficult to hold, but their cages could be kept close by. The houses of small pet animals were probably carried around and clustered in family living areas.[10] Bird owners displayed their favorites and gave them fresh air by hanging their cages in windows during warm weather. Bay windows were good places to hang the canary's cage among a collection of houseplants, and thus a tiny indoor paradise was created. Cold and the absence of central heating meant that birdcages, like fish globes, were moved into heated family sitting rooms or placed near the kitchen range, which radiated warmth continuously during cold months. Women also brought cage birds into their kitchens for company during long workdays, a practice that survived in my family through the 1940s.

While cuddling most birds was out of the question, they were sometimes let out of cages to fly freely or to play, as we have seen with the little parrot belonging to the Emerson sisters in Concord, Massachusetts. Bird owners interested in taming their birds to light on their fingers or to climb a tiny ladder could refer to guides such as *Mlle. Loretta's Art of Training Birds* (ca. 1880). Cage birds were also the first pets to be offered the array of treats and toys that we now assume are a routine part of pet care. Bird keepers added baths, sunshades, cuttlefish bones, perches on springs, or swings to cages to improve the domestic comforts of their pets. Patented innovations in birdcages and their accessories reflected this concern about kindness and some ambivalence about cage life altogether. Bradley's Bird Swing, patented in 1870 by Thomas H. Bradley of Washington, D.C., "exercises cage birds, makes them healthy, and improves their singing. . . . Actual observation has

FIGURE 2.5. *Pet pavilion from the Music Room, Gibson House Museum, Boston, Massachusetts, cotton velvet and wood, maker unknown, 1890–1910. This custom-upholstered miniature pavilion was made to match the overstuffed, Turkish-style furniture in an upstairs sitting room.*

proved that a Canary-bird, after using this swing for a while, will occupy it upwards of *three hundred times* each day, and then swing itself to sleep at night; thus clearly showing that the monotony of prison life is relieved by the use of the PATENT SWING."[11] The American Songster (patented 7 September 1880) was an expensive little gizmo that consisted of a life-sized painted figure of a bird on a perch, mounted atop a whistle with a long rubber tube. The owner was meant to put the whistle in the cage and blow through the tube, producing a warbling sound that would encourage a bored or lonely captive "to start up its best notes immediately."[12]

Not everyone approved of pets in the house or cuddling, of course. In the great era of American public health reform in the early twentieth century, some people apparently accepted the argument that animals in the house were yet another disease vector affecting vulnerable children. Henry Bishop, who operated a large bird and fish store in Baltimore, felt compelled to address this concern in his 1912 *Treatise on Birds and Aquaria*. He contended that meeting the requirements of caged pets for sunlight and fresh air actually made houses more healthful for people.[13] Other grumpy commentators fretted about the indignities of fond treatment. In 1915, the author of *Pets for Pleasure and Profit* huffed that "there is no excuse for pampering, constant fondling, dressing up in clothing, and other ridiculous customs" among pet owners.[14] He was swimming against the tide, however. Pet owners in the past knew that holding and stroking an animal was a satisfying emotional experience and that the animals themselves demanded it. Part of the fun of having a small dog or tractable cat was dressing it up (see fig. 2.6).

Naming was another symbolic way for people to express psychological closeness. Keith Thomas made giving an animal a name one of the first criteria for pet keeping, and it was important. But not all pets had names. Dogs were sometimes just called Dog, while fish in an aquarium were too numerous (and too transitory) to merit individual monikers. Animals such as working livestock, who clearly were not pets, almost always had names a farmer behind a plow or a milker had to be able to call out when giving commands. Naming animals and the kinds of names chosen were motivated by many factors: practical necessity, folk custom, humor or whim, and affection. Some owners, such as Samuel Clemens, were imaginative in naming pets. In fact, Clemens named all the family pets, a practice that resulted in dogs named Hash, I Know, You Know, and Don't Know. Letters published in children's magazines shared fanciful names such as Lucinda Virginia Daisy Petikins Josephine Snowpaws for a cat.[15] Other owners simply relied on the physical or personal characteristics of animals to cue their names (Beauty, Blackie, Bounce, Frisky). Tradition shaped many common choices. The use of the name Tom and the term "tomcat" for male cats apparently grew out of an old practice of using the nickname to represent an ordinary man; by the mid-eighteenth century it was applied to cats.[16] Lots of well-loved cats were simply called Pussy or Puss, a name that dates back at least to the first half of the sixteenth century. Parrots were called Polly or Poll as early as the late sixteenth century, and cage birds were referred to as Dicky during the late eighteenth century.[17] Sometimes pets were named after historical figures, authors, or literary characters. Quite a few dogs in the first half of the nineteenth century carried classical names like Caesar or Pompey, which reflected the classical education of boys in well-to-do families. A fad for naming dogs Carlo in the early and mid-nineteenth century may reflect the popularity of *Jane Eyre,* where a faithful old pointer named Carlo appears. Sometimes pets received the names of celebrities, such as Jenny Lind or General

FIGURE 2.6. *Jennie and Edgar Krueger's cat Tramp, dressed up in boys' clothes, ca. 1905. Photograph by Alex Krueger, Watertown, Wisconsin. Wisconsin Historical Society.*

Grant. They often bore human nicknames: Tony, Toby, Jack, Bob, Jim, and Nell. Other pet names were, by modern standards, insulting; black cats and dogs sometimes were named Nig, for example. Looking for patterns in naming animals reveals less order to the practice than anticipated. In fact, naming was only one index of pet keepers' attitudes, and many other measures of social distance or closeness have to be factored in.

Play

How people play with pet animals is another measure of changing attitudes. Although many toys for playing with pets were—and still are—improvised from bits of string or weathered balls at hand, by the 1870s pet owners could purchase toys and other gifts intended specifically for their favorites. In 1876, a small advertisement appeared in the back of *Harper's Weekly* announcing, "Fun for Kitty! Toy Mouse! Cheapest Toy in the World. Is the size and color of a MOUSE, and will run for 35 or 40 feet." Interested parties were instructed to send 25 cents (no small sum at the time) to the Bridgeport, Connecticut, address of a firm called Smith & Egge.[18] By the turn of the century, some veterinary medicine companies offered catnip balls for their tonic or medicinal properties (see fig. 2.7), a claim that sounds like what temperance-minded people said about wine consumption at the time. In 1916, *Novelty News,* a trade paper devoted to the owners of gift shops, picture stores, and other small businesses, praised a Pawtucket, Rhode Island, novelties manufacturer for introducing Catnip Mice, a classic pet toy. It recommended that shop owners keep catnip-crazed felines in their front windows to encourage the passing cat owner to "plot for his own tabby's spree."[19] In 1915, the

FIGURE 2.7. *Back cover of* The Cat, *Dr. A. C. Daniels Co., Boston, 1917 and 1924. Author's collection. The company's Summit Catnip also contained other "health giving herbs," while its patented catnip ball was guaranteed to be stimulating and amusing.*

catalog for Brooks Brothers offered rubber rings and balls for dogs in its Sporting Department. By the 1930s, however, the toys offered for pets had become more imaginative. The Sunrise Pet Supply Company of Hempstead, New York, offered both catnip toys and what seems to be the first cat scratching post (for a dollar), suggesting that more cats may have been living in places where they could no longer wander outdoors and sharpen their claws. Dogs could play with the Tug-o-War Exerciser and rubber squeaky toys shaped like fish, cat and dog heads, bones, and rats, along with a burlap rag doll containing a squeaker.[20]

Reflecting consumer prosperity after World War II as well as the renewed availability of once-scarce materials such as rubber, by the 1950s, pet stores, five-and-tens, and even department stores were carrying lines of toys specifically for pets. These toys hearkened back to humorous pet toys as far back as the 1876 windup mouse, but inventors also developed the idea that pet toys were a visual joke for pet owners, too. Squeaky toys for dogs often took forms that recalled either typical or undesirable behavior; hence there were toys shaped like rolled-up newspapers or the shoes or gloves that well-behaved dogs were not supposed to chew on (see fig. 2.8). House cats continued to play with representations of mice, while parakeets were provided with their own noisemakers. More recently, caged animals in particular are provided with toys intended to stimulate natural behaviors such as climbing or using their beaks to explore and dismantle objects that resemble what might be found in the wild. Cat and dog toys, however, are still designed to amuse owners as well as to entertain pets.

Children's letters, diaries, and essays written for juvenile magazines suggest how important pet animals could be to the emotional and play lives of the fortunate youngsters who had the extended childhood idealized in the nineteenth century. *Our Young Folks,* its successor the long-lived children's magazine *St. Nicholas,* and *Harper's Young People* often included essays about pets and letters from readers who wanted to share stories and ask for advice about their animals. They reported on the numbers of pets they owned: "I have a little kitten; its name is Tippet, and my little sister has one named Muffet. We have a lovely black dog . . . Rex, and my brother has a Skye terrier named Dandy. I have four pet ducks; they are all white, and one has a top-knot, and I call him Jimmie. My brother has three rabbits; one is an Angora, and he is beautiful, and one has two little ones. . . . We have a big black cat; his name is Toby, and he is just as old as I am, twelve years."[21] Letter writers reported pets' amusing habits, recounted the special tricks their dogs could do or how they kept their cats

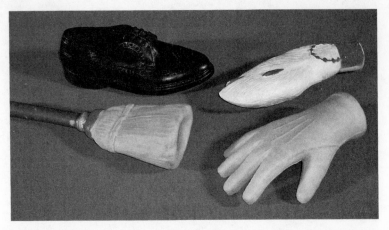

FIGURE 2.8. *Rubber squeaky toys for dogs, in the form of a shoe, a lucky rabbit's foot, a glove, and a whisk broom, 1950s, makers unknown. Author's collection.*

from bothering birdcages, and described unusual pets they had: an "old Dorking rooster named Jack," a parrot from South America that spoke only Portuguese, a pet fox that had been nursed by a cat when it was young, or a collection of newts kept in an old washbowl. They even shared disasters and pet deaths: "My cousin Ned brought a St. Bernard puppy from New York last week; but the first day [the puppy] was here he fell out of the hammock where he was swinging and broke his neck."[22]

Pets were obvious subjects for children's creative writing, too. In 1850, Helen Kate Rogers of Philadelphia wrote a poem to her squirrel Chickey, a parody on a popular verse titled "Beautiful Spring":

> How shall I woo thee dear little chick
>   What shall my offering be
> Shall I search out the woods
>   were [sic] the hickory grows thick
> And a basket of nuts bring to thee.[23]

Alice Stone Blackwell, the only child of suffragists Lucy Stone and Henry Blackwell, also wrote an ode to her cat Toby (she described her poem as "very dripping") and was much put out when her mother published the poem in the *Women's Journal* in 1872 without her permission.[24]

Other children wrote stories or playful letters in the voices of their animals. In 1838, Frederick Seward of Auburn, New York, sent a letter to his cousin Frances Adeline Worden that included a note from his cat Chitterbob to hers, named Buttercup: "My dear cousin Buttercup, I want to see you very much but I cannot come to Canandaigiua [*sic*] for the same reason that you cannot come to Auburn. I am a handsome cat and love to purr."[25] Lionel Lovering, a Newfoundland dog from New York, informed the readers of *St. Nicholas* that he could carry his own dinner of scrap meat home in a basket in his mouth.[26] In 1901, twelve-year-old Emily Rankin and her friend Grace Cogswell corresponded to each other not only in their own voices but in those of Grace's spaniel Rex and Emily's pet rooster Miles Standish; Rex even sent Miles his picture.[27] Using an animal's voice was a writing convention that had become increasingly popular among children's authors as a way of shaping perceptions of animals as sentient individuals with biographies of their own, so it is no surprise that youngsters adapted the technique for their own writing.

Keeping pet animals provided a common interest for animal-loving adults and children. Some parents were extraordinarily tolerant even by modern standards. One *St. Nicholas* letter reported on a family's pet sparrow named Bob, who had never been confined in a cage, was allowed to take "anything he wants" from the family dinner table, and slept at night in the globe of a gas lighting fixture.[28] Pets' activities and lives provided a topic for conversation and letters between parents and children, demonstrated by the 1854–55 correspondence from Peter E. Elmendorf, a doctor and gentleman farmer, to his eleven-year-old daughter Hattie while she was attending school in College Hill, Ohio. An important part of Dr. Elmendorf's reportage of everyday life at their Albany farm was about the animals on the place. (His wife, Harriet Maria Elmendorf, who shared his enthusiasm, later owned the infamous cockatoo Polly.) In a letter of 27 September 1854, he sent love to his daughter from "Pusseys, Lilly [dog], Brave [dog], chickens, Pigeons, Pompey [dog], Jenny Lind [cow], Dolly, Spot, and all the rest of the cattle." Fifteen years later, letters written to Dr. and Mrs. Elmendorf by Catherine (Kittie) Putnam, the only child and orphan of Harriet's cousin, whom the Elmendorfs raised as a daughter, also focused on the household's various pets: "I think Ned [dog] is quite lonesome without Uncle Dr. to go out with him every minute. Tip has got a sore foot and he goes on three feet. . . . The birds are very well but Eddy and he is moult-ing. The little Doves are out of the nest. . . . Ned and I went to town yesterday and every time he got in to a big mud puddle he would grumble. . . . We all send much love, also Ned and Tip."[29]

Children's play involving animals could be casual or elaborate. Emily Marshall Eliot of Boston relied on her dog Bounce as a walking companion, but he was also a playmate. In 1869, twelve-year-old Emily recorded costuming him in "my old red plaid shawl, and then I tied a handkerchief on his head and tied an old veil anon and then we played organ grinder." Bounce was a char-ter member of the Free and Easy Club (Emily, the family cat, Emily's doll Nina, and her brother Willy were the others).[30] Girls and boys played elaborate games of hide-and-seek with dogs, taught them how to fetch or do other tricks on command, and trained them to pull wagons or sleds in imitation of working horses (see fig. 2.9).[31]

The Civilized Pet

In the eighteenth century, some pet owners must have dedicated time to training their pets (surely Elizabeth Drinker would have house-trained her small dog Tartar), but information on such practices is nonexistent or fragmentary. In 1794, George Washington's

FIGURE 2.9. *Charles J. Van Schaick (American, 1852–1946), boys with dog pulling wagon, Black River Falls, Wisconsin, ca. 1900. Wisconsin Historical Society. This dutiful dog, wearing a put-upon expression, is playing the role of a horse.*

step-granddaughter Nelly Custis wrote to a friend that she had trained her parrot to sing a French song, "Pauvre Madelon," and jokingly praised his "harmonious voice."[32] Training of pet animals was informal, methods were passed from person to person, and owners did not have a literature of advice to guide their efforts.

Information on training pets became available as advice guides of all sorts appeared on American bookshelves. In the second half of the 1800s and the early 1900s, authors of training advice relied on the metaphor of "educating" or "civilizing" the animal, language that suggested both the appropriate behavior of the person doing the training and a proper understanding of the meaning of the results. The ideal of civilization, one of the guiding principles of both eighteenth-century cosmopolitan culture and Victorianism in America, perceived socialization of all kinds as a process of "raising" an undeveloped mind into a state of concord with other, cultivated members of the community. Of course, how far the uncultivated mind in question could be raised depended on its place in the natural hierarchy of creatures, a hierarchy that existed whether one believed in the old Great Chain of Being or the new Darwinian evolution. Popular writing about pets presumed, however, that the best and the happiest pet was one fully developed due to thoughtful cultivation of its physical characteristics and mental powers by a human being. While writers agreed that there were limits to the training to which most pets could be subjected, they still shared stories about felines that opened doors, squirrels that rode happily in shirt pockets, and parrots that greeted them by name. Such stories delighted their authors because they suggested that their pets had entered a special kind of membership in civilized society as companions to humans.[33]

The pet most susceptible to the civilizing process of training was, of course, the dog. The author of an 1878 book on animal training argued that because "the dog is the most domesticated and (next to the horse) the most intelligent of all animals" and "a favorite of mankind," it was our duty to "educate him in such a manner that he will not only reflect credit, but become useful to his master, besides being an agreeable inmate to all members of the household."[34] This idea of "raising" the dog into civility carried into discussions of dog training as late as the 1920s. It even included an argument paralleling an old idea about human development, that the very physiognomy of the dog was transformed for the better by civilization: "The effect of training is evidenced in the dog by his refined and dignified appearance. He develops a keen, intelligent expression as compared with the dull, stupid, sleepy look of the undeveloped dog. He becomes attractive and wins the admiration and love of all who come in contact with him."[35]

Creating a "developed" dog or cat required training in "clean habits." If animals were allowed in the house for more than short visits, they had to be taught to control their excretion. It is clear that people did house-train cats and dogs—and even an occasional rabbit—but the practice, like most kinds of pet training, was passed along by word-of-mouth and practical experience.[36] Nineteenth-century dog-training manuals had long been directed only at men who kept hunting dogs; the pet dog, especially the small lap dog, was plainly considered beneath the notice of a serious dog trainer. When dogs lived more of their lives outdoors, house-training was a casual process or perhaps never even took place. But raising a house dog required owners to be more attentive to, and able to interpret, the behavior of puppies. In 1900, one book pointed out that if a puppy had been indoors for some time and "seems to be uneasy and be smelling around, put him out at once."[37] Pet owners probably developed an informal shared knowledge of tricks such as confining puppies to kitchens or basements and training them to relieve themselves on newspaper or in a box containing sawdust, a practice that became popular as more middle-class city dwellers chose to live in apartment buildings without access to even a small back garden. Authors differed on the efficacy of punishments such as rubbing puppies' noses in their feces, but writers that scolded owners for punishing puppies too long after the offense or yelling and chasing puppies when they piddled were probably commenting on well-established human behaviors.[38]

Evidence that cats were house-trained can also be found occasionally. On 1 June 1895, Hattie Gould of Orange, New Jersey, wrote to her mother in Albany that her kitten "sleeps down stairs now. & goes to its box and scratches like an old cat."[39] However, the popularity of cats as pets clearly was compromised by the fact that their owners faced the unpleasant problem of a world without cat litter. Until Edward Lowe began to market Kitty Litter (kiln-dried granulated clay originally marketed for soaking up grease spills in factories) in 1947, families kept pans of dirt, sand, sawdust, or torn paper that had to be changed frequently. City-dwelling cat lovers were faced with the problem of having box fillers delivered in large barrels that had to be stored in the ever-smaller living spaces of apartments, which may be one reason why even urban cats were often allowed to roam.[40] By the early 1940s, some pet stores stocked the E-Z Klean Kitty Toilet, a porcelain-enamel metal pan that contained "disposal sheets" (of paper) and could be hidden from view with an optional Powder Room toilet screen. Nothing beat clay litter for absorbency, however, and Lowe packaged his product in five-pound bags that could be carried home with ease.

Notable family pets had accomplishments beyond cleanliness. Canary lovers with extra money could purchase canaries raised in special "training rooms" containing especially good singers known for their "rolling" songs.[41] Parrot owners loved their charges because of their ability to mimic sounds, sing songs, and say words like "please" and "thank you" at appropriate moments.[42] The well-educated dog was capable of "an unlimited number of amusing performances," such as shaking hands, sitting up on command, "playing dead," and balancing a treat on its muzzle, as well as more complicated tricks (see fig. 2.10).[43] In the

FIGURE 2.10. *"My pet 'Tony' 1879,"* tintype in original paper mount, photographer unknown (American). Author's collection.

1920s, newspapers and dog food companies sponsored articles and booklets by celebrity dog trainers from the Ringling Brothers Barnum and Bailey Circus and, by the 1930s, trainers from the movies, where millions of people saw dogs like Rin Tin Tin doing remarkable things.[44]

If the proliferation of advice on dog training is any guide, by the 1920s, the companion dog was an increasingly regulated creature with a wider range of typical behaviors—chasing cars, approaching other dogs, pulling on a leash, and urinating on a neighbor's shrubbery—defined as unacceptable. Training books with titles like *Dog Etiquette* (published by Ralston Purina Company in 1944) proliferated accordingly. In 1936, the American Kennel Club instituted standards for highly codified "obedience" competitions.[45] While only a handful of family dogs ever competed, this development suggests even more self-conscious involvement in dogs as an outlet for leisure time and hence expenditure. At least a few dog owners now felt they needed the advice of multiple experts when once they had simply known what to do with their pets.

Limiting Pet Numbers

One of the signal ways in which pet keeping in the past differed from modern practice is found in people's attitudes toward and methods of coping with sexual maturity and fertility. Although unwanted cats and dogs remain a significant problem in many communities, a recent survey suggested that most modern pet-lovers do not want to own sexually intact cats or dogs. At least three-quarters of the cats and dogs kept as pets are spayed or neutered, and in the last two decades animal welfare organizations have made spaying and neutering a universal requirement for adoptions.[46] Until the early twentieth century, pet owners, no matter how loving, simply had to cope with the realities and results of their animals' sexual maturity. Surplus pet stock like rabbits and pigeons could, of course, be eaten, although by the 1870s this was becoming an uncomfortable proposition for many children. Because so many cats and dogs spent much of their lives outdoors, they were more likely to have contact with others of their kind in the first place. The sexual maturity of adult cats and dogs probably had real implications for these animals' living arrangements in families. Males can be aggressive with other animals, wander in search of mates, and often mark territory, both indoors and out, while females in heat leave stains, wander, and attract numbers of ardent suitors. Wandering female dogs in heat and their admirers were also a public nuisance, perhaps even an embarrassment to high-minded people. The 1855 dog control ordinance of Philadelphia, for example, allowed licensed, collared male dogs and female dogs not in heat to "go at large," although it required them to wear a wire muzzle during the warm months. However, any "bitch when in heat, whether muzzled or otherwise," found roaming "shall be taken up and destroyed."[47]

Although castration was performed routinely on male livestock, it seems to have been rarely performed on male cats and dogs until well into the twentieth century. Skirmishes between intact male dogs and the sound of competing tomcats singing in alleys were both an annoyance in neighborhood life and a standard joke in newspaper and magazine cartoons. The presence of a class at the 1878 National Cat Show for cats of "no sex" does suggest that a few people neutered their pets. One way cat owners dealt with a pugnacious pet tomcat was simply to let him go about his business. In 1879, Hattie Gould of Albany wrote a number of chatty letters of household news including the nighttime adventures of their particular Tom-the-cat: "Tom is well, but *so* dissipated! Never comes home before two or three in the morning—sometimes later."[48] Sometimes cats disappeared "a-courting" for weeks at a time.

Despite these inconveniences, there were reasons to think twice about neutering even if a willing veterinarian was available. Taking their cues from the castration practices of livestock farmers, vets who treated small animals were sometimes cavalier about sanitary precautions for the operation. An early discussion of the surgery on cats reminded practitioners to shave the hair around the genitals, use antiseptic, and "be careful not to excise the penis by mistake." Anesthetic was considered optional, although the text warned that without it, care had to be taken not to suffocate the animal when subduing it. One textbook illustrated a tomcat restrained by being pushed headfirst into a rubber boot.[49]

Techniques for surgical spaying had been perfected before 1900 by European veterinary surgeons, but the practice seems to have been rare in the United States until the 1930s. Former large-animal veterinarians, compelled to convert their practices to pet clinics by the disappearance of the urban horse in the 1910s and 1920s, did not know how to perform the operation. One influential small-animal veterinarian even traveled the country during the 1920s demonstrating his "easy spaying and castration techniques" for novices.[50] The rarity of surgical sterilization was also due to the fact that it was, after all, major surgery—expensive, risky because of the techniques used and difficulties in controlling postoperative infection, and marked by a much longer recovery period than it is today. It is noteworthy, and unusual, that the commercial seedsmen Johnson and Stokes, who offered "rough Coated Scotch Collie Dogs" through their poultry supplies catalog at the turn of the century, suggested that customers consider spayed females, which they offered at the same price as un-neutered males ($10–15). The caption explained, "Many prefer these to any others, and they make very satisfactory housedogs; keep at home and attend to their business."[51]

As they sometimes are today, people were ambivalent about the effects of neutering their pets. Many dog and cat owners were apparently reluctant to interfere with what they viewed as natural and inevitable. They believed that the health of the animal, particularly the female, depended on its opportunity to have at least one litter, a notion that survives today despite the best efforts of animal welfare groups. (The idea's persistence is more understandable when one considers that women's health advisors routinely argued that a human female who had not borne children was less healthy than one who had.) Some early small-animal vets also argued that neutering debilitated the unfortunate subject of the operation. John Lynn Leonard, a New York City small-animal vet whose book on dog care was promoted by the popular authors Fannie Hurst and Albert Payson Terhune, argued that while spaying a bitch was "not to be recommended when avoidable," it did make more families willing to accept female puppies as pets. However, neutering males was "altogether inadvisable" because it made the male dog "exceedingly fat, lazy, and unattractive in appearance" and shortened his life.[52] Supporters insisted that cats were better pets for being "altered" and that both male and female dogs were "much less desirable as a house dog after breeding. . . . Breeding is by no means necessary to the maintenance of health, for it is possible for dogs of either sex to pass through a very vigorous existence without having a single intercourse."[53]

Even the most careful pet owners had to deal with kittens and puppies. Female cats in particular had repeated litters, since their behavior was more difficult to control than that of female dogs, who were easily confined to a cellar with occasional potty breaks or even put up on the roof of a building, like canine Rapunzels, for a little fresh air. The most common method of dealing with unwanted animals was to drown most of the newborns, sparing one infant for the mother to nurse. This practice was often implied in discussions of pets—Samuel Clemens's black cat Satan had but one kitten, Sin—but specific instructions are occasionally found. As Harriet Beecher Stowe prepared to depart with her husband, Calvin, to Florida for the winter of 1876, she corresponded with the women who would be tenants in her Hartford, Connecticut, home about her cat's impending delivery: "As to my cat—do you like cats, She has been made quite a pet of—& is going in the way of all the earth to have kittens. . . . The best way would be to have William [the handyman] kill all but one of the kits when they are a day old & then that matter will be disposed of."[54] Helen M. Winslow, a popular women's author of the turn of the century and the editor of the national magazine *The Club Woman,* was as foolish over her cats as any besotted owner today, yet she did not blink at drowning newborns. In *Concerning Cats: My Own and Some Others* (1900), her remarkable collection of anecdotes about feline lives, she discusses her own social engineering efforts frankly. She admitted that when her first cat had kittens, she had thoughtlessly drowned all three of them. The mother's suffering from her milk was so acute that Winslow gave her an otherwise doomed kitten from a neighbor's cat. Winslow kept all four of her prized Angora cat's kittens and farmed out two of them to another of her cats, a "commoner strain" whose kittens had "promptly disappeared" after their birth.[55] Of course, cats could and did foil these efforts by disappearing when the hour of birthing approached and then later returning home with a parade of vigorous older kittens less easily captured and drowned. This was so common a story that the famous New York printmakers Currier and Ives published a print called *Pussy's Return* depicting a proud mother cat followed by a parade of six bright-eyed kittens.

Excess puppies do not seem to have suffered the same fate quite as often as kittens. For one thing, there were fewer of them, since owners were more likely to be able to shield their female dogs from amorous attentions. Photographs of dogs seem to illustrate a disproportionate number of males, evidence that females were more likely to be drowned than males. Even writers on purebred dogs sometimes suggested with candor that breeders choose which puppies would be "given to the bucket and which to the world" to increase the chance that the best puppies would survive.[56]

Of course, there could be advantages to exposing children to the fecundity of the animals around their households, at least from their point of view. Bellamy Partridge, the son of a lawyer in Phelps, New York, a prosperous village near Rochester, recalled that "the mechanics of reproduction were commonplace" where animals were concerned.

Things just didn't grow—they had to be planted. Some seeds went into the ground and some went into other places. But there must always be seeds. And if there was to be a mother there must always be a father. For our cat to have kittens was no more of a miracle to us than to have radishes grow in the garden. I was well aware of the preliminary steps in either event. In the case of our cow, even the guesswork was taken out. Her affairs became vital statistics written down on a paper and tacked to the side of her stall. The name and residence of the father was there, his

age and nationality, the date of the marriage, and even the
probable birthday of the offspring.

Despite this, Partridge recalled, the adults in his life acted as if
there was "a great and mystifying difference" between human reproduction and the "goings on at the stable and the henhouse."
Children had to draw their own analogies between the realms,
because no adult allowed "even the slightest mention of the reproductive facilities or functions of human beings."[57]

Well-Being

Another way to gauge the changes in pet-keeping practices over
time is to examine people's efforts to maintain the general physical well-being of animals through feeding, pest control, and medical care. Gradually, over the course of the nineteenth and early
twentieth centuries, American pet owners engaged in more intensive routine care. They increased their use of commercial products to improve animals' well-being, and they relied more on
experts for information on the best way to preserve the health of
pets. However, as with any changing cultural practice, while the
trend is clear, its progress was uneven. Differing standards of care
did not necessarily reflect less regard on the part of pet owners.
Rather, the mixture of old practices (feeding them scraps, bathing
them with homemade soap, and doctoring them at home) and innovation found in many families was associated with limited
budgets, the absence of small-animal veterinarians, and long-
standing traditions of animal care generally.

Until the early 1900s, the only pets who regularly received
food that was prepared for sale specifically for them were cage

birds and goldfish. Bird owners could purchase bottled seed mixtures and packaged dried ant eggs and mealworms by the 1840s;
fish could be fed on commercially made wafers by the 1880s.
Even with these preparations, dedicated bird keepers and aquarists knew that the health of their charges required additional fresh
food, and they often had to provide it out of their own larders or
collect it in the wild. Fish fanciers, for example, skimmed stag-
nant ditch and pond water to collect daphnia, a minute crus-
tacean that provided food for many small predators, such as
minnows, in the wild.

The practices associated with feeding cats and dogs well into
the twentieth century suggest both the traditional role animals
played in many American households, where no food scraps were
allowed to go to waste, and new concerns that beloved pets eat
what was best for their particular needs. Commercial dog food in
the United States had its modest origins in the late 1860s; the rise
of the pet food industry is discussed in more detail in Chapter 7.
Until the prosperous decades after World War II, however, most
pets were still part of households that were used to minimizing
waste of food scraps, even in urban places, and they lived mainly
on "people food." Dogs and cats owned by poor families probably
were as malnourished as their owners. In nineteenth-century
cities, dogs and cats owned by working people were part of the
netherworld of urban scavengers that included poor people. Wandering cats kept down the numbers of rats, and cats and dogs
could dine on uncollected garbage, the offal from abattoirs and
butcher shops, and the assortment of dead animals that adorned
city streets for much of the nineteenth century. But middle-class
pets, who were also more likely to be confined at least part of the
time, thrived on the same good, plain food that their owners lived

on, either as leftovers or incorporated into specially prepared "stews" or "puddings" that added one more cooking task to women's daily routine. Butcher shops offered "dog meat," and to a lesser extent "cat meat," for sale, and there is some evidence that city dog owners collected meat scraps from local restaurants for their pets.[58]

In the early 1900s, magazine and newspaper articles directed at middle-class women published information on improving family nutrition based on the new science of home economics. This new concern for a healthy diet also encouraged interest in the nutritional well-being of family pets. The companies that produced dog food published advertisements and booklets alerting dog owners to the consequences of bad diet. Animal welfare groups such as the American Humane Association distributed free leaflets on the recommended healthy food for dogs: beef, mutton, boiled fish, stale bread, zwieback, wheat cereals, boiled onions, spinach, beans, peas, garlic, carrots, asparagus, dairy products, and meat or vegetable soups. One imagines that the daily fare for family dogs was even more varied than this. The association's listing did include "puppy cakes" and "dog cakes," the earliest kinds of commercial dog food, but only as a way of augmenting the diet.[59] Jacob Biggle, author of the *Biggle Pet Book* (1900), shared this attitude toward packaged dog food. He warned his readers to avoid feeding their dogs some kinds of people food, particularly "cake or anything sweet and greasy" (a suggestion probably honored more in theory than practice) but believed, as did most authors of advice through the 1930s, that the best practice for "dogs that have free range" was table scraps, excepting small splintery bones. Commercial dog "biscuits" (dry dog food) were "good for special occasions, but not as a steady diet."[60]

Apparently cats did not always receive the same nutritious diet as dogs because owners assumed that cats' hunting provided the meat they needed. Their kills were augmented occasionally by table scraps. But then, as now, cats were choosy about what they ate. One child reported to *St. Nicholas* that her cat would eat "dough, sweet corn, cooked potatoes, and turnips, but does n't like them very well."[61] In popular Victorian prints of a little girl feeding a cat or in children's poetry about cats, the animals receive only a saucer of milk or bread soaked in milk. Biggle represented progressive thinking about cat care when he disagreed with this custom. He recommended giving cats that caught and ate rodents a saucer of milk at milking time as a conditioner. However, he recommended that even working cats "should be fed regularly; they should have regular access to grass or catnip, which they use as medicine, and also to fresh water." Furthermore, a diet of milk and bread alone, while economical for owners, caused "indigestion and fits." Biggle argued that cats liked warm food: "a mixed diet of scraps, such as comes from the table, is the best feed for cats," along with "rice pudding" and cooked meat and fish.[62]

By the 1930s, more family cooks were unwilling or unable to service family cats and dogs. Despite the Great Depression, dog food in particular grew in popularity, and by the 1950s, the decade when women wished to spend less time in the kitchen than had their mothers, canned and bagged pet food was an important convenience food. Because pet food was regulated by the federal government, its apparent wholesomeness also helped to overcome any lingering reservations. However, since the 1970s, a handful of natural-food advocates have argued for "natural diets" for pets. Recently, the large-scale pet food industry has been questioned by both owners and some veterinarians, who argue that the quality and proportions of animal and plant proteins, along with other nutrients, are causing a new rise in chronic diseases including morbid obesity, diabetes, and kidney failure among American pets. Some owners have responded by purchasing commercially prepared organic, "human grade" pet food. Others have brought back home cooking for pets, albeit they do not use leftovers.

Increased interest in chemical pest control is another element of growing concern for pets' well-being. Even if their pets were otherwise well cared for, owners struggled with fleas, lice, and various contagious skin problems that plagued pretty much everyone in households, human or animal. The chemical methods of pest control we rely on to make indoor life with pets tolerable were unavailable to nineteenth-century families. This is another reason why many pets seem to have spent more time outdoors than their modern counterparts, especially in summer and in warmer climates where fleas are abundant.

Through most of the nineteenth century, owners of cats and dogs had few choices for controlling fleas. They could pick or comb them out of their pets' fur every day with a fine-toothed comb. Recall from Chapter 1 that young Kittie Putnam fed the fleas she pulled off her dog to her aquarium fish. Owners could also bathe their pets in the strong lye soap they used for housecleaning. By the 1880s, however, some new chemical methods for control were available. One of the most common approaches was the use of medicated soaps (see fig. 2.11). Phenol (a hydroxyl derivative of benzene), also called carbolic acid, was one of the only effective disinfectants available to hospitals and households in the late nineteenth century. The first medicated soaps for dogs contained phenol, which was also used for human skin ailments. Buchan's No. 11 Carbolic Disinfecting Soap promised to kill "all parasitic life on man and beast," while Morris Little and Son, makers of Little's Dog Soap, also produced Little's Sanitary Phenyle Toilet Soap, which it promised would both cleanse and beautify the (human) skin.[63] Medicated soap was also used to treat mange on dogs, which was much more common than today. Bathing an animal with medicated soap was a humane alternative to coating the affected animal with kerosene or turpentine, a practice that survived into the mid-twentieth century among country people. (People also used to dunk their own heads in kerosene to treat head lice.) By the turn of the nineteenth century, Lever Brothers, the makers of Lifebuoy, had realized that their product was adaptable for dog use and actually promoted it at the Westminster Kennel Club show in Madison Square Garden.[64] By the 1930s, pet owners could buy dog scrubbers that attached to a bathtub faucet and dispensed flea soap.

Another breakthrough for controlling vermin on pets was the discovery of pyrethrum (also called Persian Insect Powder), an effective botanical insecticide still in wide use by organic gardeners. Made from the crushed flowers of members of the chrysanthemum family, pyrethrum was usually the effective ingredient in preparations such as Sterlingworth Flea Killer ("For Pets That Wear Hair") and Sergeant's Infallible Flea Remedy, which was advertised for use on cage birds and poultry as well as cats and dogs in the early twentieth century.[65] Pyrethrum powder was a boon to birds because it controlled lice so effectively, and makers of bird remedies sold specialized squeeze containers to blow the dust into cages. Pet owners had to be careful not to use it near the family aquarium, however, since it was toxic to fish. By the 1930s, flea

FIGURE 2.11. *Trade card for Ricksecker's (Late Taylor's) Dog Soap, Theo. Ricksecker, New York, chromolithograph, 1880–1900. Author's collection. The advertisement on the back of the card told the story of a dog whose three baths with "that 25 cent soap" did more good than all the medicines he had been dosed with. "He feels chirp and frisky, and is handsome as a picture—no fleas, no smell." The company recommended that dogs be bathed once a week in the soap, which was about as often as many people bathed themselves at the time. Why the other pets are watching and have not hidden under the bed is a mystery.*

powders for dogs contained another botanical agent, rotenone; by the 1940s, they included the deadly pesticide DDT.

All these treatments lasted a few days at best and required continuing vigilance and repeated applications by owners. The obvious solution was to develop a way for cats and dogs to carry the means of killing fleas on their own bodies. By the late 1930s, inventors had begun to patent collars containing pads soaked in insecticides.[66] More sophisticated delivery systems had appeared by the 1960s, when pesticides were integrated into disposable plastic collars. The important breakthroughs in flea treatment since the 1980s have had two features: a pesticide for killing adult fleas and chemicals that prevent flea larvae from reaching adulthood. These include topical, monthly preventatives, which are also intended to kill ticks. Especially in warm climates, where flea control has been difficult at best, the new products have made keeping cats and dogs indoors much easier, encouraging more physical closeness to pets. Some pet owners concerned about the health effects of the new products on the animals and themselves have returned to the use of the old techniques of controlling fleas. The success of the new topicals, however, suggests that owners calculate that the benefits outweigh any potential hazards.

Assuring the well-being of pets also required that their illnesses be treated. Until after the Depression, pet owners in America were in most instances their own small-animal vets, and they relied on pet shop owners or their own druggists for practical advice. Home doctoring had mixed results. Infectious disease was the greatest killer of pet animals, just as it was for people until sulfa drugs became available in the late 1930s and penicillin arrived in the late 1940s. Even the best-tended pets rarely lived as long as they often do today.

What is interesting about home doctoring of pets, however, is not its lack of efficacy (human medicine suffered from the same difficulty) but the commonsense view of the similarity between animal and human bodies that shaped the practice. This sense of commonalities in how diseases acted on bodies underlay practices such as vivisection for the purposes of medical research, but it also contributed to the development of a popular ethic of kindness to animals (the subject of Chapter 3). People just knew that animals felt pain as they did and that the underlying causes of diseases were the same, too. Until the germ theory of disease was widely accepted, pets suffered from "overstimulation" or "excess heat" in their systems (just like people); they had surfeits of bodily fluids requiring the use of emetics, purgatives, or even bleeding (just like people); and they required bland "sickroom diets" to get back on their feet (just like people). People doctored their pets as they doctored themselves, using traditional remedies and patent medicines, some of which were intended for use by both human and nonhuman sufferers, and alternative forms of medical treatment, such as homeopathy. There was one important difference: the decision not to treat and to end the life of a suffering animal often came sooner than it does nowadays. Still, even here the parallels with typical attitudes toward human disease and death are clear. People seem to have been more willing to accept death as an inevitable outcome, and while family members did not euthanize people, it seems clear that they often had to accept nature taking its course.

Dog owners particularly feared distemper, which is caused by a virus in the same family (morbillivirus) as human measles. It was widespread and fatal at least half the time in puppies, which may be why many people favored purchasing adult dogs. One booklet on dog diseases reported, "About the first question the buyer of a dog asks a seller is, 'Is it over the distemper?'"[67] Distemper was a particular problem in cities or wherever dog populations were concentrated, because the virus not only passes through the mucous and waste products of dogs but is subsequently borne through the air. Distemper was no respecter of fine breeding. People interested in entering the dog fancy were advised not to bring young purebred dogs to shows unless they had survived the disease.[68] Remedies for treating dogs with distemper were an important part of the product range of companies making over-the-counter veterinary medicines, but most antidotes probably did little to relieve the symptoms except to knock the patient out. The fever, vomiting, diarrhea, and seizures from a full-blown case were often so severe that euthanizing the sick dog was the merciful thing to do. My mother recalls that her father, a gentle man who loved dogs, felt compelled to shoot their spitz Chincapin in 1930 because her suffering was so terrible.[69] Dogs that did survive distemper, which took several weeks to run its course, were often permanently weakened by the experience. Some were subject to other opportunistic infections; others suffered from chorea (permanent tremors). The best hope lay in prevention through immunization. Successful research to find an effective vaccine against distemper was funded in Great Britain by sporting groups in the 1920s. American vaccine research was prompted partly by response to this triumph and partly by the fur industry, where the virus swept through fox farms. A number of effective vaccines were available by the 1930s, including one for feline distemper, which is actually a different disease called feline panleukopenia.[70]

Rabies was always fatal, of course, although much more rare. Because it was transmitted to humans through animal bites and the resulting disease was a death sentence, public fear of the malady led to campaigns every summer during which stray or wandering dogs were shot or clubbed by working-class men or boys for bounty payments. Community dog laws also authorized police to shoot stray dogs or dogs that bit anyone. However, owners could protect their dogs by signaling both ownership and harmlessness with collars and muzzles. The 1828 and 1855 Philadelphia dog ordinances required that dogs wear both a metal or leather collar engraved with the owner's name and address and "a substantial, safe, wire-basket muzzle, enclosing the whole mouth" during warm months.[71] Dogs in certain "rural districts" within the city limits were exempted. The spread of muzzling laws probably inspired *Godey's Lady's Book* to provide the instructions for a small crocheted dog muzzle in 1868. Although they seem to have been enforced sporadically, laws requiring muzzling for pet dogs that were not confined survived well into the 1930s. By then, several effective killed-virus vaccines were available, and during that decade communities created rabies control programs that mandated regular vaccination, at least for dogs.[72]

Pets suffered from respiratory infections, infectious mange, and other ailments passed from one to another wherever animals were allowed to roam, but especially in towns and cities where animals frequently came in close contact. Cat and dog epidemics paralleled human ones. Elizabeth Drinker reported a "Sickness and Mortality" among the cats of Philadelphia (perhaps feline distemper), with animals lying dead in the street, in the summer of 1797.[73] Pets got into fights and developed infected sores; they were accidentally burned by hot water from wash kettles or stove pots; they broke bones; they ate poisons. Poor living conditions caused another set of problems. Cage birds suffered from diarrhea, constipation, colds and asthma, and sores on the feet from spoiled seed, drafts, and dirty cages. Rabbits in dirty, damp hutches got the "snuffles." Especially in the South, dogs developed "black tongue," or pellagra, a nutritional deficiency that also plagued people. Like people, cats and dogs also suffered from several kinds of worms because of contact with the feces from other infected animals.

For most owners confronted with these health crises, the only option was home nursing. A handful of small-animal specialists appeared as early as the 1880s, but few veterinarians were interested in the problems of "useless" pets.[74] Even college-trained practitioners, who were, in effect, the mechanics for the urban transportation system's engine, the horse, were uninterested in the problems of the family dog, cat, or canary.

As a result, pet shop owners often became "doctors" because they had more practical experience with the diseases of small animals than did veterinarians. In 1884, George Walton, a Boston dog dealer whose regular advertisements in city directories suggest his ambitions for his business, described himself as both "Dog Doctor, and Dealer in Choice Breeds of Dogs . . . Sick dogs visited at their Homes at the Request of Owners." (He also sold "Dog Biscuits, Dog Medicines, Dog Muzzles, Imported Dog Collars, Mange Cure and Flea Soap.")[75] Pet shop owners were the only practitioners available for other small animals. They dispensed proprietary medicines, offered written advice, and did the hands-on doctoring. They remained the primary care providers for rodents, small exotics, and reptiles until quite recently. Edward S. Schmid, owner of Schmid's Bird and Pet Animal Emporium in Washington, D.C., included lengthy instructions on caring for rabbits with colic, constipation, and "snuffles or influenza" in his catalog and price list for

1903. Owners nursing a rabbit with flu were advised to give it a vaporizer treatment with steam containing oils of eucalyptus and camphor and "sanitas oil," a disinfecting compound, inserted into a hutch covered with sacks: "Treat in this manner for ten or fifteen minutes, care being taken that the invalid is not suffocated by the operation."[76] In the late 1920s, *Pet Dealer,* a trade magazine for the business, noted with approval that pet shop owners added to their incomes by doctoring the animals and birds they sold.[77] By that time, shops also carried an increasingly complex array of patent medicines for small animals, some of which store owners had developed themselves.

Money, more than sentiment, probably inspired the first veterinary education directed at treating dogs. As the canine fancy developed and purebred dogs became very expensive and valuable, breeders pressured veterinary schools to include canine medicine in their programs. The University of Pennsylvania Veterinary Hospital had a ward for dogs soon after it opened in 1884. When the college established a new veterinary hospital in 1908, it contained a small-animal section with "a canine operating room, instrument room, sterilizing room, a dark room for diseases of the eye," and "three large non-contagious wards and two separate wards for contagious diseases." By that time the hospital was already serving more dogs and cats (2,929) than horses (2,334), a fact that suggests a latent demand among pet owners.[78]

By 1900, some large-animal vets in cities had expanded their practices to include smaller creatures. Dr. J. J. Maher's Veterinary Hospital for Horses, Dogs, and Small Animals, located in a livery stable building on Marshall Street near the Sixth Street Farmer's Market in Philadelphia, offered both evening clinic hours and free ambulance service for dogs. Maher was not the only vet with a dog ambulance. Around the same time, Robinson's Veterinary

Hospital in Washington, D.C., bought a miniature wagon from the Connecticut Pie Company of the same city and used it to transport sick animals (see fig. 2.12). By the early twentieth century, the biggest and most advanced small-animal veterinary practices were located in big cities and were often associated with the animal welfare organizations that had been founded beginning in the late 1860s. The most famous, George S. Angell Memorial Animal Hospital, was opened by the Massachusetts Society for the Prevention of Cruelty to Animals in 1915.[79]

FIGURE 2.12. *Photograph of dog ambulance for Robinson's Veterinary Hospital, Washington, D.C., ca. 1897. National Museum of American History, Behring Center, Smithsonian Institution. This miniature wagon was built for the Connecticut Pie Company and was later sold to Dr. Robinson. It is now in the collection of the Smithsonian Institution.*

By the 1910s, however, private small-animal clinics were still often crude facilities whose sanitary arrangements did not parallel those in hospitals for people. Because so many vets had been large-animal practitioners first and were used to working in barns, they did not understand that human clients expected a different level of comfort for their small animal companions. Guidance on setting up and managing small-animal practices began to appear in the journal of the American Veterinary Medical Association in the 1910s. According to one expert, the modern pet hospital of 1928 contained "reception rooms, office, examination-room, operating-room, kitchen, store and drug-room, washroom, and wards for the patients." Its windows and runs were screened to keep out flies, its hot water and heat were plentiful, and its walls and ceilings were painted with easy-to-clean white enamel. Further, the clean and neat appearance of the vet himself, as well as that of his attendants, was newly important.[80]

Just as they nursed themselves and called on doctors for only the most serious ailments, however, pet owners diagnosed and nursed their own sick animals at home. People fell back on the techniques they used on themselves when treating their pets. In 1847, the sailors aboard the barque *Hollander,* bound from New York City to Rio de Janeiro, discovered that the captain's dog had eaten some rope and was constipated, so they gave him an enema using what was probably the same syringe they used on themselves. What makes this case so unusual—and worth citing even though it is not, strictly speaking, an example of home doctoring—is that one man onboard preserved the episode for posterity with an ink sketch in a log book (fig. 2.13).[81]

People also dosed their pets with the same over-the-counter remedies and coddled them with the same invalid cooking they used on themselves. When Pixie, a tiny puppy belonging to the

FIGURE 2.13. *"The Dog Jack becoming constipated by eating rope yarns is operated on by the Captain," journal of John Codman (1814–1900), recording the voyage from New York City to Rio de Janeiro of the barque* Hollander *in 1847. Courtesy of Historic New England/SPNEA.*

Gould family of Orange, New Jersey, fell through the balusters of the stairs, her owners rubbed her with Ponds Extract (a trade card from around that time called the remedy "the Unequalled Vegetable Pain Destroyer").[82] Dr. George Watson Little, perhaps the first American celebrity small-animal veterinarian and author of the popular *Dr. Little's Dog Book* (1924), informed his readers that a number of the remedies in their own medicine chests were suitable for their canine charges. He recommended paregoric (a mild opiate) for teething puppies; it was also used at the time for babies in the same unhappy state. Castor oil and milk of magnesia were both recommended for canine constipation, and La Grippe tablets, cough syrup, and chamomile or creosote steam baths were prescribed for respiratory infections.[83] Owners were advised to feed sick cats and dogs on rice gruels and beef tea, standard "strengthening" foods for human invalids at the time.

While makers of veterinary patent medicines in the United States were offering a variety of commercial remedies for livestock by the mid-nineteenth century, it was some time before they discovered that there was a lucrative market for cat and dog medicines. Lines for pet animals often began as preparations compounded and sold to clients by veterinarians or druggists. Their apparent (or devoutly wished-for) efficacy eventually led their makers to prepare them in quantity and brand them. By the 1910s, companies such as Polk Miller Products Corporation (the maker of the Sergeant brand) of Richmond, Virginia, the H. Clay Glover Company of New York City, Dr. George W. Clayton of Chicago, and Dr. A. C. Daniels Company of Boston were selling full lines of medicines for dogs through feed stores and neighborhood drug stores. They also offered a lesser selection for cats, who were often simply dosed with small quantities of dog remedies. Medicines for distemper, respiratory infections, mange and other skin diseases, ear canker, and worms were the most common. Enterprising neighborhood druggists also put up their remedies for sale using guides such as A. Emil Hiss's two-volume *Domestic and Veterinary Remedies* (1908). Hiss devoted half of the second volume to medicines for livestock and pets, including rheumatism remedies for old cats and dogs and asthma medicine for canaries.[84]

The booklets that makers of veterinary remedies distributed for free also reveal how closely popular understandings of animal disease and human disease were linked to one another. At the turn of the century, for example, medicine makers suggested that pets suffered from overstimulation of the nervous system just as middle-class people did. The digestive systems of delicate dogs required pills containing pepsin or "pepsinated" foods, just like those of people with similar proclivities.[85] In the 1930s, canaries debilitated by molting needed Hartz Mountain Pep Tonic to "re-build" their blood; people dosed themselves with tonics for the same reason. One of the jokes about old-time patent medicines still in circulation regards remedies that claimed to cure "both man and beast," but even the joke suggests how deeply this intu-itive understanding of the similarities of animal and human bod-ies ran in the culture. As late as the 1940s, T. L. Marney, a Los Angeles veterinarian who produced a wide range of medicines for cats and dogs, recommended his Stimulating Liniment, Penatol Paste for clearing nasal passages, and Nu-Kote Skin Lotion, a remedy for eczema and dandruff, for both humans and pets.[86] Today, pet owners still dose cats and dogs suffering from allergies with some of the over-the-counter antihistamines people take; we use the same ointments from our own medicine chests for their wounds; and sometimes we even use liniments and ointments in-tended for animals on ourselves.

The alternative treatments or "health reforms" that swept America in the decades before the Civil War also shaped house-hold pet doctoring. Homeopathy, one of the most important forms of alternative medicine in the nineteenth century, rejected the "heroic" philosophies of allopathic medicine and its techniques of bleeding and purging to restore "balance" to internal systems. The manufacturers of homeopathic remedies for human beings sold veterinary kits containing medicines for both livestock and dogs and published their own manuals through the 1930s. Pet owners improvised home treatments that reflected other popular ideas about health reform, too. In 1866, when Harriet Beecher Stowe's Pomeranian, Bogy, had a fit, she diagnosed the problem as "too much meat," following progressive medical thought about human diet and disease. A recent convert to hydrotherapy, the "water cure," she administered a "warm bath" to the dog, and he apparently recovered.[87] Cage birds suffering from apoplexy were also subjected to hydropathic cold showers or "plunge" baths.[88] These days, pet owners interested in alternative therapies can consult websites for advice on herbal remedies and veterinarians trained in practices such as acupuncture and chiropractic manipulation.

Rituals of Family Life

Over the course of the nineteenth century, the important social occasions that marked everyday life gradually incorporated ways to display the bonds between pets and people. Two events, the important occasion of having a portrait made and the rituals surrounding death, suggest the interplay of emotions, motives, and commonsense understandings that marked pet keeping as a practice (see fig. 2.14). Pet owners were pragmatists who understood that human beings shaped the lives and deaths of animals. But they were also tied to at least some of their pets by bonds of real affection, and many wished to record for posterity the special nature of those ties.

Since the seventeenth century, having portraits made of family members has been one of the most important ways that Americans made statements about their feelings toward one another, their status in their communities, and their desire to preserve the history of their families for posterity. Our lives are now so saturated with pictures of all kinds, and so many of us live with overflowing drawers and shoeboxes of snapshots and tabletops full of school pictures and family portraits, that it is almost impossible to imagine a world where only a minority of people could own even a single image of the people they loved, much less pets that they

FIGURE 2.14. *Charles J. Van Schaick (American, 1852–1946), collie dog being posed in the photographer's studio, Black River Falls, Wisconsin, 1890–1910. Wisconsin Historical Society.*

cherished. However, until the arrival of photography in America, that was the case.

After the 1790s, in both city and countryside, thousands of Americans had their portraits "limned" by artists who were forced to travel to earn a living and who often painted signs, striped wagons, and did other kinds of decorative work to make ends meet. These pictures ranged from black silhouettes to almost life-sized views, although smaller, bust-length pictures predominated. Even the smallest portraits were relatively expensive, however. One recent discussion of popular portraiture in New England estimated that perhaps one in five households owned pictures of any kind, so portraits were scarce commodities. Still, the thousands that survive are impressive, and a rough count demonstrates a marked increase between 1800 and 1840, the year photography began to displace the painted portrait.[89]

The rarity of painted portraits in relation to all households, however, means that portraits of pets were even more scarce. Occasionally portraitists recorded being asked to render a likeness of an animal, as when Augustus Fuller wrote to his father on 1 August 1842 that he was moving from Brattleboro to Antrim, New Hampshire, "to paint Luke Woodbury some portraits and one dog."[90] Provincial artists often included pet animals in portraits of children. In some cases it is impossible to know whether the animal really existed or was simply painted in because of the increasing association of pet keeping and childhood. In other instances a specific pet animal was indeed recorded and was an important part of the picture, as in William Mathew Prior's portrait of the Morse children with their spaniel Minny (see fig. 3.11).

Once oil paints became available in tubes and no longer had to be ground, self-trained and aspiring artists were able to create likenesses of their favorites. Amateur portraits of pets are usually images of the entire animal, rather than head-and-shoulders vignettes, but painters often used other visual formulas common to portraiture of people, including the addition of pastoral backgrounds and drapery. Well-to-do customers sometimes asked local artists to make portraits of family pets. Hanna B. Skeele (1829–1901), who made her living as a painter in St. Louis, Missouri, and Portland, Maine, made a number of such portraits in the 1870s and 1880s.[91] As the dog fancy spread in the last quarter of the nineteenth century, owners of valuable purebred dogs often had paintings made of important champions, following the practice in Great Britain. Such images, which often show champion

FIGURE 2.15. *Martha Ann Knowles, age ten, with her dog, 1852. Sixth plate daguerreotype #D.6.111, photographer unknown. Courtesy of Historic New England/SPNEA.*

field dogs at work, have more in common with paintings of champion horses than with sentimental portraiture of pets.[92]

One of most remarkable aspects of the rapid spread of photographic portraiture is how soon and how often people brought animals, particularly dogs, into studios to have likenesses made (see fig. 2.15). In the 1840s, daguerreotypes were relatively expensive, but they were cheaper than a good-quality painted portrait.

Tens of thousands of ordinary Americans hied themselves to studios for "sun pictures." Individuals often had themselves depicted with things that they valued: the tools of their trades, their books, and their dogs. The mid-1850s saw the advent of the less expensive tintype, in which an image was developed directly on sensitized, thin sheets of japanned or varnished iron. The cabinet card of the 1860s, produced when a glass negative allowed multiple copies of an image to be printed onto photographic paper and mounted on cardboard, soon followed. Both processes allowed people of very modest means to possess pictures (see fig. 2.16). Exposure times necessary to capture the images were much shorter for these newer methods, too. By the 1860s, some pet owners were bringing especially calm, prized cats to photo studios. In a typical cat pose the animal was displayed on a lap or draped tablecloth, although Tiger Summers of Norwalk, Connecticut, the magnificent, eighteen-

FIGURE 2.16. *Tintype of a chubby, happy dog, photographer unknown, 1870–1900 (American). Author's collection. Notice that this dog is wearing a collar with a lock, one way that dog owners tried to prevent dogs from being stolen.*

FIGURE 2.17. *"Tiger Summers, Weight 18 lb 3 oz,"* carte-de-visite *photograph, W. A. Judson, New Britain, Connecticut, ca. 1870. Author's collection.*

pound, three-ounce subject of a *carte-de-visite,* was posed on his own small chair (see fig. 2.17).

The most common studio portraits of pets depicted owners and animals together. Sometimes dogs were posed at their owners' feet. But in a large number of pictures the subjects were carefully arranged so that the pet and the owner were shown with their heads close together, a composition also used with people and one that implied friendship or love. Posing an animal alone, however, suggested that it was a full individual in its own right. A surprising number of studio portraits of pets and their people are deliberately playful and humorous (fig. 2.18).

When photography was simplified enough to become a common amateur pastime in the 1880s, people began to document their pets in both ordinary activities and humorous poses and situations (see fig. 2.19). After 1900, the first mass-marketed camera,

FIGURE 2.18. *A pair of sports: an unidentified man and his dog posed with a clay pipe in the dog's mouth. Sixth plate daguerreotype #D.6.346, photographer unknown, undated. Courtesy of Historic New England/SPNEA. Notice that the dog has been tied to the chair to keep him in focus; however, he has moved his head (and the pipe).*

the Kodak Brownie, made casual picture taking a routine part of social life. By 1901, photographic postcards, where amateur photographs were printed onto postcard stock suitable for mailing, encouraged people to share casual pictures (see the portrait of Alice and her rabbits, fig. 1.9). "Don't you miss Barry?" asked the writer of a postcard depicting a slightly out-of-focus Boston bull terrier climbing onto the running board of an auto around 1905.[93] By that time, photographs of pets were an essential part of family archives. By the 1940s, pets were appearing in home movies; today, with the widespread ownership of video cameras, pet owners have a new genre in which to document the history of pet keeping. The ease of making videos has meant that pet owners now routinely record behaviors that rarely appear in the historical record.

The death of a pet animal presented families simultaneously with a dilemma, a lesson, the experience of grief and mourning, and an opportunity for another ritual that, like portraiture,

FIGURE 2.19. *Members of the Hawes family, Sherborn, Massachusetts, and their dogs, snapshots mounted in album, 1910s. Courtesy of Historic New England/ SPNEA. The Haweses had fun stacking their dogs on a Morris chair on the front lawn.*

marked the membership of a pet in a family. More difficulties arose when an animal's health or behavior or a family's changing circumstances raised the issue of hastening the pet's death. The practice of euthanasia marked a boundary and a fundamental difference between the pet and the members of its human family. The possibility that an animal could be euthanized labeled even the most cherished animal as not-human, a being whose claims to life depended on the people who controlled its life. Euthanasia of unwanted, old, or sick animals presented people with several awkward choices. Partly the problem was practical: how could it be done, especially in cities? So many cats and dogs were drowned in Philadelphia's Fairmont waterworks head-race that an 1828 city ordinance warned that any person who "shall entice, throw, lead, or conduct any dog or animal therein . . . shall forfeit and pay" between $5 and $50, depending on the number and size of the victims.[94] After the introduction of chloroform as the first effective anesthetic in the 1850s, animal lovers quickly discovered that it could be used to kill a suffering creature mercifully, but it was also expensive. Owners were instructed that the animal to be euthanized had to be confined in a tin box or under a tin tub with a sponge soaked in the substance.[95] Some individuals simply held chloroform-soaked rags over the muzzles of their dying pets. Shooting larger animals was commonplace; but not all Americans had access to guns, and firing them within cities was not encouraged by the authorities. Owners were not always sure exactly where to aim to cause the least amount of suffering. This difficulty led the American Humane Education Association to include instructions, with diagrams, for shooting horses and dogs inside the front cover of its famous paperback edition of *Black Beauty* in 1904.

Human emotions were the source of another dilemma. We have already discussed euthanasia of unwanted baby animals as a sad and difficult-to-avoid commonplace in households. Drowning kittens or puppies was not easy for tenderhearted people to do. Elizabeth Drinker had avoided drowning kittens for years (her sister or a servant probably did the deed). In 1805, however, fearing that her servant Peter would not do the job quickly, she "assisted to day doing what I never in my life did before, drowning 3 kittins, 3 days old. . . . The poor little things were soon out of pain. . . . I know not how it happen'd I could have an hand in such an undertaking."[96] In the 1820s, Sophie du Pont and her siblings were unable to bring themselves to drown excess kittens. Instead, they allowed them to grow up, then carried them across the Brandywine Creek and left them, hoping that they found homes with cousins and friends.[97]

Anticruelty tracts and stories suggested to children that euthanizing unwanted animals was, in fact, a particular duty of kind people. Abandoning pets as the du Pont siblings did was a practice that Harriet Beecher Stowe attacked in an essay for children titled "Aunt Esther's Rules." The wise old woman (a fictionalized version of young Harriet's own beloved Aunt Esther) informed children that "when there were domestic animals about a house that were not wanted in a family, it was far kinder to have them killed in some quick and certain way than to chase them out of the house, and leave them to wander homeless, to be starved, beaten, and abused." Taking responsibility for the deaths of such animals (here Stowe used the universal example of unwanted kittens) was "real brave humanity," but it was important that the method used be "the kindest and quickest method of disposing of one whose life must be sacrificed."[98] When she chose the word "sacrifice" to describe an unpleasant household task, she implied that killing unwanted animals was a moral act with religious overtones because it was an act of mercy, and that even the death of some animals might be for the greater good of others of their kind.[99]

Pet deaths also provided a relatively harmless rehearsal for the experience of human death. Printmakers published a number of images along this line, with titles like "First Loss." This popular print depicted a sorrowful young girl holding her dead canary. As many readers know from their own experience, children who keep small animals are presented with dead bodies frequently, and the experience rarely leaves a permanent emotional scar although it is an occasion for sorrow. However, the death of an animal regarded as a special friend or peer was a significant event in the life of a nineteenth-century child, just as it is now. When nine-year-old "Fred T." wrote to the editor of *Harper's Young People* in 1887 about the death of his dog Jack, "run over by the [street]cars last week," he said simply, "I feel as though I had lost my best friend."[100] Little Alice Hughes of Buffalo, New York, also had her first taste of personal tragedy with the death of her dog Dick. Although the dog was the Hughes children's "constant companion, gentle and dependable," he disliked strangers—and thereby he met his downfall.

> Complaints poured in, and at last he bit the postman and tore his pants and that was the finish. Buffalo didn't have an S.P.C.A. in those days but any policeman on the beat would get orders to shoot on sight when complaints came in. . . . I remember . . . seeing a crowd in front of our house looking down at something in the street, and a policeman standing with a revolver in his hand. It was poor Dick. That

I was brokenhearted goes without saying, and I wrote a long poem to commemorate the event. I can't recall it all but just the last verse:

> And they laid him to rest,
> With his paws on his breast,
>   Far, far from his own sunny home.
> And the night dew falls,
> And the breezes sigh,
>   And none but the angels and God are nigh.[101]

Alice's poem used images characteristic of the era's sentimental death poetry; she probably knew the genre well through both school readers and popular magazines. The fragment of verse suggests how bereaved pet owners appropriated and adapted the rituals and the rhetoric of funerals and mourning for people to their own needs and ends. Sometimes this was done with a certain amount of embarrassed self-consciousness, especially among adults. Most of the time, however, pet funerals were treated seriously. They allowed children to contemplate the mystery of death on a more intimate scale and to rehearse the ceremonies of their society. And pet funerals provided an occasion for children and adults to express their understanding of the place of a particular animal in their lives.

Though rare, pet funerals appear in the historical record as early as 1800. By the 1830s, both children and adults routinely marked the passing of beloved animals with ceremonies of mourning and burial. Sometimes these included homemade coffins, as when six-year-old Frederick William Seward recorded in a letter to his father the death of his "old cat": "Peter made her a box and put her in and buried her in the snow."[102] The funerary rituals accorded pets in the nineteenth century incorporated the same symbols as the funerals of people. When their dog Carlo was "murdered" in 1855, the family at Cherry Hill in Albany, New York, went into "official mourning," with both animals and people "wearing crape."[103] Sometimes pets were buried under weeping willows, an emblem of mourning.[104] In 1851, Luther Spaulding Bancroft (1804–72) of Pepperell, Massachusetts, a farmer and lifelong bachelor, did this for his dog Byron, who had lived a remarkably long life. Bancroft also recorded other details of his private ceremony and his feelings:

> Pepperell Dec 26th 1851. My Faithful Dog Byron Died this morning, Aged 18 years, I burried him this afternoon, between the hours of three and four o'clock on Mount Lebanon Hill—near a weeping willow—When I had placed his body in the grave—I fired three vollies over it and bade him farewell forever! Tears rolled down my cheeks like rain—I was alone, and I felt as though I had lost one of my best friends. That Dog [illegible] more than one half of the human race—Ah! Reader the Affections of a Dog, has made the stoutest hearts melt—Even Napoleon who could dictate the order of battle, (where it would cost the lives of ten thousand men,) with a dry eye—was once moved to tears, by the affections of a *Dog*! . . . "His Monument shall be his name alone."

> > The faithful Dog which I have loved,
> > I have followed him to his last abode,
> > The booming gun, the mournful sob,
> > Have said to him their last farewell!

> For him, far hence his Master will sigh,
> And fancy comforts yet to come;
> He'll never caress his "Faithful Dog",
> He'll only hear the booming gun.[105]

Bancroft, like young Alice Hughes, used common literary conventions—a sentimental poem, a telling anecdote, and even an epistolary address to his "Reader"—to give form to his grief.

A similar exercise in adapting conventions of mourning is found in the untitled obituary for Ponto, a manuscript dated 8 February 1866 (see "A Dog Obituary of 1866").[106] The obituary is both humorous and serious, suggesting the deep attachment of its anonymous author to its subject while making light of the inability of a second, younger dog to comprehend the meaning of Ponto's death. The author discusses the character and intellect of the dog as well as Ponto's physical beauty in youth. Ponto is described using the same literary conventions (from the perfection of his limbs to his lustrous eyes) applied to depictions of beautiful people in sentimental fiction of the era.

Funerals required graves, and graves required tombstones. H. H. Delong's memoir of an upstate New York boyhood in the 1850s and 1860s included an account of the burial of a monkey named Jocko, who was accidentally killed by a blow from an ax. His homemade headstone "recorded his virtues and a pathetic account of his taking off, embellished with a free hand picture of the axe that laid him low."[107] The Canby family of Wilmington, Delaware, had established a "family burying ground" for cats and dogs by the 1830s. It featured "two painted boards giving the names of favorite cats" and a white-painted wooden obelisk dog monument about five feet high bearing the names of Faithful Carlo, Blanquo, and others.[108] Families of means sometimes paid to have simple stone markers made for pets, such as those in the pet burying ground on the lawn of the Rundlet-May Mansion in Portsmouth, New Hampshire. Although none of these stones contains birth or death dates, the graves seem to span several decades. One of the graves is for a dog named Flora, who was carried north as a living souvenir of the Civil War.[109]

By the mid-nineteenth century, the grounds of some houses contained complex pet graveyards. Sometimes these were created by children during a period of active pet keeping but were later abandoned. At the instigation of their mother, who had been "chief mourner" at dog funerals during her own childhood, Harriet Beecher Stowe's children marked the demise of each family dog with "a canine funeral with all the requisite pomp and circumstance." The backyard of one house the Stowe's lived in was pocked with "a number of mysterious mounds" that puzzled the subsequent tenant.[110] The Rankin children had a special "bird semetry" at Cherry Hill and a separate plot for other pets.[111] Mrs. Annie Waln Ryerss and her son Robert, animal-welfare activists in nineteenth-century Philadelphia, maintained both dog and horse graveyards with headstones. They still survive on the grounds of the house, which is now a museum.

Another mourning ritual in which some Victorian pet owners indulged was having a posthumous portrait made of the deceased (see fig. 2.20). Cats do not seem to have been so honored very often, as the examples located to date have all been of dogs. Prior to photography, provincial painters sometimes made pictures of dead children so that some image would be left for the bereaved family. These pictures presented the subject as he or she was in life, although some contain inscriptions or visual clues that they were made following death—angels peek out of clouds or open gates in the background, for example. Posthumous photographs, on the other hand, clearly depict dead children.[112] Photographers often tried to soften these images, however, by taking advantage of the popular euphemism for death, eternal sleep. They arranged the limbs of their subjects as if they were asleep and sometimes posed them on a sofa or chair as though they were napping. Pictures of dogs taken after death depict the same formula. The subjects were carefully posed as if curled up for a snooze, sometimes against a rustic backdrop or on a rug, although some remarkable photos of dogs in their coffins also survive. Posthumous pet photography still survives, as does posthumous photography of people taken during viewings, as a deeply personal type of snapshot photography.

FIGURE 2.20. *Posthumous portrait of a dog, cabinet card. Photograph by K. M. Mann, Bloomfield, New Jersey, 1880–1900. Collection Judith Murphy Grier.*

Not all memorialized pets were accorded the dignity of a burial, however. In some instances, they became their own monuments through the art of taxidermy. While bird stores and natural history shops offered to stuff all kinds of pets for their owners, birds were the most likely candidates. From a technical standpoint, they were the easiest to preserve and hence were less expensive to mount than four-legged creatures. Taxidermic birds under glass were already common in Victorian interior decoration. The high cost of exotic pets such as parrots may also have encouraged a heartbroken owner to at least recoup a small part of his or her investment by converting a pet into a decorative object. While taxidermy was rarely chosen as the technique for commemorating a beloved pet, like the practice of euthanasia it serves as a reminder that the treatment of pet animals was guided by a complex set of emotional, moral, and practical discriminations. Americans would have abhorred the idea of keeping a taxidermic mount of a dead colleague or relative, but many pet animals could easily be shifted back and forth from subject to art object.

In congested cities that had no space for animal graves, most dead pets simply went out with the household trash or perhaps wound up at a rendering plant. This undoubtedly caused much distress, but there were no alternatives. By the end of the 1890s, however, well-to-do pet lovers in greater New York City without access to a plot of land had a new option. In 1896, a small-animal veterinarian practicing in Manhattan, Dr. Samuel Johnson, allowed a grieving client to bury her dog in a corner of his apple orchard on his farm in rural Hartsdale, New York. After this burial was publicized by a reporter friend, Dr. Johnson received many requests by pet owners to use his orchard. The orchard began to look like many picturesque cemeteries for people of the era, with

FIGURE 2.21. *A section of Hartsdale Canine Cemetery, Hastings-on-Hudson, New York, as it looked in 2001. Photograph by the author.*

tombstones surrounded by wire or stone "grave beds" planted with blooming plants. Pet owners were responsible for caring for their own plots until 1914, when Hartsdale Canine Cemetery became a corporation to guarantee its existence in perpetuity. Hartsdale was followed by other commercial pet cemeteries such as Francisvale in Philadelphia, founded in 1908 in association with a no-kill shelter; both cemetery and shelter are still in business. In the early twentieth century, animal welfare organizations also developed pet cemeteries on the same plots of land where they had their shelters.

Hartsdale is still a thriving cemetery in the Victorian "picturesque" tradition (see figs. 2.21 and 2.22). The epitaphs on the grave markers show that, while some dogs were celebrated as

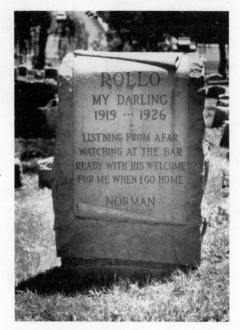

FIGURE 2.22. *A grave marker at Hartsdale Canine Cemetery, Hastings-on-Hudson, New York. Photograph by the author.*

champions or for their bravery and sense of duty (the cemetery also contains monuments to dogs used in combat and police dogs), the vocabulary of mourning associated with most cats, dogs, parrots, and other pets reflects two ways of thinking about the deceased. Many were described as friends: "Mignon, dearest and most beloved friend," "Our pal," "My Only Friend," and "Adios Amigo." An equal number present the pet as a child: "Love from Momma and Poppa," "Our Big Girl," and "Our Precious Baby." Graves sometimes depict the toys associated with the childlike animal. On recent graves at Hartsdale, it is common for pet owners to leave toys along with flowers.

How did animals become "friends" or "children"? In Chapter 3, I explore the development of what I call the domestic ethic of kindness to animals and the ensuing social and cultural changes that encouraged such personal investment. The domestic ethic of kindness changed how Americans thought about many, although not all, animals and made gentle treatment a necessary part of the character of respectable people.

THE LIFE AND DEATH OF PONTO

Departed this life, at his residence in Gorham, between the hours of ten last night, and seven this morning, the Good Old Dog PONTO, at the advanced age of fifteen years; he retired to his bed in the evening apparently in his usual health; and nothing more was known of him by the family where he resided till morning, when what remained of him that was mortal, was found by his friends lying "in the cold ground" (snow). Wheather the poor old dog suffered much while in the agonies of death, is not known; but from appearances we must come to the mournful conclusion, he had no friend near to close his eyes, or place the big Copper Cents over the dim orbs, for in the morning they were wide open, with a mighty big *Stare;* nor was that friend near to lay straight his [illegible] and comly limbs, for he was found pretty much *sprawled* about. No blame is attached to this friend, but his death is solely attributed to the visitation of the Black God of Dogs, who cometh in the night and stealeth away the life of the whole canine race, and there is no help for it.

A watcher was left with him when he retired at night, but we are sorry to say, that we fear the watcher is a gay thoughtless dog, much more given to fun, frolick, and feasting, than to looking after the sick infirm and dying. We wish not to reflect on the living, whose character has thus far been papably good it will not help the dead, we can only say, the darkness of night shrouds the whole affair, and the particulars of our old dog friend's last moments will never be known "till the last DOG TRUMP shall sound."

It was a solemn sight, this afternoon, to see that *Solitary* procession winding its way in the snow leg deep, down through the orchard, under the shadow of the stately old appletrees, followed by only *one mourner*, and as if purposely to add to the solemnity of the scene, he looked as if he was marching to his execution, head and tail down, continually lifting up his cold feet and whining most piteously. But when the last sad rites were fully performed, and the last shovel full of snow was piled up, it would have done you good to have seen this disconsolate mourner turn tail too, and make a line for warmer clime—I expect he was thinking of the *"Cold Wittles"* he should inherit, and said to himself, "there will be no division hereafter, this dog has the whole, such is life."

All of the surviving friends appear as well as could be expected under the trying circumstances. Old Ponto was a fine old dog, of the War-Horse breed, descended in a direct line from the Dons and Cavaliers of Andilusia in Spain, his ancestors were once amongst the great and noble of that far famed land, but by the viscissitudes of fickel fortune were compelled to migrate, and took up their residence in that Heaven of islands known as Cuba in the sunny climes of the West Indies, where Ponto first saw the light of the sun. When young Ponto was a dog of noble carriage and stately mein, remarcable for the beauty and symmetry of his form, his every limb was fashioned after the most perfect model, with an eye of the pure lustrous Spanish cast, made expressly to shoot love to the hearts of all, with a noble heart always yearning toward his friends, and good living. Anxious of doing right he knew no fear and was full of bravery. When excited the courage of a lion was not equal to his.

Ponto early in life shew a remarcable intelligence and desire for information, but was somewhat of a roving disposition, and becoming acquainted with a foreign sea captain was indused to take a voyage to New England, and finally settled in Gorham in the State of Maine, where he made a large circle of acquaintances, and many fast friends where he spent most of his useful life, never loosing his dignity of character, doing good continuously, to all around him, he has left many sincere and disconsolate friends to mourn his loss. But what is their loss is his gain, he has gone to his reward, and there is probably a great rejoicing in that happy land where all Good Old Dogs go to, over the safe arrival of Old Ponto.

[illegible] to Old Ponto
Gorham Feb 8th 1866

FIGURE 1. *Eddie, Emily, and Herbert with their bunnies, summer 1899. Historic Cherry Hill.*

THE BUNNIE STATES
OF AMERICA

Edward Elmendorf (Eddie), Herbert, and Emily Rankin grew up in an Albany, New York, household with a habit of pet keeping (see fig. 1). Catherine (Kittie) Putnam Rankin, their mother (who was mentioned in Chapter 1 as she considered the pleasures of her aquarium in 1870) became less enthusiastic about pets over time. Perhaps she just outgrew them, or perhaps she had been permanently traumatized by fate of her doomed pet sheep Billy (see Chapter 5). But Kittie's "aunt and uncle," Dr. Peter and Harriet M. Elmendorf, and their daughter Harriet Van Rensselaer Elmendorf (Gould), remained very fond of animals. Harriet Elmendorf, who acted as the children's maternal grandmother, was the doting owner of the infamous cockatoo Polly. Kittie and her husband, Edward W. Rankin, a lawyer, lived in her family's large, Georgian-style house, "Cherry Hill," after their marriage in 1884. They purchased the place in 1896 and remained there the rest of their lives. Edward W. Rankin had also kept pets as a boy, and he was a tolerant father. So the three Rankin children played with a changing cast of household pets, including felines Muff, Blacky, and Grahame, "the first queen of the cats"; dogs Trixy, Rover, and Stray; and other small animals. They even had two pet cemeteries, one for birds and one for other pets. The death of their pet Birdy "in fits" in March 1897 and his subsequent interment in the "bird semetry," was recorded in fragmentary notes by one of the children.[1]

In August 1897, the children were temporarily without pets; even the beloved Grahame had passed on, killed by a stray dog. Ten-year-old Herbert and twelve-year-old Eddie convinced their mother to let them have a pair of young rabbits. The rabbits did not come from a pet store, however. According to a "history" written in Eddie's characteristic scrawl and with his creative spelling, the boys had "sean them in a cage, and . . . we asked mama if we might not have them she agreed and we bought them of a butcher or seller of all traids Mr. Wassabach."[2] Thus the rabbits were rescued from their fate as someone's dinner. The children apparently already had a club, called the Browny Society after an earlier pet, and they renamed it the Bunnie Society. Papa Bunnie was crowned King, and Mama was Queen. The royal couple's accommodations were improvised; at first they were housed in the bathroom, but by mid-October they had been relocated to the dirt-floored basement of a house addition, and the dynasty began.

The story of the Bunnie Society and its business spin-off, the Bunnie States Fowl and Garden Company, can be reconstructed from a collection the children's mother later named the Bunnie Papers. Carefully gathered and saved among the family's voluminous personal papers, the handwritten minute books, legal documents, business reports, newspapers, and other scraps, along with a handful of snapshots, offer a look at the imaginative play of children at the turn of the century and reveal how the children felt about their pets. The papers also show how instructive the experience was, as Edward Rankin encouraged his children to create and manage a small enterprise that provided the family with vegetables, chickens, and eggs beginning in 1899.

The progenitors of the rabbit realm, Papa and Mama Bunnie, had four litters in rapid succession before Mama died on 14 June 1898. In December of that year, Eddie wrote a history of the bunnies and noted that "she was probaly worn out she had so many children." The first litter included Kleine, who was given to Emily; Whitie I, who was reluctantly shared with Nettie Reed (probably a young relative of the family's housekeeper, Hattie) but eventually returned to the kingdom; Whitie II; and Maltie, who escaped. All but three of the next two litters and Whitie II met a tragic end at the paws of a marauding cat. After Mama Bunnie died, the children dug the fourth litter out of the rabbits' underground burrow and tried unsuccessfully to feed the babies with a bottle and a spoon. They still had five rabbits, members of a "race" (the children's own term) that included such distinguished individuals as Kleine and Whitie I and, in time, Brownie III, Greylecka, and Richard, who bit people. The death of so many of the bunnies left the children preoccupied with royal succession, however, and they produced the "Will of Papaa Bunniy": "The throne shall be left to Whitiy If she dies to Kleine and if he dies to Malltiy and he dies to Baby Bunie and then to Whitiy's children, and then let them decide who shall have it among them selvs. . . . I grant to any pet who shall come next, to go any where on this place I grant that my belonging shall be equaly devided among my children."[3]

During November 1898, the Bunnie Society was renamed the Bunnie States, and the kingdom was reorganized as a republic on a trial basis, perhaps reflecting civics and history classes that the boys were taking at school. Kleine won the presidential election, and Papa Bunnie was demoted from king to an elected representative. During the next month, the children held a census and divided the land into states. Government officials were appointed, and Herbert was made postmaster general of the newly established national post office. In a Declaration of Independence dated 9 December 1898 (see fig. 2), the citizens of the Bunnie States declared themselves "free of Kings and queens." President Kleine assured his citizens of a good government through a "National Consil" on which "responsibility should fall." The new government levied taxes, wrote more laws, and fined the boys for speaking "ruff."[4]

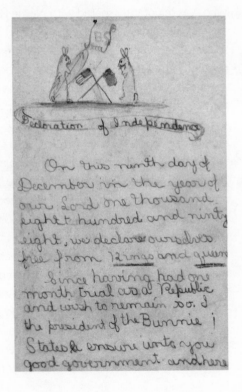

FIGURE 2. *"Declaration of Independence," paper, ink, and watercolor.*

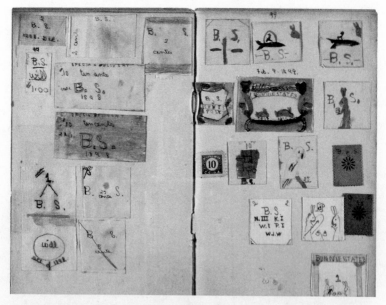

FIGURE 3. *Bunnie States stamps in "album," paper, pencil, ink, and watercolor.*

Over the winter of 1898–99, Herbert and Eddie began to produce postage stamps and money marked "Bunnie States of America" (see fig. 3). This activity may have been inspired by the boys' new enthusiasm for collecting real postage stamps, but it was also important for a republic as completely imagined as was the Bunnie States to have its own medium of exchange and mail service. The boys even made up trade cards for a B. S. Supply Co. with a jingle and a trademark (see fig. 4).

Papa Bunnie died in January 1899 of "chin trouble" and was buried in the animal cemetery, but his remains were desecrated by cats and dogs (the children thought). The children declared war on stray cats and dogs, noting that the "Bunnie Mascre" of a year earlier had never been "wholly revenged."[5] The children were also troubled by the negligent mothering of Whitie, who had "lost many citizens for the B.S." In a position paper titled "The Whitey Children Case," Eddie worried that "sonething ought to be done to provent any more from being lost." He proposed an inspection of the rabbit burrow, "the best of

FIGURE 4. *B.S. Supply Co. trade card, paper and ink. Note the jingle, apparently set to the ragtime tune "Hot Time in the Old Town Tonight."*

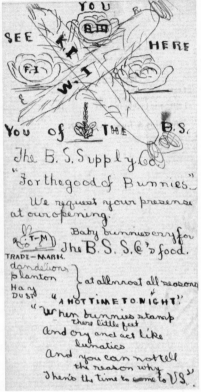

FIGURE 5. *Coat of arms for the bunnies, 1898 or 1899, paper, pencil, ink, and watercolor.*

food," and little handling, "for if the B.S. dose not have more Citizens it will die out or another race will take its place." He proposed that Whitie had been taken from her mother at too tender an age: "She sertainly did not get her carlessness from Mama Bunny."[6]

At the time of its construction in 1787 for the Van Rensselaer family, Cherry Hill had been a 900-acre rural estate. The city of Albany grew up around it as family members inherited or sold off parcels of the land over the years. By the late 1890s, urban row houses occupied by working-class families had closed in on three sides of the property, but the Rankins were too deeply attached to their home to move. The old house still had a couple of acres of grounds, an array of small outbuildings, and room for a new set of pets: chickens. In the early summer of 1899, the Rankin children's interest in the Bunnie States was enhanced by the addition of three incubator chickens named Joe, Betty, and Elizabeth.[7] One had arrived as an egg dropped by a neighbor's wandering hen. In the summer of 1899, the Rankin children initiated the Bunnie States Fowl and Garden Company (B.S.F.&G.CO.), for the purpose of making their own pocket money. Two months earlier, they had "purchased" the family vegetable garden for $100.[8]

From the start, the venture mixed play and humor with juvenile enterprise. The boys began to produce a "monthly" titled *The Speaker,* which reported on company and national news such as the declaration of an annual "legal holiday" called Fish Day on 14 May. The event was celebrated by the "fine sight" of the children's single goldfish and twenty-six minnows "swimming in the big tub" (probably the bathtub), a vacation the bowl-bound creatures were treated to every few weeks during the summer.[9] One issue included the following full-page advertisements:

B.S.S. CO.

FOODS & SUPPLYS

2d. STORY OF CHICKIE'S HOUSE

WE HAVE NOT FAILED.

Pres. E. E. Rankin

Wholesale & Retail

WHITIE & CO

FINE MAPS OF THE B.S. MADE TO

ORDER with the number of feet as

nearly correct as possible.[10]

A Whitie map company map survives marking out the Bunnie States geography, including Elm Street (where dead bunnies were buried, perhaps under the hedge) and the Rankin's carriage road re-named Walnut Street. The B.S.F.&G.CO. property was located in the dirt floor basement of a house addition where there were chicken "perches," "Bunnietom" (home of Mrs. Whitie and Brownie III), and a "race course" under the front piazza (see fig. 6). "Houston" (House Town) is Cherry Hill itself.

With this expanded citizenry, the children realized that the im-provised quarters in the basement were unhealthy for their pets, whose manure also made the north hall of the house smell bad. They were getting few eggs ("at present our chickens are not pay-ing for themselves"), and the rabbits continued to find ways to es-cape.[11] So the company planned to move everyone to new quarters on the sunny lawn up the hill and behind Cherry Hill. At the end of June, Herbert wrote to his brother, who was visiting relatives in Yonkers, about the problems he and Emily had on their first con-struction attempt: "We are not getting with house very well we haven't got any of either front or back walls done we began at the back we could not find a long enough board so we tried at the top and we could'nt make it stick so we began to put the paper on and after that it rained so that all for the house."[12]

The death of Emily's pet chicken at the paws of a stray cat on 18 July 1899 was softened by the arrival a week later of a young Plym-outh Rock rooster, appropriately dubbed Miles Standish. He was friendly and gentle and allowed himself to be picked up for several photographs in Emily's arms (see fig. 7). With the addition of two Cochin hens that the children convinced their mother to purchase and a couple of bantams donated by a Van Rensselaer cousin, the children had a flock and could produce enough eggs to sell, at least to their mother. They had also begun to grow a big vegetable gar-den.[13] The children even learned to doctor their flock. The Bunnie States Medical College awarded a special medal and certificate to Herbert as an "able doctor" for curing the "little brown hen" on 25

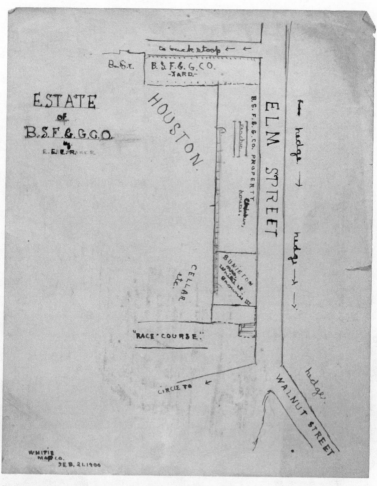

FIGURE 6. *Map of the Bunnie States of America, 1899, by Eddie Rankin, paper and ink.*

October; it was one of a number of prizes and honorifics (see fig. 8).[14] By November, the inventory of chickens included "one Plymouth-rock rooster who has just learned how to crow two Cochin hens, two game banties one black and white banty and

FIGURE 7. *Emily Rankin and Miles Standish, summer 1899.*

FIGURE 8. *Bunnie States medals and cases, 1899, cardboard, pencil, pen, and ink. These include a medal, badge, and case presented to Eddie Rankin, an "able doctor," for saving the life of a chicken, and a medal with case presented to Herbert Rankin for "elocution."*

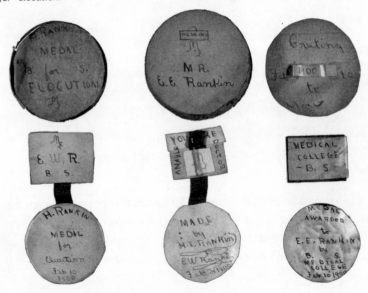

another little chicken which is a mixture of different kinds."[15] The boys produced a financial prospectus on the state of the B.S.F.&G.CO., "the best and one of the firmest companies in the B.S. [Bunnie States]," with a charter that cost "$500 B.S. money," "$1.28 cents U.S. in the Treasury," "10 chickens a fine house and corn, plates, food, and other articles" worth around $14.00.[16]

The purpose of the company, whose motto was "Slow and Steady / Quick and Ready / Win the Race," was to sell eggs and produce from the children's garden to Mr. and Mrs. Rankin and family friends. However, fresh eggs also made lovely gifts. A letter from Grandmother Rankin in Newark, New Jersey, to Emily dated 15 January 1900 thanked the children for "the wonderful eggs which were so mysteriously hidden in the pure white cotton in the little box." They had been hand-delivered by their father, who was visiting.[17]

Meanwhile the Bunnie States of America continued to thrive, especially with the addition of Mr. Brownie IV in April. The children published handwritten papers covering events among the rabbits and chickens and neighborhood news. Encouraged by their father to try their hands at practical business methods, in May 1900 the boys set up the B.S.F.&G.CO. Egg Account No. 1, with a page for each chicken: Brownie, Dott, Simpus, Black with White Face, Joe, Big Cochin, Delhi, Croppy, Gamy, Winged, Darkey, Topnots, and Croppy II.[18] They kept track of babies hatched as well as the vegetables and eggs bought by their parents and the supplies and birds purchased.

The children also drafted a constitution for the B.S.F.&G.CO., which included as Article 1 the stricture that "no one can sulk in meeting" as well as arrangements for annual elections, special meetings, and the passage of laws.[19] Two minute books survive that contain deliberations from the Saturday meetings, which followed Robert's Rules of Order—more or less. The tongue-in-cheek minutes include "passing of the candy box" and time for "declamation" by officers of the company, who were clearly studying rhetoric in school. A declamation (which may date from 1898) from Herbert suggests what these speeches may have been like: "Think of those famous Bunnies who have past away with the greatest grief of all shall not there history be written? Will not any of you take the time and labor? Why why will you refuse? It is not too great a task; it will not take a life-time."[20]

Little sister Emily had always been a follower rather than a leader in the Bunnie States of America game, although she did hold office and attend meetings. By 1901, however, she was a full participant, especially when the boys were away. In her diary, she kept careful track of new baby rabbits, who now enjoyed improved living conditions in a rabbit house with a loft.[21] In April, she recorded spending some of her spring vacation working on a "B.S. language" and drew stock shares for the company while the boys began building another new chicken house. She also recorded when Eddie created wills for Richard and Brownie III.[22] Mr. Brownie instructed his executor, Herbert, to settle his debts and that "all personal property shall go to a museum." With the help of Annie the housekeeper, Emily took over all animal and garden care when her brothers traveled to Yonkers to visit relatives that June. She found herself coping with such problems as impromptu chicken fights between Miles Standish and the game rooster owned by the keeper of the saloon on the corner of Pearl Street and First Avenue. Her mother reported in a letter that she had complained to the man that "his rooster . . . was not behaving at all like a gentleman, . . . and every time I looked out of the window I had to see a cock fight which I did not enjoy."[23]

Between 1901 and 1903, the B.S.F.&G.CO. was run more and more as a small business. The number of chickens had grown to thirty by 1903, and they no longer all bore names. Bunnie State minute books from these months are full of debates about fattening hens for sale to Mrs. Rankin, selling hens that were no longer laying, and buying new stock.

In the fall of 1903, Herbert, age sixteen, and Eddie, eighteen, began a final year at Albany Academy; fourteen-year-old Emily continued her genteel education at Misses Cooper School in Albany. The Bunnie States year of 1903 had gotten off to a bad beginning when someone, presumably from the neighborhood, stole eighteen of the chickens. With their more complicated teenage social lives, the children decided to dissolve the B.S.F.&G.CO. In a special meeting on Valentine's Day, with their father presiding, the children voted for "Dissolution of company on account of the loss."

Several animals remained, however, and Emily, who was often at home without her brothers, continued as a dedicated chicken and bunny keeper. She wrote to Herbert and Eddie about the adventures of escaping bunnies, life and death in the hen house, and selling eggs and "pie plant" (rhubarb). She graduated from Misses Cooper in 1906 and prepared to leave for Northampton School for Girls prior to attending Smith College. Someone dug out the old Bunnie States minute book and recorded a Special Meeting called to order on 14 September at 3:45 P.M., with the children's father presiding. "All members present. The president here stated the object of the meeting viz What should become of the company." Herbert, Eddie, and Emily decided that the company would become the Association of the B.S.F.&G.CO., with meetings at Thanksgiving, Christmas, and Easter. They agreed that "the live stock should be indefonately transferred to Mr. John R. Ayre," a relative who lived in western Massachusetts. The descendants of Papa and Mama Bunnie, Miles Standish, and the rest emigrated from their ancestral homeland. And so ended the childhoods of Eddie, Herbert, and Emily Rankin.[24]

Prepared with Maxine Lorang, Researcher, Historic Cherry Hill, Albany, N.Y. All Bunnie States illustrations courtesy Historic Cherry Hill Collections, Albany, N.Y.

⇥ 3 ⇤

THE DOMESTIC
ETHIC OF KINDNESS
TO ANIMALS

𝓙n 1838, Lydia H. Sigourney (1791–1865), a prolific author of sentimental poetry, fiction, and advice, published *Letters to Mothers*, which included instructions on training very young children in a "moral code of infancy." This code had three "primary lessons." The first and third lessons, obedience to parents and telling the truth, were intended to create good order in families. But the second was quite different, for it made even the very young directly responsible for the welfare of others. Sigourney's discussion of this second rule, which she called "kindness to all around," captured a complicated but increasingly powerful set of ideas that had a lasting impact on the history of American family relations, animal treatment generally, and pet keeping in particular. "The rudiments," she wrote, "are best taught by the treatment of animals."

> If it [the infant] seizes a kitten by the back, or pulls its hair, show immediately by your own example, how it may be held properly, and soothed into confidence. Draw back the little hand, lifted to strike the dog. Perhaps it may not understand that it thus inflicts pain. But be strenuous in confirming an opposite habit. Do not permit it to kill flies, or to trouble harmless insects. Check the first buddings of those Domitian tastes. Instruct it that the gift of life, to the poor beetle, or the crawling worm, is from the Great Father above, and not to be lightly trodden out. A little boy, who early discovered propensities to cruelty, was so thoroughly weaned from them by his mother, that when attending to infantine lessons in Natural History, long before he was able to read, and hearing of a bird that was fond of catching flies, he lisped, with a kind of horror upon his baby-face, "Oh! kill flies! will God forgive it?"[1]

This quotation, written in a style more flowery than that of modern parenting advice, bears close attention for two reasons. First, that there were many editions of some of Sigourney's advice books suggests that she had her authorial fingers firmly on the pulse of her readership. Thus her writings are good places to look for clues about what respectable folk—the new American middle classes who bought books, subscribed to magazines, and could pay for the use of subscription libraries—were thinking and worrying about at the time she wrote. At least six editions of *Letters to Mothers* had appeared by 1846.

This passage also introduces the assumptions and principles that guided the interactions of many people in their relations with animals in the 1800s—and that still underlie many consensual ideas about good relations between humans and animals. Kindness to all around meant not only that children should be restrained from harming others but that they should be encouraged to act as agents for good through gentle treatment (soothing the kitten). Sigourney pointed out that learning to be kind to "all around" required rehearsal, and that household animals were useful to the very young as stand-ins for the wider world of social relations. She also took care to point out that the animals living in each household had the ability to respond to kindness with "confidence," or trust, and that they were entitled to kindly regard in their own right because they shared the same divine spark of life with human beings.

Sigourney was of two minds about the sources of childhood cruelty. She acknowledged that cruelty to animals by infants (at the time she wrote, "infancy" continued until around age seven) needed to be understood in terms of child development and that it sometimes occurred without understanding. But she also labeled

FIGURE 3.1. Household Pets, *chromolithograph, George Stinson and Company, Portland, Maine, 1870s. Author's collection. Following Lydia Sigourney's advice, the woman in this print socializes her toddler by encouraging kindness to pet animals.*

childhood cruelty "Domitian," after a Roman emperor remembered, at least by people with classical educations, for his calculated brutality to his opponents. Thus she suggested that cruelty
could easily become a considered preference.

In her discussion of kindness as a fundamental rule for living,
Sigourney outlined a domestic ethic of kindness that was already
changing the way some people treated animals in nineteenth-
century America. Fully articulated by the 1820s, this ethic made
kindness to animals one of the identifying traits of respectable
folk. It also connected this trait to other desirable characteristics
in a properly home-centered society. Kindness to animals was one
part of an expanded sense of stewardship for dependent others
who could not survive in the world without special attention and
care. The ethic of kindness even gave the pleasurable routines of
pet keeping high moral purpose.

The domestic ethic of kindness redefined some common behaviors toward animals as cruel. Beginning with the passage of a
handful of state laws in the 1820s, abuse of livestock and "blood
sports" such as dog fighting were also the focus of the earliest animal welfare efforts.[2] However, the ethic also addressed casual
cruelty to dogs, cats, and other small animals that seemed commonplace in everyday life, including in children's play. It made
two principal arguments. First, although children were born with
natural feelings of kindness and an innate moral sense, they had
to be carefully socialized into self-conscious tenderness to other
beings. This was necessary because thoughtless cruelty to animals opened the door to the "passions," a dangerous substrate of
human nature that could only be controlled by imparting self-
discipline. Cruelty to animals was one outward expression of in-
ward moral collapse, and unchecked childhood cruelty, no matter

how casual or unknowing, was a predictor of antisocial behavior in adulthood.

The second principal argument of the domestic ethic of kindness was that animals themselves deserved special care. Not only did they have the capacity to feel physical pain, but they expressed recognizable feelings—joy, distress, sorrow, and most important, devoted love—to their mates, between parents and offspring, and to people who sometimes did not deserve their devotion. Animals themselves were both emotional and moral beings occupying recognizable social roles. Some were willing servants and watchful guardians; others were the source of as much delight as beloved children; still others were caring parents whose families paralleled the best human ones. Further, animals possessed a sense of right and wrong that, it so happened, was very much like the moral sensibilities of respectable people. So children could learn and adults could be reminded of the rules for right living from close contact with the animals in and around households. People could even experience love through their relationships with animals.

By locating the origins of their feelings and their morals in nature, middle-class Americans demonstrated to their own satisfaction that their "family values" were universal rather than the specific products of a particular culture at a particular moment in history. People also began to argue that kind treatment of all dependents was not simply the absence of abuse. Kindness was also the fostering of a broader concept of well-being for the self and others, including actions that helped beings who needed humane care to thrive. This belief in the importance of active stewardship shaped the formation of animal welfare organizations beginning in the 1860s, but its most profound impact took place in individual families. As families abandoned keeping livestock, another change that took place gradually well into the 1900s, pet keeping became the only way many could directly express kindness to animals.

The domestic ethic of kindness evolved from ideas that defined middle-class, or "Victorian," culture in America: gentility, liberal evangelical Protestant religion, and domesticity.[3] Each idea helped to define the other two, and all converged in promoting self-cultivation and self-control in individuals, and in their articulation of such principles as social hierarchy and progress. For the sake of clarity, however, gentility, liberal Protestant thought, and domesticity will be treated separately. As is the case with all sets of powerful cultural ideas, their expression in daily life was marked by apparent contradictions between ideals and practice. In the case of kindness to all around, comparing real stories of people and the animals in their lives to the ideal relationships prescribed in stories, poems, and pictures yields some tensions worth exploring. How, for example, could people love some dogs as family members yet eliminate stray dogs so ruthlessly? How could they justify drowning newborn kittens and puppies? How could they love a pet lamb and then slaughter and eat it?

While some critical assessment of the limits of the domestic ethic of kindness must be part of any account of its history, simply looking for evidence of hypocrisy on the part of ordinary people does not offer much insight. What is interesting, and important, is how popular spread of the domestic ethic of kindness justified new ways of relating to animals and increased self-consciousness about animal treatment. This occurred at a time when human life was absolutely dependent on the labor of animals and on the products of their bodies, and when almost no one doubted that human beings had the divine right to be in charge of all the world's creatures. The ethic grafted new ideas onto an old and complex legacy of ideas about animals and long-standing patterns of human use for animals. In making arguments for kindness, ordinary people grappled with big questions about the nature of the good person and the good society, sometimes successfully and sometimes inconsistently. Even so, the domestic ethic of kindness propelled an important step forward in popular concern about the well-being of animals.

Arguments on behalf of animals were not new to the nineteenth century, and they did not originate in America. In a pioneering study of changing attitudes toward the natural world, historian Keith Thomas has identified a persistent, minority voice for kind treatment running through the intellectual life of England between 1400 and 1800, and concern for animals was part of the eighteenth century's cult of sensibility. The fact that so many public voices for kindness were now feminine was new, however. The women whose voices are heard in this chapter include Sarah Josepha Hale, the influential editor of *Godey's Lady's Book,* and some of the era's best-selling authors—Lydia H. Sigourney, Lydia Maria Child, and Harriet Beecher Stowe, among others—along with a cohort of now-obscure figures. The distribution their writing enjoyed was a new phenomenon, too; the spread of the domestic ethic of kindness was enhanced by the new mass print media of the early and mid-nineteenth century. Magazines, newspapers, and books of advice for parents took up the issue. Authors spoke directly to children through Sunday school lessons, poetry, songs, and stories that promoted kindness and discussed the consequences of cruelty. Even the visual media of the era joined in, as inexpensive prints, illustrated juvenile books, and objects such as children's dishes and toys depicted the new standards for animal-human relationships (see fig. 3.2). Even after the domestic ethic of kindness was widely accepted, updated versions of the same tales

FIGURE 3.2. "The Favourite
Rabbits," child's plate, 1825–50
(English). Author's collection.
"How joyous at each sunshine
hour / I haunted evry green
retreat / Of forest, garden,
heath & bower / Their cell to
store with clover sweet."

and images were published for the socialization of later generations
of children. Stories promoting kindness to animals became part of
the ordinary instruction of American childhood through a variety
of tools for what was called humane education. Some tales were
the product of organized efforts beginning in the 1880s, but others
were simply part of the vast corpus of children's stories that has
persisted to the present. During the 1960s, for example, I spent
many childhood hours poring over a Classics Comics edition of
Black Beauty, and I read old copies of Marshall Saunders's *Beautiful Joe: The Autobiography of a Dog* (1894) and Ernest Thompson
Seton's *Wild Animals I Have Known* (1898) that belonged to my
parents and grandparents.

Gentility and Feelings

It seems clear that the breakthrough in popular attitudes about
animal treatment, at least in Anglo-America, coincided with the

rise of a society that embraced the concept of gentility, the standard of personal excellence that elites on both sides of the Atlantic adopted with enthusiasm in the 1700s.[4] Gentility linked two separate phenomena: a high standard for individual self-presentation from courtly life (physical grace, beautiful manners, accomplishments, and taste) and influential ideas about human nature and moral development articulated by Scottish common-sense philosophers such as David Hume and Adam Smith.

The truly genteel person exhibited two characteristics as he or she moved through the world: cultivation and benevolence. The idea of cultivation, originating in agriculture, suggested that the fine manners and the delight that genteel people took in the world around them were the results of steady effort and self-care. Further, genteel people were marked by their expansive benevolence, the disinterested desire to promote happiness among all beings capable of the feeling. Benevolence was the product of the undamaged, properly cultivated moral sense with which each human being was born. Benevolence itself required only "sensibility," the innate capacity for deep feelings and "quickness to display compassion for suffering."[5] Even people who were only conventionally pious (or, shockingly, did not profess any religious beliefs at all) could still display benevolence and act correctly on their impulses to relieve the suffering of others. What is important to our genealogy of the domestic ethic of kindness is that "others" was almost always defined as including animals. "It is grievous to see or hear (and almost to hear of) any man, or even any animal in torment," observed one author as early as 1731.[6]

Advice books promoting gentility in the nineteenth century informed readers that ordinary people could train themselves into it. American interpretations of the genteel ideal were ambiguous on the role "good breeding" (social class) played in the creation of the refined person, which made sense in a society where social class was perceived as, and to some extent was, porous and a question of self-definition. Advice authors even suggested that sensitivity to others could be enhanced through self-cultivation. Defining benevolence simply as "a quick sense of what may give pleasure or pain," the anonymous author of *A Manual of Politeness* (1837) assured readers that the benevolent impulse could be developed through rules that could be studied and mastered.[7] The author did not specify whether the pain under discussion was physical or psychological because both were unacceptable, and even the etiquette book version of benevolence did not indicate that the experience of pain or pleasure was reserved for humans alone.

Religion and the Individual

Liberal evangelical Protestantism, the second set of ideas that influenced the domestic ethic of kindness, attracted converts beginning with the Second Great Awakening, an era of religious revivals in the 1820s and 1830s. Its optimistic theology argued by evangelists such as Charles Grandison Finney, a lawyer and Presbyterian minister whose published sermons reached a national audience, argued for the ability of individuals to determine their own fates. Whether or not one had been "elected" to salvation by God, one could choose to be a better person, succeed at the task, and be saved. This meant that individual progress—and by extension broad social progress—toward perfection in the millennium was possible. The argument that individuals could choose and work toward spiritual perfection and salvation was a lot like the proposition that individuals could work toward becoming genteel. In this case, though, progress required the presence of the divine as well as self-discipline (this time, the self-discipline of active faith).[8]

Benevolence was also an important theme in this thought. However, the compassion of the Christian and the benevolent sensibility of gentility differed in one important way. Finney argued that the latter was "simply a feeling of pity in view of misery. . . . It is not a virtue. It is only a desire." He propounded a "compassion of will," a morally grounded, rational "choice or wish" that "misery might not exist." This benevolence required action "in relief of suffering."[9] Thus Finney's brand of benevolence guided believers toward a wide variety of organized social causes, from antislavery activism to prison reform and eventually to organized animal welfare work.[10]

Simple, kind actions at home were acts of benevolence that carried families closer to the "Eden of Home," where each household became a microcosm of heaven on earth.[11] For centuries, a small number of Christian thinkers had commented on the nature of humankind's obligations to animals ("a righteous man regardeth the life of his beast") and emphasized good care, but the new vision of a perfected society explicitly included animals. Charlotte E. B. Tonna, an English evangelical whose writings seem to have been widely available in the United States by the 1840s, argued that animals had fallen alongside Adam and Eve. Thus restoration of kind relations between humans and animals was an important step toward rebuilding paradise.[12] Forty years later, Harriet Beecher Stowe still argued that "the care of the defenceless animal creation is to be an evidence of the complete triumph of Christianity."[13]

Domesticity and the Qualities of Men and Women

The third set of ideas shaping the domestic ethic of kindness was what historians now call domesticity. Domesticity reflected and interpreted changes in home life, in men's and women's daily tasks as family life was increasingly separated from earning a living, and in the definition of what was appropriate behavior for men and women (see fig. 3.3). It adapted and embellished some of the conventions of gentility and liberal Protestant theology in describing two idealized spheres of moral and material authority in the world, male and female. Everyday life could not be, and never was, divided into such tidy domains, but the ideal of separate arenas for male and female authority set the parameters of the normal.

In domesticity's map of the ideal world, the realm for men was rational, commercial, and primarily public. The other realm, life in the household, provided a safe, private space for tender qualities that were considered fundamentally feminine. Strong feeling, for example, had once been a mark of genteel sensibility for both men and women in the eighteenth century. In the domestic ideal, having a nature dominated by tender feelings was a mark of womanliness. Domesticity gave the household a new importance in the world as the primary setting for rearing the self-disciplined adults that American society needed. It was a refuge from the world of economic competition in the developing American economy. And it was a model of the world as it should be, where physical and economic power was softened, or even supplanted, by moral influence and love.[14]

The private household became the laboratory for building better humans, especially a new kind of man, disciplined and able to

FIGURE 3.3. *Charles R. Passons and Lyman W. Atwater,* The Four Seasons of Life: Middle Age, "The Season of Strength," *lithograph, published by Currier and Ives, New York, 1868. Library of Congress, Division of Prints and Photographs. This image offers a concise statement of the ideals of domesticity. Both father and son arrive home, to be greeted by mother and daughters—and the family dog, who takes the master's cane.*

succeed in his own sphere yet capable of deep feeling and inculcated in domestic values, including Sigourney's kindness to all around, by his mother.[15] Over time, popular authors such as Harriet Beecher Stowe even made an argument for domesticating the entire world. Applying domestic values to public life meant kindly care for an enlarged "household circle" of dependent beings who could not defend themselves in the world: the insane, the worthy poor, the orphan, the aged, the penitent prostitute, the slave— and the animal.

The first task, however, was good order. The domestic community of love and care was inclusive but not democratic. Each household was a "little world" where the principles of good social order were "as operative . . . as in the town, state, or kingdom." However, domesticity limited the use of power in families, especially the traditional rights of men to run things as they saw fit. It emphasized service as a duty and used the concept of dependence ("the weak upon the strong, and the ignorant upon the wise") to explain good family relations.[16] Harriet Beecher Stowe's sister and fellow advice author Catharine Beecher argued that children's desire for "social usefulness" grew from parents' demonstrations of this "law of human kindness."[17]

Hierarchy, Power, and Animals

In fact, according to gentility, liberal evangelical Protestantism, and domesticity, inequality in social relations was natural and even desirable, and, of course, this assumption underlay discussions of animal-human relations. Both classical and biblical texts supported the notion that every plant and animal had been created for the purpose, directly or indirectly, of meeting human needs. However, two somewhat divergent ideas about human power existed within this general tradition of anthropocentrism, the pattern of thought that places humans at the center of the world. These ideas have been called, to be concise, dominion and stewardship. The former pressed unqualified human rights to use animals without apology; the latter emphasized what Keith Thomas has called "a distinctive doctrine of stewardship and responsibility for God's creatures" while still acknowledging that human beings ran the world.[18] The discourses that promoted kindly stewardship toward animals actually paralleled domesticity's discussion of good family life in Victorian America, which is why the issue of kindness to animals resonated so strongly. In preindustrial America, the first principle of household order had been the undisputed power of fathers to control the daily work and lives of the family; in effect, fathers had dominion. The new domestic view of relations between family members paralleled the gentler notion of stewardship to animals by emphasizing the obligations of the strong to the weak.

The domestic ethic of kindness used the same strategy for prescribing good relations between people and animals. Uncomfortable with naked expressions of power over animals, it softened the realities of humankind's ability to coerce animals and to deprive them of life with a similar rhetoric of religion, duty, and service. Its supporters generally agreed that "the revealed will of God" gave humans the right to use animals "to promote our comfort."[19] However, just as power in families was softened by self-discipline and love, so advocates of kindness to animals tried to soften the implications of divinely ordained hierarchy. The author of A Natural History of Animals (1828) took a common position when he argued that abuse of animals "given to us for the purpose of promoting our convenience and comfort" was "foul ingratitude" to God for his generosity.[20]

Good stewardship required that humans acknowledge their power while understanding that it was a temporary gift. Understanding the full implications of stewardship toward animals even allowed humans to contemplate their own relationship to God as his dependents. The author of an 1867 essay titled "An Apology for Dogs" argued explicitly that full appreciation of stewardship led to recognition that humans were to domesticated animals what God himself was to humankind. Enlightened ownership of dogs encouraged people "to imitate the divine character" and be just and merciful in exercising power over their animals. It taught humans "from ruling inferiors, to submit to Superior rule" by analogy.[21]

This Christianization of human relationships of power over animals was strikingly like earlier attempts to Christianize slavery through an argument for stewardship and restraint on the part of masters to the benefit of their less-civilized human chattel. It also suffered from similar limitations as an argument, since both enslaved people and animals were defined fundamentally by their legal status and value as property rather than by their place in the human heart.[22] (In general, pet animals did not even qualify as property. Gradually, in legal precedent and law that is still evolving today, more kinds of animals became legal property. This meant that their ownership could be contested legally, their actions could cause owners to be fined, and loss of their services could be compensated through the courts.)[23] Some authors tried to get around this deep contradiction by euphemizing ownership. Thus Harriet Beecher Stowe, the most influential literary voice against slavery in the 1850s, called owning animals "a sacred trust from our Heavenly Father."[24] *Kindness to Animals; or, the Sin of Cruelty Exposed and Rebuked* (American ed., 1845), a book that was distributed through the American Sunday-School Union, went so far as to argue that animals were never really owned by people, which was "one of the things that we are apt to forget when we have a beast, or a bird, or a fish, or an insect, in our power." Rather, each was "a creature of God's, not of ours; and if we do any thing that he does not approve of, he will surely recon [*sic*] with us for it."[25]

Put these ideas together: increased sensitivity to the suffering of others and belief in an innate human drive to relieve suffering; the ability of properly disciplined and principled people to per-

fect themselves in both secular or religious terms; the moral ob-
ligation of self-aware people to make society a better place for
the lost, the weak, and the dependent as well as for themselves;
and the belief that private family life was the best place to train
children into the discipline of kindly stewardship. In nineteenth-
century America, they added up to a formula that made kindness
to all around an important characteristic of respectable people
and that, from its beginning, explicitly included animals as part
of "all."

Kindness to All Around

Advocates of kindness to animals assumed that human infants
were born with a natural moral sense that inclined them toward
the good. This idea reflected significant changes in theories
of child-rearing among progressive parents, reaching back to
philosopher John Locke's *Some Thoughts Concerning Education*
(1693). Locke argued that children were born unformed, ready to
be shaped, for good or ill, by the world; he used the metaphor
"white paper," which suggested both their purity and their blank-
ness.[26] Because children's values were imparted by experience,
parents had a particular responsibility to raise their offspring
using kindness, consistent discipline, and carefully guided education. Later thinkers, particularly the Second Earl of Shaftesbury,
Locke's own pupil, and the practitioners of Scottish moral philos-
ophy such as David Hume and Adam Smith even took this a step
further. They believed that experience shaped character but that
parents had a head start because children were born with a conscience that already made moral distinctions and pointed humanity toward benevolence.[27]

Parents who practiced progressive child-rearing in the first half of the nineteenth century inherited this legacy of thought, supported by books, sermons, and influential periodicals. They now believed that infants had a moral sense that required direction.[28] But while the moral "clay" of the young child was easily molded, it was also easily misshapen. Children needed shelter from the rough-and-tumble of the public domain. In the household's small world, practice in channeling inborn moral impulses and sensibility into adult benevolence could be limited to household members: parents, siblings, other relatives, carefully selected servants—and to animals; this brings us back to Sigourney's kindness to all around. Inside the Eden of Home, the animals already present as guardians, workers, companions, or ornaments had a special role to play in the all-important task of civilizing children.

Because of this, parents had to be careful about their own everyday relations with animals. Adult authority should never include brute force, since the flexible nature of children was warped by every bad example seen or experienced firsthand.[29] When authors of advice to both fathers and mothers suggested to readers the powerful "influence of example," they often used as illustrations behavior toward animals rather than bad conduct toward other family members. Jacob Abbott, one of the most popular children's authors of the time, discussed a father's behavior toward a wild robin, arguing that "if a boy hears his father speaking kindly to a robin . . . there arises at once in his own mind, a feeling of kindness toward the bird, and toward animal creation, which is produced by a sort of sympathetic action. . . . On the other hand, if the father . . . goes eagerly for a gun, in order that he may shoot it, the boy will sympathize with that desire, and . . . there will be gradually formed within him . . . a disposition to kill and destroy all helpless beings that come within his power."[30] Lydia Maria

Child, author of the best seller *The American Frugal Housewife,* offered the case of a young mother laughing as her toddler pulled a kitten's tail, then beating the animal when it scratched the child. The boy was "encouraged in cruelty" by seeing his mother's thoughtless amusement, and the woman taught a "lesson of tyranny to the boy" by engaging in physical retaliation.[31]

Remember, warned one author, that "all the larger cruelties of mankind have their origins in the cruelties of infancy and youth."[32] Some took particular pains to embrace all animals, no matter how lowly. This included frequent criticism of what one writer called the "wanton sport of torturing poor insects."[33] Lydia Maria Child concurred. Like other nineteenth-century proponents of kindness, Child borrowed from earlier writings to bolster her arguments. She quoted the eighteenth-century poet William Cowper, a favored source of quotations for exhortations to kindness, to the effect that "I would not have for my friend . . . one who carelessly sets foot upon a worm" and warned, "If I see even a young child, pull off the wings of an insect, or take pains to set his foot upon a worm, I know that he has not been well-instructed, or else there is something wrong and wicked in his heart."[34]

The Progression of Cruelty

One of the axioms repeated by the proponents of kindness was that the practice of cruelty was incremental: the boy who tormented animals would in time become the man who tormented other people. Like the discussion about the nature of stewardship, this proposition that the cruel child begat an even worse adult was not new to the nineteenth century. The formula, which had appeared in Christian commentary as early as the thirteenth century, was revived during the eighteenth century in the new

FIGURE 3.4. Fidelity, *lithograph, Kelloggs and Comstock, Hartford, Connecticut, and New York; Ensign and Thayer, Buffalo, New York, ca. 1850. Harry T. Peters, "America on Stone" Lithography Collection (60.2349), National Museum of American History, Behring Center, Smithsonian Institution.*

discussion of human moral development.[35] Success in socializing the child should result in the "man of feeling," a being whose innate goodness had not been damaged in youth and whose "tender-hearted susceptibility to the torments of others" marked his "deeply virtuous nature."[36] The inverse, the man who did not feel, was to be feared.

The most compact eighteenth-century narrative of progressive cruelty was William Hogarth's famous series of engravings *The Four Stages of Cruelty* (1750–51). The first, most famous print depicts gangs of boys, including Tom Nero, whose path is being plotted in the narrative, hanging cats, cockfighting, gouging out the eye of a small bird with a wire, and sexually molesting a dog, among other outrages.[37] Eventually Nero commits a murder and is hanged. By the 1780s, this narrative, including its dire conclusions, had moved to the new realm of children's literature. The Reverend C. G. Salzmann's *Elements of Morality for the Use of Children* (1782), translated into English by Mary Wollstonecraft and in circulation in America by 1800, used a variation on the theme when a young boy is scolded by his father for proposing to punish a mouse as a "little thief" by cutting off its ears and tail (a crude copy and indirect critique of mutilating punishments for human criminals). His father shames him as a "cruel boy" and warns, *"He who can torment a harmless animal . . .* accustoms himself by degrees to cruelty, and at last he will find a savage joy in it: and after tormenting animals, will not fail to torment men."[38] Eighty-five years later, "Cruelty and the Gallows," a particularly hair-raising admonition in the children's newspaper *Youth's Companion,* still used this formula. It informed readers that a famous murderer, recently hanged at age nineteen, had admitted that, as a child, he had liked killing animals "better than anything else": "Youthful reader! whenever you find yourself delighting in cruelty to any of the creatures which God has made, think of Prescott—think of the *gallows*!"[39] While modern understanding often interprets youthful cruelty to animals as evidence of "borderline personality disorder," the voices of the domestic ethic of kindness based their interpretation on a different premise: cruelty to animals was the private act of the underdeveloped or damaged moral sense.[40] Furthermore, in a religious context, it was a sin, bearing eternal implications like other sinful behaviors.

Moralizing children's literature that focused on animal treatment proliferated in the decades before the Civil War. Authors intended these stories as acts of intervention, believing that they were effective because children experienced a sympathetic identification with the characters. Sigourney even demonstrated to mothers how they worked by recounting an anecdote of a boy, noted for his kindness to dogs, who attributed his good behavior to having heard a "simple story" of a faithful dog when "almost an infant."[41] (In this sense the function of these tales was similar to—and in fact some seem to have predated—popular published narratives of slavery that, by inspiring pity and identification on the part of readers, expanded the concept of individual rights and the definition of cruelty in the 1830s and 1840s.)[42] Identifying with the childish perpetrators of cruelty in the stories enabled children to escape the firsthand experience of cruel behavior and to "reform" themselves alongside their fictional peers without actually committing evil deeds.

A few selections from the early decades of the *Youth's Companion,* a popular and long-lived children's weekly paper founded in 1827 by the publisher of the Boston Congregational newspaper *Recorder,* offer a good sample of both the content and tone of these tales.[43] Sometimes the injury done to an animal was mild, as when the protagonist of a "*true* story" titled "The Puppy" was mortified by the fear and mistrust forever manifested toward him by a dog he had once thrown in a pond as a joke.[44] However, repentance often came only after the death of an innocent creature. Forcing a woodchuck trapped in the water between groups of boys to swim until it drowned, the protagonists of "The Woodchuck" remembered how "he had approached them as though he considered them friends, but they proved to be his murderers." They are haunted by the image of the dying animal, "motionless on the bank, now and then looking at them with an expression which seemed to denote nothing but forgiveness."[45] In "The Wounded Bird," Henry and Alfred, "two thoughtless boys," go gunning for songbirds. When Henry returns home with three dead songbirds and a wounded oriole and presents them to his mother with pride, he is stunned by her response: "'Poor bird!,' said she, taking from Henry the wounded oriole, and handling it with great tenderness. 'Can it be possible that my son has done this?—that his hand has committed so cruel a deed?' and the tears dimmed her eyes." Henry's heart is "touched in an instant" as he has "a glimpse of the truth that it was wrong to sport with the life of any creature" and dissolves into repentant tears. Not only does he pledge never to "hurt any animal in sport," but he convinces the gun-toting Alfred to sell his prize and purchase "a handsome little juvenile library of good books."[46]

The Habit of Cruelty

Given the way that the era's medical concept of "excitability" described the impact of behavior on human bodies, small and seemingly unimportant actions could easily foster a more serious, lifelong "habit of cruelty." In sermons reprinted as *Lectures to Young Men* (1844), Henry Ward Beecher, one of the most influential preachers of the mid-nineteenth century and the brother of Catharine Beecher and Harriet Beecher Stowe, offered a vivid explanation of the physiology of sin, explicitly identifying "blood sports" involving animals as examples of the evil that men grew to crave. In a state of normality or balance, the nervous system preferred the "moderate but long continued excitement" of ordinary work and leisure. The body could, however, absorb without harm short periods of "intense but short-lived excitement." The problem came from the fact that such "intense thrill" was physically addicting. Beecher warned that once "this higher flavor of stimulus has been tasted, all that is less . . . must be continued, or the mind reacts into the lethargy of fatigue and *ennui*. It is upon this principle that men love *pain;* suffering is painful to a spectator; but in tragedies, at public executions, at pugilistic combats, at cock-fightings, horse-races, bear-baitings, bull-fights, gladiatorial shows, it excites a jaded mind as nothing else can."[47]

Despite this physiological interpretation, succumbing to the craving for extreme excitement was still a failure of self-control. It could, however, have large-scale consequences. Some advocates of kindness to animals even tapped into a widespread conversation on political virtue, apparently hoping to make the case irresistibly compelling by connecting it to national politics. They argued that boyhood cruelty not only portended private tyranny at home; it had worrisome implications for the future of the American republic.[48] For example, Sigourney pointed out that "Benedict Arnold, the traitor . . . in his boyhood loved to destroy insects, to mutilate toads, to steal the eggs of the mourning bird, and torture quiet, domestic animals."[49] If boyhood cruelty to animals

FIGURE 3.5. The Cruel Boys, *colored lithograph, artist unknown, from* Picture Lessons, Illustrating Moral Truth, *American Sunday-School Union, 1840–50. Courtesy, The Winterthur Library: Printed Book and Periodical Collection.*

and political treachery were indeed linked, thousands of failures in reading boys would, in the aggregate, harm the American republic. Anxiety about the fragility of public order did indeed make a number of traditional social practices, including the blood sports singled out by Beecher and public executions, into problems for respectable Americans, who increasingly cherished self-discipline and emotional control as the basis of a good society.

The Problem with Boys

Yet everyone knew children were not naturally cruel; in fact, they were blessed with "natural feelings of kindness."[50] So how could the abuse even infants apparently heaped upon the animals in their paths be explained? Did the theory of overstimulation apply even here? In fact, small children did have passions that could find expression in a number of ways, from refusing to eat supper to throwing stones at the family dog. Fortunately, childish passions were relatively weak, and early cruelty was simply "careless" and could be counterbalanced by training. Stories such as *Master Henry's Rabbit,* published in the United States around 1840, encouraged children to put themselves in the place of their pets and suggested ways parents could safely punish misbehavior without physical chastisement. When young Henry forgot to feed his rabbit, he was sent to bed without his supper so that he could experience the same pain of hunger as did his neglected pet.[51]

The children's stories about cruelty and kindness discussed so far featured little boys, and, indeed, relatively few tales in this genre took girls as their principal protagonists, especially as the nineteenth century passed.[52] On the rare occasions when fictional little girls were the thoughtless perpetrators of cruelty, they reformed immediately; in fact, they sometimes reformed themselves without adult intervention. In one 1833 story, a naughty nine-year-old girl smashes a meadowlark's nest without being caught; at four in the morning, she is found by her father praying for God to forgive her sin.[53] As the untutored voices of sympathy and conscience in the children's literature promoting kindness, little girls rehearsed the role they would play as mothers. What has been called "the most famous children's poem in the English language," Sarah Josepha Hale's "Mary's Lamb" (1830), was a call for children to follow the example of a little girl whose love for her pet encouraged its love and patient loyalty in return.[54] Jacob Abbott's *Friskie the Pony; or, Do No Harm to Harmless Animals* (1865) also relied on a female exemplar, an older girl who teaches younger boys to be kind to a toad and admonishes a younger girl not to take a bird's nest and eggs. She demonstrates a concrete benefit of kind behavior when she gentles a pony that has been tormented by boys and is able to ride him when they cannot.[55]

Given how common and apparently popular these children's cautionary tales were, the question is whether they reflected the actual behavior of children, young boys in particular. In fact, these stories did have some grounding in reality. While we have seen children engaged in peaceful games with pets in Chapters 1 and 2, childhood pretend-play with animals sometimes had a dark side. For example, the American comic actor G. H. "Yankee" Hill recalled in his 1853 memoir that reading a biography of Napoleon Bonaparte as a boy had inspired "all sort of juvenile military mischief," including "hanging traitor cats and dogs on the trees or clothes-lines."[56] In a world without organized sports or video games, observers of children knew that the healthy boy was constantly "tempted" to throw rocks or aim an arrow at an animal as "a trial of his skill" or "a proof of his strength."[57]

The domestic ethic of kindness found boyhood hunting as play especially objectionable. "Sport shooting," a leisure pursuit for middle-class men, was already suspect because it dealt in blood for the purposes of amusement, which made it dangerously exciting. Some advocates of kindness also targeted boys' "fishing and hunting for mere sport" as an early introduction to the "exciting and pernicious amusements" of the senses.[58] One author admonished mothers neither to smile on "these juvenile murderers" nor ever to "eat the fruit of their doings."[59] As the earlier discussion of the right of humans to use animals suggests, the issue was not that humans were not entitled to kill them for food or other human necessities. The difficulty came when people exhibited a love of killing, a fundamental breakdown in empathy and self-control that hardened the heart and could graduate the practitioner into "rapine, murder, and war."[60] The belief that killing animals must never be "passionate" was even applied to discussions of household rats and stigmatized animals such as snakes; extermination must never be torture or be undertaken in the "spirit of war and murder."[61]

Many respectable families, however, the very people who supported kindness to animals, did not hold to the most extreme positions against boyhood hunting. Young boys of all social classes spent more time outdoors than their modern counterparts, and hunting and trapping small wild animals and barnyard pests offered outlets for youthful energies, provided pocket money, and imitated widespread adult practice in both town and country. William Lyon Phelps (1865–1943), the son of a Connecticut minister who became a professor at Yale University, recalled how he "delighted in shooting and killing birds, any bird, edible or otherwise," especially after he received his first double-barreled shotgun at age twelve, although "I was not cruel by nature, and could

not bear to see any animal ill-treated or in pain."[62] Boys trapped
muskrats to earn pocket money from their pelts; they killed barn
rats for target practice. Even Henry Ward Beecher acknowledged
that the sight of a woodchuck in his youth had caused attacks of
"venatorial perturbation," and he winked at his own sons' efforts
to catch and kill them despite his sermonizing on the progressive
nature of the passions.[63] Killing small wild or nuisance animals
was often done with adult approval, and sometimes it was clearly
a rehearsal for the activities of manhood.[64]

Even the thoroughly respectable "rational amusement" of natural history involved killing. It almost always involved collecting
animal "specimens" and awkward attempts at taxidermy.[65] By the
1870s, books of advice on hobbies and healthful recreation for
boys routinely included instructions for methodically raiding
birds' nests to collect the eggs or for capturing and killing small
animals. Collecting insects (the explicit concern among some of
the advocates of kindness) became a staple of the "nature study"
movement of the late nineteenth and early twentieth centuries.[66]
Daniel Beard's *American Boys' Handy Book* (1882) simultaneously
offered advice on keeping pets and invited children to try their
hands at shooting and stuffing birds and a few small quadrupeds.
Thus, in criticizing boyhood hunting, authors sent ambiguous
messages to parents about how boys should be reared. This kind
of killing also exposed one of the irresolvable tensions in the domestic ethic of kindness, where new ideas collided with long-
standing traditions of leisure and education that used animals.

Still, adults did try to define for children which behaviors
toward animals were cruel or kind. In 1856, Caroline Cowles
Richards, a girl of fourteen in Canandaigua, New York, recorded
her grandfather's admonition to her when she "stepped on a big

bug crawling on the sidewalk" as they strolled downtown. "Grand-father said I ought to have brushed it aside instead of killing it. I asked him why, and he said, 'Shakespeare says, "The beetle that we tread upon feels a pang as great as when a giant dies."'"[67] In 1885, Olivia Clemens, a mother who followed the child-rearing practices in which she herself seems to have been raised, would only allow her youngest daughter, Jean, to create an insect collection with specimens the child found already dead. This approach lacked a certain charm, and Jean soon fed her collection of dead flies to Sour Mash, one of the family cats.[68]

In its completeness and its absence of retrospective moralizing, Samuel Canby Rumford's memoir of life in Victorian Wilmington, Delaware, offers a clear sense of how complex ideas about cruelty and kindness could be in everyday practice. The Canby Rumford family was fond of dogs and cats (their pet graveyard was discussed in Chapter 2). The Rumford children kept a wide range of other pets and even ran an impromptu animal hospital in their playroom. Their father was a sport hunter, however, and Samuel and his brother received slingshots and then small hunting rifles. The boys used the guns to shoot barn cats and to hunt bullfrogs to provide their families with tasty frogs' legs for dinner. Like many boys, Samuel and his friends also made collections of birds' eggs by raiding nests. But young Samuel was also learning that other behaviors toward animals were unacceptable because adults considered them cruel. For example, he recalled one misadventure resulting from his desire for a goat that could pull a cart. Samuel, his brother, and a friend managed to scrape together one dollar to buy a "well grown young Nannie" (they could not afford the Billy they wanted) from an Irish woman who kept a herd. They rigged up a homemade harness—the bit consisted of two buttonhooks—and tried to hitch Nannie to their old toy wagon. The ensuing bucking and uproar attracted the attention of the adults, who issued "an edict . . . that we must get rid of the goat at once, since cruelty to animals would not be tolerated." Sam also learned that attitudes about cruelty and kindness differed from neighborhood to neighborhood (that is, by social class). He often visited the local livery stables where fighting dogs and cocks were trained, and he watched both conditioning sessions and sparring matches. Fascinated by the beauty and aggressive natures of gamecocks, Sam raised several and even learned how to "dub" or trim their combs. When he flirted with fighting them, his parents forced him to sell off his flock—for family dinners.[69]

The Reality of Violence Against Animals

In other, larger ways, too, the discussion condemning violence against animals was more than an imaginative exercise by a collection of overly sensitive souls. Concerns regarding cruelty to animals were grounded firmly in crude realities of animal treatment that were visible every day. Violence enacted upon the bodies of animals in public was routine in both rural and urban America throughout the eighteenth and nineteenth centuries. But much of the daily violence visited upon animals was what might be termed violence by community consensus. Some of it, such as slaughter for food, was part of the cycle of life as Americans understood it. Other violent acts were associated with the traditional demands of using animals for motive power. Even city folk were intimately familiar with animal death caused by humans, and they accepted that animal bodies were irreplaceable as sources of nourishment and raw materials for manufactured products (remember that this was a world without plastics or other modern substitute materials). Sometimes animals—the fox or cat raiding the chicken flock, the dog killing the sheep, or the rat raiding the larder—were in direct competition with people for scarce and valuable resources. Winning this contest usually meant killing the competition. Living close to animals also meant that sometimes people simply lost their tempers with the antics of household animals pursuing their own interests.[70]

A gradual breakdown in the unspoken community consensus about the permissibility of some violence against animals began in the United States as early as the late eighteenth century. At that time, a few sensitive folk began to object to behavior that had once been unworthy of comment. In 1794, Elizabeth Drinker was "really distress'd . . . to see the cruelty of the Dray-Men to their Horses, in forcing them to drag loads to heavy for them up the Hill." Her diary indicates that she had been troubled by this conduct for some years, although as a Quaker and a woman she took no public action against what she saw.[71] Brave individuals sometimes acted on their sympathy in an ad hoc manner. Mark Twain recalled his mother spontaneously upbraiding a carter for beating his horse—she even took his whip from his hand—on a visit to St. Louis in the 1840s.[72]

The first statutes against cruelty to animals appeared as early as 1828, although they were rarely enforced, and it is only fair to note that these bills were introduced by men and passed into law by deliberative bodies of men. They focused on some kinds of abuse that took place every day in public spaces, such as transporting calves trussed and piled in wagons to market or beating an exhausted horse pulling a too-heavy load.[73] However, some violence against animals was actually organized and rewarded by governments. Rural communities had long used bounties to encourage extermination of wild predators or "nuisance" animals. In cities, stray and feral dogs were annually the object of a unique kind of urban mayhem. In hunts during the "dog days" of summer to prevent the spread of rabies, mobs of working-class men and boys roamed city streets clubbing animals for bounty payments. Writing from New York City in 1841, Lydia Maria Child deplored the practice, and she connected it explicitly to possible breakdowns in social order:

> Twelve or fifteen hundred of these animals have been killed this summer in the hottest of weather at a rate of three hundred a day. The safety of the city doubtless requires their expulsion; but the *manner* of it strikes me as exceedingly cruel and demoralizing. The poor creatures are knocked down on the pavement, and beat to death. Sometimes they are horribly maimed, and run howling and limping away. The company of dog-killers themselves are a frightful sight, with their bloody clubs and spattered garments. I always run from the window when I hear them; for they remind me of the Reign of Terror. Whether such brutal scenes do not prepare the minds of the young to take part in bloody riots and revolutions is a serious matter.[74]

Even routine control of strays in cities was done with considerable cruelty. The contractors of city dog carts strangled their victims with wire lassos and sometimes clubbed or shot them on the spot, and frantic captured dogs often tore each other to pieces within the confines of the dog wagons.[75]

Blood sports, singled out by Henry Ward Beecher as "desperate excitements of debauched men," were also part of everyday life in city and country.[76] Setting packs of dogs on tethered bears and panthers (baiting); giving the starved lions in traveling menageries cats, dogs, sheep, and goats to tear to pieces before a paying audience; organizing dog and cock fights for money; and shooting at tethered fowl for prizes were all part of leisure around taverns, town commons, and other places men gathered through the early decades of the nineteenth century. Such activities attracted largely male audiences from all levels of society.[77] If they did not see these events firsthand, women certainly heard about them, for they were commonly reported in newspapers.[78] By the 1820s, large-animal blood sport, such as bear baiting, had largely disappeared in eastern towns, but dog- and cockfighting and ingenious "sports" such as ratting competitions continued to thrive, even where they were declared illegal, in the clubrooms and backrooms of taverns that also supported activities such as bareknuckle boxing. Some forms of sporting violence to animals even remained the special province of the well-to-do, as in the case of pigeon shooting, where captive birds were released from traps to be gunned down in competition. (The captive pigeons in such contests were eventually replaced with clay birds.)

The violence perpetrated on animals that probably spoke most clearly to the early advocates of kindness, especially women, was individual and casual, reflecting a rough world of male privilege that regarded the suffering of the powerless as a joke. While this way of living was increasingly stigmatized by middle-class culture, it was still common and visible enough to stand in some imaginations for the violent potential of all men. The remarkable autobiography of William Otter (1787–1856), a plasterer, tavern keeper, sometime slave hunter, and occasional horse dealer in southeastern Pennsylvania and Maryland, offers numerous examples, since it is built around a lifelong series of "scrapes" and cruel practical jokes perpetrated on both people and animals. Otter recounts tormenting a "very large baboon" owned by a tavern keeper in Lititz, Pennsylvania; drowning an immigrant's pet dog as a joke; running a herd of horses nearly to death; almost scorching a monkey to death on a hot stove in a tavern; and stuffing a live turkey down a chimney.[79] Otter may or may not have been a singularly cruel man; he recorded fondness for his horse and his dog. His scrapes represented long-standing uses of living and dead animals as the medium for a coarse humor that commented on the realities of physical and social inequalities between people or communicated displeasure at the conduct of others. Such commentary often relied on cruelty to make its point, and the tormented animal bodies were intended as metaphors for what could happen to human ones. Male perpetrators such as Otter understood well the pain they administered. They did not, in fact, care about it and expected to suffer pain themselves if they were unable to assert their wills over others.[80] This was the cruelty that was, in the end, most threatening to the ideal of kindly stewardship toward dependent others that was fundamental to the domestic ethnic of kindness, and to the ideal of a society where kindness ruled.

Until the late 1860s, when middle- and upper-class men and women became active in chartering and running anticruelty groups such as the American Society for the Prevention of Cruelty to Animals (1866) and the Massachusetts Society for Prevention of Cruelty to Animals (1868), no welfare organizations dedicated to animals existed in the United States. Until then, the most important public forum for advocates of the domestic ethic of kindness was the printed media they used with such enthusiasm and in which they identified the origins of cruelty and tried to remedy cruel practices through love and example. In their eyes, cruelty to animals was fundamentally a social malady that grew out of individual failing, especially on the part of men of any class who were victims of their own passions.[81] The best cure for such cruelty was socializing children to be self-consciously kind to animals. While a consensus seems to have developed among respectable people of the desirability of kindness to all around, we have seen that families differed from the most strident advocates of the domestic ethic of kindness in their definitions of what constituted unacceptably violent or cruel behavior toward animals.

This discussion has traveled some distance from simple stories of pet animals and their people. Still, understanding why pet keeping became such a rich and complex form of interaction with animals requires, in part, an understanding of how the domestic ethic of kindness to animals was grounded in a broader set of cultural concerns about defining good relations within families, between men and women, and between the powerful and the powerless. The way the ethic addressed animal-human relationships was shaped by new definitions of normality in family life. By saying this, however, I do not want to suggest that animals were only a medium for socializing children and interpreting the lives of human beings, or that cruelty to animals in "kind" families never took place. People are never able to reach the heights mapped by their social ideals. Further, violence to animals, whether interpreted as cruelty or not, was a routine part of daily life in America. Now, however, respectable people understood the origins and human consequences of certain kinds of violence to animals in new ways.

There is another facet to this new self-consciousness about relations between people and animals. Household animals had been appreciated as valued servants and workers, and sometimes as companions, long before the domestic ethic of kindness became part of middle-class culture in the United States. In fables and folktales, they had been the sources for lessons on living for centuries, and a significant body of popular literature and imagery generated in the 1800s continued along this line. Thoughtful people who spent time around animals had long recognized that these members of their households had feelings, quirks, and preferences. However, the domestic ethic of kindness encouraged people to think more deeply, and with less embarrassment than before, about animals as individuals. Humans always think about one thing in terms of another, and the domestic ethic of kindness now made available an expanded array of metaphors for understanding the place of animals in the household.

An Increase in the Family: Four Metaphors for Animals

Stories, poems, children's books, and anecdotes in advice books about kindness to animals almost always described a small world, the Eden of Home, and focused tightly on the behavior of individuals and within families. When authors showed cruelty as a failure of an individual character with an identifiable victim, they also made the important argument that the victimized animal was an individual, too. In a properly domestic world, recognizing the animal as an individual meant that its value had to be calculated on more complex grounds than the economic worth of the products from its body or the energy of its muscle power. Determining value had to include the "sacred right" (a phrase used by the advocates of kindness) of an animal to enjoy the life given to it by a benign Providence.

Advocates for kindness insisted that animals were entitled to special care because of their wholeness as sentient beings, including the emotions they clearly felt and the moral standards that seemed to guide their behavior. This was not a matter of anthropomorphizing animals—that is, making them into people. Nor were the written and visual narratives that promoted this view simply fables in which talking animals were vehicles for telling stories about human foibles. Rather, popular narratives about animals seemed to describe universal qualities. Many of the behaviors in which pet owners engaged, and the ways they talked about their animals, demonstrate that they, too, saw their pets as beings with feelings, desires, temperaments, life trajectories, and even souls. These practices and ways of speaking constituted a popular theory of what scholars now call "animal mind."

In a culture where an idealized family life set the standard for human relationships, the domestic ethic of kindness defined the place of household animals by using metaphors that transformed them into members of those families. In the first half of the nineteenth century, the word "family" still meant all the people who lived together under the authority of a father, including relatives, apprentices, and other household workers. By the second half of the century, the use of the word was generally limited to inhabitants sharing blood ties. The ethic of kindness continued to use that older understanding of family, however, by routinely comparing some animals favorably to trusted and loyal servants. It also drew on a second metaphor (one that had appeared intermittently for centuries) whereby animals' own families were discussed in terms of their resemblance to human parents and offspring.

A third emotion-laden metaphor described animals, including adult animals, as beloved children who, within the limits of their capacities, were entitled to the same care and attention as human offspring. This metaphor made a new emotional language available to pet owners and encouraged them to express their feelings about animals in the same way that people ordinarily spoke about children. The comparison of children to pets also received a considerable amount of material reinforcement from thousands of formulaic popular prints, and it quickly became a staple of photographic portraiture.

Over time, a fourth metaphor, the animal as friend, saw increasing use in relation to pet keeping by both children and adults. With its suggestion that some pets were social peers and that friendship occurred across the boundary of species, this description grew especially important by the late nineteenth century. At that time, it became part of the common language of the humane education movement, which targeted elementary students with a variety of storybooks and other educational materials about animal friends.

All four metaphors permeated popular fiction and magazine stories and proliferated in popular images, reinforcing the sense that they were a good way to think about animals. For example, prints depicting young children with pet animals at play or comparing animal and human mothers with their infants were popular and appeared in many editions. Such images helped both to articulate and to promote the view that animals were part of, according to the title of one image, "an increase of family" in a properly domestic America (fig. 3.6). When consumers purchased and displayed prints, statuary, or other objects that compared animal and human families or that depicted babies and pet dogs as equals and playmates, they ratified the particular cultural values that made these images possible. Further, these artifacts suggested what normal interaction with pet animals should look like in very literal terms.

It is impossible to say which came first, the gradual appearance of a more emotionally engaged kind of pet keeping or the published arguments on behalf of pet animals in the household. The practice of pet keeping and the ethic of kindness seem to have reinforced and amplified one another. Pet keeping became more complicated, with owners intervening more frequently in the lives of their animals. Pet keepers now had a more complex framework for interpreting their own behavior, and they may have felt more free to open themselves wholeheartedly to pet keeping as an emotional experience.

The Animal as Individual

One of the most important changes in the history of relationships between animals and people occurred in the eighteenth century with the debate about whether the experience of physical pain was an inevitable part of the cycle of life.[82] Recognition that all sentient beings were capable of sensation, hence pain, underlay pioneering arguments for kindness articulated by utilitarian philosophers such as Jeremy Bentham, religious thinkers inside both mainstream Anglican Protestantism and new sects such as Quakerism, and other intellectuals.[83] This new abhorrence of pain, and the belief that people should go to great lengths to avoid inflicting pain, dovetailed with what folks already knew about the similarities between the diseases and ailments they suffered and those endured by the animals in their care. People were also becoming more reluctant to accept pain as their own lot in life. Recall that home doctoring of pet animals was based on the unspoken belief that human bodies and animal bodies reacted the same ways to disease or injury and benefited from the same kinds of treatment.[84]

The intellectual move from recognizing the physical similarity of bodies to acknowledging alikeness in other ways was not difficult for people to make. The belief that animals were emotional and moral beings capable of inspiring the finer feelings in humans was an important justification for welcoming other creatures into the household. In previous chapters I described how much pet owners felt for some of their animals, including how they grieved when pets died. This intensification of feeling becomes especially apparent when we examine two instances of mourning for an animal and compare the language used by two Philadelphia women five decades apart.

The first subject is Elizabeth Drinker, whose beloved cat Puss has already been mentioned. On 20 September 1800, Drinker noted in her diary the death from a "disorder among the cats" of "our poor old Puss . . . in the 13th year of her age." Drinker's servant Peter "dug a grave 2 feet deep, on ye bank in our garden, under the stable window, where E. S. [her sister], myself, and Peter saw her decently interred." Recall that Puss had been held in high enough regard to be transported in a basket to Germantown, where the Drinkers fled to escape the yellow fever epidemic of 1797, when most animals in the city had been left behind. Yet Elizabeth Drinker closed her account of Puss's simple funeral (apparently the only pet that merited one) with the remark, "I had as good a regard for her as was necessary."[85]

The second example is a diary entry made by Anne Hampton Brewster (1818–92), an author and journalist. On 9 May 1859, she recorded the last moments and death of her small dog Beauty from a respiratory disease in as much detail as any account of a human death. Brewster wrote, "No one can tell how I miss him and grieve too at night. I feel his little paws scratching me and his little tongue on my hand asking me to take him in my arms. . . . I come up to my now silent room & have no noisy loving bark to greet me—Oh I am very lonely."[86] This is a very different way of speaking, but its full implications are not clear until we compare Brewster's diary to Fanny Longfellow's writing of the death of her daughter Fanny in 1848: "Sinking, sinking away from us. Felt a terrible desire to seize her in my arms and warm her to life again at my breast. Oh for one look of love, one mood or smile."[87] The similarity of these two entries shows that Brewster mourned the death of her dog Beauty in the voice of a bereaved mother while taking care to present the dog as an expressive, loving being.

Even granting that Drinker's remarks on the death of Puss were tempered by a characteristic Quaker restraint, her words are still a useful starting point for considering the apparent differences in perceptions between pet keepers in early America and increasing numbers of their nineteenth-century counterparts. Drinker's emotional restraint in the face of obvious deep regard suggests her sense that there was appropriate social distance between human beings and animals. Expressing too much affection for an animal violated this distance and was embarrassing, as this journal entry from Virginia planter Landon Carter of 15 April 1758 also suggests:

I can't but take notice of the death of my little Canary bird [probably a goldfinch], an old housekeeper having had it here 11 year this month and constantly fed it with bread and milk, and I wish the heat of this weather did not by Souring its food occasion its death, for it sung prodigeously all the forepart of the day. At night it was taken with a bark-ing noise and dyed the night following, vizt, last night. I

FIGURE 3.6. An Increase of Family, *lithograph, artist unknown, published by Currier and Ives, New York, 1863. Library of Congress, Division of Prints and Photographs.*

know that this is a thing to be laught at but a bruit or a bird so long under my care and protection deserves a Small remembrance.[88]

Advertisements for lost animals in eighteenth-century newspapers also suggest the ambiguities of human feelings. Here is an example from the *Pennsylvania Packet* of 15 September 1796: "Lost. A Half bred pointer bitch, stands low and very square before—the colour is a kind of dusky white, her ears marked, a pale liver color, and one of them a good deal cut or torn away—answer to the name of Romp. As she is valued only as an old servant, three dollars reward and no more will be given upon her being returned to the owner. Enquire at the office of the *American Advertiser.*"[89] Although Romp's owner clearly was worried about the dog and had supported it long past the time of any utility as either a watchdog or a hunting dog, he took pains to describe Romp only as a decrepit dependent supported by the household out of a sense of duty. This description may have been devised, at least in part, to limit the amount of ransom a dog thief would have to be paid, but the defensiveness of the reward statement suggests that the owner also worried that apparent affection was a personal weakness. His reasons cannot be recovered, of course, but we can note that three dollars was a very large sum of money at the time.

The metaphor used in this advertisement for Romp—the animal as servant—encompassed much early thought about animal welfare and remained one of the organizing tropes for anticruelty work throughout the nineteenth century, too (see fig. 3.7). It made good sense in a world where animals did so much of the physical work and provided so much material for human comfort in the products derived from their bodies. However, by the end of the eighteenth century, arguments for kindness that emphasized human obligations to servant animals did so by granting animals emotional lives and a sense of fair play along with the ability to experience pain and exhaustion. Early appeals such as "The Address of the Superannuated Horse to His Master" (subtitled "Who, on account of his [the Horse], being unable, from extreme old age, to live through the winter, had sentenced him to be shot") drew on contemporary discussions of benevolence and sensibility when they suggested that no feeling person would abandon an incapacitated servant, whether two or four legged:

> And hast thou fix'd my doom, sweet Master, say?
> And wilt thou kill thy servant, old and poor?
> A little longer let me live, I pray,
> A little longer hobble round thy door.[90]

Servant animals were easy subjects for benevolence in part because they were ideal servants. Poetry and stories never depicted them as balky, grumpy, or vicious—only disappointed and sad if their masters failed to recognize the obligations of stewardship that came with their position.[91]

Giving animals voices was a particularly striking and effective literary technique for making the case for kindness. It became one of the most important tactics used by animal welfare organizations in their first public education programs of the 1880s. When servant animals such as the superannuated horse spoke, they made claims that went beyond simple survival. The horse calls on his "kindest master" to recall the rides "we both enjoy'd," claiming pleasures, including good memories, that are as fully experienced as human ones. In these poems and stories, a new idea that animals were entitled to enjoy their lives was added to old conceptions of animals as emotional and moral actors. Here, popular thought was in direct opposition to the ideas of some academic moral philosophers of the era, who insisted that, whatever their capacity to feel pain and whatever their right to be spared physical suffering, animals were "destitute of any moral faculty."[92]

To make this expanded claim for animals, the apologists for kindness drew on, and added to, a long tradition of stories, folk beliefs, and popular natural histories wherein animals were agents of their own lives. They argued that human beings, especially young ones, actually benefited from daily contact with animals because of animals' exemplary qualities.[93] Children could learn respect for the family dog hearing their mother describe "the virtues of his race . . . their fidelity and enduring gratitude"; they also learned that these qualities were valued in people as well.[94] Cats were "very neat" and observant of changes in their environment (a trait "very useful for boys and girls and every body to imitate").[95] Even the ubiquitous dooryard chicken provided a useful model for children, in part because of its direct connection to a scriptural metaphor that emphasized a maternal Jesus.[96]

This formulaic comparison of particular animals to particular categories of people is consequential. Commonplace metaphors really do shape the way their subjects are perceived and treated. All cultures use metaphors to guide perceptions of the world, and the contents of the metaphors meaningful to any particular group of people are shaped by shared cultural assumptions. (For example, in some cultures, dogs are suitably compared to pigs, in that they are scavengers that also happen to be good eating; other cultures compare dogs to lovable, innocent human infants. Both metaphors have practical implications for the treatment of dogs.) The conventional metaphors in everyday use by a culture—the comparisons that people use without a second thought—address some big questions: How is the world beyond the boundary of my own body organized? What is it like to be a human being, compared to other beings in the world? How am I to describe the desirable and undesirable emotions, qualities, experiences, and relationships in my life? These are questions that all human beings pose both self-consciously in ritual and less so in the routines of daily living, and to which they must find workable answers. However, the forms of understanding they choose, including the metaphors used to suggest answers to these fundamental questions, are historical, specific to time and place. The increasing or declining popular usage of a particular metaphor (such as "the pet animal is a like a young child"), along with the appearance of new metaphors, indicates changes in the culture that uses it.[97]

While successful commonplace metaphors become so conventional that their origins are no longer remembered, they do have some basis in observation. Cats really do work to keep themselves clean, and, as predators, they are indeed observant. But discussion of the qualities of animals resonates in two directions. While a particular metaphor comparing people and animals may be used as part of a broader discussion about human qualities, good and bad, the animal is clearly present and real as one of the two terms in the comparison. The metaphor can, and does, shape the way animals are regarded.

Thinking back to the nineteenth century's preoccupation with home life, increased use of metaphors comparing children and pet animals, or animal families and human ones, grew out of the particular ways that middle-class culture defined sound relationships within families. Comparing human families and animal families, and "finding" monogamy and loving care of infants in both, reinforced the cultural norms of domesticity by, paradoxically, giving the virtues of middle-class family life origins in the nature world. Denying any gap in moral standards between people and certain animals also helped to open the door to widespread acceptance of the idea that both parties shared feelings and ways of being.[98]

Stories, anecdotes, and poems featuring virtuous and loving dogs were the most common narratives of the emotional and moral qualities of animals. As the print *Fidelity* (fig. 3.4) suggests, some dogs seemed to blend the characteristics of good servant and loving parent. In a typical example, a shepherd discovered that his dog had been feeding the man's lost son until the child could be rescued from a cave. Sacrificing his own small ration of bread, the "faithful dog guarded him like a father, and fed him with a mother's tenderness."[99] In 1848, the General Protestant Episcopal Sunday-School Union even published a children's book titled *The Dog, as an Example of Fidelity*.[100] Further, both domestic and wild animals provided models for receiving benevolent treatment, since they had the capacity for gratitude.[101]

The animals whose stories were recounted in thousands of "true" anecdotes published in magazines and newspapers and collected into children's books and gift books and in popular fiction displayed a full range of emotions, from their ability to love deeply to their capacity for anguish and sorrow. Such depictions implied that emotions were the same, whether experienced by a dog or a man, and that animal emotions could easily be recognized by anyone whose heart had not grown cold and hard. (Writing with this same agenda, directed mostly to adult audiences, has enjoyed a renaissance with the publication of best sellers like Jeffrey Moussaieff Masson's *Dogs Never Lie about Love* [1997].)

Expressions of maternal grief were particularly compelling. An "Anecdote of a Cat," published in *Youth's Companion* in 1828 and *The Cabinet of Natural History and American Rural Sport* in 1832, recounted the attempts of a favorite cat to make her master follow her from a room. When her efforts proved to be of no avail,

FIGURE 3.7. *Reward of Merit, Massachusetts Society for the Prevention of Cruelty to Animals, chromolithograph published by John H. Bufford (1810–70), Boston and New York, n.d. (1868–70). Author's collection. This small reward card for children used a copy of a painting by Sir Edwin Landseer,* Waiting for Master, *to depict willing domestic servant animals. The back contained a poem and text commenting on the painting and pointing out that domestic animals were entitled to kind treatment because of their "usefulness, intelligence, affection, and fidelity, and because Religion requires it."*

the cat brought "the dead body of her kitten, covered over with cinder dust," to his feet. The stricken man "now entered into the entire train of this afflicted cat's feelings. She had suddenly lost the nursling she doated on, and was resolved to make me acquainted with it—assuredly that I might know her grief, and probably also that I might inquire into the cause . . . and divide her sorrows with her."[102] (Unspoken, of course, is the probability that the cat had only one kitten because the rest of the litter had been drowned by someone in the household.)

Because of this interest in the apparent resemblance between human and animal families, sentimental prints about animal families were popular throughout the nineteenth century. They were a commentary on and a celebration of the universality of family life, especially maternity, for their purchasers. For example, *An Increase of Family* (fig. 3.6), versions of which were published by several different firms, invites comparisons between several sets and generations of mothers and infants, both biped and quadruped. The title can also be interpreted in two ways: progeny represent increase, but the cat and her family can also stretch the boundaries of the middle-class family.

One of the most fully developed, and culturally loaded, comparisons between animal and human families involved songbirds. Wild birds, like caged ones, occupied a special position in the catalog of animal kinds in Victorian culture. They had become "honorary pets," entitled to a level of interest and care other wildlife did not enjoy. Birds had been praised for their apparent familial sentiments for centuries, but the conventions of domesticity gave this formula new, deeper resonance. The "untiring devotion" of bird couples to each other, the "care and tenderness they show to their young," and the "ingenuity with which they construct their nests" mirrored the qualities young couples were supposed to exhibit in building and caring for their own households.[103]

Given the emotional quality of these accounts, it is not surprising that some children's stories about bird families were also commentaries on the dangers faced by human families. Moralizing poetry, stories, and even Sunday school lessons commented on the destruction of bird families and made clear the parallels between human and avian families. *Picture Lessons, Illustrating Moral Truth*, a set of large, colored pictures with didactic captions published by the American Sunday-School Union, included *The Cruel Boys Robbing the Bird of Her Little Ones* (fig. 3.8). The caption

THE CRUEL BOYS ROBBING THE BIRD OF HER LITTLE ONES.

Harken!! my boys. Would a mother like to have a cruel robber come, and take her little ones out of the cradle, or the crib while she has gone out, to get bread for them? Answer this question before you touch these helpless birds.

FIGURE 3.8. The Cruel Boys Robbing the Bird of Her Little Ones, *from* Picture Lessons, Illustrating Moral Truth, *American Sunday-School Union, 1840–50. Courtesy, The Winterthur Library: Printed Book and Periodical Collection.*

chided, "Harken! my boys. Would a mother like to have a cruel robber come, and take her little ones out of the cradle or the crib while she has gone out, to get bread for them? Answer this question before you touch these helpless birds."[104] (The irony here is that the birds were probably being captured to become pets.) Birds deprived of their mother became "orphans," and stories and poems cataloged in excruciating detail their suffering as they slowly died of hunger and cold.[105] Such rhetoric suggested that both animal and human families were entitled to special consideration because of their vulnerability to the predations of heartless people.

Children and Animals

While nineteenth-century Americans were surrounded by literary and pictorial representations of animals as devoted servants or watchful, loving parents, discussion of the individuality of pet animals in their own households also drew heavily on the development of more complex, and more sentimental, understandings of childhood. When the relationship between mothers and children became a paradigm for the best human relationships, it also became available as a description of the loving relationship possible between sensitive people and certain animals. Hence Anne Hampton Brewster's diary entry on the death of her dog Beauty. This metaphor deserves particular attention because it has survived—even flourished—in present-day talk about pets. E. B. White's *Stuart Little* (1945) even featured a mouse "born into" a human family. Americans today routinely discuss their pets as their "furry children," a metaphor that receives constant reinforcement in contemporary advertisements for pet products and the popular commercial images published in greeting cards, framed prints, and tabletop figurines.

Parents in the seventeenth and early eighteenth centuries had compared their own children to beasts and found them uncomfortably, rather than charmingly, close in the kinds of sounds they made and their predilection for crawling on all fours. Upright posture and walking were fundamental signs of full humanity in children; the connection was so deep that by the late sixteenth century, the adjective "upright" was also used to describe an honorable person.[106] When more liberal philosophies of child-rearing described children as innocent beings inclined to good rather than evil, the physical "animality" of babies was less troubling because it would, in time, disappear. The old, unfavorable comparison of children and animals was supplanted by one that found children and animals both good and innocent.

If young children and household animals shared many physical characteristics, from crawling on all fours to lacking speech, they also apparently shared loving hearts and a need for gentle guidance. Children and household animals were dependent beings that required "raising" into society (recall the discussion of animal training in Chapter 2) but had special contributions of their own to make. As a result, child-rearing and anticruelty literature sometimes paralleled each other in startling ways. Around the same time that Lydia Sigourney described a boy who ran to his mother crying, "My goodness grows weak . . . help me to be good," Charlotte E. B. Tonna informed her readers that the animal "wants the help of your reason to keep him from doing wrong; and he wants you to explain to him how he may please you."[107] This language even gradually penetrated the rather hardheaded men's world of dog training. The author of *Woman in Her Various*

Relations (1851) noted that children "are peculiarly creatures of imitation, but they can also be trained to a certain course of action, with judicious care and effort." The author of *Practical Training of the Shepherd Dog* (1891) echoed this description of young children, informing his readers that "the shepherd pup is much like a child; he is a great imitator" whose training required "imperturbable patience."[108]

Harriet Beecher Stowe, whose novel *Uncle Tom's Cabin* galvanized popular feeling against slavery in the 1850s, was one of a number of authors who routinely compared pets to children in her fiction and essays.[109] In the 1850s, 1860s, and 1870s, she published stories and didactic essays for children with dogs as protagonists. She even used dogs as plot devices in several sentimental novels for adult readers.[110] Stowe published fictionalized accounts of her own family's relations with pets, including "Our Dogs," which first appeared as a series of stories in the children's magazine *Our Young Folks* in 1866 and was collected in book form in 1867. Her anecdotes are notable for their vivid depictions of pet dog behavior, from chewing shoes to frantically enjoying carriage rides. However, her descriptions of the personalities of dogs are particularly interesting. Throughout the texts, the children of the household and the dogs are described in the same tone and vocabulary: both boys and dogs are "rovers," and both puppies and children commit "youthful errors." Each dog is described as a person with a distinctive nature: one mannerly dog is "a highly-appreciated member of society," another is "a friend and playfellow," and a third is "a little black individual . . . not very prepossessing in appearance and manners, but possessed of the very best heart in the world," a formulation that sounds suspiciously like descriptions of some of the enslaved characters in

Uncle Tom's Cabin.[111] In the follow-up to the series, "Dogs and Cats," Stowe pointed out to her readers that each of her dogs "had as much his own character if he had been a human being," and that such individuality was a potential characteristic of every animal, given proper family raising and love.[112]

Texts such as Stowe's were only one medium reinforcing the favorable comparison of children and animals. Inexpensive printed pictures that decorated rooms throughout Victorian America represented children and their pets as similar beings. While prints depicting animals as devoted servants or showing the love between animal parents and offspring were common, images of children and animals were the most popular. Even today, a cursory search on eBay suggests that uncounted thousands survive, an unscientific but powerful demonstration of how far the metaphor had percolated into American society. Linking children and animals metaphorically had distinctive limits, of course. Children were twinned with selected pet animals, most commonly lambs, which had a biblical basis, but also cats and dogs and songbirds and chicks.[113] The growing American picture trade called these images "juveniles," suggesting that publishers believed the pictures primarily suitable for the young, who were also the market (through their parents) for the era's expanding array of children's books and self-consciously educational toys. Some images were also marketed as "domestic scenes," suitable for home display.[114] Three types, or genres, of images that were published many times in inexpensive prints, trade cards, book illustrations, and stereoscopic views reveal how apt the metaphor comparing children and pet animals seemed. While individual titles vary, the three most common image types were Play with Me, Little Pets, and Can't You Talk?

The genre Play with Me (which included titles such as *Play-mates*, *My Little Playfellow*, and *My Little Favorite*) typically depicts the happy greetings of a pet, usually a small dog, and a young child beginning a day of play together. *Good Morning! Little Favorite* (fig. 3.9), for example, was published by Currier and Ives after 1857 as one of a pair with the same dog and child. The images were so popular that they were reproduced as *carte-de-visite* photographs suitable for display in the photo albums that graced parlor tabletops. All the variations of this genre are striking as depictions of a special kind of equality. Roughly the same size, the dog and the child are friends and equals who look at each other

FIGURE 3.9. Good
Morning! Little Favorite,
lithograph, artist unknown,
published by Currier and
Ives, New York, ca. 1860.
Library of Congress,
Division of Prints and
Photographs.

GOOD MORNING! LITTLE FAVORITE.

with delight while the viewer peeps in on the action. *Good Morning! Little Favorite* depicts the beginning of the story, and its paired image shows the end, when the baby sleeps safely while the tired dog takes up another role as servant and guardian. A variation of the genre that was especially popular later in the century depicted somewhat older children, usually girls, giving a tea party or playing school with their pets. In these images the animals are surrogate children, the girls stand in for adult women, and the idea of play with pets as a way to socialize children takes a humorous turn.

The second group, Little Pets (variant titles include *Household Pets, Our Pets,* and *Papa's Pets*), includes many images that may be regarded as generic portraits. The prints typically depict an imagined child, usually an infant or a preadolescent girl, holding one or more animals in her arms; several more may gather around her.[115] Like any portrait, *Little Pets* (fig 3.10) invites an exchange of looks between the viewer and the subjects of the image. However, because the child is no one in particular, she is intended to be a typical child; the same can be said for the animals. Often all the figures in the Little Pets genre look directly at the viewer, their expressions suggesting innocent confidence in his or her goodwill. That the child holds the animals so close suggests emotional intimacy. However, it is also a conventional maternal gesture, and the composition and the child's direct gaze at the viewer recall images of the Madonna and Child. The titles of these prints are also important, since the use of "pets," a word that suggested both trusting and pliable dispositions and dependence on the indulgence and care of adults, is deliberately ambiguous. The titles invite the viewer to apply the word "pet" to both the children and the animals; they may even suggest that they are, on some level, siblings.

FIGURE 3.10. Little Pets,
*colored lithograph, published
by E. B. and E. C. Kellogg,
Hartford, Connecticut; Phelps
and Watson, New York; Geo.
Whiting, New York, 1842–48 or
1855–67. Library of Congress,
Division of Prints and
Photographs.*

By the second quarter of the nineteenth century, the visual
conventions of Little Pets were a common formula for portraiture
of real children. Take, for example, itinerant painter William
Mathew Prior's famous painting *Two Girls of the Morse Family and
their Dog Minny* (fig. 3.11). Prior painted the children and the dog
so that their heads are the same size and at the same height. All
three are sitting and look directly at the viewer. The artist also
linked the three subjects by a pink ribbon that runs through their
hands and Minny's collar, on which her name is engraved. By the
1870s, these portraiture conventions were so common that they
could even be burlesqued, as in the cabinet card in figure 3.12,
which parallels an unidentified tough little boy and his tough dog.
The convention continued in formal studio portraiture, and well

into the 1900s it also appeared in commercially produced stereographs, the paired images mounted on cardboard that appeared three dimensional when viewed through a special device.

Can't You Talk? (fig. 3.13) was one of the most durable of the images pairing animals and children. This image is different from the others because it can be traced to a particular source, a long-lived but obscure British artist, George Augustus Holmes, who was active between 1852 and 1911. His work was pirated by the pictorial press and American printmakers, who seem to have

FIGURE 3.11. *William Mathew Prior, Two Girls of the Morse Family and Their Dog Minny, oil on canvas, 1840–45. Old Sturbridge Village (B20708).*

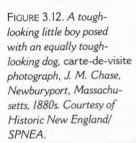

FIGURE 3.12. *A tough-looking little boy posed with an equally tough-looking dog,* carte-de-visite *photograph, J. M. Chase, Newburyport, Massachusetts, 1880s. Courtesy of Historic New England/ SPNEA.*

known as little about Holmes as we do now. How *Can't You Talk?* first reached the United States is unknown. Popular from the 1870s to the 1920s, versions appeared as wood engravings, lithographs, photomechanical prints, and even trade cards, the brightly colored scraps of paper distributed as advertisements by American merchants in the last quarter of the nineteenth century. One early reproduction, a trade card for Dr. Jayne's Tonic Vermifuge, Sanative Pills, and Expectorant, contained a text praising

"THE very popular picture—'CAN'T YOU TALK?'" and suggesting that "the appeal made by the original picture to sympathies as tender as they are universal, will not, we trust, be deemed any less acceptable in the miniature copy offered for your approval."[116] Stereograph publishing companies made and sold photographic variations. *Can't You Talk?* was printed on cloth and molded out of ceramic and plaster, it was cast in base metals, and in the 1920s, it was produced for use as an electric lamp base. Consumers even reprocessed the image into other home crafts. *Can't You Talk?* has been embroidered onto a quilt in the collection of the Smithsonian and has formed the motif for a hooked rug.[117]

Can't You Talk? depicts the encounter between a crawling baby and a collie outside an open doorway while a kitten (who is absent from three-dimensional versions of the image) looks on from inside. Both the baby and the dog are on all fours; this emphasizes the idea that the baby is a young animal like any puppy or kitten. It is unclear from either the composition or the provocative caption whether the dog or the baby is asking the question, and therein rests the power of this picture. *Can't You Talk?* is similar to the Play with Me prints in the way it suggests a story; in the direct gaze of the baby and the dog, who do not realize that they are being watched; and in the position of the viewer, who looks in without disturbing them. *Can't You Talk?* suggests that the dog and the baby see each other as equals and are equals in important ways, especially in the absence of speech. The baby, however, can grow in a way even the best-trained, most developed dog never can, and the baby must, in time, become the dog's master or mistress.[118]

Can't You Talk? resonated so deeply with certain audiences that it became a staple of two genres of reform-minded elementary school textbooks at the turn of the nineteenth century into

FIGURE 3.13. *[George Augustus Holmes]*, Can't You Talk?, *chromolithograph published by George Stinson, Portland, Maine, 1879. Author's collection. At the time this print was published, copyright laws were so weak that Stinson could publish* Can't You Talk? *without credit to the painter and could copyright it in his own name.*

the twentieth. The first was dedicated to organized humane education, an important part of the larger animal welfare movement that began in the late 1880s with the importation of the English concept of Bands of Mercy clubs for elementary schools.[119] The image experienced another life in the picture study movement associated with public schools in the Progressive Era, a period marked by intense social reform activity in American cities in particular. Classroom picture study, using reproductions of narrative paintings such as *The Gleaners* and heavy-handed discussion questions, was intended to awaken pupils to "the good, the true, and the beautiful in everything about them" through contact with art deemed suitable for children. Flora L. Carpenter described *Can't You Talk?* thus: "What a busy life this baby has with so many things to do and so much to learn. She tries hard to understand. I suppose she thinks, 'Good old dog, you seem to know so much more than I do. How does it happen that I can talk and you cannot?'"[120]

This interpretation reinforces the idea that some of the image's power lay in the notion of speech itself. Advocates of kindness to all around often used the potent idea of speech—or, more precisely, the inability to speak—to emphasize the helplessness of animals. What made some categories of dependents especially worthy of defense was their inability to speak for themselves, as the title of *Our Dumb Animals,* a popular monthly published by the Massachusetts Society for the Prevention of Cruelty to Animals, made clear. Social reformers associated with causes such as abolition or women's rights already knew that speech was empowerment. However, the claims of animals to protection, like those of young children, were both qualified and given special urgency because animals were, by their nature, a "helpless class who can neither speak, read, nor write, but who have no capacity for being taught any of these accomplishments."[121]

Anecdotes of the intelligence or devotion of animals often made the case for kindness through the use of an outside narrator's voice. But the most powerful strategy for creating "voices for the speechless" was allowing animals to speak for themselves. Some creatures, such as the superannuated horse, already had clear voices of their own by the end of the eighteenth century. Poems and stories using animal narrators appeared now and again through the 1860s. However, the animal "autobiography" was used most effectively beginning in the 1870s, the decade when *Can't You Talk?* was first published. What made animal autobiographies different from the typical children's stories promoting kindness was that young readers were invited to assume the identity of the suffering animal through the "I" in the story. Providing a powerful emotional experience, the first-person voice of the animal became a standard tool in organized humane education, especially following the publication in America of Anna Sewell's *Black Beauty* (1877). Once the book had been called to the attention of animal welfare activist George Angell by a woman sympathetic to his work, he christened it "the *Uncle Tom's Cabin of the Horse.*" Angell's American Humane Education Society (founded 1889) printed and distributed 3 million copies by the early 1900s.[122] Other authors chimed in with tales such as *Beautiful Joe: The Autobiography of a Dog* (1893) and *Dicky Downy: The Autobiography of a Bird* (1899), a story that opposed caging wild birds and decorating women's hats with feathers. Eventually even Mark Twain got into the act with his sad *A Dog's Tale* (1903). The narrator tells a heartrending tale of the blinding of her puppy by her master in a scientific experiment, even after the dog had saved the master's child from a fire and been terribly wounded.[123]

In these examples, animals not only testify to their own blamelessness but describe *themselves* as servants, children, and parents—the same comparisons used in the prints. And they add one more characterization: they are unappreciated friends to humans. This fourth metaphor, the animal as friend, became increasingly important as pet keeping became a larger part of Victorian childhood. It added another layer of description to Play with Me and Can't You Talk? Calling an animal "friend" provided a comfortable way for adults, particularly men, to interpret cherished relationships. The diary entry by Massachusetts farmer Luther Spaulding Bancroft regarding the death of his dog Byron (see Chapter 2) mourns the end of a long and comfortable friendship.

Describing an animal as a companion or friend had a couple of important implications for that relationship. First, the metaphor suggested active relationship building on both sides, by peers. To have an animal as a friend was to live in an enlarged community of voluntary social ties shaped by mutual recognition across the boundary of species. By the late nineteenth century, children's books about all sorts of animals, including the plethora of books intended for nature study classes with titles such as *Friends and Helpers* (1899), emphasized the idea that most animals were indeed friends to humans, if only their role in a shared community was understood. Second, a pet-friend may have been dearly loved, but just as human friends could come and go from one's life, so could pets. The use of the metaphor could have a slightly distancing effect that was enhanced by adjectives such as "four-footed." Hence it may also have been a better reflection of the practical realities of animal life and death—realities we have seen in previous chapters—and the limits of human stewardship for most people. The metaphor of friend may also have reflected some gender differences in perceptions of animals; women may have been more comfortable viewing animals as fur-covered children than were men. Certainly the thousands of images of men or boys and their dogs posed side by side suggest that the pet in the photo was first and foremost a pal.

Prescribing "Furred and Feathered Friends"

If animals could teach human beings important lessons about love, loyalty, duty and stewardship, and friendship, then keeping them as pets was a worthwhile part of family life. In the 1690s, John Locke had made what was perhaps the first explicit association between childhood pet keeping and cultivating the instinct for benevolence when he noted that interest in small animals could be turned to good purposes. Through caring for animals, children could be taught "diligence and good-nature" and "to be tender to all sensible creatures."[124] Nineteenth-century commentators echoed this sentiment and also argued in favor of pet keeping as a "rational amusement," play that did not overstimulate children's passions but improved them by inspiring interest in natural history. They also agreed that the most important human quality nurtured by pet keeping was the capacity for love. "Indeed, love in any form, and to any thing," thought the Reverend A. B. Muzzy, "is an elevating motive. . . . Who can doubt that many a heart, both of the happy and sad, has been made better by the multitudes of parrots, lap-dogs, canaries, &c., which have been objects of affection."[125] In a letter, J. L. V. Lesley, a distant relative of the Elmendorf family of Albany, New York, wondered, "Where would we be without our pets. I really think it makes us human to have them about and how wonderfully kind the Creator is to establish the law of love as to bind his creatures together—creatures of all kinds—speaking and nonspeaking—even the animals with the inanimate. I love my flowers & my domestic animals."[126]

The capacity of pet animals for love made them especially satisfying playmates. Catharine Beecher took pains to point out that it was animals' own displays of affection that would "awaken corresponding tenderness and care" in children.[127] Pet keeping was particularly important for boys, of course. In 1868, Sarah Josepha Hale, the magazine editor and sentimental author of "Mary's Lamb," published an essay that encouraged parents to permit their sons as many animals as they could care for. Pets "humanized" boys and offered "a great preventative against the thoughtless cruelty and tyranny they are so apt to exercise toward all dependent beings!" (As civilizers-in-training, girls benefited from pet keeping because "as sisters and mothers, they must help and teach boys in whatever things are good, tender, and lovely.")[128]

These opinions, along with the fact that pet keeping was already established in many households, meant that when the Victorian "golden age" of children's magazines and books began soon after the Civil War, pet keeping and the lives of animals generally formed one of the most important subjects for young readers. The editors and authors of *Our Young Folks, St. Nicholas,* and other periodicals were members of the first generation raised on the domestic ethic of kindness, and the editorial content probably reflected their own childhood experiences. Yet they also knew well the interests of their readers, a generation of urban and suburban children whose play with pet animals was now a hallmark of childhood. Letter Box columns featured lively correspondence from young readers who shared stories about their animals, creating a national public of pet-keeping children. By the 1870s and 1880s, children's magazines also regularly printed articles on topics such as canary care and making and stocking an aquarium.[129]

At the end of the nineteenth century, justifications for pet keeping were split between the high rhetoric of the domestic ethic of kindness and a more relaxed approach to pet keeping and children's play. By the 1890s, a few educational reformers argued that pets were "a powerful weapon for good" in "the hands of parents and teachers," whose instincts in favor of pets were supported by "statistics, carefully gathered from training-schools and prisons, that very few men who in boyhood owned or cared for a pet animal . . . are to be found among criminals."[130] By then, however, much of the literature promoting pets had moved away from the earlier arguments on the dangers of cruelty. Writers in favor of keeping pets in late Victorian America continued to agree with Jacob Biggle, author of the popular, hand-sized manual *The Biggle Pet Book,* that "the character of the young person is formed" by caring for and training pets. They no longer, however, made explicit arguments connecting pet keeping to, say, the future of the American republic. For his part, Biggle condemned poor treatment, but he suggested that most carelessness about the needs of pet animals was merely a function of age. Children simply needed to be "old enough to care for them properly" before receiving pets.[131] Pet keeping now taught simple "responsibility" rather than the appropriate dynamics of power in families.

Periodicals, children's books, and advice literature promoting pet keeping were on the front end of what may be called an institutionalization of the practice beginning in the late nineteenth century. Beginning in the 1880s, organizations such as the American Humane Education Association introduced school clubs formed with the mission of promoting kindness to animals. Texts promoting kindness to animals became part of classroom reading in the early twentieth-century curriculum of nature study, and an increasing number of elementary school classrooms began to keep sturdy and relatively undemanding pets like rabbits and guinea pigs, a practice that continues in schools and early childhood education centers today. The Boy Scouts had added a merit badge on dog care by 1930; the Girl Scouts added pet care to their merit badge array in the 1940s. Animal welfare groups also began to sponsor pet shows, where children could receive praise for their good care for animals.[132] Today, groups such as the Pet Care Trust sponsor humane education programs in public schools, children's museums, and shopping malls. These efforts not only address the well-established topic of kind treatment but promote other issues such as limiting dog and cat populations through spaying and neutering.

Pets as Friends for Lonely Adults

While childhood was the primary interest of pet-keeping's literary proponents during the nineteenth century, some people also argued for the therapeutic value of pets as friends and even as surrogate children in the lives of lonely adults. As early as 1845, one author had observed that pet keeping was "something that childless people are apt to do, if they are wise."[133] Catharine Beecher

believed that pet animals had "intuitive perceptions of our emotions which we cannot conceal," giving them characteristics that
her readers would have recognized as similar to those of close female friends or relatives.[134] In 1894, Olive Thorne Miller, author
of a number of books on animals, argued for the therapeutic
power of pets to a society that was more responsive to the idea
than ever before:

> The use of the pet as an aid to health has not been consid-
> ered as it deserves. No instinct is truer than that of the un-
> married woman of lonely life to surround herself with pets.
> The companionship of cats and birds in solitary lives has
> unquestionably kept more people than we suspect out of
> the insane asylum; and if friendless men took kindly to
> them, there would be fewer misers, drunkards, and crimi-
> nals than there are now. It seems to be the divinely ap-
> pointed mission of our furred and feathered friends, who
> never grow gloomy with care, never suffer from envy, am-
> bition, or any of our soul-destroying vices, to make us for-
> get our worries, to inspire us with hope, and thence with
> health.[135]

Other advocates of pet keeping by adults discussed the role
pets played in creating a "pleasant home," the playful cultivation
of expertise through competition in various amateur "fancies,"
and the relief from the stresses of business that an animal "hobby"
could provide.[136]

In 1956, the Equitable Life Assurance Society published the
Assurance of a Fuller Life booklets, a series with a public health
focus. Alongside titles on vacationing and safety in kitchens, the

fifth volume was devoted to pet keeping: "Ask any pet owner. You will find that the work involved in choosing, training, and keeping a pet healthy seems like nothing when you add up the countless hours of enjoyment your pet gives you."[137] Pets were now firmly associated with the increasingly therapeutic focus of American society. Once they had improved our moral character; now pets were a leisure pursuit that made us feel better and improved quality of life.

Since the 1970s, a growing number of scholars in the social sciences have made the interactions of people and pets the focus of their research, exploring the impact of relationships with animals on both human development and the physical and psychological well-being of adults. Some of the early writing from this new era of research has very strong echoes of the old domestic ethic of kindness, cloaked in therapeutic language. In 1990, Gail Melson, a professor of child development at Purdue University, proposed a research agenda on the role of animals in healthy child development. She identified the "beneficial effects of pets" to family life. Care for animals allowed children to develop "internal working models" of healthy nurturing relationships; she even argued that it was particularly beneficial for boys because it was "gender-neutral" as opposed to care for infants, which very young boys identified as an activity for girls.[138] While Lydia Sigourney and her peers would not have understood the lingo, they certainly would have seconded Melson's working assumptions.

The institutional catalyst for much of this early research is the Delta Foundation (1977), which became the Delta Society in 1981. Its mission was to "understand the quality of the relationship between pet owners, pets, and care givers." In time, the society refocused on what it calls "animal-assisted activities" and "animal-assisted therapy." The Delta Society took the institution-alization of pet keeping even further by establishing the Pet Part-ners program for groups of volunteers who bring their animals into a variety of therapeutic settings. The organization has contin-ued to serve as the lobbying group on behalf of animal-assisted therapy programs throughout the United States. Anecdotal infor-mation on the positive impact of visits from pets to groups such as seriously ill children or patients suffering from Alzheimer's dis-ease abounds, although these benefits have been difficult, if not impossible, to "prove" scientifically. Popular belief in the thera-peutic value of pets is wide enough, however, that progressive nursing homes often contain resident pet animals—cages of birds, aquariums, and small dogs—for their patients. In my com-munity, the residential ward of the local Veteran's Administration hospital has its own cat.

Over the course of the nineteenth century, pet keeping devel-oped its own set of intellectual, social, and emotional justifica-tions that included, but went far beyond, simple pleasure. Yet pet keeping was not the only relationship children or adults had with animals. I noted earlier that pet keeping developed into a complex and popular practice while human society was utterly dependent on living animals as workers and on animal bodies as both food and raw material for manufacturing. Surely, then, not all animals could be regarded as children or even as friends.

In the next chapter, I explore the complicated boundaries of pet keeping. When the domestic ethic of kindness elaborated the meaning of owning a pet, it actually made the constructed char-acter of all animal categories more visible. Some children and adults found this truth uncomfortable. Most children learned to accommodate the commonsense rules as part of the process of growing up and accepted them as inevitable in a society where long-standing tradition and social and cultural change coexisted. As animals were increasingly drawn into industrial processes in ways that separated them from everyday contact with people, the limits of the domestic ethic of kindness as a guide for all human-animal relations were revealed even as pet keeping became the most important relationship that many people had with living creatures.

THE EDGES OF PET KEEPING AND ITS DILEMMAS

$\mathcal{B}$y the 1860s, the domestic ethic of kindness to animals was widely accepted by American families who embraced Victorian culture's ideals of gentility, liberal evangelical theology, and domesticity, and their attendant beliefs in social progress and moral uplift. Gentle treatment of animals was regarded as an important attribute of good character and a useful test for distinguishing a good neighbor and citizen from a bad one. However, Americans had a long history of complex animal-human interactions that predated the middle-class vision of the home as a "little world" and the ideal society as "home-writ-large." Although they were increasingly popular, the metaphors examined in Chapter 3 were ways of thinking about relationships with animals that existed side by side with other ways that categorized sentient creatures into a number of kinds.

The word "kinds" suggests something other than scientific categories, the taxonomies of genus and species. "Kind" recalls older ways of regarding animals, based on habit and information that came from observation and contact. Anthropologists have long been interested in how cultures around the world categorize animals; they may be wild or tame, edible or inedible, useful or useless, or friend or foe according to the purposes of humans.[1]

These are descriptions of how animals fit in relation to human communities rather than the niches they occupy in nature. Historians have also begun to consider the complex ways people in the past thought about animals. For example, in England between 1400 and 1800, ordinary people classified animals according to their utility and edibility. But they also ordered animals in ways that mirrored social standards of the time—as handsome or ugly, disgusting or attractive, or of noble pedigree or low lineage. Animals were sorted by the values their behavior seemed to embody, such as their cooperation for the good of community (bees) or their bad behavior in preying on weak and helpless creatures (foxes). Scientific classification into orders, genera, and species was the last approach to sorting to appear in the history of human thought about animals, and it was (and probably still is) the least common way that people think about the place of other creatures in everyday life.

In the 1800s, ordinary Americans still mentally sorted animals into a dizzying array of kinds, and a considerable amount of overlapping and complexity characterized the ways they thought about a particular animal. Some animals were wild, that is, beyond human control except insofar as their movements could be limited by obstacles like fences or their numbers reduced by hunting and trapping. The animals people knew best were tame, which meant not only that they were under human control but that they were docile and could, to some extent, be trained. Tame animals could be further sorted into stock, creatures whose fertility and life courses were controlled so that their muscle power could be harnessed for work or their bodies eventually consumed as raw materials or food. Other tame animals, such as watchdogs, were not stock, but they were household workers. Most of the representatives of the animal kind that interests us here, pets, depended on human care throughout their lives—just like stock—but their presence in a household was usually associated with private leisure and pleasure rather than work.

However, even pet animals sometimes occupied ambiguous places at the intersection of several customary categories. Were house cats that hunted rodents really fully civilized and subject to human direction? Or were they, in some fundamental way, still wild? Cage birds may have been dependent on human care and tolerant of a certain amount of handling, but they would fly away if they escaped their cages; so were they fully tame? And what of dogs and cats that had lost their identities as household workers or pets and lived on the margins of human communities? Were they now vermin, too? Even the smallest pets could embody a number of categorical complexities. Most mice were pests, but unusual-looking mice, inbred to encourage the recessive trait of albinism, were sold as children's pets in this country as early as 1870. So even the basic ways of sorting animals by their proximity or relation to civilized living were full of ambiguities. Insect-eating wild birds were recognized by many as useful workers; some wild birds became honorary pets, entitled to particular protection and care even though they did not come when called or permit themselves to be handled. But other wild birds were vermin that preyed on human resources, including animals under the care of people. Could these be killed without regret? Differences in perception of wild animal pets could also lead to conflict among people. And as in the case of my great-grandfather's groundhog (discussed in Chapter 1), differences in perception could mean that one man's wild animal pet could be another's supper.

Nineteenth-century Americans also continued to sort animals into kinds that echoed social categories. Animals could be regarded as part of family social networks. In 1829, Sophie du Pont wrote to her brother Henry that "it is the fashion here to call dogs by their master's names, for instance, Brandy *Wiliams,* Prince *Dixon,* Cupid *Biderman* etc."[2] Sometimes animals had a public role as community members. This could be as simple as being recognized as "the neighbor's cow," but some creatures had a special role as a representative of a community or group, as in the case of firehouse dogs. Especially in cities, however, most animals that people encountered were nameless strangers: anonymous workers who did hard labor in the streets, sojourners whose passing through town was as little noticed as that of any other traveler, or vagrants and tramps who made nuisances of themselves and threatened good social order.

Pet keeping developed into a richly complex activity at a time when people were still intimately acquainted with all these animal kinds. Regarding some animals sentimentally—as loyal family servants, children, or friends—did not require that people be unfamiliar with traditional uses or categories. People made the necessary discriminations, just as they did among the kinds of people they encountered. Further, an individual animal could oc-

FIGURE 4.1. The Farmer's Pets, *lithograph, Kelloggs and Comstock, New York and Hartford, Connecticut, 1848–50. Harry T. Peters, "America on Stone" Lithography Collection (60.2339), National Museum of American History, Behring Center, Smithsonian Institution.*

cupy several categories simultaneously, or its identity could change over the course of its life; a stray animal might become a pet, for example. Perhaps the best way to summarize this complexity is to note that most thinking about animals did not require that a creature be only one thing. Real identities in the world were more often a matter of "both/and" rather than "either/or." The community identities of animals were fluid, changing as settings and circumstances shifted. While the domestic ethic of kindness did make people self-conscious about at least some of their behavior toward animals and taught them new ways of behaving, most ideas about animal kinds were learned as part of living. Within daily life, ordinary situations were loaded with potential contradiction when an animal's identity crossed several categories at once.

One of the arguments that appears repeatedly in current talk about pet keeping is a classic either/or proposition: the development of pet keeping is not possible except where people are unfamiliar with strictly utilitarian uses for animals. Yet anthropologists have repeatedly demonstrated that pet keeping also takes place in small-scale, preindustrial societies whose members know very well and practice a wide range of uses for animals. Furthermore, the (admittedly fragmentary) historical record suggests that pet keeping has been a constant, if minority, practice among people in both the East and the West, and that it has taken place among people who were neither members of ruling elites nor materially well-to-do as well as among aristocratic households.[3] Each case, whether Amazonian tribal society, Japanese court life, or middle-class family in the United States, is special and grows out of different social and cultural conditions.

Many of the anecdotes of pet keeping recounted in previous chapters have indeed been set in towns and cities, settings that seem ideal for raising the question of the growth of pet keeping versus animal utility. Did city dwellers, including the middle-class and elite families mentioned previously, have much routine contact with other kinds of animals, particularly working and food animals? In fact, until the 1930s, when the urban horse had largely disappeared and municipal reformers finally pushed at least the largest working animals out of cities and sizable towns, they did. Townspeople often owned livestock as a way of guaranteeing fresh milk, eggs, and meat for their own use. Whether one lived in a small town or a large city, stepping out one's front door meant entering a complex, multispecies community where the needs and bodily functions of domestic animals shaped both formal and informal living arrangements for people and supported the lives of other creatures, too.

American artist Francis Guy's *Winter Scene in Brooklyn,* painted between 1817 and 1820, suggests what this community of people and animals was like in many towns and less densely settled cities until the end of the 1800s (see fig. 4.2). Guy painted this picture of his neighborhood from his studio window at 11 Front Street, which was actually the commercial center of small-town Brooklyn. In a key to the painting published in 1869, many of the people going about their business are identified as Guy's friends and neighbors; some of the animals are depicted with so much detail that they may be specific individuals, too, although their identities are now lost. Three dogs follow people on their errands, but three others are simply running loose and socializing. A dignified, homely old sow also makes her way up the street unimpeded, either searching for a meal or ambling home. The urban farmyard owned by Abel Titus is at the center of the picture. Titus feeds chickens before the open gate while a freely wander-

FIGURE 4.2. *Francis Guy (American, 1760–1820),* Winter Scene in Brooklyn, *ca. 1817–20, oil on canvas. Brooklyn Museum of Art, Gift of The Brooklyn Institute of Arts and Sciences.*

ing cow looks on; another cow feeds from a tub in the barnyard. Capitalizing on grain that the horse drops, more chickens peck for food in front of the open barn door where the Titus family horse resides. The two-wheeled carts pulled by horses were the light trucks of their day, hauling the coal and firewood that Brooklynites needed as fuel. A few people ride horses, but most are on foot, and the wandering animals, fellow pedestrians, do not attract particular attention. Guy's image is bucolic, of course, and does not depict the conflicts that occurred between people and animals living in close proximity. But it does suggest the multispecies character of town life, where some animals could even pursue their own interests away from the immediate supervision of their owners.

The Urban Horse

Because horses are large animals and played such an important role in town life, they provide a good starting point for this brief look at the lives of animals in human-animal communities. In towns and cities, relatively few people owned horses, but everyone relied on them. Extraordinary developments in transportation—harnessing steam for ships and trains beginning in the 1810s, adapting electricity for trolley lines beginning in the 1880s, and firing up experimental internal combustion engines by the end of the 1890s—characterized the nineteenth century. However, horses were the most flexible mode of transportation (other than human foot power) until the appearance of the modern bicycle in the 1890s (see fig. 4.3). Horses and wagons carried freight within cities; horses provided the power for cabs, streetcars, fire engines, refuse collection carts, and police wagons. In fact, the numbers of horses in American cities steadily increased until the 1910s, the first decade that automobiles were widely available, and horses remained the source of motive power for a declining number of small businesses and some urban services into the 1930s.[4]

Both large and small communities contained buildings and streetscapes created to accommodate the presence of horses, along with businesses dedicated to their needs. Cities in the Midwest and West were often designed with streets wide enough to accommodate the wide turning radius of wagons hitched to multiple teams. (The narrow streets of the oldest neighborhoods in

eastern cities reflect the fact that almost everyone walked everywhere in early America; as horses became more common and
commerce accelerated, the old streets of cities like Boston and
lower New York suffered from traffic jams.) Streetside hitching
posts, raised curbside steps for entering carriages, and water
troughs all marked the equine presence. As animal welfare organizations pushed governments to provide more streetside sources
of fresh water for cart horses, manufacturers of plumbing fixtures
and garden furnishings ceremonialized the act of dispensing public water by selling elaborate drinking fountains with separate
spigots and basins intended to serve people, horses, and dogs.

FIGURE 4.3. *Street types of New York City: Hansom driver standing in front of
horse and cab. Photograph by Elizabeth Alice Austin, ca. 1896. Library of Congress,
Division of Prints and Photographs.*

Such amenities suggested that all who used city streets were equally entitled to basic comfort.

Even small towns had a few livery stables and blacksmiths, but large communities had entire neighborhoods devoted to equine services and care. The places horses occupied had their own small ecosystems. They had to be provisioned with large quantities of hay and grain, and the presence of this food in barns and scattered on the ground attracted rodents. These, in turn, required the presence of other animals, such as cats and ratting terriers, to control them. Boys of all classes found horse environs irresistible places to loiter, comparable to boys of subsequent generations hanging around garages to watch the mechanics. Harvard professor Samuel Eliot Morrison grew up in what he called the "horsey end of town," and his memoir offers a rich picture of what that distinction meant.

> Almost the entire square between the backs of Beacon, River and Mt. Vernon Streets, and the river, was occupied by stables big and little—livery stables, which let out "seagoing" hacks and coupés; boarding and baiting stables, where gentlemen who drove in from the suburbs behind fast trotters left their rigs during the day; club stables where individuals could board one or two horses; dozens of private stables. . . . Near the corner of River Street was Joe Pink's harness shop, redolent of saddlery, where horse tack was made and repaired, and the fraternity made horse deals around the pot-bellied stove. On Lime Street, there were at least two blacksmith shops, where the cheerful ringing of hammer on anvil could be heard from 7 a.m. to late afternoon. There was Chauncy Thomas's carriage fac-

tory on lower Chestnut Street, where beautiful sleighs, victorias, broughams and other horsedrawn vehicles were built. . . . All this afforded abundant opportunities for an inquiring small boy to advance his education by picking up learned opinions from stablemen, coachmen and black-smiths on how to select and breed a horse, on equine maladies, proper horseshoeing and the like. . . .

This horsey atmosphere, delicious to the rising genera-tion, was less favorably savored by our elders. It gave the air a rich equine flavor, especially on days when the stablemen were pitching manure into the market gardeners' trucks which came to take it away. Swarms of flies penetrated 44 Brimmer Street [his house] in spite of the screens. . . . My grandmother, in desperation, offered me a cent for every fly I could kill indoors.[5]

Away from the horsey part of town, pedestrians could not help but recognize the ubiquity of the horse. The vehicles horses drew dominated street traffic, and the occasional run-away was a real safety hazard. The sounds of horseshoes on pavements, the rumble of ironclad wheels, and the shouted commands of drivers were part of the ambience of street life— as were the mounds of manure and puddles of urine that mixed with the dirt of unpaved streets and clogged gutters. In 1889, the author of *The Family Horse* estimated that the United States had 13 million horses, 2 million of which lived in cities.[6] Each produced an estimated twenty pounds of manure and several gallons of urine each day. The numbers kept increasing until the 1910s, when more than 3 million horses and mules were urban animals.[7]

The lives of most city horses, the "horses of slow work" who were the short-haul and delivery trucks of their day, were brief. Once they arrived from the countryside and were introduced to city work, their life expectancy was only two to four years. Fifteen thousand died in New York City in 1880 alone, and their carcasses often lay in the street waiting to be carted off for rendering, another city business that was part of the domestic animal economy. New York City's famous horse market even included a section where debilitated or old horses were sold to renderers and killed on the spot.[8] The fictional Black Beauty's downward spiral to cart work that touched the hearts of millions of American readers in the late nineteenth century was an accurate rendition of what happened to many city horses in the United States.

Yet Anglo-American culture had a great deal of respect and affection for horses and considered them noble and intelligent animals. The plight of urban working horses was one of the most important issues tackled by the first American animal welfare organizations, with some real success.[9] Some perceptive individuals also made the connection between the working conditions of horses, who lived a "short and miserable life" and their "overworked and underpaid" drivers.[10] In fact, both drivers and horses were anonymous, often ignored urban workers that cities could not do without. Just how important horses were was confirmed in the equine influenza epidemic of 1872. The *Live-Stock Journal* pointed out that the epidemic had caused "a suspension of street cars, omnibuses and express wagons, and blocked the wheels of commerce by preventing the transfer of freight from one locality to another." Deliveries of groceries, coal, and other necessities, transportation of bodies to cemeteries, and even delivery of the U.S. mail ground to a halt in cities from Philadelphia to Chicago.[11]

Despite their admiration for and dependence on horses, few townspeople actually owned them. Many people did not know how to care for a horse or ride any but the most gentle animal; in large cities, many probably did not know a horse by name. Around 1890, there was one horse for every five people in the United States; in cities the number was one for every ten or eleven, and most of these horses were draft animals.[12] Keeping a horse was an expensive luxury. Surviving receipts from big city livery stables indicate that 50 cents per night or $4.00 per week for boarding one animal were typical charges.[13] This was equivalent to per-night charges in all but the best hotels. Unlike cars, horses required daily care; they needed feed, their stalls required cleaning, their feet needed trimming and shoeing, and they even required periodic dentistry.

People who wanted private transportation for a special occasion borrowed a horse or hired a rig from a livery stable. Gentle, tough-mouthed horses used to novice drivers and a variety of carriages were available for hire by the hour; Alfred H. Bates of Utica, New York, guaranteed "Horses, Kind and Gentle, with Low, Easy Phaetons for Ladies's Driving."[14] Many women preferred a carriage with a driver.[15] It was possible, however, for townsfolk to go for years without setting foot in a carriage. William Lyon Phelps, who was born in New Haven in 1865, recalled the excitement of going on his first carriage ride in a hired hack—at the age of six. In 1871, his sister died of typhoid, "and when I was told that I was to be taken to the funeral, I leaped up and down and shouted and laughed with glee. I was not rebuked for this. My parents knew that I had no real notion of the tragedy of my sister's death, and that the excitement of going somewhere in a carriage overcame every other sensation."[16] Residing in what was at the time a semirural suburb of Pittsburgh at the turn of the nineteenth century, the Spencers, an upper middle-class family, still did not own a horse. If they could not walk or ride the street-car, they hired a livery stable carriage to transport them to parties, weddings, or funerals, or their Grandfather Acheson sent his own carriage, pulled by his old horse Dan. Decades later, Ethel Spencer remembered as "sheer joy" the occasional opportunities the children had on Saturdays to drive gentle Dan by themselves.[17]

Even in smaller towns, most people borrowed or rented a horse and buggy when some special occasion required it.[18] Some-times families shared a "partnership horse," since not everyone required use of the animal every day.[19] Writing from the perspec-tive of the 1920s, sociologists Robert Lynd and Helen Merrell Lynd took pains to point out that the "horse culture" of pre-automobile "Middletown" (Muncie, Indiana) had never been "as pervasive a part of the life of Middletown as is the cluster of habits that have grown up overnight around the automobile. A local carriage manufacturer of the early days estimates that 125 families owned a horse and buggy in 1890, practically all of them business class folk. . . . But if few rode in carriages in 1890, the great mass walked. The Sunday afternoon stroll was the rule."[20]

The relative rarity of the experience of driving and riding for city and suburban folk made owning a good, fast "road horse" a fantasy for young men, like owning a fast car is today; but the dream was much less accessible. The richest 5 percent of Ameri-cans owned highly bred carriage horses, and their equipage of fast horse and fancy vehicle was a well-understood symbol of their success. The author of *The Private Stable* (1899) estimated that keeping a "small stable" of good horses and a couple of vehicles required an initial investment of $3,000 and annual upkeep of an-other $2,000 to $4,000.[21] Typical annual middle-class incomes at that time were $1,000 to $2,000. Fancy horses were the expensive, high-status performance cars of their time. The animals were both admired athletes in their own right and a medium for dreams of power and money.

As new suburban developments appeared, especially in the last quarter of the nineteenth century, moderately prosperous urban folk who never would have been able to maintain a horse in a city began to look for an animal to buy after they relocated. Thus a new kind of suburban equine appeared. For the households that purchased one, the family horse (such as Grandfather Acheson's Dan) could cross several kinds: servant, ambulatory status symbol, and family friend. The family horse was no longer an anonymous worker in the hubbub of town life. Further, the arrival of the family horse coincided with the increasing importance of pet keeping and its ways of feeling and talking about animals in the late nineteenth century.

Given the general lack of experience among these new horse owners, the family horse required its own genre of advice literature. Family horse literature differed from the traditional advice directed to farriers and stable owners in its focus on the basics: how to buy a gentle but healthy horse, how to build an appropriate one-horse stable, how and what to feed your new friend, sanitation and exercise requirements for a horse confined largely to a stall, and basic directions for safe driving and riding.[22] The reassuring tone was different as well. In her 1903 *Encyclopedia of Household Economy,* directed to residents of quasi-rural suburbs, author Emily Holt titled her chapter on keeping cows and horses "Four-Footed Friends" and guaranteed her readers that "anybody—man, woman, boy, or girl—can attend to a couple of animals." Like the authors of advice on pets, she suggested that suburban husbandry was as useful a character-building enterprise as it was a contribution to familial well-being.[23]

Thus the family horse was not only a worker; it became a pet. A little volume of humor and advice on suburban life by M. E. W. Sherwood, *Home Amusements* (1881), described the best family horse as "a great pet . . . ready for the most timorous to drive. . . . The boys can harness him, the girls can drive him. . . . He has that instinct of a good family horse—he stops when anything is wrong." Blossom, the horse in Sherwood's essay, could go fast "when papa wishes to catch the train" but normally would "never do anything but walk and trot gently." Of course, no one was allowed to whip him.[24] Blossom, whose personal quirks were noted and cherished, represented a relatively new way of thinking about the most important source of transport power in American cities prior to the 1920s.

The quirks of Blossom point up the most important distinction between a horse and a motorized vehicle: when you look at an engine, it does not look back, and it does not have to be trained to respond to commands. While an engine may sputter and refuse to turn over, it never takes off at a dead run for home. In 1861, for several days the Emerson family's "submissive" horse Dolly, for example, was startled by the horse-drawn trolley cars that ran back and forth to Boston from Concord. She "ran away, broke the sleigh, hurt Mr. Craig's hand (the family man-of-all-work), and galloped back to her stall."[25] Still, while street accidents featuring horse-drawn vehicles shared some of the features of auto accidents, they were never as common as were accidents involving motor vehicles, partly because the speed of traffic was so much slower.

By 1910, articles in magazines such as *Country Life* were turning against the family horse. They offered comparative cost analyses of owning a horse versus an automobile. *Success in the Suburbs* (1917), a book that generally promoted suburban livestock, suggested that a flivver was more practical as a train greeter and mode of travel for holiday trips.[26] The status of the family horse was increasingly that of the leisure-time pet. While some family horses were allowed to spend their remaining days in the paddock or were used gently until their deaths, many were undoubtedly sold off—perhaps to be slaughtered for use in the new canned dog food of the early twentieth century. In effect, they "reverted" to their status as livestock.

The family horse sometimes survived in miniature form, however. The Shetland pony became increasingly popular as a pet for privileged children in the first decades of the twentieth century (see fig. 4.4). Hardy draft animals bred to thrive on an inhospitable island environment, Shetland ponies were (and still are) often bad tempered and stubborn, but the idea of a child-sized equine was so seductive that women's magazines advertised ponies as good suburban pets. Sometimes stores sponsored contests for children with ponies and their tack as the prize, and eventually even the Chicago mail-order companies Spiegel and Sears, Roebuck sold ponies through the 1950s.[27]

Workers and Sojourners

While only a minority of families owned horses, other animal workers were common in towns and cities. Many were transients, nameless strangers whose labors were witnessed only in passing. As American industrialization gathered momentum in the last quarter of the nineteenth century, populations of livestock grew exponentially. In 1900, the United States had an average of

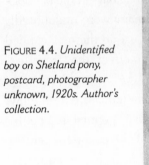

FIGURE 4.4. *Unidentified boy on Shetland pony, postcard, photographer unknown, 1920s. Author's collection.*

25.6 people per square mile; large animals (not including dogs, cats, or poultry) numbered 72.8 per square mile. And one in eleven American factory workers and tradespeople were involved in industries processing animal bodies—for meat, textiles, fat and oil, and other raw materials that were made into hundreds of commercial products (tallow for soap, hooves for gelatin, and hides for leather).[28] While large herds of stock animals did not live permanently in cities, they passed through and spent time in the pens of abattoirs, which were increasingly pushed to the edges of towns as the century passed (see fig. 4.5). This meant that the well-to-do no longer lived with the stench of large quantities of manure and the smells of butchering and rendering, but working-class families still did, since they needed to live within walking distance of their places of employment.

Despite the gradual trend toward large-scale livestock operations, many city people were also on a first-name basis with individual animals. As late as 1900, 25 percent of all barns, stables, and other animal enclosures in the United States were still located in cities and towns of 2,500 or more people.[29] Townspeople often kept flocks of chickens or a pig or two; both working- and middle-class families kept a family cow and made extra income by sharing milk with their neighbors. (Recall that the Great Chicago Fire of 1870 was supposedly caused by "Mrs. O'Leary's cow," who kicked over a kerosene lantern during milking.) While town and city centers gradually grew more compact in the Northeast in particular, many communities consisted largely of neighborhoods where houses were supported by complexes of small buildings—sheds, chicken coops, and small barns—along with small yards for livestock and space for family gardens. Other livestock did not need the array of businesses associated with horse keeping, but local feed stores still supplied grain and hay, along with over-the-counter veterinary remedies and other supplies. Local livestock dealers and butchers traded in excess animals that could not be sold to or bartered with neighbors.

Chickens were the most common urban livestock, since they were relatively easy to keep in family-size flocks. Having chickens meant plenty of fresh eggs, an otherwise expensive luxury in some seasons. Allowing hens to "set" also led to a supply of new layers and cockerels for Sunday dinner, and old hens could be killed for stewing after their egg-laying declined. In Samuel Canby Rumford's Wilmington, Delaware, of the 1880s and 1890s, "most families had flocks and in every part of town the crowing of roosters

FIGURE 4.5. *Bill Payne driving hogs through town, Black River Falls, Wisconsin, early twentieth century. Photograph by Charles J. Van Schaick. Collection Wisconsin Historical Society.*

could be heard." In Rumford's own family, as in rural families for generations prior, his mother's "big Brahma chickens" fed on table scraps and vegetable peels. Working-class Wilmingtonians let their chickens scratch in the streets so they could feed entirely off the undigested grain from horse droppings.[30] Chickens and other poultry were popular children's pets, too. Bantam chickens were small and docile, and many children seem to have owned one or two at some time (see fig. 4.6). In her memoir of growing up in a streetcar suburb of Baltimore in the 1910s, Nan Agle recalled that her family kept chickens for eggs and meat. Two bantam chickens, Billy and Jenny, lived in the flock but were her older sister's pets.[31] This meant that they were protected from the fates that awaited the rest of the Hayden family's poultry. Killing a chicken (by wringing its neck or cutting off its head) for Sunday dinner was a common event, one that most children and adults witnessed at some time, if they did not do the slaughtering themselves (see fig. 4.7).

Like chickens, pigs were relatively easy to keep in town because they did not require much space. They could even be turned out to wander and were trusted to find their way home, like the old sow in Francis Guy's painting. Roaming pigs were a problem in some compact American cities such as New York throughout the first half of the nineteenth century (see the discussion of animal vagrants later in this chapter). Towns found pigs, like chickens,

FIGURE 4.6. *Paul A. G. Johnson (b. 1908) and his pet bantam chicken, East Los Angeles, California. Collection of Paul E. Johnson.*

FIGURE 4.7. Her First Refusal, *photoprint by R. J. Cracker, 1909 (American). Library of Congress, Division of Prints and Photographs. This photoprint, which was offered for sale, represents the dilemma faced by some of the children who had been raised to treat animals kindly and who may have had livestock animals as pets.*

useful because of their unbridled enthusiasm for waste of all kinds. In an era before systematic refuse pickup, they converted garbage into meat. H. H. Delong's best friend, the son of a widow, spent a good part of each day scavenging Danville for food scraps for the single pig, "old Bristles," the family raised each year in a shed behind their house. The boy amused himself by keeping a pet turtle in the animal's "swill barrel" (the collection point where the food waste was added to water to make a kind of soup).[32]

An extraordinary number of cows also lived in cities and towns. In the largest cities, commercial dairies kept cows sequestered from the public eye, often in miserable conditions, but the routine of caring for a "backyard cow" was part of family life in cities until the early 1900s.[33] H. H. Delong recalled that "about every fifth citizen kept a cow and supplied a few neighbors" in his town in the 1850s and 1860s.[34] In Wilmington, Delaware, in the 1890s (a city of 61,000), the Rumford family kept cows in a vacant lot across the street from their downtown house.[35] Because cows "freshened" by the birth of a calf had so much milk to give, families often shared an animal. Young Nan Hayden's family outside Baltimore had the barn; their neighbor Mr. Griffith supplied Bess, the cow; and both families shared the milk.[36] Cow keeping was also part of life in tonier suburban developments, especially for families concerned about the healthfulness of milk from commercial dairies. The extended Acheson-Spencer family, who had moved to the new Shadyside suburb of Pittsburgh in 1877, kept two cows in the 1890s, when the Spencer children were young. The family cow pasture was ornamented by a row of cannas, and Ethel Spencer recalled that as a child she loved the ritual of mixing the cows' daily mash and helping with the milking and skimming.[37]

Like the suburban family horse, the suburban family cow generated a literature of advice directed to new owners. It was never as large, however, perhaps because expertise on cow keeping was more widespread than skill at horse care. *Keeping One Cow*, a newsy collection of essays first published in 1888 and expanded in a new edition in 1906, recorded the amount of daily labor involved in the practice but suggested that it was not difficult. "The family cow is a usual, if not indispensable part of the domestic outfit of the village or suburban dweller," announced the publisher. "It is not a question of dairy farming, but of dairy gardening."[38] In their essays, enthusiastic cow-keepers from all over the United States discussed how to maintain an animal successfully on a property as small as half an acre (even, in one case, in a stall in a carriage barn on a town lot). Some reported relying on help from a handyman (the Acheson-Spencer family did so), but for most the cow was a family project. Henry E. Alvord of Easthampton, Massachusetts, provided a year-by-year journal for 1875–80. He described his routines of milking and experiments with timing calving so that the cow would produce milk through the winter, and he included plans of his village lot, the stable he adapted for June (the cow's name) and a small flock of chickens, and a small adjoining meadow he rented.[39]

Working with the family cow, which included twice-daily milking by hand, required a level of physical closeness literally unmatched by work with other livestock. Yet keeping even one cow also meant facing the facts of animal birth, life, and death. Cows required calving in order to freshen, and since half of newborns were male, keeping them was out of the question under any circumstances. (A family might keep a she-calf if the mother was approaching the end of her productivity.) The comments of one of the authors in *Keeping One Cow* suggest the discomfort that family cow-keepers sometimes experienced when scruples about kindness to animals and the metaphor of animal families being like human ones collided with the realities of livestock ownership. "The disposal of the calf depends on circumstances, of which the owner is the best judge," he noted. "If the calf is not to be raised, it ought to be sold before it is a week old, because the milk that it drinks before it is ready for the shambles [butchering], is worth more than the price it will bring. If a purchaser for the calf cannot be found while it is so young, it is most profitable to kill it. . . . I simply state this as a fact, without recommending it to be done, for it is cruel work; but so is any butchering." This author also acknowledged that the mother would "grieve for its loss," although the sooner the calf was "removed" from the cow, the shorter this period would be.[40] Finally, no matter how beloved the family cow, in time she would stop giving milk, and her care would be an expense with no payoff. Even if family cows were, in that same author's words, "the pet and delight of the household," they were eventually sold off and killed, their bodies rendered for meat and the raw materials of other consumer goods.

The Livestock Pet

Keeping livestock meant that people were used to making routine decisions about animal life and death based on practical concerns. Some families faced what they perceived as unpleasant dilemmas, as the discussion above regarding the necessity of killing young calves suggests. Because they were still learning the commonsense rules of animal kinds, children in particular questioned the practices they saw around them. They were socialized to be kind to animals and were encouraged to keep numerous pets, and they lived in everyday contact with stock animals. Now these children had to learn to accept killing and eating animals they knew well. Sometimes they had chosen to regard stock animals as pets without the blessing of their parents; sometimes their parents encouraged the familiarity and were the agents who created the problem. Conflict over livestock pets reveals the qualified and human-centered nature of the pet kind, elements of the definition that most discussions of pet keeping avoided treating explicitly. Pet status was something given to animals, and it could be taken away.

Understanding the dilemma of children with livestock pets requires learning something about attitudes toward meat as part of the human diet. While the effects of eating animal flesh on human well-being were debated by diet reformers and a handful of ethical vegetarians, almost all Americans accepted the idea that meat was a necessary, if potentially volatile, part of the diet and were candid about its origins. It was a "stimulating" food that strengthened people who did hard physical labor. Recuperating invalids were encouraged to ingest gallons of "beef tea" as an important element of their convalescent diet.[41] Presenting meat to guests was an essential (and ancient) part of celebrations and feasting of all kinds, including the American ritual of the family Sunday dinner. In everyday life, salted pork (the most common meat until the development of the modern beef industry beginning in the 1870s) seasoned otherwise bland food, and animal fats were the only fats available to cooks. In contrast to the ready availability and cheapness of meat in the modern American diet, meat in nineteenth- and early twentieth-century America was expensive, although the gradual industrialization of livestock production did bring its cost down over time. Its comparative high cost can be detected in period cookbooks, where recipes made routine use of cuts and parts that few Americans eat today, and in the "family budget" studies undertaken by the first generation of social workers in the early twentieth century. Thus growing one's own meat sources was highly desirable, even for relatively well-to-do families.

When advocates of the domestic ethic of kindness encouraged people to regard animals as individuals of worth, killing and eating livestock became a practice that had to be actively justified rather than simply accepted. Popular prints in which the denizens of the barnyard were labeled "the farmer's pets" (see fig. 4.1), however, may have added to children's confusion. Authors who tried to tackle this problem were generally reduced to the sort of weak argument published in *Right and Wrong; or Familiar Illustrations of the Moral Duties of Children* (1834). Presented as a conversation among three siblings, the lessons in this small book included one discussion based on the youngest child's discovery that meat comes from "oxen and lambs and pigs." He asks, "Is n't [*sic*] it wicked to kill them?" His older sister replies, "No, God gave them to us to eat. . . . God gave man *dominion* over the cattle, and over the fish, and over the fowls. *That* means, that we may use them as we please, only we must not hurt them, when we can help it. We have to kill the oxen, and the lambs, and the pigs sometimes, or else we should have no meat for dinner."[42]

Alert children wondered about the fairness of these arrangements, however. Samuel Clemens kept a flock of Pekin ducks at his Hartford, Connecticut, suburban house in the 1880s; they were intended for eating, and the children knew it. Once Jean Clemens, who must have been five or six at the time, observed a new hatch of ducklings and asked her father, "I wonder why God gives us so much Ducks as Patrick [the handyman] kills so many."[43] Sometimes eating pets was even a punishment, as when Samuel Canby Rumford had to sell his illicit gamecocks for family dinners.

One parental strategy for dealing with the attachment of children to livestock pets was to make the animal disappear. Six-year-old Clara Clemens got too attached to a calf named Jumbo after P. T. Barnum's ill-fated elephant (see fig. 4.8). Patrick the handyman had informed her that if she brushed Jumbo enough, the animal would turn into a pony, and she tried several times to ride the calf. Fearing that she would be hurt, Patrick simply "disappeared" Jumbo from the barn. Clara's grief brought Jumbo a temporary

FIGURE 4.8. *Clara Clemens and Jumbo with the family dog Hash. Photograph by H. L. Bundy, Hartford, Connecticut, 1884. Courtesy, The Mark Twain Project, The Bancroft Library.*

reprieve, as Samuel Clemens insisted that the calf be bought back. However, it is telling that Clara's story about Jumbo, told decades after the fact, neither explains why the calf was there in the first place nor reveals what eventually happened to the animal.[44] Given the attention span of small children, time was often on parents' side.

Another sad story of a livestock pet was recorded in an unpublished memoir by Emily Rankin of Cherry Hill. It concerned a pet ram named Billy, dead a hundred years, who had been given as a "tiny white lamb" to Emily's mother, Kittie Putnam, as a child. "Billy grew into a splendid ram friendly to all the family but he did not like Fred the hired man. He would catch him under the knees when Fred was going down hill." Kittie's uncle Peter Elmendorf asked the girl "if it would be all right if she found a ten dollar bill on her pin cushion and never saw Billy again." Kittie "knew the ram was a great care and that her uncle was not very young any more and she consented. But for years she would not eat a piece of mutton for fear of eating Billy."[45]

This informal protest—refusing to eat an animal one knew socially—appears to have been common among children with livestock pets. An 1877 letter to *St. Nicholas* offered the story of "Misery," a pet goose who was killed and eaten because he "seemed so unhappy in spite of all we did for him" and was growing thin. The ten-year-old author concluded, "P.S. I did not eat any of the goose"; she mentioned that her family was soon going to have a "little dog."[46]

A story that demonstrates how a number of practices, including the informal lessons taught by parents, worked together to teach children the rules of relationships between people and livestock may be found in the children's book *Victoria: A Pig in a Pram* (1963), by Mary Ellen Chase. Chase wrote it as a memoir with invented dialogue recounting an incident when its author was ten years old around 1897. Daughter of a lawyer and judge in a small town in Maine, Chase grew up in a household that kept pets, a horse for her father's work, and a sow whose annual litter provided the family's supply of pork. The children disliked the sow and her progeny, who lived in a muddy sty under the barn, but they still dreaded the coming of winter, when "a brave man, known throughout the country side as 'Mr. Leach, the pig-sticker,' would come to carry out his grim duty." When slaughtering time came, "we children all ran upstairs to bury our heads in our pillows so that we might not hear the shrieks" of the young pigs.

One year, however, Chase's tenderhearted father, who routinely rescued stray cats and dogs from the roadside, impulsively saved a newborn piglet after the sow rolled over on it and broke its back. Chase's mother bandaged the piglet and turned it over to the little girl for care. Chase and her father distinguished the piglet from the rest of the litter by keeping it clean, allowing it in the house, and naming it Victoria after the queen of England. The girl gave Victoria, who slept in the kitchen in a laundry basket full of pillows, a daily bath with Castile soap and taught her how to eat oatmeal from a spoon. Victoria wore a crocheted baby bonnet, pinafore, and pink booties on her hind feet without complaining and became the talk of the town when Chase wheeled her around in an old English pram donated by her aunt. The young girl was convinced that the piglet enjoyed "all the things that separated her from her filthy and forgotten family in their odious sty." She had been "raised" into a civilized and better life.

Victoria's inevitable future, however, loomed over the little girl. As she cared for her charge, "somewhere in the dim future, I sensed tragedy; but I resolutely put all such dark fears out of my mind." Her mother admitted that she wished the piglet wasn't growing so fast. Finally her father proclaimed that the piglet was "reverting to type." Chase's sister explained, "He meant that she's just a pig after all. He meant she'd become just like her family if you put her down with them under the barn." Her parents "softened the tragic blow" by allowing the piglet to be sold to a local farmer. Victoria's fate would now be unknown rather than certain, and her meat would not be consumed by the Chase family. Her father, who had initiated the saga, pronounced the situation a "collision of worlds." The only possible resolution was returning Victoria to the category she had been born into—it was "just the way things are."[47]

In Mary Ellen Chase's household, Victoria made the entire family pause and consider its categories for animals self-consciously, even if the end result was simply the ratification of usual behaviors. Other children recognized and struggled with their feelings alone as they learned to live with the realities of animal life and death. An example of this can be found in the childhood diary of Margaret Harding Tileston (1867–1912).[48] Raised on a farm in Concord, Massachusetts, Margaret Harding was the second of seven children of a Harvard-educated farmer who, a generation after Thoreau and Emerson, seems to have sought out farming as a virtuous alternative to city living. Margaret was eleven years old when she began to record her daily activities and some of the work on the farm. She was aware of the discussion of animal treatment found in magazines such as *St. Nicholas* and *Our Dumb Animals,* since she recorded receiving copies of both as gifts from her visiting grandfather on six occasions in 1878.[49] On 9 August 1878, Margaret began an account called "Animals," where she provided a genealogy of animals she had known on the farm: 35 cats, 42 cows, 62 calves "born on the farm" and 37 more bought "from the butcher," the dog Jock, and the farm's four horses. She updated this part of her diary until December 1880.

The routine farm practice of selling very young calves to the butcher made Margaret deeply uneasy. Margaret and her sister Mary had named each calf, perhaps without their father's approval. In her account, Margaret listed each by name and recorded its sex, color, mother if known and date born, and its fate, usually "sold to butcher," and the date. Some entries included a brief observation of the calf's nature; others commented on the girl's feelings. After Highlander, a red-and-white bull calf born in 1879, became meat for the family, she noted, "We had some of his veal, but I didn't eat any."

At the end of the first volume of her diary, Margaret included a section titled "Anecdotes of Cattle," where she poured out her heart about the fate of the calves. The most dramatic entry, on 5–6 February 1879, concerned the fate of Bright-eyes, a calf that the girl had, in an earlier entry, called her pet:

> Bright-eyes is the sweetest bossie that ever was born. She will kiss with her little gray nose, and she used to play with me bunting my knees. . . . Tomorrow the butcher is coming to take my Brighteyes away. He will probably take Daylight too. I have planted a great many kisses on the pretty white star in Brighteyes forhed. She will alway be a dear, little calf in Heaven. . . . Brighteyes and the pig were sold to the butcher this morning February 6th 1879. I dreamt twice about her going. The butcher came at six-oclock. I was awake in the night.[50]

There is a gap of several months in the surviving record, but something had changed by the opening of a new volume of Margaret's diary in 1881. The girl had stopped chronicling the births and subsequent fates of cattle, although she noted their departures in passing. She had been given complete responsibility for the farm's flock of poultry (she called them "my hens") and earned small amounts of money from occasionally selling eggs. She received an allowance of twenty-five cents a week on top of that.[51] As she had done with the calves, Margaret named the chickens. But while she refused to eat the veal that had once been Highlander, she had no such qualms about the cockerels slaughtered for dinner: "White Knight, Young Man and his twin brother, three of our cocks, were killed at night. . . . We ate the three cocks for dinner and they were very nice and tender."[52] By then, Margaret had concentrated her loving attention on a single pet bantam chicken who would not be eaten, and by the summer she was preparing to go away to school and her father was trying to sell the farm. Like Mary Ellen Chase, Margaret had come to accept "just the way things are."

Alice Stone Blackwell, the only child of suffragists Lucy Stone and Henry Blackwell, took principal responsibility for raising chickens for both eggs and meat on the family's property in the new suburb of Dorchester, Massachusetts. She also won first prize for her school in the Massachusetts Society for the Prevention of Cruelty to Animals (SPCA) essay contest for 1872; the theme was Kindness to Animals. The girl's understanding of the ethic of kindness clearly led to an expanded sense of stewardship toward her little flock and ambivalence about consuming the excess roosters. On 14 September 1872, her birthday, Alice Blackwell wrote that "there was a splendid sunset, but I was worried in my conscience because I was to have a rooster killed, and did not go up to see it." On Thanksgiving of the same year, she noted that the family "dined off my massacred roosters."[53]

For some sensitive youngsters trained in the domestic ethic of kindness, ingesting the body of any familiar continued to cause discomfort even as they accepted the distinctions among animal kinds. Children's literature may only have compounded this confusion. Editors of magazines such as *Harper's Young People* persisted in publishing items that used the first-person animal voice—the technique employed to promote sympathy—and made stock animals fully conscious of their fates. One poem, written in the voice of a Thanksgiving turkey, ended by promising, "If you'll quit eating turkey, / I'll send you a kiss."[54] By the end of the century, even advice books recommending livestock rearing as a good hobby for middle-class children admitted that "it makes one feel like a cannibal to have an animal you are attached to slaughtered and eaten."[55] Few children, except those who participate in the rural and suburban livestock-raising clubs of 4-H, the national agricultural education program, face this dilemma today. The children who raise calves or sheep are socialized to separate themselves from the animals they sell at the end of each season, but there is an important difference between the past and the present. Members of 4-H rarely see their projects slaughtered or are asked to eat the meat; the animals' fate is known, yet it is also unseen.

Art, Pet, Meat

Among the difficulties associated with defining animals on the edges of the "pet kind," "pet stock" may have presented the most complex case. This special animal kind appeared by name in advertisements for pet shops by the 1870s. It generally embraced purebred poultry and pigeons, "fancy" rodents (rabbits, cavies, and white mice and rats), and goldfish. Pet stock animals could be treasured companions, cosseted aesthetic objects, or animal resources providing meat or fur and feathers. Because pet stock animals were small and most were relatively inexpensive, they were perfect for cramped quarters in town lots. While children raised and enjoyed pet stock, thousands of men and a smaller number of women also engaged in a more intensive practice called "fancy breeding" as a pastime. For an animal species to become this sort of ornamental pet stock, it had to display a range of genetic variability, and it had to breed frequently enough and mature quickly enough that fanciers could experiment with crosses and see the results in a few months. Fanciers exhibited their best animals competitively, with prizes awarded on the basis of published "standards of perfection" developed by national clubs of fanciers.

Fancy pigeons are perhaps the best example of the richly ambiguous world of pet stock (see fig. 4.9). Pigeon breeding is an ancient practice that dates back at least to the Roman Empire. The 150 breeds of fancy pigeons all derive from one common ancestor, but their widely distinctive looks and behaviors are the result of deliberate inbreeding in closed populations to encourage recessive traits to emerge. The word "fancy," an old contraction of "fantasy," suggested to people in the past that something was capricious and imaginative, yet pleasing. Applying the term to special breeds of animals or cultivars of plants in the nineteenth century suggested that prized standards of appearance were based on artifice—on intervening in nature, reshaping the qualities of the natural object in ways that were pleasing and entertaining.[56]

Purebred pigeons were kept as living ornaments in a few American households by the early nineteenth century. American interest in showing fancy pigeons competitively had its roots in European clubs, particularly the English groups whose refined breeding practices engaged the interest and participation of Charles Darwin as he worked out the implications of what he called "artificial selection" for his theory of evolution.[57] By the 1840s, the same decade that progressive American farmers became deeply interested in importing chickens from Asia and Europe to improve the American dooryard flock, fancy pigeons were turning up in surprising places. In June 1842, a large advertisement in the *South Carolina Temperance Advocate and Register of Agriculture and General Literature* announced the arrival in Columbia of a collection of eight different breeds of fancy pigeons, which were offered for sale "back of the Barber's Shop, second door below THOMPSON's Shoe Store." The text praised the birds in this "extensive, rare, and beautiful collection" for their "peculiar beauty and innocence" and described each variety in detail, which suggests that the pigeons would have been something new to the paper's readership.[58] As early as 1852, fancy pigeons were given space in the large, important

FIGURE 4.9. *"Group of Fancy Pigeons,"* American Agriculturalist, *December 1868. Author's collection. This image introduced some of the most common types and suggested that they be housed in a decorative dovecote.*

poultry shows of New York, Boston, and other cities.[59] But like the craze for purebred dogs, the American pigeon fancy seems to have received a boost at the Centennial Exposition, where 500 coops of 34 different breeds were displayed alongside the cream of American livestock.[60]

This timing is important, for the rise in pet stock fancies was not only associated with the growing popularity of pet keeping generally. It was also linked to expanding popular interest in self-expression through the practice of avocational fine and applied arts: china painting, "art needlework," ornamental woodworking, and a score of other activities that middle-class Americans had enough time and spare money to pursue as a form of leisure. While women were encouraged to explore a wide variety of arts and crafts as accomplished amateurs, middle-class men were more constrained in their pursuit of these pastimes because so many were regarded as female avocations. The typical leisure pursuits of men—woodworking, gardening, and fancy breeding—had some symbolic relationship to men's traditional livelihoods as craftsmen and farmers.

Fancy breeding of small animals (first pigeons and, in time, rabbits, cavies, and goldfish) also offered a parallel artistic experience for men. For the true fancier, it was husbandry for art's sake alone. The pigeon fancier's work was the creation of "living pictures," one breeder noted. He was motivated by "the same longing that incites the painter, the sculptor, or the connoisseur." He even argued that the activity had a refining influence on men precisely because its purpose was "solely to maintain the fancy points of color and outline, with no reference to utility." Although poultry fanciers were always able to argue that their efforts to improve breeds were useful to farmers, New England pigeon fancier William G. Barton pointed out with pride that his chosen fancy was purely aesthetic, "allied to that for roses, dahlias, and tulips; and I will venture to assert, that in grace of form, and beauty of color and marking, those flowers have in pigeons formidable rivals."[61] Another author insisted that fancy pigeons offered lessons in beauty for children. He gave his "Littlest Girl" pairs of Fantail and Runt pigeons, and subsequently added others to the family coop. "I am tempted to doubt if the over-burdened magnate who pays half a million for a Rembrandt masterpiece derives any greater, or higher, esthetic satisfaction than we have experienced from the daily sight of 'Fannies' mincing forward with tail-feathers set," he wrote.[62] The ritual of the pigeon show reinforced the comparison between fancy pigeons and art objects. Some varieties, particularly the pouter, were shown on small wooden pedestals, and the standards for connoisseurship were as elaborate as those for a work of art.

Raising and racing homing pigeons also became an American pastime in the 1880s. This hobby differed from the fancy in that athletic performance, rather than appearance, was its goal. But it was like the aesthetic hobby in that it involved constant cultivation of the animals, efforts to breed toward a standard of excellence, and the steady expenditure of money to support a leisure pursuit involving small-animal husbandry.

While fancy breeders in the past did not know the genetic science behind breeding, they did understand that creating controlled lines for inbreeding resulted in some offspring in each generation that had the special characteristics they desired. From the standpoint of genetics, all animal fancies are based on breeding in a closed population to encourage recessive traits, and breeders deliberately inbred to attain ever more exaggerated looks. As the contemporary debate over dog breeding practices suggests, this is not necessarily in the best interest of the genetic health of a species. In the case of fancy pigeons, some breeds were (and remain today) so "manmade" that they would quickly disappear without human intervention (like the English bulldogs that are now unable to deliver their large-headed puppies vaginally). The most dramatic examples of this in the pigeon world were the "short-faced" breeds, whose tiny beaks and bulging heads meant that they could not successfully regurgitate pigeon milk (partially digested food) into the open mouths of their newly hatched "squeakers." Fanciers kept ordinary pigeons (their own young were removed from the nest and presumably destroyed) that served as nurses to the fancy babies. Another prized breed, "tumblers," were unable to fly in a straight line but "fell" through the air in somersaults, a characteristic that would have quickly disappeared in wild flocks. To the fancy, this high degree of artificiality was precisely the point. A British guide to pigeon breeding pointed out that the fancier regarded the "natural bird with slight esteem" and that the most "high-class birds" were the ones with the greatest "structural peculiarities."[63] Artificiality is a theme that appears repeatedly in other pet stock fancies of the period. There was an interest in fancy goldfish with delicate, long fins and fragile, bulging eyes (reportedly first imported from Japan at the height of the craze for "Japonisme" in the late 1870s) and a much smaller craze for fancy mice. The latter took pains to retain such recessive traits as "waltzing" (the animal travels in circles because of a defect in its ability to balance itself), albinism, and even hairlessness.

By the late nineteenth century, the men who took up the pigeon fancy included businessmen, professionals, white-collar workers, and skilled artisans. On 25 December 1898, the Syracuse, New York, *Herald* featured a two-page spread titled "Some

Pigeon Fanciers of Syracuse and their Collections," discussing a group of men who bred and showed unusual pigeons "merely for the pleasure to be derived from the pursuit." Mr. F. J. West, the "best known" of the group, spent "the greater part of his spare time . . . watching and caring for his pets"—as many as 140 birds at a time—in a purpose-built, two-story loft with stove heat, electric lighting, and running water. West, the proprietor of a wholesale and retail millinery business, collected and showed white birds only from a number of breeds: turbits, dragoons, Burmese hen pigeons, fantails, owls, and Japanese frillbacks. He segregated his stock by show quality, trading away his second-rank animals. While West undoubtedly enjoyed an advantage in being able to purchase highly rated birds, the possibility always remained that his colleagues with more modest pocketbooks could breed their own champions with some careful planning. The community of local fanciers to which West belonged included a grocer, a church sexton, a bookkeeper, a real estate agent, and a pattern maker—respectable men in respectable occupations.[64] More research is needed, but a similar pattern seems to hold for the other small-animal fancies, too. Rearing fancy goldfish, and later tropical fish, and showing them competitively seems to have been popular among white-collar professional men (see Chapter 5) before the practice was accessible to less-affluent men.

The literature of all fancies tended to downplay the necessity of culling or the possibility of eating the rejects. Pigeon fanciers then (and now) also had to deal with birds that were not good enough to show or reproduce and that could not be traded to other fanciers. If no pet shop wanted these rejected birds, the question was, How should the fancier dispose of them? The literature of the pigeon fancy was notably quiet on the subject, al-

though pet stock was increasingly promoted as a way for townsfolk to produce meat for the family table and to practice commercial husbandry on a small scale. It may have been considered
improper to eat culls.

As pet keeping expanded, so did rearing pet stock for sale. By
the 1890s, promoters of pet stock pronounced that "no industry offers a more favorable field, especially for women who must support themselves."[65] A short-lived magazine called *Pet Stock World*
featured successful stories of pet stock breeders in the mid-1910s.
In the early 1900s, breeders also promoted pet stock with an emphasis on meat. They encouraged a fad for raising Belgian hares
and squabs (young pigeons) as a profitable addition to suburban
small farms, but American cooks never embraced rabbit and pigeon meat as a major part of the family diet.[66] More important, the
relationship of the pet stock world to laboratories was also clearly
established by the early twentieth century, when middlemen
began to purchase animals directly from amateur breeders.[67] Pet
stock animals—aesthetic objects, pets, and meat sources—now
had another identity as scientific tools; by the mid-twentieth century, this was the dominant role played by a number of species.

Tramps and Vagrants

Throughout the nineteenth century and well into the twentieth,
town and city streets in the United States were full of animal
strangers—pigs, chickens, dogs, cats, and at the dark edges, mice
and rats—pursuing their own interests. Free-roaming "vagrant"
large animals, sometimes deliberately turned out to scavenge or
graze in vacant lots, were common enough to require control by
ordinance. This was not a new problem. Colonial governments

had passed hundreds of laws to control the movements of large animals and push them to the margins of increasingly crowded city centers. Such laws, one historian notes, were honored "far more in the breach than in practice."[68] Hogs were critically important urban scavengers in growing American cities. They consumed the mixture of garbage, manure and human slop, offal from butchering, and dead animals that filled open gutters and converted it into flesh to be consumed by the people who owned them. In New York City, for example, tenement dwellers relied on these animals as a principal source of meat, and butchers "ran" pigs to fatten them for free.[69] In the 1840s, pigs were still a prominent feature of New York street life, even in the best shopping districts; in a famous passage from his *American Notes,* Charles Dickens dubbed them the "gentleman hogs" of Broadway.[70]

Philadelphia's laws against roaming livestock suggest the complexity and mixed character of the animal population of most cities. In 1855, the city passed a resolution that listed the creatures that citizens were used to meeting in their daily rounds. It forbade "any horse or horse kind, cow heifer, bull or steer, sheep or sheep kind, pig or goat, to go at large in any of the highways of the City, nor in any of the public squares or parks thereof, or upon any unenclosed field, common or piece of land therein." The city council did not forbid outright ownership of pigs in the central, most urban wards of the city until 1912, and abattoirs were still allowed to raise hogs, although not within one-half mile of churches, schools, and hospitals. Clearly, urban husbandry that relied on the use of open land within city boundaries was still common.[71]

Wandering cows and pigs were the largest animal vagrants in mid-nineteenth-century cities, but they were never the most numerous, only the most obviously destructive to property. American city streets were also full of wandering dogs and cats, despite early animal control efforts. Like the underclass of people who traveled around begging for their livings or doing odd jobs for a meal or a place to sleep, ownerless cats and dogs were called "tramps." The use of the term is important. It suggests that people regarded such animals, despite their misfortunes, as somehow still the masters of their own lives. This idea and the name still lingered as late as 1955, when Walt Disney released the cartoon musical *Lady and the Tramp*. Tramp was an unowned, unneutered male mutt who roamed the city at his pleasure and escaped from the city pound whenever he was captured.

Not all wandering dogs were tramps. Some were simply following their owners around town or patrolling their immediate neighborhoods. Like Francis Guy's picture of 1820 Brooklyn, prints and paintings of city streets almost always contained wandering dogs, and this was not just an artistic convention. Sometimes the status of a dog was a matter of perception. In large cities, for example, working-class dog owners seem to have been more willing to let their dogs run because the animals could scare up at least part of their own living by scavenging. In any event, whether owned, abandoned, or truly feral, tramp dogs wandered cities—fighting, socializing, accosting people carrying market baskets, and eating dead animals and trash in the gutters. While rabies was relatively rare, the American public was terrified of the disease and regarded strange dogs with suspicion, especially during the summer. Thus cities paid for horrendous dog killing sprees, where dogs were clubbed to death in the street or taken back to crude city "pounds" and either bludgeoned to death or drowned after brief stays. The pound keepers made exceptions for dogs that were obviously well fed; they were held for a day or two in anticipation that their owners would bail them out for a dollar or two (see fig. 4.10). Municipal pound workers seem to have been a rough lot, exactly the sort of violent men whom advocates for kindness feared. In 1877, two New York City dog-catchers were even sued for assault and battery on a dog owner. In any event, they treated dogs as vermin rather than as moral exemplars and faithful friends.[72]

When local governments recognized wandering dogs as a public nuisance, they began efforts to control their numbers by creat-

FIGURE 4.10. At the Dog Pound—The Rescue of a Pet, *drawn by W. A. Rogers, wood engraving,* Harper's Weekly, *16 June 1883. Library of Congress, Division of Prints and Photographs.*

AT THE DOG POUND—THE RESCUE OF A PET.—DRAWN BY W. A ROGERS.

ing dog taxes and requiring licenses. As early as 1809, Philadelphia required that a census be taken each year of "all dogs of upwards of one month in age, owned or possessed by any person or
persons." It created a sliding annual licensing fee of 25 cents for
the first dog, $1.00 for the second, and $2.00 apiece for the rest.
This was a very large sum, and it was intended to squelch the
multidog household, at least among poorer citizens.[73] Because
city police forces were small and licensing fees were high, most
people probably did not license their dogs. Well into the twentieth century in smaller communities, licensing laws simply required that dogs be registered, not confined (see fig. 4.11).

Local governments and humane organizations were slow to
turn their attention to cats. Cats were not likely to attack people,
and they usually conducted their lives at night, away from human
eyes. Small businesses and even government offices relied on cats
to protect their contents from rats and mice. The U.S. Post Office
relied on what one observer called "quite an army of cats" to protect the mail; postmasters in large cities even had budgets for "cat
meat."[74] Anywhere grain was stored to service livestock, cats were
present. But cities were also full of half- or wholly wild tramp cats
that performed an important if unacknowledged service by at least
partially controlling larger urban rat populations, especially in port
cities. The old cartoons of battered-looking tomcats singing and
fighting in alleys at night represent another truth about the complex urban human-animal community. Even in big cities, most cats
were routinely allowed out to wander, and owners expected fights
between their own animals and feline invaders. John W. Gould of
Orange, New Jersey, was pleased when his cat Mike matured
enough to have "his experience fighting outside. He has licked all
the Tramps but one & I think he will whip that one next time."[75]

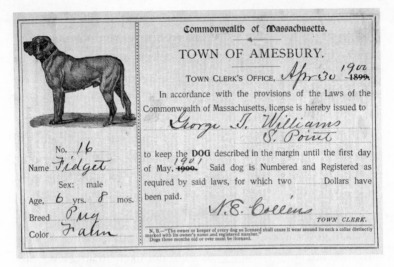

FIGURE 4.11. *Dog license for Fidget the Pug, owned by George T. Williams, Amesbury, Massachusetts, 1901. Author's collection.*

By the early twentieth century, public health professionals in the largest urban centers had turned their attention to remaking cities into orderly, healthier environments with safe water, clean streets, and regular trash pickup. In this context, the urban tramp cat was no longer a joke or even an unpleasant yet acceptable fact of life. Cities had needed them, but now the misery of half-starved feral cats and increasing, if misguided, public concern about cats as carriers of diseases, including poliomyelitis, led to new efforts to control their numbers. Whether or not populations of stray cats had increased dramatically in those years, as advocates of control claimed, it is true that hundreds of thousands of cats were captured and killed between 1890 and 1910.[76] In 1911, the New York SPCA killed "upwards of three hundred thousand cats," most of which were kittens. Philadelphia disposed of 50,000, and Boston destroyed another 25,000 that same year. The author of the *McClure's* magazine article that startled readers with those figures excoriated pet owners who abandoned their cats for the summers or refused to euthanize unwanted kittens: "It does not fit in with the decencies of civilization that so much living and dying should go on casually, in lofts and cellars and drains and coal-pockets and vacant houses. Neither does it accord with a decent humanity that so many sentient and dependent creatures should be left so completely at the mercy of circumstances."[77]

Did society owe anything to these small animal strangers living in its midst? Soon after its founding in 1869, the Women's Branch of the Pennsylvania SPCA, based in Philadelphia, argued that it did: it owed them kinder, more rational methods of control, the possibility of adoption, and a death that minimized suffering. At only its third meeting, in 1869, the membership passed a motion to found "a Refuge for lost and homeless dogs, where they could be kept until homes could be found for them, or they be otherwise disposed of."[78] In a remarkable move, the women decided to lobby Philadelphia's mayor for control of the municipal pound. They succeeded, and they built a new facility in 1870 that they called a "shelter." They also changed the methods of capturing stray dogs and cared for the canine prisoners with adequate food, water, and shelter. Rejecting the annual summer dog roundup, they instituted routine control activities throughout the year, regularized the accounting process for dog fines, and by the mid-1870s, created multiple drop-off points where citizens were encouraged to relinquish animals for whom they could no longer care, rather than abandoning them to the streets. The Women's Branch also instituted "painless killing," first via chloroform and then by the construction of a euthanasia chamber using "carbonous oxide gas." Puppies and cats were chloroformed in a sealed box (see fig. 4.12).[79]

The Pennsylvania SPCA was ahead of its contemporaries in acting on behalf of stray animals, but a second wave of humane organizations, founded several decades after the first SPCAs, increasingly took up the cause of both dogs and cats. (Prior to this, one of the interesting offshoots of humane concern was the ad hoc work of small groups of women who patrolled some cities looking for strays, especially cats, and euthanizing them with chloroform.) These later groups developed comprehensive approaches to feline and canine welfare, including new clinics and "dispensaries" that served working-class pet owners, relinquishment programs that encouraged people to turn in rather than abandon unwanted cats and dogs, the first systematic adoption programs for abandoned or unclaimed stray animals, and technologies for humane euthanasia. What is interesting for our purposes is that these groups—the Animal Rescue League of Boston (1899), Chicago's Anticruelty Society (1899), the Bide-A-Wee Home in New York (1903), and many others—were committed to restoring the status of pet to as many animals as possible.[80] As is the case today, however, they could not begin to place all the wandering, abandoned, or feral animals their agents captured.

Abandoned and feral cats continue to live on the margins of human communities, although their role in urban rat control is unclear. While numbers of feral dogs are apparently quite low, the national population of feral cats appears to be in the tens of millions, perhaps as high as 40 million.[81] Unadoptable because of their wildness and sometimes carriers of diseases such as feline

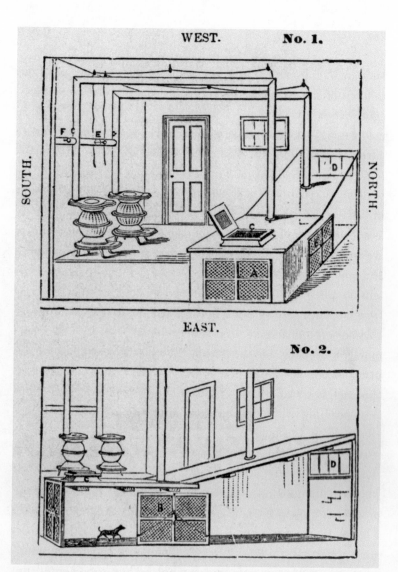

FIGURE 4.12. *"Illustration of the Mode of Killing Dogs by Carbonous Oxide Gas,"* Twelfth Annual Report of the Women's Branch of the Pennsylvania Society for the Prevention of Cruelty to Animals, for the Year Ending December 31, 1880. *The Library Company of Philadelphia.*

leukemia, feral cats probably account for a high percentage of the millions of cats euthanized in municipal shelters each year. In recent years, the debate over approaches to the welfare of feral cat colonies has taken an interesting turn. Feral cats now have their advocates, including the group Alley Cat Allies based in Washington, D.C., and San Diego's Feral Cat Coalition.[82] These organizations support a policy called Trap-Neuter-Return that originated in Europe. The Alley Cat Allies website describes the approach as a "comprehensive management plan where all healthy feral cats are sterilized and vaccinated, and then returned to their habitat and provided with long-term care. Adoptable (tame) cats and kittens are placed into homes." This management technique is controversial because of the continued dependence of feral cat colonies on human caregivers, the presence of feral cats as community nuisances, and the impact of feral cats on wildlife, particularly songbirds. Whatever its problems, the Trap-Neuter-Return approach is striking in its effort to define a place that is neither tame nor fully wild for cats in communities.

Community Pets and Honorary Pets

The final animal kinds examined in this chapter were wholly the product of human social life. Community pets and honorary pets differed from other animals on the edges because of the deliberately public nature of their roles.[83] Community pets were simultaneously living animals and symbols. They represented the special ties in a community of people—a company of soldiers, a group of workers, the members of a club, the customers of a store, or even a whole town—and sometimes were selected to embody characteristics that the entire group claimed. The ambiguity of the community pet's position between living subject and symbolic object was often expressed in the way that particular animal's body was treated after death: it was stuffed and displayed rather than buried with ceremony. Until the rise of the deliberately promoted animal celebrity, community pets were made by circumstance or by tradition.

Honorary pets, on the other hand, were wild animals or particular species of wild animals whose lives seemed to reflect values that a human community regarded as especially important or worthwhile. In the nineteenth century, the most important honorary pets were wild birds, who have already been mentioned as animal role models for family life; these days bottlenose dolphins and wolves are two of the most important species enjoying the status. The honorary pet expanded the idea of stewardship to wild animals without fully embracing their wildness, however. In nineteenth-century America, this hybrid kind extended into nature the ideas of domestic love and concern that created pets in the first place; today, this habit of symbolically domesticating wild animals through naming, providing biographies, and encouraging identification is still one technique used by conservation groups and mass media.

Most community pets were known only within their immediate neighborhood or community. Their status was a matter of circumstance; they were clever or knew special tricks or were particularly prized by their owners. The antics of the community pet punctuated the routines of daily life and offered a topic for collective humor and storytelling. A good example is Shellbark, a large poodle owned by Walter A. Corson, a grocery store owner in Doylestown, Pennsylvania, at the turn of the nineteenth century. Corson trained Shellbark to run on a beautifully decorated treadmill that was part of an apparatus for grinding coffee in the store. Shellbark became an important a part of daily life in Doylestown. After the dog died, amateur anthropologist, collector, and ceramicist Henry A. Mercer collected Shellbark's treadmill and adorned it with a studio portrait of the marvelous dog "riding" a small high-wheeler bicycle while holding a basket of flowers in his teeth. Mercer displayed the composition in his museum. Sometimes community pets were famous enough to be the subject of a collectible photograph. Kitty Burnham, a cat who probably belonged to Boston photographer Thomas Burnham, and her kittens were the subject of a *carte-de-visite* that went through several editions in both Boston and New York. McKinley, a very large tuxedo cat presumably named for the portly president, was the subject of a souvenir postcard for Farmington, Maine (fig. 4.13).

Other community pets were defined by tradition and were associated with working groups of men. By the mid-nineteenth century, fire companies often owned dogs. Firemen believed that dogs calmed the company's horses and allowed the canines to run alongside or ride to fires in the engines. By the early twentieth century, Dalmatians, traditionally an elite coaching dog, began to be called "firehouse dogs," but most company dogs were mutts, either the dog of a particular fireman or a tramp dog who adopted the firehouse. Firehouse dogs were well loved. When the Vigilant Fire Company in Georgetown lost its "Old Fire Dog" Bush to poison in 1869, the company placed a brass plaque on its building in memory of him.[84]

Troop pets were a genre of community pet common during the Civil War, and some garnered a measure of fame in their lifetimes. Old Abe the War Eagle, for example, a bald eagle who was carried by Company C of the 8th Wisconsin Regiment, was wounded twice during the war and was exhibited around the country after the conflict.[85] Next to Old Abe, the most famous Civil War pet was Sallie Ann Jarrett. The 11th Regiment of Pennsylvania Volunteers cared for and traveled with the female bull terrier, who had been presented to their captain during training near West Chester, Pennsylvania. She attended daily drills, guarded the bodies of wounded or dead members of the 11th during battle, and was killed alongside her soldiers at Hatcher's Run near Petersburg, Virginia, on 6 February 1865. "We buried her under the enemy's fire," noted the official report of the battle. Sallie is commemorated by a life-sized statue in

FIGURE 4.13. *"The Largest domestic cat 'McKinley' weight 35 pounds. Souvenir of Farmington, Maine,"* 1907. *Postcard copyrighted by Warren W. Seavey. Author's collection.*

The Largest domestic cat "McKinley" weight 35 pounds.
Souvenir of Farmingdale, Maine.
Photo copyrighted 1907 by Warren W. Seavey.

the 11th Pennsylvania Monument at Gettysburg National Military Park.[86]

In the late nineteenth century, the most well-known community pet was Owney, a terrier mutt who was cared for by the occupational community of railroad clerks of the U.S. Post Office (see fig. 4.14). The little tramp dog took up residence in the Albany, New York, post office in 1888. On his own volition he began to accompany sacks of mail on the postal railroad cars and traveled with the U.S. mail (even making one round-the-world circuit) until his death in 1897. The clerks made Owney a coat with his Albany home postal bag seal on it, and workers at other locations attached the metal seals from their home offices to the garment. (It became so heavy that its decorations had to be removed several times.)

Why did men take on this kind of group pet keeping? Apart from any utility such animals had, Owney, Sallie Ann Jarrett, and Bush the firehouse dog (there are hundreds, perhaps thousands of other examples) offered a safe place for men to focus their affections and attention and provided a release from the tension of dangerous work. Sometimes community pets also seemed to embody the qualities the group wished to have identified with itself: courage, insouciance, and devotion. The symbolic function of community pets is foregrounded when we examine responses to their deaths. Community pets were more likely to be stuffed and their bodies put on display. (The other animals typically preserved as taxidermic mounts were natural history specimens, hunting trophies, or freaks of nature, all animals whose symbolic value—as representations of creatures in the wild, emblems of sport, or evidence of the mysterious hand of the Divine—formed the largest part of their identities in relation to human beings.) Old Abe the War Eagle, who died in 1881, wound up as a taxidermic

Wheeler 𝒲𝒮 JEWELER AND PHOTOGRAPHER PITTSFIELD MASS.

FIGURE 4.14. *Owney, the community pet of U.S. mail carriers, seated on a mail bag. Photograph by Wheeler, Pittsfield, Massachusetts, between 1888 and 1897. Collection Mary Thurston, Animal Image.*

display in the Wisconsin state capitol building. After Owney's death, some clerks apparently agreed that the dog deserved greater commemoration than a simple burial, and his body still resides at the U.S. Postal Museum.[87] The firemen of the Active Hose Company of Rochester, New York, mounted the body of their curly-coated firehouse dog on a wooden plank and displayed it in their elaborate session rooms.[88]

In the twentieth century, the community pet has often been a created celebrity, adopted by the diffuse public audience that followed its deeds or performances through the new mass media of print and, by the 1920s, film and broadcast. Since the eighteenth century, audiences at theaters, taverns, and even museums all over America have been entertained by trained animals. Some, such as the Grecian Dog Apollo, who toured the United States in the 1820s, even became celebrities of a sort. However, the mass medium of film provided audiences with a new kind of community pet, the animal hero of movies, whose image was as carefully cultivated as that of a human movie star. The studios that cranked out silent film serials had featured animals in story lines for years, but in 1925 the *Saturday Evening Post* reported the presence of "two horse stars of the first magnitude in the film colony now, three dog stars, twenty featured dog players whose weekly salaries run up into the hundreds," and a shifting population of barnyard and wild animal actors. Children were the "greatest admirers of dog pictures," the most popular of which featured German shepherds, such as Rin Tin Tin, whose training for police work and service as "war dogs" in World War I had already contributed to their popularity.[89]

Pet animals belonging to the president of the United States or his family also became community pets beginning in the early twentieth century. While First Families all the way back to the administration of George Washington had been pet keepers, White House pets became celebrities with the administration of Theodore Roosevelt from 1901 to 1909. The patriarch of a rambunctious pack of six children who attracted considerable attention in the era's assertive national press, Roosevelt himself liked animals. The White House was home to rodents of all kinds (including five guinea pigs named Admiral Dewey, Dr. Johnson, Bishop Doane, Fighting Bob Evans, and Father O'Grady), birds, cats, dogs, wild animals such as a young bear and a badger named Josiah, snakes, and a Shetland pony named Algonquin, whose claim to fame rests with his famous trip up the White House elevator to visit Archie Roosevelt during an illness.[90]

The most famous White House pet, however, was Fala, Franklin Delano Roosevelt's beloved Scottish terrier (see fig. 4.15). The offspring of two Scotties belonging to Roosevelt's cousin Margaret L. Suckley, he arrived at the White House in November 1940. Fala was lively and cunning; he escaped the White House grounds a number of times but was returned by citizens of Washington, D.C., who recognized him or read his gold-plated tag (which read, "Fala, the White House"). He was devoted to Roosevelt, who soon realized that the dog was a public relations asset. The press published many pictures of the dog on the presidential train, riding with Roosevelt in the car, and sitting at the president's feet during meetings. The president even talked about the dog during his fireside radio chats. In 1942, Fala's breeder and Alice Dalgleish published a popular children's book called *The True Story of Fala,* which described the dog's daily routine with the Roosevelts, including his attendance at press conferences and meetings. Like his owner, Fala received letters and gifts from the

FIGURE 4.15. *Franklin Delano Roosevelt and Fala aboard the USS* Tuscaloosa, *Charleston, South Carolina, 14 December 1940. Franklin D. Roosevelt Presidential Library and Museum.*

public; these have been preserved at the Franklin D. Roosevelt Library in Hyde Park.

Community pets such as Fala offered a point of common relationship between famous people and the public. Roosevelt realized that Fala made him more approachable, and White House public relations departments have been using presidential pets for this purpose ever since. Barney, the Bush family dog (also a Scottie) is featured on the extensive educational websites maintained by the White House. Movie and television "star" animals also became part of the collective life of the imagination created by mass media in the twentieth century. In a society that promoted pet keeping and practiced it widely, petless children could dream of owning an animal as smart as Lassie or as funny as Petey in the *Little Rascals* movies. It was a benign and presexual form of celebrity worship. In real terms, Rin Tin Tin and Fala also inspired crazes for their breeds among prospective dog owners, a trend that has been repeated with mixed results for featured breeds.

Dogs became a formal part of the U.S. military during World War I, when they served as bomb sniffers and guardians; they have continued to serve this function to the present. The soldiers who handled working dogs share a particular identity as veterans and have commemorated their canine charges in a variety of ways, including the War Dog Memorial at the Hartsdale Canine Cemetery. Recently, however, working dogs of a new variety have become heroes and community pets. These include the Drug Enforcement Agency's "sniffer dogs," who were honored with a set of collectible cards in Milkbone dog biscuits in the late 1990s, and rescue dogs, particularly the dogs who searched for survivors and bodies in the wreckage of the World Trade Center in 2001. The subject of a number of news stories during their work, especially after one dog died in the line of duty, these 9/11 dogs and their handlers were lauded at a special ceremony at the finals of the 2002 Westminster Kennel Club dog show.

Honorary pets were different, however. They were wild animals chosen for special attention and care because of qualities that Americans regarded as worth protecting. Wild birds were the most important honorary pets of the nineteenth century. Their beauty, songs, and apparent virtues, along with arguments on behalf of their utility in insect control, inspired the first widespread public efforts at wildlife protection.

The cultural significance of birds, along with interest in socializing children to be kind to animals, underlay the remarkable rise of one of the first organizations dedicated to saving wildlife, the Army of Bird-Defenders promoted by St. Nicholas beginning in 1873. Naturalist C. C. Haskins wrote that he had been "thinking for a long time of writing a plea for a large family of our friends who are wantonly destroyed or abused by impulsive persons without good reason, and, very often, thoughtlessly." He announced a plan for "an army of defense, without guns" for birds, which would conduct a war of "example and argument and facts, instead of powder." The goal was "perfect peace" for birds.[91] Subsequent communications from "Commander-in-Chief" Haskins continued to use military metaphors, suggesting both unity of purpose and resolve. Like other early supporters of bird preservation, Haskins also offered an argument that combined ecology and human utility by emphasizing songbirds as "good" species that helped to control insects.

Children who wished to join were encouraged to copy and sign the special bird-defenders' pledge and to vow to "abstain from all practices as shall tend to the destruction of wild birds," and to "advocate the rights of all birds at all proper times, encourage confidence in them, and recognize in them creations of the Great Father, for the joy and good of mankind."[92] The children who read St. Nicholas were thrilled to be included in a great cause that connected with their own daily experiences. The magazine published "Musters" of thousands of children's names until 1876, when the organization seemed to run out of steam.[93] During its

heyday, however, the editors not only encouraged children to or-
ganize clubs but created space in the magazine for individuals
and groups to communicate with one another. This published correspondence makes the bird-defenders particularly interesting
because children's letters revealed the special dilemmas this hybrid of the wild and the pet animal kinds provoked.[94]

Letters supporting the new group first appeared in *St.
Nicholas* in February 1874. Many simply listed names of recruits,
while some reported on specific activities to help birds. Other letters from young bird-defenders suggest how children faced difficulties in figuring out which wild animals to succor and which
were "enemies" in a world where all animals were, in theory, entitled to kindness and were also potential pets. Encouraged to be
kind, children struggled to make appropriate ethical discriminations, particularly where predation was concerned. One child
asked if it was acceptable to kill a snake that attacked a bird's
nest. The editors said yes, even though the snake was a natural
predator. Did hunting ducks for eating purposes disqualify one as
a bird-defender? Not if the hunting was done only to procure
food. Was collecting birds' eggs for a natural history collection
begun the previous summer acceptable? The editor thought not,
although natural history was a rational amusement. Could a bird-
defender "take a bird's nest after the bird has left it?" Yes, if the
nest was indeed abandoned. How could cats be kept away from
birds? The editor advised feeding pet cats until they became "too
lazy" to hunt; on the other hand, tramp cats, apparently no one's
pets, could be shot.[95]

How many young bird-defenders grew up to become adults
who supported bird preservation can never be known, although
the history of groups like the Audubon Society is well documented.[96] In any case, songbirds have continued to be privileged

honorary pets, entitled to feeding, special housing, and other protections that other wild orders do not receive. In its pitch to potential franchise buyers, Wild Birds Unlimited, a company with more than 300 stores devoted to backyard bird and wildlife feeding and watching, reports that 54 million Americans spend $3.1 billion on food and another $732 million on feeders, baths, and nesting boxes each year.[97]

In the early twentieth century, Ernest Thompson Seton's *Wild Animals I Have Known* (1898) and *Lives of the Hunted* (1905) offered sympathetic biographies of wild animals that emphasized their possession of what Thompson Seton called "the virtues most admired in Man." The goal of the author was to encourage his middle-class readership to preserve wildlife.[98] Thompson Seton's biographies emphasized the wildness of his subjects, although he gave them names like Lobo and Krag, and most of his stories ended with the death of the protagonist. By the 1950s, a new type of honorary pet appeared as the wildlife documentary film took its modern form, a biographical narrative of particular individuals that built on this earlier narrative legacy. Beginning with Walt Disney's famous Secrets of Life series of the 1950s, documentaries seemed to swing between emphasizing the wildness of their subjects and presenting them as lovable creatures for whom audiences could root. Public attention to issues of wildlife protection still seems to be best focused by storytelling that makes many wild animals into honorary pets. This is exemplified in the recent case of Keiko, the killer whale who was returned unsuccessfully to the wild after a long and expensive campaign to remove the animal from the Mexican aquarium where he lived, resocialize him to other whales, and return him to his pod off the coast of Norway, where he died in 2003. Modern mass media "created" Keiko as a public figure twice over, first as a movie star in the popular movie *Free Willy,* then as an object of public concern as the whale's off-camera living conditions were revealed.

Lessons from the Edges

Anonymous workers, food sources with names and personalities, vagrants and tramps, living art objects, local or national celebrities, and embodiments of ideal community life: what conclusions can be drawn about animal kinds, and about the characteristics of Americans' changing relationships to animals, from these cases on the edges of the expanding practice of pet keeping? One assumption seems clear: the continued primacy of human purposes over the trajectories and quality of animal lives. Most people—at least once they became adults—were confident of the appropriateness of animal categories and did not worry about the ability of humans to bestow and to withdraw the protection of a particular status such as "pet." The case of the livestock pet demonstrates that sensitive children could and did identify the apparent arbitrary character of animal kinds and were sometimes uncomfortable about the implications of the distinctions.

One hundred years ago, animals' identities in communities were just as complex as those of people. The emotional characteristics and daily practices of modern pet keeping developed at a time when even city folk were closely familiar with the range of roles animals played in society. In what may be termed the "circle of concern" in daily life, both people and animals were usually ranked according to their distance or closeness to the person making the discriminations. However, just as reform efforts to improve the quality of life for human strangers in need represented a more complex imagining of community, so did efforts to improve the comfort of (or provide a relatively comfortable end of life for) anonymous animal workers and animal strangers. Community pets and honorary pets also represented expansions of human communities, but the treatment of these two kinds also reflected the complicated everyday ethics of regard for animals.

Pet keeping urged a particular way of thinking about animals as individuals who lived complicated lives, and it clearly affected how people thought about other animal kinds. Because of the way it framed responsibilities toward animals, the nineteenth-century's domestic ethic of kindness had distinctive limitations, despite its potentially universal claims, when it confronted cases on the edge. It was unable to propose satisfying answers to important questions about human obligations to animals in a rapidly developing economy that created new ways to exploit large numbers of animals. Traditional thinking in terms of kinds and the gentle ethic of kindness could not adequately describe or prescribe against the industrialization of animals, a process that was well under way in the late nineteenth century but became the principal mode for the production and consumption of animals by the middle of the twentieth century.

At the same time, the pet kind increasingly dominated the imaginative lives of Americans, particularly children, while the dynamics, routine practices, and emotional structures of pet keeping sometimes changed the ways people regarded animals that had been considered workers, as in the case of the suburban family horse. Thus pet keeping affected the process of reconsidering human relationships to the rest of the sentient world, a reimagining that is still under way. Today, prompted by decades of new writing on animal rights beginning with the publication of

Peter Singer's *Animal Liberation* in 1975 and the activism of animal rights and animal welfare groups, some Americans are less confident of the old categories and some relatively new ones (such as "laboratory animals"), along with the behaviors that accompany them.

By the late nineteenth century, however, pet animals themselves had two new roles to play. Some were now a unique kind of merchandise, produced in quantity for the modern pet trade. Pets were also vicarious consumers, through the owners who purchased a new array of products and supplies created and sold by small businesses and, in the twentieth century, a handful of large corporations that saw profit in serving pets. These two aspects of pets in America are considered in the next two chapters.

❧ 5 ❧

A Pet
in Every Home

$\mathcal{S}$o far, we have seen that pets in America were regarded as servants, children, friends, and family members. Some bore the burden of being moral exemplars; others were objects of art. Sometimes household animals could be members of the pet kind temporarily but lost this protected identity when their age, sexual maturity, or size presented difficulties to their owners. Still others became strangers and vagrants presenting problems to the communities where they wandered. No matter how complex the social identity of the individual animal, however, being one of the pet kind was a conditional status.

As the United States became a modern industrial and commercial society, pet animals occupied another, increasingly important role. They were commodities, reared specifically for the purposes of sale, to be purchased as inventory by store owners and as goods by customers. Pets differed from most other products, however, in their requirements for both presale and post-purchase maintenance and the possibility for emotional investment they offered. People buying pet animals were also buying a relationship, one that could be short or long lived, harmful or beneficial to one or both parties, a simple matter of basic physical care on the part of owners, or a major investment of emotional energy.

Between 1840 and 1940, all the elements of the modern pet industry gradually came into being, from specialized producers and manufacturers to dedicated retail outlets and service providers. The term "pet industry" is worth pausing over, for it vibrates with the fundamental tension between sentiment and commodification that characterizes the enterprise. Its most important products, animals, were produced and acquired in a variety of settings. Until the early twentieth century, families acquired many of their pets from friends and neighbors. Most of these transactions involved no cash; sharing a kitten whose mother was a good mouser, the puppy of a favorite dog, or a home-raised canary was a form of neighborliness. Sometimes people hunted up their own pets, as when children engaged in the controversial activity of raiding birds' nests for fledglings or fished in ponds and streams for creatures to live in their aquariums.

By the mid-1800s, however, small animals were also the objects of a slowly growing commerce supporting a community of entrepreneurs who often combined trade in animals with other kinds of work. City markets had been the sites of casual buying and selling of cage birds and other small animals in the eighteenth century, and so they continued in this role into the nineteenth. Two kinds of pet sellers emerged by the mid-nineteenth century, however. Dog dealers provided working, fighting, and pet dogs. As prosperous American consumers became more interested in European breeds and purebred dogs, some dog dealers became respectable importers and even breeders of purebred animals. So did other individuals, including well-to-do women who found in dog breeding a business genteel enough to fit expectations for women's proper roles. By the 1840s, a new kind of small business, the bird store, dotted larger American cities. Bird stores offered a full array of supplies for the care of caged songbirds. Their owners sold both the American birds that were captured for sale in city markets and an imported bird, the canary, that had been cage-reared since the 1600s.

By the 1890s, the modern pet shop had appeared in cities. It supplied both the animals and special supplies and equipment to facilitate their care, and its services included boarding, grooming, and medical care. By the turn of the century, even department stores had added bird sales to their miscellaneous household goods departments. By the 1920s and into the 1950s and 1960s, five-and-tens had become places to purchase hardy canaries and parakeets, as well as the less demanding aquarium fish and other ephemeral childhood pets.

In the late nineteenth century, a handful of ambitious pet store owners worked to reach a national market, thanks to the speed and reliability of shipping by rail. However, the retail pet business in America was mostly made up of small, family-owned stores serving a local market. Still, they tried to keep up with modern techniques for building trade in their living merchandise. They stocked animals with "brand names," offered various sales gimmicks such as guarantees, advertised in local papers, and kept up with periodicals like *Pet Dealer* and *Pet Trade Journal*. Pet store owners were not necessarily kind to the creatures they sold, and their talk within the trade press emphasized the economic problems they faced squeezing profits out of small operations rather than the emotional satisfactions of caring for animals for a living. Pets also became a sideline for other, larger retail operations, including five-and-tens and department stores.

Studying the production of pet animals for sale means looking at backyard hutches as well as international import specialists. Growing purebred kittens and puppies, show pigeons, and fancy rabbits remained in most cases a cottage industry conducted on a small scale by enthusiasts. However, the growing American interest in purebred dogs led to a small but significant trade with breeders in Europe and even Asia, especially after the 1870s. The trade with Europe for large numbers of hand-raised canaries and a few other species was highly organized by the mid-nineteenth century. By the late nineteenth century, international trade in captured parrots from Mexico and South America was so brisk that it undoubtedly began to have a serious impact on wild numbers. By the early twentieth century, budgerigars and other exotic birds were being raised on farms in California and Florida. These operations, along with the goldfish farms that dotted Indiana and Maryland by the turn of the century and the southern tropical fish breeders who raised guppies and a few other species amenable to captive breeding by the 1920s, can be compared to other forms of commercial livestock production. Sometimes commercial production of small animals was intended for other purposes, as in the growing trade in laboratory animals that brought the hamster to the United States in the 1930s. Further, some pet animals were immune from commercial "farming" of their species until relatively late. Increasing interest in purebred dogs, especially after World War II, combined with the success of vaccines and other drugs that made keeping large populations of dogs in close contact feasible for the first time, created the puppy mill.

In February 1929, the editor of *Pet Dealer* proclaimed the magazine's business motto for the year: a pet in every home. Pet-less households, he claimed, were a symptom of old-fashioned business methods, since "if a sufficient amount of money was spent in advertising . . . a pet could be sold to every home." The editor reminded his readers, the members of the American Pet Dealers Association, that pet owners tended to buy more than one animal and that they required a constant stream of supplies, "all of which means more business."[1] Pet store owners were lucky. Their customers were already what modern retailers craved: dedicated repeat customers driven to make purchases not only by necessity but by emotion. But was the living inventory of pet stores like any other consumer good? Pet stores such as Albert and Henrietta Greenberg's Supreme Brooklyn Pet Emporium were unlike

FIGURE 5.1. *Albert and Henrietta Greenberg and an unidentified employee at the Supreme Brooklyn Pet Emporium, 1939. Author's collection. Albert Greenberg is working with tanks that probably contained tropical fish, ideal pets for local hobbyists in small apartments. The middle shelf of the case contains some new ideas for dogs, including a low pottery dog dish and dog toys stacked in and around it. The bottom shelf displays a large electric air pump for aquarium use and a jumbled array of accessories for fish keepers. According to a relative, the business existed until the 1970s.*

most other retail businesses (see fig. 5.1). Inside pet shops, living animals, some the fragile products of a specialized husbandry, began a remarkable transformation from object to subject, from consumer good to individual and even family member. Pet shops were thrilling and ambiguous sites where customers determined the life course of animals by choosing one over another and where store owners themselves coped with life and death in front of their clientele.

Dealer talk on animal wholesaling was often practical, focusing on acceptable rates of mortality during transportation and cost per unit. Facing the public, however, store owners manipulated the emotions of passersby through techniques such as displaying the animals most likely to interact with customers in front windows and keeping one or two shop pets that were not for sale. Pet shop owners also faced the possibility that they sold animals to customers who would neglect or abuse them, or that their trade in a particular species could endanger its future in the wild. Particularly at the level of wholesale production, the pet industry seemed to ignore these possibilities. It did not offer advice to its members on the subject of purchasers who mistreated their animals. It neither suggested that pet shop owners not sell their living goods to everyone nor hinted that owners themselves might be engaged in careless or even cruel practices. As with other consumer goods businesses, the neutral medium of cash tendered released the businessperson of responsibility for the use of the goods and freed the purchaser from future interference, too.

Early Trade in Pet Animals

In the late 1700s and the first decades of the 1800s, hawking songbirds and small animals to be kept as pets was part of the rich scene around city markets. On 31 December 1798, Elizabeth Drinker noted in her diary that her bachelor son William had "bought a flying squirrel in market, brought it home to please the children. . . . I should have been better pleased had it remained in the woods."[2] Deborah Norris Logan's beloved red bird Reddy had been a gift from her son, purchased in the early 1820s at the "Jersy market" in a "little corn stalk cage."[3] This kind of trade was seasonal and opportunistic. In a memoir of his profession from the 1820s to the 1870s, Philadelphia butcher George Bates recalled that Jake and Bill Lake, two sheep butchers he knew, had in their youth been called the "yellow bird boys" because they "used to catch yellow birds [probably goldfinches] and sell them in the Market Street Market."[4] The spring was the time to buy goldfinches, cardinals, grosbeaks, purple finches, and even rice buntings. They were brought to the market in the "trap-cages" that cost them their liberty and were sold for as little as 25 cents per pair.[5] It seems likely that city markets were good places to obtain cats and dogs as well. Farm families and butchers who occupied booths probably brought in extra puppies and kittens on market days. Sales of exotic pets were similarly informal in these years. Parrots and monkeys could be had at city wharfs, where captains and sailors also supplied commercial exhibitors with larger wild animals. Today, selling pet animals through informal channels—newspaper ads, advertisements in agricultural extension service newsletters, word-of-mouth, and notices posted on the bulletin boards of grocery, feed, and local pet supply stores—is still a very important, although unmeasured and unmeasurable, avenue for buying and selling pets.

Small businesses occasionally made selling pet animals a sideline. In 1828, John Fox, a barber in the Erie Canal boomtown of Rochester, New York, offered "A few pair of Canary Birds, good singers and beautiful plumage, warranted to breed the next season, for sale."[6] These may have been the surplus of Fox's own hobby or trade from a canal boat. Either way, it is interesting to note that Fox believed that a market already existed for the most genteel of cage birds. His notice was probably an effort to reach women who would prevail on the men in their lives to visit his establishment and purchase canaries. By the 1830s and 1840s, sales of canaries and goldfish were also part of the florist's trade. As merchandise, these pets were grouped with potted plants and hothouse flowers as both gifts and middle-class parlor ornaments.

Frances Ann Butler, the young English actress whose tour with her father in 1832 and 1833 resulted in a published journal, recorded a visit with a Scottish immigrant florist whose greenhouse and "seed shop" was ornamented by "the voice of a hundred canaries resounding through it." It also contained "a tank [probably the greenhouse cistern] full of beautiful gold fish, as they indiscriminately called them." An 1843 advertisement for Bernard Duke's Seed and Horticultural Warehouse on Chestnut Street in Philadelphia offered canaries and other songbirds, the available range of their supplies, and "Chinese Gold-fish and Glass Globes of all sizes."[7] Trade cards from the last quarter of the nineteenth century inform us that in smaller cities the bird business was still often combined with some other gracious trade, as in the case of Campbell's Picture Frame and Bird Store of Manchester, New Hampshire, and the McClunie Bros. Original Bird Store and Flower Shop of Hartford, Connecticut.[8]

In the 1800s, urban dealers of small animals fell into several recognizable types with particular class identities. One familiar character was the working-class dog dealer who provided watchdogs, fighting and ratting dogs, and hunting dogs, as well as other animals on occasion. It was not uncommon for dogs of value to be stolen from their owners and their appearance altered by clipping and the application of dye, or more seriously by ear and tail docking, to disguise them for resale to dog dealers. Henry Wadsworth Longfellow's small, rough-coated terrier Trap—who suffered from chronic canine wanderlust—was stolen several times within a few days in 1867. Trap was only recovered "through the intervention of a dog-dealer in Boston," who apparently located the dog after Longfellow appealed to him: "I put a new collar upon him, and had him fed; whereupon he ran away and was stolen again on the same day. I have recovered him again. . . . He has hair dye put all about his eyes to disguise him, and is quite abject and forlorn. He evidently thinks Cambridge is a dull place. At the dog-dealer's they gave him rats to kill. That is the charm, which he cannot resist. He has been trying to sneak away this afternoon, and will be stolen again tomorrow, no doubt."[9] Dog dealers could be rough characters. An 1874 story in the *New York Times* recounting a visit to "a dog fancier's cellar" found a "menagerie of dogs" presided over by "a very large man" who was missing part of his nose, the result of a dog attack. His stock included an imported English bloodhound, fighting bulldogs, Scotch terriers, and a few poodles for the carriage trade. The reporter noted that dog theft and disguise were common in the trade and that some dogs were stolen and returned to their sellers repeatedly.[10] City directory entries for dog dealers are rarely found (and terse when they do exist), but occasionally one suggests the class identity of the dealer and nature of the business. The only dog dealer listed in the 1868 Boston city directory was Harry Jennings, who lived at his saloon on 38 Portland Street.[11]

Early pet shops sometimes developed out of the activities of working-class dog dealers, who also recognized that there was money to be made from expanding their lines to include other animals. In 1881, the *Children's Museum,* a short-lived monthly published in New York City, printed a lengthy account of one such business. The Cockney immigrant proprietor, Mr. Jennings, operated out of "a rambling, curious old house on Broome Street," a section of the city that was no longer fashionable. He described himself as an "Exterminator of Rats. Importer and Breeder of Dogs, Ferrets, Animals, Birds, and Fowl." He also doctored and boarded dogs. The shop was a room "partitioned around the sides with kennels and wire enclosures, which are filled with . . . all sorts of pigeons, rabbits, squirrels, Guinea pigs, woodchucks, badgers, foxes, and dogs of high and low degree," including ratting dogs, and cats "kept for sale or hire" as mousers. It is clear that Jennings participated in the masculine netherworld of blood sport and that some of his animals were kept as prey (and it is striking and usual that the author of this piece neither hid these activities from young readers nor condemned them). Like the dog dealer who had Longfellow's terrier, Jennings kept live rats for the purposes of terrier rat-killing exhibitions. He sold them for $15 a hundred and commented coyly that "as to what is done with 'em, you must guess for yourself." He also imported and sold bulldogs from England, some presumably for fighting purposes. (He even displayed the taxidermic mount of a "celebrated dog which he had owned, named 'Old Turk' who had last fought in 1865, representing the city of Boston.") Finally, Jennings kept "hundreds of common pigeons, for sale at twenty-five cents each for shooting matches," a genre of sporting match that was condemned by anticruelty advocates.[12]

A second category of dog dealer, who self-consciously worked to attract a genteel clientele, began to appear by the 1870s as prosperous Americans became more interested in owning unusual purebred animals. In 1876, George Walton of 121 Haverhill Street in Boston advertised "Dogs and Pigeons, Imported Every Week. N.B.—Best of References."[13] By 1884, Walton had become a "Dog Doctor" and "The Oldest Dog Dealer in Boston [Established 1846]," selling both "Choice Breeds of Dogs" and their supplies.[14] Eventually purebred dog breeding was dominated by specialist kennels that were as often avocational pleasures as serious moneymaking enterprises. These were part of the developing national subculture of "dog fanciers," including women, who participated in an annual round of bench shows and field trials. The old assumptions about the trustworthiness of dog dealers may account for the promise *Country Life* made to its readership that advertisers in its monthly Kennel Directory, begun in 1904, were "reliable."[15]

Middle- and upper-class women played an important role in the late Victorian purebred dog trade, especially for the smaller companion breeds. Gwendoline Brook's 1907 account, "How Japanese Spaniels Paid on the Farm," may be taken as a typical example of both the motivations for and the logistics of getting into the breeding business. Brook undertook the breeding of Japanese spaniels after a life spent owning "almost all varieties" of dogs; she decided that "with a little planning their acknowledged popularity would insure ready sale at good prices." Following complicated negotiations through a San Francisco general importer, she brought her start-up stock of five bitches and a male directly from Japan at a cost of $175, with additional expenses for care and shipment from Seattle to New York. The animals were severely debilitated and "a good deal upset" by their ordeal, but all survived and were subsequently removed to Brook's small farm. Three bitches subsequently whelped, and the twelve surviving puppies and two unbred adults sold for $610. Touting her experience as a model for her readers, Brook reported,

> For my original investment of $226 I have received cash dividends of $310, and I still have stock left of the actual value of $275. This is looking at it from the merely mercenary point of view; only those who have been themselves deeply interested in dogs can appreciate the enjoyment and true happiness there is for an earnest dog-lover in first taking the animals in the rough as imported, getting them into perfect condition, passing through the stages of hope and

fear in the matter of breeding, the arrival of the puppies and the watching of their daily development from mere rolls of fur and fat to lively, sprightly, and intelligent little dogs, the opportunity for the exercise of the commercial instinct when the question of selling the stock comes up, and finally the feeling of relief that the experiment has turned out so well and that time and pains and money have not been spent in vain.[16]

Thus a successful kennel operation for companion dogs could offer women a respectable business opportunity that was both a safe avenue for "exercise of the commercial instinct" and a chance for emotional fulfillment. The differences between the expressed motivations of Brook, a genteel woman on the margins of America's burgeoning business culture, and the traditional motivations for canary breeding and other animal fancies also are worth noting. Early efforts to promote home canary breeding emphasized the practice as a "rational amusement" that could be used for larger ends (the cultivation of the self and contact with the natural world), and Brook's male contemporaries who bred fancy small animals for exhibition argued explicitly that their motivations were anticommercial and aesthetic. Breeding pet animals seems to have offered both men and women access to worlds of experience that gender conventions otherwise denied them.

The "Graceful Trade" in Birds

Forerunners of the modern pet store, specialized bird stores appeared in city shopping districts by the early 1840s. They serviced the middle-class passion for singing cage birds, especially imported canaries. While no business records survive from early bird stores, an occasional glimpse can be had of small operations where men and women who took pleasure in birds sold them out of their houses or tiny shops. An 1877 article in *St. Nicholas* noted that New York City's neighborhoods were dotted with small shops kept by "kindly old Germans": "The deafening chorus which is kept up from dawn till dark by a hundred or two birds singing at the top of their voices in a single room, added to the din of a small menagerie of other animals, is something surprising."[17] However, small bird stores were not always healthy places for the creatures sold there. On 3 July 1871, the Philadelphia Society for the Prevention of Cruelty to Animals received a complaint from "Many Neighbors" of "the filthy condition that birds are kept in—some being alive with vermin—at the bird store of G. Pavanarius 463 Nth 8th St."[18]

The handful of businesses about which some detail can be reconstructed were larger, owned by ambitious entrepreneurs whose operations could attract the attention of the Dun reports, the forerunner of Dun and Bradstreet in rating the creditworthiness of nineteenth-century businesses. These pet shop owners, who operated in larger cities from Boston to Omaha, left a trail of credit reports, trade catalogs, and books of advice either written or published by them and containing their own advertisements. They even took out the occasional patent for cage bird equipment. These go-getters actively imported large numbers of birds from Europe and, later, from Asia and South America, along with a smaller number of other animals such as monkeys. They also served as wholesalers to small neighborhood businesses. Several also operated significant export businesses, contributing to the decline of native populations by shipping tens of thousands of American songbirds to Europe each year until the end of the century. Although numbers of European and American wild birds and canaries had been transported back and forth long before the advent of successful transatlantic steamship travel, the shorter travel times certainly made successful movement of such fragile cargo less difficult and encouraged the development of regular import businesses.[19]

Charles Reiche, dealer and author of *The Bird Fancier's Companion* (1853), and his brother Henry were among the first of this new type of pet shop owner. Immigrants "late of Braunschweig, Germany," the Reiches were selling birds in New York by 1843. Three years earlier, they had paid for a full-page advertisement in an advice book by another author, guaranteeing that their shop kept "constantly on hand and for sale, from November to May of each year, a CHOICE COLLECTION OF HEALTHY YOUNG BIRDS . . . consisting of German and French Canaries, and other European Song Birds," including linnets, bullfinches, thrushes, nightingales, and "European robins," and American wild birds including goldfinches, "Black Caps" (chickadees), and mockingbirds.[20]

In the 1867 third edition of *The Bird Fancier's Companion*, Reiche offered an account of just how many canaries he had brought to America during his early years in New York: more than 20,000 in the decade before 1853, 10,000 in 1853 alone, and 20,000 each year by 1867. At that time the Reiche brothers claimed to be the country's single largest importer, accounting for two-thirds of the birds shipped into America. By 1870, an R. G. Dun credit report on the business noted that the brothers "have made money from a very small beginning" and had a business worth $30,000 to $40,000. Charles Reiche had returned to Germany permanently to make purchases for a business that continued to expand, while Henry managed things in America.[21]

Not only were the Reiches importing large numbers of birds, but by 1873, the transcontinental railroad allowed the brothers to ship canaries to Salt Lake City and Denver for sale. By 1871, the brothers had opened a second branch store in Boston at 9 Bowdoin Square, a storefront attached to and owned by the Bowdoin Square Baptist Church. This was an advantageous location for a business that appealed directly to middle-class women and children. The Bowdoin Square New York Bird Store was directly across from the Revere House and near the Coolidge House, two elite hotels where families also boarded, and near other shopping that developed after the Union Railroad ran its first horse cars to the square in the 1850s.[22]

Charles Reiche & Brother introduced itself to Boston with a tenth edition of *The Bird Fancier's Companion* in 1871. A full-page advertisement in the volume showed how the business had expanded and changed. By the 1870s, the brothers had become "Importers and Dealers in all kinds of Rare Birds, Reptiles, Sea Shells, Stuffed Birds, and Curiosities." From his office in Europe, Charles was able to provide "Birds of Plumage" and exotic animals for "Zoological Gardens, Menageries and Private Game Parks." The advertisement also noted that the Boston store provided a "Department of Taxidermy," which not only mounted "Pet Birds or Animals" as funerary monuments to themselves but also allowed the business to profit from the demise of some of the merchandise: "A good assortment of STUFFED BIRDS constantly on hand."[23] Providing taxidermy services seems to have been an important sideline for larger city pet stores until the early twentieth century, when changing attitudes toward the use of mounts as interior decor and as emblems of sentiment made this part of the business decline.[24] Clearly, the Reiche brothers were moving away from their retail business and emphasizing their wholesale trade. They also undertook management of the New York Aquarium at

Coney Island in 1878. The Reiches sold their New York Bird Store in Boston to their partner and manager George H. Holden in May 1876.[25]

Holden was another entrepreneur who opened stores in Providence, Rhode Island, and even New York City by 1879. A Dun report for that year noted that he claimed to have "an agency in Germany for the purchase of foreign birds" (probably the Reiches) and typically carried $10,000 to $12,000 worth of stock in his three stores. Marketing was his forte and the way he differentiated himself from the small neighborhood bird seller; his "principal bills" at the time were for advertising.[26] Given the American penchant for advice books of all kinds, the Reiche brothers realized that the medium was still a good way to promote business. Thus they published *Holden's Book on Birds,* written by George's brother Charles, in 1873. Holden then published his own *Canaries and Cage Birds* in 1883, along with heavily illustrated catalogs promoting an expanded stock not only of birds but his own brands of bird seed, medicines, and cages. He even deployed the classically American business strategy of taking out and publicizing patents, in this case Holden's Patent Cups. These were feeders that prevented birds from scattering their seed or bathing in their drinking water.[27] Holden's New York business was so long lived and successful that it occupied a stylish modern Fifth Avenue storefront by the late 1920s (see fig. 5.2).

The Reiche brothers and George H. Holden represent the changing nature of the pet business at the higher levels of the trade in the nineteenth century. While the modest neighborhood bird store serving a local clientele was now a fixture of city life, the business of dealing in small animals was developing along the lines of other consumer goods enterprises of the time. It now had

FIGURE 5.2. *George H. Holden's storefront at 300 Fifth Avenue, New York, postcard, 1922. Author's collection. The abundant glass windows in this choice corner storefront were full of cages displaying the stock.*

its own import/export specialists and wholesalers. International shipping was improving, and pet animals could be sent around the interior of the United States via the rapidly expanding rail lines that crisscrossed from coast to coast by the 1870s. The pet business demonstrated an increasing reliance on publishing and advertising that would culminate with national branding and advertising of live animals by the 1920s, several decades after this strategy appeared for processed foods and other consumer goods. In 1929, the descendants of these first ambitious pet entrepreneurs organized a professional trade association, the Pet Dealers Association, and supported the national trade magazines *Pet Shop* and *Pet Dealer*.

The business also had its network of wholesale producers, large and small, who were capable, given a little time, of changing their production to meet special greater demand. Before 1901, figures for the importation of cage birds to America are fragmentary, but the numbers that are recoverable do offer a sense of the expanding import trade. In 1873, humorist Benjamin Franklin Taylor published an essay on birds that praised what he termed the "graceful trade" and marveled at its extent: "Who would think, without thinking, that more than seventeen thousand songbirds are annually sold in New York (City)?"[28] The U.S. Department of Agriculture (USDA) kept importation records by 1906, when it reported the arrival of 322,000 cage birds, 275,000 of which were hardy European canaries. After World War I, bird importation climbed to 825,736 (562,980 canaries) by 1930.[29] Even these accounts, with their staggering numbers of birds, cannot give an accurate picture of the extent of American bird selling, keeping, and breeding. So much of it, especially in small towns, seems to have been informal, an opportunity for bird owners to have the pleasure of watching their little avian families grow and to give home-reared canaries as gifts.[30]

Canaries had been pets for hundreds of years, and their breeding was a European cottage industry that no longer affected the wild populations of the Canary Islands. The canary business consisted of an international network of small entrepreneurs and specialist wage laborers. The importers with offices in Germany and England worked with "pickers," who selected birds from village breeders who might raise a hundred to sell in a season, and "travelers," who accompanied and cared for shipments of birds as they crossed the Atlantic on steamers (see fig. 5.3). Breeders in the Harz Mountains of Germany, the region that provided the largest numbers of birds, had standing arrangements with wholesale dealers; raising canaries was a lucrative seasonal sideline to their principal livelihoods. Families of miners and woodcutters spent evenings making the small wooden cages used to ship birds and, eventually, to carry them home from the bird store (see fig. 5.4). After pickers selected birds (a good day's work was 200, most of which were singing males), they were carried by foot and on rail to importers' "bird houses." During the peak season, the workers in the bird houses received, graded by evaluating their health and the quality of their song, and shipped 4,000 birds weekly. George Holden informed his readers that the strongest canaries were held for the long trip to America and noted, "Few ladies, while caressing their pets, and bestowing on them their daily delicacies, imagine for a moment the dangers through which the feathered immigrants have passed in their younger days."[31] Holden was probably right about the blissful ignorance of canary owners, and he was clearly right about the dangers of transport. The winter shipments of the 1870s apparently lost from one-quarter to one-half of the birds; by the turn of the century, the number was much lower.[32]

The result of these labors, the imported bird singing lustily in its cage in a kitchen or parlor, was a middle-class luxury until the 1910s. In the 1860s, Charles Reiche sold his canaries for $2.00 to $10.00 each and up to $15.00 for a breeding pair; Holden's were in roughly the same price range two decades later. (At this time, a skilled worker such as a carpenter earned $2.00 to $3.00 per day; an imported canary was not an impulse purchase for most people.) Prices gradually declined as American-bred birds became available, and ordinary male birds—the singers—typically sold for a dollar or two by the turn of the century. In 1914, Philadelphia's Cugley and Mullen offered its best-quality birds, "Golden Opera Singers," for $5.00, and an ordinary male canary

FIGURE 5.3. *"Methods of Shipping and Testing Cage Birds," photographer unknown. Henry Oldys, "Cage-Bird Traffic of the United States,"* Yearbook of the United States Department of Agriculture, 1906 *(Washington, D.C.: GPO, 1907). Author's collection.*

cost $2.50.[33] The combined price of bird, cage, food, and other equipment was still enough that a canary was a planned purchase, often a Christmas gift, since new bird stock arrived each year in November and December.

In the United States, large-scale breeding of canaries and other small cage birds for wholesaling developed during the first two decades of the twentieth century. By the 1920s, the warm climate of California proved hospitable for raising large numbers of exotics, such as parakeets (Australian budgerigars) and zebra finches, once exclusively imported.[34] Around the same time, American breeders were producing so many low-grade canaries that their surplus of females, who cheeped but did not sing, sold for 25 cents apiece. They became "wheel canaries," common if unfortunate prizes in games of chance on carnival midways.[35] The best canaries, however, remained European imports, and their higher prices reflected both the cost of bringing them to the states and the conditions of their production. They were carefully mated for quality, and the German breeders made efforts to educate young male canaries by exposing them to superior singers in training rooms.

However harmless the canary business, the broader trade supporting the gentle pleasure of household bird keeping had real consequences for wild bird species by the late nineteenth century. American native songbirds were "extracted" from the natural world just like minerals or trees; they were always caught in the wild whether for domestic consumption or exportation. Uncounted thousands died at the hands of rural bird catchers or during the rigors of a steamship voyage and further transport.[36] Along with the shooting of songbirds—by boys for fun, by amateur naturalists for their collections, and, in the case of a few species such as the bobolink, as culinary delicacies—trapping contributed to

FIGURE 5.4. *Transportation cage, probably German, 1870–1930. Author's collection.*

the alarming declines in the populations of native birds in the second half of the nineteenth century. Responding to the threat of widespread extinctions, the American Ornithologists Union produced a model law in 1883 that protected nongame birds from interstate commerce and import, and versions were gradually adopted by state legislatures in the Northeast. These efforts were augmented by such federal efforts as the Lacey Law of 1900.[37] In 1906, the USDA's annual yearbook contained an essay on the trade in cage birds reporting, perhaps optimistically, that "the domestic and foreign trade in native American birds has been entirely abolished."

Stock lists for pet stores at that time do confirm that such natives as Kentucky cardinals, goldfinches, and mockingbirds were no longer offered for sale. However, the USDA estimated that more than 200 different species of cage birds were being imported.[38] Early twentieth-century pet businesses apparently tried to substitute related species of South American and European birds, affecting bird populations in other places as well. The 1910 catalog of the Max Geisler Bird Company, an Omaha, Nebraska, business that shipped birds anywhere in the United States, offered for sale "Mexican Mockingbirds," "Mexican Cardinals," and "Brazilian Gray Cardinals," along with "European and Russian Goldfinches."[39] Between thirty and forty foreign species of finches alone were imported to stock turn-of-the-century aviaries.[40]

The trade in imported parrots may have been particularly devastating to wild species. High prices prevailed for birds during a fad for parrot ownership in the 1890s and early 1900s, and importers worked hard to meet demand. American dealers were unable to get large parrots to breed in any numbers, so pet store birds had been snatched from their nests by South American or African peasants and sold to pickers. One author noted candidly that the "high rate of mortality" among young parrots was due to "change of food and manner of living." "Indigestion and cold" claimed most of them. He claimed, however, that most wild parrots stood no better chance for long lives, since "farmers hunt them mercilessly" to protect grain crops.[41]

Relying on foreign stock, the newly formed Pet Dealers Association of America was no friend to either American or international bird protection efforts. In 1930, George Jenkins, first president of the group, complained in a speech at the association's banquet that the Audubon Society's successful efforts to pass a bird protection bill in the New York state legislature in 1900 reflected only the legislature's ignorance of birds: "The only thing [the law] did was to take thousands of sales from the pet shops of New York." He argued that a mockingbird in captivity was better off because it lived four to six years longer than one left to fend in the wild, bypassing completely the issue of species survival and casting the argument in terms compatible with the old domestic ethic of kindness, that of the well-being of each animal.[42]

Fish Farming and Importation

The most remarkable part of the American wholesale pet animal business serving neighborhood stores was the propagation of the most ephemeral stock: goldfish and, by the 1920s, tropical fish. By the mid-nineteenth century, middle-class families typically sustained a simple glass globe with one or two (typically short lived) goldfish that served, in the words of one advice book, "the purpose of an animated ornament."[43] The goldfish (*Carassius auratus*), an Asiatic member of the carp family, was probably introduced to Europe as a by-product of trade with China. Goldfish are so hardy that they can easily become feral and breed freely in ponds in climates with moderate winters.[44] One author of an 1896 book of advice on aquariums suggested that this indeed occurred in the United States some decades earlier. Their exact date of arrival in this country is unknown, but Frances Butler's visit to that florist with a greenhouse cistern full of goldfish shows that small-scale, local goldfish raising was already taking place by the 1830s; or perhaps nature was simply taking its course.[45]

Commercial goldfish farming seems to have been the first successful commercial aquaculture in America. According to William Kampfmuller's advice book *Our Pets* (1876), by the mid-1870s farms breeding goldfish had been established on Long Island and shipped cans of fish "to every part of the United States," something that could only have become possible with the railroad.[46] In 1883, another author estimated that the annual sale of domestically raised goldfish in America amounted to 2 million fish with a value of $300,000. This was an average wholesale cost per unit of 15 cents, a price suggesting that goldfish were still small luxuries.[47]

Able to survive during the winter months as long as their pond did not freeze completely solid, goldfish could be bred for sale in large numbers outdoors. Cincinnatian Hugo Mullert promoted a method of raising fish in a series of man-made, shallow ponds for spawning, rearing, and "storage" and a deeper pond for wintering-over breeding stock. Whether Mullert was simply sharing an established method of commercial goldfish farming or whether he was an innovator, as he claimed, is unknown. But variations of his system of pond raising came into use among the handful of large commercial breeders who supplied department stores and five-and-tens as well as pet shops (see fig. 5.5). By the 1920s, Frederick County, Maryland, had between thirty-five and forty goldfish farms, producing more than 3 million young fish each year for wholesaling to East Coast cities.[48] The July 1929 issue of *Pet Dealer* featured an illustrated article on Grassyfork Fisheries of Martinsville, Indiana, the nation's largest breeder, where 160 acres was given over to a complex system of 300 ponds yielding 5 million saleable goldfish a year, "half the nation's supply."[49] By this time common goldfish were so cheap (a typical wholesale price for two-inch fish was $2.50 per

FIG. 207. BREEDING PONDS WITH BOARDED EDGES

Also showing one of the world's best-known and cheapest grass cutters—a useful adjunct on a farm with acres of ponds. Some fish farms utilize sheep.

FIG. 207a. EGG NESTS

They have just been removed from upper pond and are being placed in raised concrete hatchery tanks. Eggs are deposited on the grassy mat, which is supported by poultry netting. Fish enter through open side spaces in the bottom.

hundred) that the importation of anything other than specimen fish for fanciers hardly seemed worthwhile. Yet around this time T. Mori and Company of San Francisco, "the Golden State Goldfish Company," regularly advertised to pet stores that it had as many as a half-million acclimated imported fish in stock for "guaranteed safe arrival to any part of the U.S."[50]

Goldfish were bred in the United States in such large numbers—21.5 million in 1929 alone—that breeders and jobbers, the middlemen who collected fish from the smaller operations and held them until ordered, inevitably began to treat them as a bulk crop. Not unlike fresh fruit and other perishables, goldfish had their preservation and transport problems. Speed of transport to retailers was key. As the cost per unit dropped, however, shippers flirted with the relative costs of shipment and loss, testing the limits of goldfish tolerance for poorly oxygenated water and ignoring issues of well-being. A 1929 U.S. government report on the goldfish industry reported deliberate overcrowding of fish in shipping cans to reduce freight charges, with consequent "quite heavy" losses due to suffocation.[51]

By the early twentieth century, the cheapness of plain goldfish a few inches long also affected how people obtained them. Goldfish were the original dime-store pet. The retail prices for small fish could be fixed so low that they met the pricing requirements of F. W. Woolworth and its competitors by around 1915, when an article in *Pet Stock World* condemned the dime-store method of keeping fish in "tiny globes in which the fish soon suffocate and die a horrible death."[52] By 1916, live goldfish began to appear as loss-leader

FIGURE 5.5. *Illustrations of the pond-raising system used by large goldfish farms. William T. Innes,* The Complete Aquarium Book: The Care and Breeding of Goldfish and Tropical Fishes *(New York: Halcyon House, 1936). Author's collection.*

advertising features in drugstores; by the 1920s, they were carnival prizes.[53] One might think of goldfish as the first modern "disposable" pet—produced in high volume, casually acquired through chain retail outlets, and just as casually disposed of down the flush toilets that two-thirds of American households had by the 1920s.

A more specialized, smaller market for fancy goldfish also existed by the 1880s, with the introduction of Fantails, Fringetails, Telescopes, and Lionheads, developed in China and Japan over centuries. The fanciers for these expensive, delicate creatures may have been the market that the Reed & Barton Company had in mind when it introduced fish globes on silver or silverplate stands in that same decade (see fig. 5.6). Exhibition-quality fish cost as much as $75 apiece and represented a minute, if glamorous, segment of the market.[54] Well-to-do hobbyists routinely imported unusual fish from Japan for both competition and breeding. Fancy fish could not be turned over as rapidly as ordinary farmed goldfish. Both amateur breeders and commercial farmers had to hold on to the creatures longer to see if the requisite flowing fins and colors would appear. Fancy fish also could not be subjected to the same sorting techniques and rough handling tolerated by common stock.

Tropical fish, perhaps the biggest pet craze of the 1920s, first appeared in American aquariums as wild-caught, "extracted" resources but rapidly moved through the stages of small-scale hobbyist breeding and, finally, organized farming. After the principle of the "balanced aquarium" was articulated in the 1840s, ambitious amateur naturalists tackled its intricacies, seeking to establish self-sufficient communities of pond or seashore creatures and plants, the aquatic equivalent of the "Wardian case," the first terrarium. The experience of keeping an aquarium changed dramatically, however, by the 1920s with the popular introduction of varieties of tropical fish. The discovery of small, colorful freshwater fish suitable for aquarium confinement was an outcome of natural history exploration and collecting in South America, Africa, and Asia. One 1933 book compared "intrepid" commercial fish collectors to orchid hunters, reporting that at "the present rate of exploration . . . there will not remain a stream or pool unvisited or a species of suitable size untried."[55] It appears that many of the advances in tropical fish care and breeding also came from the passions of shopkeepers and private collectors rather than scientists. In 1928, Joseph E. Bausman, a Philadelphian who sold nothing but goldfish and tropical fish, sent his grown son to South America to bring back new kinds of tropical fish for breeding in the family

FIGURE 5.6. *Silverplate fishbowls on stands, Reed & Barton illustrated catalog, 1885, Taunton, Massachusetts. Courtesy, The Winterthur Library: Printed Book and Periodical Collection.*

greenhouses. He estimated that "within two years" the results of this expanding breeding program would be available for sale.[56]

Collecting tropical fish became a hobby for a handful of wealthy American men by the 1910s. Importing fish rarities was an enjoyable challenge. A fancier could establish direct connections with commercial breeders in Hamburg, Germany (the first in the world, in a city that was the most important international center for the wild animal trade generally). Or he could arrange for steamship stewards to pick up a few hundred dollars' worth of wild-caught fish from collectors in Asian or South American ports-of-call and care for them on the trip back to the United States. As with canaries, large shipments of tropicals traveled with their own handlers, and steamships provided rooms equipped with heaters and electric air pumps to meet the requirements of fish used to life in warm, fast-moving streams in the wild. A 1927 article encouraging pet shop owners to stock tropical fish noted that serious fanciers were still willing to pay as much as $150 apiece for rare specimens.[57]

The first species of tropical fish bred for popular sale in America was the Paradise Fish (*Macropodus opercularis*). A native of East Asia, a small number of these fish arrived in France in 1869, but it took decades for them to appear in the United States. F. L. Tappan's *Aquaria Fish: Management and Care of the Aquarium and Its Inhabitants* (1911) was still devoted largely to describing various fancy goldfish breeds but devoted one section to the Paradise Fish, noting that it was "of relatively recent importation." The home aquarist who did not want to raise goldfish still had to rely mainly on capturing small American pond fish, but Tappan recommended trying the Paradise Fish because it was hardy enough to be raised in outdoor ponds in warm weather and could be bred for sale in a greenhouse.[58] Once other species became available, male Paradise

Fish proved too aggressive for the popular "community tanks," where fanciers tried to get a number of species to cohabit, and it slipped from popularity as substitutes came along.

In large cities, fanciers of tropical fish organized their own societies, buying, selling, and trading fish they raised and competing for prizes. The greatest success an aquarist could attain was getting fish to breed in captivity. Even guppies, introduced into the United States around 1905, were once treasured acquisitions whose life cycle and mating habits had to be deciphered by a few dedicated individuals.[59] A handful of successful amateur breeders also did business directly through the mails, using outlets like *The Aquarist* to reach enthusiasts.[60]

Few neighborhood pet shops stocked tropicals until the late 1920s. By then, the common species were raised by U.S. businesses such as the Crescent Fish Farm in New Orleans and priced low enough that they could be purchased by individuals with either a more casual interest in having an aquarium or less pocket money. Beginning in 1927, a series of articles in *Pet Dealer* urged pet shop owners to stock and advertise tropical fish, creating a market for this new kind of aquarium. One Ohio breeder and dealer wrote an article encouraging pet shop owners to supplant his retail mail-order business by expanding their own fish departments. The enthusiasm of tropical fish fanciers was unparalleled, he noted: "Talk about going a mile for a Camel—They send 2,000 [miles] for a pair of Guppyis [*sic*]. . . . We know the market is there, not just in New York or Chicago, but all over the country."[61] His list of the six most popular fish sold through the mails is close to the list recommended to freshwater aquarium beginners today. Guppies, the cheapest, also were the most popular, followed by Swordtails, Paradise Fish, Zebra Danios, Rosy Barbs, and "Moons" or Platyi, all available for $1 to $3 per pair.

As was the case with consumer goods from mouthwash to safety razors in the 1920s, the market for tropical fish was created. In 1930 John Doscher of William Tricker, Inc., a "complete aquarium service for the pet shop," wrote that the popular interest in tropical fish, a hobby that had been limited to "a handful of men, whose means and positions had enabled them to gather and import these then rare fish" a "mere dozen years ago," was the result of canny marketing. "Several large dealers and breeders" had "stimulated public interest by advertising in magazines, issuing instructive catalogs illustrated in color, and offering other pamphlets with instructions."[62] Others felt that the exhibitions sponsored by tropical fish clubs had kicked off the growth. Even department stores got into the act, sponsoring local aquarists' "large exhibitions of tropicals," which were publicized by newspaper ads and feature stories.[63]

The combination of dedicated collectors, alert commercial dealers, the entrepreneurial business spirit of the 1920s, and the experimental inclinations of pet shop customers even led to fads in fish, with consequent headaches for producers trying to predict demand. The introduction of *Betta splendens,* the Siamese fighting fish, offers one example of this phenomenon. In the wild, the fish were rather nondescript unless two males heightened their colors as part of mating displays or territorial combat. A 1927 shipment from Siam to San Francisco brought a natural mutation or "sport," a "cream-colored Betta with fiery flowing fins" that was promptly set aside for breeding purposes. German breeders experimented with the species around the same time, and the results of both programs—the "modern veiltail Betta" in shades of bright blue and red—was sensational and begat the fish department star of the 1930s. The aggressive nature and delicate fins of the males meant that bettas required a more hands-on kind of husbandry (including isolation from one another) than did other common tropicals. But the extra work paid off.[64]

For tropical fish to become truly popular, however, their care had to be easy enough so their keepers did not become discouraged. (As anyone who has flirted with keeping an aquarium will attest, removing dead bodies from the surface of the tank regularly is not only expensive but depressing.) Goldfish will tolerate low levels of oxygen in the water and a wide range of water temperatures. Tropical fish, however, need steady temperatures of approximately 75 degrees Fahrenheit, and species native to moving streams require better aeration. The unevenness or lack of central heating in many houses as late as the 1920s meant that keeping aquarium water warm enough required supplementary sources of heat. Early tropical fish fanciers rigged heating systems consisting of closed copper or glass tubing filled with water heated by Bunsen burners run from illuminating-gas jets.[65] Less-dedicated fanciers simply located their tanks in the house's warmest room or atop covers over the steam radiators that were becoming common in middle-class houses. In the early 1900s, the development of small electrical heating coils (the same kinds that powered the new electric irons and toasters of the era) led in time to the development of the submersible aquarium heater. In October 1930, William Tricker, Inc., advertised the "Chil-Breaker" Electric Aquarium Heater, a heating coil in an aluminum case mounted on a handle, in 25, 40, and 70-watt sizes. It looked like, and probably was an adaptation of, the immersion heaters offered for sale by Hotpoint a decade earlier for heating soup or beverages in small containers. It lacked a thermostat, however, which probably led to some accidental fatalities. Two years later the firm announced that it carried an "Automatic and Adjustible" aquarium heater: "Superior in that it will constantly maintain any desired temperature in the tropical fish tank from five to sixty gallon capacity. Will sell readily as it is just what so many tropical fish fanciers are looking for. Made to retail at \$7.50 with a good margin of profit for the dealer."[66] Fiddling around with the balance of plants to fish and the amount of light necessary for the plants to provide enough oxygen for a tropical balanced aquarium also required more dedication than casual owners were willing to give. Manually aerating the water was tedious, and by the 1930s, small electrical pumps were in common use.[67]

Today, freshwater tropical fish and their equipment are staples of nearly all pet stores. Most of the fish come from Florida, but a surprising number of tiny, bright-colored specimens are still extracted resources from South Asian and South American waters. Saltwater tropical fish, at the high-status end of the aquarium hobbyist's world and a prized element of interior decor for restaurants and medical offices, are captured from the wild for sale, a situation that has sparked concern among ocean conservationists. The care of saltwater fish is so complex that their owners often use the services of saltwater aquarium caretakers, who make house calls to the tanks.

Living Inventories and Mail-Order Pets

Once cans of fish and crates of canaries in their travel cages were delivered to a pet store, they became part of a small business with complex problems. Pet store owners had to obtain healthy stock, care for it in crowded conditions, and cope with the inevitable demise of part of the inventory. Selling songbirds had long been the heart of the pet business; but it was inevitably cyclical, peaking around Christmas each year, and canaries were in short supply by late winter. Thus store owners relied on the sale of cages, feed, and medicines to see them through the slow period. They also turned to other kinds of pet stock, such as ornamental pigeons and chickens, rabbits, white mice, and guinea pigs. The 1874 catalog of J. C. Long & Co., a short-lived business on a block of Ninth Street in Philadelphia that was known for its row of pet shops in the last quarter of the nineteenth century, shows how varied that stock could be. Long, who had exhibited fancy pigeons and poultry at the Centennial Exhibition, offered eighteen different varieties of chickens, five of ducks, two of turkeys, "any variety" of geese to order, pheasant, pea and guinea fowls, and California quail. The list of fancy pigeons included fifty-seven different items, counting the varied colors offered for each distinctive breed. Long supplied canaries, several kinds of parrots, at least seventeen different species of "Song and Ornamental Birds" (including bobolinks, orioles, and starlings), and seven breeds of rabbits (Lop Eared, Himalayan, Angora, Silver Grey, Belgian Hare, Dutch, and Common English). Gray squirrels, white mice, and guinea pigs rounded out the offerings of pets. Finally, Long stated that he imported English Pugs, King Charles Spaniels, and Gordon Setters to order, and he could supply locally bred pointers, setters, terriers, spaniels, hunting hounds, greyhounds, and "Spitzer" dogs.[68]

Businesses such as Philadelphia's Cugley and Mullen must have relied on contacts with small-time breeders such as Gwendoline Brook (who sold the last three Japanese spaniel puppies from her first breeding experiment to a dealer in New York) to supply the thirty-four different breeds of dogs advertised in their 1900 advice book and catalog, *Hints for Pets.* Cugley and Mullen's stock also included Angora and Maltese cats, four kinds of monkeys, three kinds of rabbits, guinea pigs, seven species of squirrels, chipmunks, fancy pigeons and bantam chickens, eight different kinds of canaries, fifty-four other species of small birds, and parrots. They also offered goldfish, "Paradise Fish of India," sticklebacks and other freshwater pond fish, turtles, newts, tadpoles, mussels, and snails to fill out the home freshwater aquarium.[69] Some livestock brokers apparently served as jobbers to the pet trade. In 1910, the Grosbeck Company, Inc., of Hartford, Connecticut, general livestock brokers, also matched buyers to small breeders of fancy pigeons, cavies, Angora cats, dogs ("Pets, Street, or Hunting Purposes"), and Shetland ponies.[70]

As wholesale animal dealers and stores joined in the development of the modern pet business, they supported a more aggressive search for other animal novelties and "seasonal merchandise" in animals.[71] Novelties were often creatures that never would have been indoor pets—or pets at all—in the nineteenth century. By the 1920s, the Max Geisler Company of Omaha had added to its stock American chameleons (*anolis* lizards), which became a staple of childhood terrariums after World War II and were sold at circuses wearing little wire collars and leashes, at least through the mid-1960s. In 1928, the National Pet Shops of St. Louis, Missouri, offered to ship "TEXAS HORNED FROGS . . . Alive and Attractive . . . 25¢ each/$1.50 Dozen—$4.50 for 50. Eight Dollars per hundred."[72] As pet shops joined the quest for novelties to attract new customers, animals often faced unpleasant consequences. Seasonal and novelty pets had little prospect of long or healthy lives. Easter chicks, dyed like eggs, were too fragile to survive the rough handling of small children. The needs of reptiles also were too specialized for the casual purchaser; they, too, became throwaways. According to recent surveys, Americans now care for millions of reptiles as pets. As with most aquariums, reptiles as pets are often associated with the presence of children in the house, but a community of serious amateurs thrives; they can be described as "collectors" as much as pet owners. They sponsor special pet shows and sales and are engaged in serious breeding efforts to create genetic sports. (A trip to one of their shows is an astonishing experience, as large plastic storage containers full of very large snakes are unloaded from vehicles and stacked on folding tables for display.)

Long before tropical fish breeders were engaged in the delicate business of shipping their fragile stock to a national clientele, ambitious pet dealers had worked to reach a wider market by offering to ship pets long distances to mail-order customers. In this practice, they followed an established national trade in pedigreed livestock for farmers' breed improvement programs. Mail-order shipment of dogs, fancy rabbits, and purebred strains of poultry began with livestock importers such as N. P. Boyer & Co., located in Chester County, Pennsylvania. Boyer operated as its principal business the importation of purebred English cattle, pigs, and sheep, but a catalog from around 1870 also offered fancy poultry, pigeons, rabbits, dogs, and birds. It also contained lengthy testimonials from satisfied customers throughout the South and Midwest.[73] J. C. Long's Philadelphia catalog was clearly directed at an out-of-town clientele; the prices quoted included "boxing and shipping by Express Company." Long also voiced the eternal mantra of the pet shop owner when he insisted that, once an animal was off his premises, "my responsibility must cease." "I ship nothing known to be out of condition," he insisted, "and as all Live Stock are abundantly supplied with food and water, they should, with ordinary care, go any distance safely."[74] The exhibitors' catalog for the Centennial Exhibition dog show contained a full-page advertisement from Benson and Burpee

("Successors to W. Altee Burpee") offering "Fancy Pigeons and Thoroughbred Dogs" along with imported pedigreed English swine and sheep.[75] By the 1890s, other seed companies were offering pets and fancy poultry as a sideline.[76] Henry Bishop, a Baltimore pet dealer who specialized in birds and goldfish, shipped the fragile creatures as far away as Montreal, New Mexico, and Cuba, according to testimonial letters published in his 1912 catalog: "Fishes arrived this morning all alive and in good shape. Well pleased with them. These are better fishes than I expected to get," wrote M. F. Simpson of Sherman, Texas.[77]

The most startling experiment in mail-order pets took place almost a half-century later, however, when Sears, Roebuck and Company and Spiegel, which called itself "The Nation's Pet Shop," both offered full pet departments in their catalogs. The spring and summer 1958 Spiegel *Home Shopping Book* not only offered forty-six different breeds of pedigreed puppies but also raccoon cubs, descented baby skunks, mynah birds, and several species of monkeys. Sears added toucans, fancy pigeons, and flying squirrels to the list. Shetland ponies and Mexican burros ("$67.50 cash. Only $13.50 down") were available for purchase on installment by both companies, just like the appliances, tools, and furniture offered elsewhere in their catalogs.[78]

Using the same tactics as purveyors of other lines of consumer goods, such as groceries and toiletries, mail-order and wholesale businesses even developed brand names for animals, and some advertised directly to retail customers through national magazines.[79] The 1928 mail-order catalog of the Max Geisler Bird Company (est. 1888) of Omaha, Nebraska, emphasized its "hand-raised" parrots imported from Mexico (see fig. 5.7). Branded the "Human Talker," this Mexican double-yellow-headed parrot came

FIGURE 5.7. *Cover,* Illustrated Catalogue, Max Geisler Bird Co., *1928. This image features the company's trademarked "Human Talker" parrot. Author's collection.*

with a "written guarantee . . . to learn to talk within six months." The company also patented a brand name for its special strain of imported Andreasburg Roller canaries (a breed with a distinctive trilling song). The "Living Music Box" (U.S. Patent No. 50853) cost as much as $10 for "extra fine selected singers." In 1929, the same firm developed a national marketing campaign that offered the male, singing birds with "Max Geisler" stamped on the inside of one wing, "a 100% sex guarantee to you. . . . It takes a staff like Geisler's to pick the singers." At the same time, bird importer Henry Bartels announced a national advertising campaign in *Ladies' Home Journal, Good Housekeeping,* and the *Saturday Evening Post* for "Trade Marked, Nationally Advertised, Legally Guaranteed" canaries.[80] The Hartz Mountain Company, whose displays of small-animal foods, nonprescription medicines, equipment, and pet toys are a fixture of supermarkets today, had as its first business the importation of a high grade of German canaries in the late 1920s. Until the company got out of the live animal industry in the 1950s, Hartz Mountain brand canaries went home from the pet store in special cages with the company's label on one end; so did Geisler's "branded" canaries and parakeets. Hartz also supported its brand with a radio program and 78 rpm recordings featuring the "Master Radio Canaries" warbling along to an organ playing such tunes as "Mexicali Rose."

Pet Stores as Small Businesses

Along with being an important part of the story of the evolution of pet keeping, pet stores offer an interesting case study in the role small business has played in the United States as a consumer society. Most pet stores were indeed very small. Mussog's Bird

Store in Philadelphia began as the hobby of a German immigrant canary breeder. As the numbers of birds grew, Emil Mussog, employed as a machinist, and his wife converted their front parlor into a shop in 1916. By the mid-1920s, they were also importing birds and had purchased a small three-story building on North Twelfth Street to accommodate the business. The Mussogs also had a "country estate" in nearby Willow Grove where they bred their own canaries and fancy fish. Mrs. Mussog operated the store with help from eight clerks. The couple also created a small mail-order business and published several catalogs.[81]

The Mussogs claimed that their success was due to their stringent adherence to the Golden Rule. However, the relationships pet shop owners developed with their customers were far more complex than those enjoyed by other retailers, both because of the nature of the stores' core inventory and the support services that storekeepers found themselves supplying. Animals could never be considered simple merchandise. When pet shop proprietors sold an animal to a customer, they were selling a relationship between a consumer and a consumer good who recognized each other. (Even the owners of pets with very small brains, such as fish, will tell you that their pets recognize them, if only as the shadow dispensing food on the opposite side of the glass.)

Pet stores tended to be small, crowded, noisy, warm, and smelly. Their mysteries and pleasures were particularly attractive to children. Along with five-and-tens, pet stores were places where American children learned how to be discerning customers, saving for and choosing small animals and their supplies and equipment. Pet stores were also where a fragile product of specialized husbandry began a process of transformation, from a simple object of trade to a nameless being in a crowd and then to an individual with preferences and a biography. No one in the pet business seemed to have the language to encompass this complexity, although reportage on successful pet stores suggested that pet dealers were at least partly aware of the emotional charge of their trade. When *Pet Dealer* published a series of features on exemplary pet stores, it emphasized qualities that were decidedly noncommercial. These included store interiors that were "home-like," where women could "bring in their birds and chat about them just as they would chat to their neighbors about their babies," and windows where birds were displayed against backdrops of houseplants or fully curtained windows and wallpaper.[82] Figure 5.8 shows a Los Angeles pet store captured by a photographer on 5 June 1916. It was decorated like a mission-style bungalow, with a stenciled ceiling and painted landscape on the upper walls and framed prints and photographs hanging on the walls and leaning from the shelves. Mr. Grider, the proprietor, leans against the counter. The taxidermic mounts on display, including a parrot that may have been a former shop pet and the head of a small black bear, may have been examples of Grider's own work.

While small neighborhood pet stores continued to rely on word of mouth and community ties for most of their trade, by the end of the nineteenth century, upscale pet stores aiming for wider markets offered the same appeals to attract and retain customers as did other modern purveyors of consumer goods. They used trade cards, postcards, catalogs, and newspaper advertisements to pitch the novelty, fashion, and low price of their stock and the clean, modern character of their facilities. The 1901 *Illustrated Catalog and Price List* of Schmid's Bird and Pet Animal Emporium of Washington, D.C., opened with a guarantee like those made by dry goods and furniture stores: by "satisfactory arrange-

FIGURE 5.8. *Grider's Birdland, Los Angeles, 5 June 1916. Photograph by S. M. Grinder. Library of Congress, Division of Prints and Photographs.*

ments" with wholesalers, Schmid was "enabled to buy the latest and best specimens at the lowest cash prices, and cheerfully give my patrons the benefit of these arrangements by making the prices low."[83] Reflecting Progressive Era concerns with health and sanitation, Philadelphia's Cugley and Mullen advertised their Market Street store as "Germ Proof," featuring metal kennels "kept absolutely clean and free from disease." They also provided written guarantees for animals—that they would sing or that they would not die—and permitted exchanges.[84]

Shopkeepers' responsibilities for the animals they sold often extended far beyond the sale. Some proprietors offered the only doctoring available for small animals in their communities. They dispensed advice and proprietary medicines and performed hands-on treatments based on their practical experience. Although cats and dogs became regular veterinary patients, pet stores remained the places where sick birds received care until quite recently. When Portland, Oregon, seed merchant Ralph R. Routledge opened a new business with an expanded pet department in 1935, the space included a freestanding "bird house and hospital" run by his wife. A news item in *Pet Trade Journal* reported that "hundreds of people . . . from all parts of Oregon and parts of Washington" traveled to the shop because of Mrs. Routledge's "knack of treating canaries."[85]

Just as they provided medical services, enterprising shop owners also began to bathe and groom pet animals, especially dogs, and they provided a home away from home by taking in boarders. For the owners of birds, the only boarding service available was in pet shops. Freestanding boarding kennels for dogs and cats appeared near big cities like Boston and New York by the end of the nineteenth century; they were another business that women could pursue with approbation and success. However, businesses such as the High Ball Pet Shop (see fig. 5.9) in Syracuse, New York, worked to make themselves into one-stop destinations for all pets' routine needs.

Pet shop owners were sometimes held accountable for events beyond their control, including the deaths of pet animals long after purchase. Business lore included anecdotes of the "bum

FIGURE 5.9. *Postcard for High Ball Pet Shop, Syracuse, New York, 1930s, photographer unknown. Author's collection. The High Ball Pet Shop offered grooming and boarding services for dogs as well as pet supplies and equipment. While the architecture of the store was blocky and modern, the kennel entrance emphasized its hominess.*

SYRACUSE NOW HAS A DOG BEAUTY SALON.
OF COURSE, IT'S AT HIGH BALL PET SHOP. 225 EAST ADAMS STREET
THE MOST COMPLETE IN CENTRAL NEW YORK.

CORNER OF SALON SHOWING MRS. H. E. RAWLINGS, PROPRIETOR,
PERSONALLY OILING ONE OF HER CUSTOMERS' DOGS;
AND HER FAMOUS KENNELS AT 5614 SOUTH SALINA STREET.

sport, who blames all his troubles and losses on the dealer, and who wants to exchange dead pets for live ones."[86] Store owners also struggled with ignorant owners demanding free advice and the "time-consuming curiosity seeker" who treated the shop as a zoo with no admission fee.[87] Despite these concerns, pet store owners wanted and needed to manipulate the curiosity and emotions of passersby, encouraging them to enter and, perhaps, to leave bearing a new pet and its appropriate supplies purchased on impulse. In the 1890s, the pet stores on Philadelphia's Ninth Street attracted attention by piling cages on the sidewalk outside their doors, thus enticing small crowds of men and boys who occasionally had to be dispersed by the local beat cop.[88] Display windows often featured the animals most likely to interact with customers or play with one another. Owners also kept one or two named shop pets, typically monkeys, talking parrots, or even a python, that were not for sale. Shop pets demonstrated the husbandry skill of the proprietor, gave the shop a community identity, and euphemized the store's commercial purposes. Their presence also suggested the appropriate nature of the pet-owner relationship—beyond commerce, companionable, and affectionate (see fig. 5.10).[89]

The advertising for many pet businesses simply assumed that the motivation for pet keeping was self-evident. However, by the 1920s, overtly psychological appeals, a genre perfected by a new generation of copywriters and agencies, began to appear in advertisements from the companies that made pet products. The most suggestive was a series sponsored by the Andrew B. Hendryx Company, the largest and most savvy manufacturer of birdcages at the time. Hendryx inserted half-page advertisements into national magazines where its own product played second fiddle to the rela-

FIGURE 5.10. *Unidentified pet store owner and his shop pet monkey, Denver, Colorado, between 1920 and 1930. Photograph by Harry Mellon Rhoads (1880/81–1975). Courtesy Denver Public Library, Western History Collection (RH1664).*

tionship of the caged bird and its owner. Each featured a story about the therapeutic benefits of pet ownership. One presented the tale of a "great physician" who "could count on one little friend to help him forget sorrow and suffering." Another appealed to women who felt bored or underappreciated: "His Sunrise Song chased away the Morning Blues. . . . When Mother was given a canary as a birthday present, she laughingly remarked, 'Now, at last, I'll have someone to feed on Monday morning who will be cheerful about it.'" In a third ad, a restless young wife received a "lively songster" from her husband and found new pleasure in housework and staying home, thanks to "the Feathered Guest that kept a home together."[90] Hendryx also published a free booklet, titled *The Feathered Philosopher,* featuring an extended story about an invalid musician whose canary encouraged her to take up the violin once more.

Becoming adept at the use of advertising and other forms of publicity was increasingly important for neighborhood pet stores as their proprietors faced new competition from department stores and chain stores such as F. W. Woolworth. In the 1920s, department stores also added pets to their home furnishings departments. In 1926, the John Wanamaker branch in New York City alone sold 18,000 canaries and 5,000 lovebirds.[91] The Jones Store in Kansas City, Missouri, set up a "rustic two room cottage" among the bed linens and china. The cottage was surrounded by new cages; in front was a large goldfish tank and several tables of fishbowls and supplies. The most extraordinary feature of the Jones Store "Bird House" was the constant presence of "a negro maid in uniform of black and white" whose job was to keep the cages and birds "in sanitary condition" and display them to interested customers. The manager of the "housefurnishing" department of a St. Joseph, Missouri, store praised "the stimulating effect" the presence of live birds had on the sale of cages, which cost more than the animals themselves. Stores often had "bird sales," where the cage and bird came as a package for holiday giving; an Omaha store manager noted that these sales events sold "as many as 200 birds in a single day."[92]

In the trade literature of the pet business, the ambiguous nature of animals as nationally distributed consumer goods, destined to be transformed into possessions of a very special sort, was generally unremarked. The publications and lore of the pet trade sometimes promulgated cartoons or stories that relied for their humor on the disjunction between the pet-loving consumer, who was purchasing a creature that might later be regarded as a family member or special friend, and the pet store proprietor, a harried businessman who struggled with eccentric customers who refused to think of the pet store as a commercial space. In its May 1928 issue, *Pet Dealer* printed a British cartoon that suggested that the joke was on the consumer: Salesman (to old lady buying goldfish): "These small ones are one-and-three-pence each, and the larger ones half-a-crown." Old Lady: "Which do you think would be the better company for me?"

Pet store owners relied on emotions; in fact, they worked to encourage feelings in their customers. But live animals were also the most "ticklish" part of pet store operations, their purchase a "constant problem," according to a 1953 book on pet store operations: "Just when you think that you have lined up some good breeders who will supply you with the quality and quantity you will need at the prices you can afford to pay, something happens and you are out looking for breeders again." Fish farms provided the most reliable and steady, if most ephemeral, of pet store live inventory. Because of their annual breeding cycle, birds were either abundant or scarce, but they were "fairly durable stock and if given proper care they can be kept on display year-round." Buying and selling puppies, however, was "the most perilous operation in a pet shop." "Mongrel" puppies were uncertain sales; commercial breeders of purebred puppies were sometimes "undesirable," and the stock itself had a very limited and complex display life. Along with their constant demands for care, puppies had to be sold "soon after you buy them," or they grew into "gangly looking adolescents that nobody wants."[93] The pet store literature, like the literature of the animal fancies, was coy on the subject of disposing of unwanted or ailing animals. The author of *Pet Shop Manual* did urge his readers to "prevent needless suffering by the humane destruction of ailing, aged, or crippled stock that will not respond to treatment," although he did not provide instructions on the methods to be used.[94]

Further, pet stores were not always good places for animals. There were, undoubtedly, always operations with poor sanitation and care practices. Issues associated with the poor condition of pet store stock drew a new level of attention, however, as pet stores entered a new era of competition in the 1960s with the arrival of the franchise. Franchising seemed to offer modernity to the old-fashioned retail pet trade. In 1964, the magazine *Pet Industry* reported on the efforts of the Docktor brothers, owners of a successful Philadelphia pet store, to "introduce the franchise idea to the pet business. If all goes well, dealers and newcomers to the trade will be able to walk into a canned operation, much like a Howard Johnson or One-Hour Martinizing drycleaner—for a price, of course."[95] Docktor Pet Centers were placed in shopping centers and the new enclosed malls, where they could capitalize on lots of passersby, and they attracted customers by filling their large front windows with puppies. The Docktor chain had a troubled history, including near-bankruptcy in 1972, but in 1990 it still had 153 stores in thirty states, generating $80 million in retail sales.[96] However, the company's practices led to repeated lawsuits in the 1970s, 1980s, and early 1990s because it continued to rely on puppy mills to keep the front windows of its franchisers stocked; failed to take adequate care of puppies, cage birds, and other animals; and used cruel methods to euthanize ill and dying stock. The *Special Report on Abuses in the Pet Industry* published by the Humane Society of the United States in 1974 noted, "With the sale of dogs and cats expected to reach $310 million annually this year, animals are being handled more and more like merchandise instead of the living creatures they are."[97]

"Breeding factories" or "puppy mills" probably grew in number as Americans' interest in owning purebred dogs increased, particularly after World War II. Puppy breeding operations may have seemed like an inexpensive way for small farmers to add income to their struggling operations, and the regularity of canine estrus cycles guaranteed two crops a year. The run-down facilities of many of these operations reflected the relative poverty of the rural people who undertook them. Complaints to the Humane Society of the United States and subsequent lobbying by the organization and other animal welfare groups led in 1970 to amendments to the Animal Welfare Act (AWA). The AWA had been passed to focus on the production and use of animals in research and industry, but the new amendment required that commercial dog breeders supplying to the pet trade be licensed and inspected regularly by the USDA. By the early 1980s, however, another investigation by the Humane Society found that an estimated 5,000 puppy mills, most in rural America, produced a half-million puppies. Few were inspected by AWA enforcement officers, who also bore responsibility for inspecting the living conditions of large stock animals.

Not all of what the American Kennel Club (AKC) calls "high-volume breeders" are guilty of the cruelty and neglect that characterize these rural puppy mills. Some large puppy farms meet health and safety requirements and even include staff to handle puppies and play with them during a crucial developmental window between six and fourteen weeks. However, an AKC report on high-volume breeders acknowledged that home dog breeders, who are still the source of most puppies, and large commercial operations have "sharply different values and motivations" for being in the dog business. All large puppy-breeding operations, whether a run-down rural puppy mill or a scientifically managed puppy farm, treat dogs as livestock, violating public expectations about the status and appropriate treatment of dogs. However, these public expectations are not applied to other commercial breeders of animals intended to be sold as pets, with the notable exception of cats. Further, the AKC has successfully fought efforts to further restrict commercial breeding operations on the grounds that additional regulation is an infringement on dog owners' property rights.[98] Regulatory efforts have been more successful in relation to pet stores; most states now require special licensing to enter the retail trade and regulate many store operations.

In the 1980s, the "big box" store concept of K-Mart, Wal-Mart, and other retail chains arrived for pets, too. The most important of these companies, and by far the largest today, is Petsmart. In 1987, the company opened its first two stores; it began expansion in the western United States almost immediately. In 1993, the year of its initial public offering on NASDAQ, the company had 107 stores in nineteen states. In 1994, Petsmart launched its new slogan, which echoes the old metaphors of the past: "Where pets are family." One corporate policy that made the company unique was its decision not to sell dogs and cats, although it still handles birds, fish, and some small animals. Instead, Petsmart helps local shelters place homeless cats and dogs at in-store adoption centers; in 2000, the millionth homeless pet was adopted this way. Throughout the 1990s, Petsmart gobbled up a number of other chains, including the sixty Petstuff superstores. In 2002, the company had 600 stores; its net sales that year for products and services totaled $2.7 billion, almost one-tenth of the estimated value of the American pet industry. By then, the company had announced its goal to become the "preferred provider for the total lifetime needs of pets." It trained its own canine obedience instructors, provided grooming salons, and even offered veterinary clinics at its largest sites.

Back in 1929, when the editor of *Pet Dealer* proclaimed the motto "a pet in every home," he was not only thinking about the profits in animals. Although animals were the most potent goods pet stores offered, they were not, in fact, the most profitable part of the pet business. Equipment and supplies were the products that capitalized on the desire of customers to care well for the animals they purchased. While a few items such as dog collars and cages had been manufactured for centuries, between 1840 and 1940, pet keeping gradually supported production and sale of an elaborate array of products and a select group of services intended to enhance the experience of pet ownership and improve the well-being of pets themselves. Pets were friends, family members, servants, art objects, moral exemplars, occasional food sources, and consumer goods; through their owners, they also became consumers in America.

❖ 6 ❖

BUYING FOR
YOUR BEST FRIEND

𝒥n December 1907, Lathrop's Pet Stock Shop in downtown Rochester, New York, sent a postcard to its customers. The message on the back invited them to patronize the store for the "best appreciated Holiday gifts," including the "Finest Song Birds in Rochester" and "Pets of all kinds" (see fig. 6.1). The front depicted Lathrop's interior viewed from the front door; it was a long, narrow space with shelves running from floor to high ceiling and multiple glass-fronted display counters. Banners hung from the ceiling, advertising feeders, incubators, and other supplies for the urban poultry keeper. Once customers passed the case of cigars, the table of newspapers, and the rack of postcards—goods intended to catch a bit of extra trade from passing businessmen and travelers—they were surrounded by products and supplies intended for household pets. Brass birdcages were suspended from the ceiling or from decorative stands on the shop floor. Dog leashes, wicker beds, animal carrying cases (see fig. 6.2), and shelves of over-the-counter remedies were found on the right. On the left wall, fishbowls and shelf after shelf of aquarium ornaments suggested how important fish were to the pet shop's bottom line. Notice, however, that no living creature was visible in this portrait of a prosperous pet business. The animals that provided the rationale for Lathrop's existence were either confined to the rear of the shop or located on another floor altogether.

Even if they were successful in attaining the Pet Dealers Association's goal of "a pet in every home," pet shops like Lathrop's could not survive on sales of animals alone, and the store's layout showed it. As mentioned earlier, creative store owners diversified their live inventory with novelties like Easter chicks or horned toads to compensate for the seasonal availability of "fresh" animals such as imported canaries, but equipment, supplies, and

FIGURE 6.1. *Postcard for Lathrop's Pet Stock Shop, 27 East Avenue, Rochester, New York, published by the Rochester New Company, postmarked 18 December 1907. Author's collection.*

services allowed pet stores to stay in business year-round. Over time, the cost of a handsome cage, special food, over-the-counter remedies, and toys or other accessories far exceeded the price of an animal, assuming that it was store-bought rather than a stray or a gift from a neighbor.

As the United States slowly developed as a consumer society—that is, a society where the needs and purchasing abilities of individuals drive the economy—ordinary practices such as pet keeping spawned constellations of purchasable objects. This trend toward innovation and growth in the new objects added to ordinary households was well established by the late eighteenth century, but change was gradual. In the late nineteenth century, a striking period of innovation in making, distributing, and marketing consumer goods began. This development was slowed by the

Depression and World War II, but the pace picked up again in the postwar period, when an era of new prosperity spawned another burst of innovation and proliferation.

This trend can be seen in the history of products for pets, but the objects that survive and the advertisements that promoted them also suggest other changes. The forms and functions of the artifacts and the images and texts that their makers directed at pet owners support my argument that the ways people thought about pets changed significantly. The first pet equipment, collars and cages, was intended primarily to restrain, identify, and control animals. A few wealthy owners purchased decorative or novelty cages as ornaments or handsome collars as a small statement of their means. However, by the 1840s, the proprietors of the first bird shops were selling new products intended to enhance both the physical and psychological well-being of their stock, from tonics and special foods intended to help canaries pass through the annual trial of molting to packaged materials for nest building. By the 1880s, pet stores, feed stores, leather goods and sporting goods shops, and druggists carried food, medicines, and equipment, including special feeders, toys, carriers, and beds, that were meant both to improve the lives of pet animals and to enhance the interactions of people and their pets. A new category of goods—dog furnishings—no longer simply labeled or restrained dogs but turned them into fashionable dressers like their status-conscious owners.

The trade literature and advertisements used to promote pet supplies and equipment are also worth a closer look. Their pictures and texts suggest an ongoing conversation among manufacturers, store owners, and consumers and demonstrate how changing perceptions of the needs of animals often paralleled a

FIGURE 6.2. *Travel case for pet, wicker, maker unknown, ca. 1900. Author's collection. Intended for a cat, small dog, or rabbit, this case opened from both the top and the front.*

new understanding of human needs. The theories of nutrition be-hind commercial pet foods and the advertising marketing these new products often employed the reasoning and the rhetoric of human diet reform efforts or reflected the owners' new attitudes toward pets as members of their families. Other pet products, such as vitamin supplements and spring-upholstery beds, were congruent with products introduced for people. Pet toys reflected the desires of owners to give animals, particularly those confined to cages or small urban living spaces, pleasure. In the early twentieth century, the makers of these goods encouraged owners to give pets Christmas gifts of special foods, new clothes, and toys, just as they presented such gifts to family members. These goods and the practices of giving reveal the increasing complexity of the obligations that pet owners felt toward their animals.

Where pet supplies and equipment were available also says something about the ubiquity of pet keeping. Pet stores carried the widest range of goods, but products for pets also became part of the inventory in stores supplying analogous goods for people. Patent medicines for pets were also sold by druggists; pet food, by grocers; collars and leashes, in leather goods shops; and pet coats and beds, in department stores. Once the five-and-ten or variety store became a site for purchasing pet supplies and equipment, buying goods for pets became part of the shopping rituals of Americans with very modest incomes.

The photograph of Grider's Birdland in Los Angeles (see fig. 5.8) shows in more detail the nature and distinctive aesthetics of early twentieth-century pet equipment. A plain, sturdy parrot cage stands beside the heavy counter, but smaller cages shaped like minarets or having the roof lines of cottages predominate. Aquariums, including one in a fantastic "rustic" style, and the ceramic castles and statuary to furnish them line a high shelf in front of the landscape frieze. Not every object in the imposing front case can be identified, but the top shelf contains paperbound books of advice, glass and ceramic feeders and waterers for birdcages, faux eggs to encourage fancy poultry or pigeons to set a nest, floating ceramic duck ornaments for fish globes, and tins of fish food. The middle shelf displays dip nets, leather dog collars and harnesses decorated with metal studs and contrasting linings of wool or chamois, dog sweaters, wire seed guards for birdcages, and a tiny mouse cage with exercise wheel. The bottom shelf contains another row of brass birdcages with visible price tags. These cages were relatively inexpensive, but their delicately shaped wire frames, shining brass trays, and sparkling milk glass feeders were made of the same materials as the ornaments in many middle-class dining rooms, and they were intended to display just as nicely.

The owners of Lathrop's Pet Stock Shop and Grider's Birdland did not make what they sold. Instead, they drew on the specialized production of scores of small companies, where workshops with a few machines and some skilled hand laborers could produce a variety of styles and shapes for each kind of pet product. The display at Grider's emphasized three of the oldest kinds of pet equipment: cages, containers, and collars. Dog collars have been found in Egyptian tombs and were depicted on Roman sculpture, and birdcages date back at least that far. However, by the 1870s, the small companies in the pet product business had begun to produce a wider variety and greater numbers of things. They used the era's important business techniques of taking out patents for both manufacturing innovations and new designs, publishing trade catalogs and giveaway trade cards, and advertising in the new national magazines that appeared in increasing numbers at the turn of the century.

Other small entrepreneurs, including pet shop owners, druggists, and a few prescient veterinarians, found a livelihood in pets by creating and marketing their own special foods and proprietary remedies. Their boxes, bottles, and tins were also an essential part of all pet store trade. In 1915, Grider may still have been compounding and bottling his own remedies and special foods for birds. In 1927, when his daughter Idella Grider Manisera published *Birds and Pets,* a sensible little paperback book on pet care, Grider's Birdland sold its own Cage Cleaner, Oil-E-Tonic (a "marvelous remedy" for "desperately ill birds"), Condition Powder, and Diarrhoea Remedy. As late as 1950, Birdland's Copyrighted Remedies, "used successfully in the largest BIRD HOSPITAL in the U.S.A." (Manisera's own shop), were available wholesale to the national trade.[1]

Pet owners in the late 1800s and early 1900s probably would have agreed that the products sold by the Lathrop Pet Stock Shop, Grider's Birdland, and the Supreme Brooklyn Pet Emporium were essential to the well-being of their animals. Pet products continue to evolve, however, reflecting changing social, cultural, and scientific understanding of the needs of dogs, cats, rodents, birds, and fish. As the range of exotic animals kept by some Americans expands, so, too, does the array of specialized supplies and equipment sold for pet care. Reptiles, for example, need full-spectrum lights and electrically heated surfaces, which are often shaped and colored like the sun-baked rocks on which their ancestors lolled. Even so, most of the thousands of products stocked at my local pet store are simply iterations of the old standbys.

Pioneering Bird Supplies

The front countertop of the Supreme Brooklyn Pet Emporium (see fig. 5.1) contained two cardboard displays supplied by the Max Geisler Company (see Chapter 5). The advertisement on the right featured a message from a canary, its wings outstretched in a pleading manner: "PLEASE help me! I need GEISLER'S MOULTING

KIT To Grow Bright New Feathers!" The animal first-person voice, used so effectively in earlier generations to plead for kindness, had become commercial. The Geisler canary claimed that its well-being now depended not just on kind care but on products made especially for it. While Max Geisler's original trade was in cage birds themselves, selling food became part of his Omaha bird business soon after he sold that first shipment of canaries he carried home in 1888 from Germany, where he had traveled to find a wife.[2]

In fact, bird dealers were the pioneers of the American pet supply business. By the 1840s, they had introduced the first packaged, commercial foods and medicines made specifically for pets. The how-to books they published and the bottled remedies they sold built on the long history of bird keeping and its practical lore. At first, bird sellers such as Charles Reiche (see Chapter 5) assumed that bird owners were their own provisioners. Live food eaters like mockingbirds, a very popular captive throughout the nineteenth century, had demanding requirements; successful care required real dedication. The caretaker of a captive robin, for example, needed to provide homemade "German paste (a mixture of cooked grain and chopped egg), crumbled bread, bruised hemp-seed, and poppy-seed," along with occasional feedings of insects (ant eggs, mealworms, wood lice, spiders, and earwigs were recommended) and "a few bits of raw beef occasionally." A recommendation for "hay-saffron" or a rusty nail in birds' water once or twice a week must have been intended to provide missing minerals, especially iron.[3] Reiche informed his readers that birds who ate seeds still needed "plenty of green food," a challenge when the ground was covered with snow and most people were not getting much in the way of green vegetables. But he also pronounced "very healthy" "some bread and milk, and a little smoked bacon, scraped off with a knife. . . . And for soft-billed birds, a meal worm dipped in sweet oil [olive oil], some berries and ant's eggs."[4]

These instructions challenged genteel urban bird keepers to find a source for seeds and to collect bugs. Mealworms were probably available in poorly stored flour at home, as was the occasional tasty spider or fly plucked from corner cobwebs. Shops like Reiche's offered a variety of bulk seed, but they also sold ant eggs and mealworms for insect-eating birds; someone was either busily collecting or actively propagating insects for customers who either could not or would not do it themselves.[5] Soon bird stores offered packaged, prepared products such as "mocking bird food" in glass jars and put their names on the mixtures they sold. Holden's New York Bird Store of Boston offered, along with the usual collection of canary seeds, its own "Red-Bird Seed, half each unhulled rice and hemp" and "Reiche's Prepared Food" for soft-billed birds; it also sold dried mosquitoes, flies, and ant eggs by the pint and mealworms by the dozen or hundred.[6] At the turn of the century, the Philadelphia Bird Food Company offered a variety of brand-name seed mixes, special Bird Manna to see cage birds through their annual molt, and Nestling Food to replace homemade German paste.[7]

Given the simplicity of the manufacturing process, bird food makers tried various tricks to differentiate themselves. Henry Bishop, Baltimore's "Bishop the Bird Man," marketed a variety of foods that used the Progressive Era's interest in safe, sanitary packaged food for people as a marketing tool for pets. "Bishop's Best Mixed Canary Seed" was "Guaranteed under the Food and Drugs [sic] Act, June 30th 1906. Serial No. 2489." "Bishop's Bird Dainties" were a "Luxury and Upbuild" for listless pets. His special

Parrot Biscuit and Parrot Seed, Red Bird Seed, Orange Color Food (which contained cayenne pepper to make canary feathers a darker orange-yellow), and Mocking-Bird Food (which came in two varieties depending on the age of the bird) were, he noted, "my own invention" and "Sold by Progressive Druggists and Grocers Everywhere."[8]

Grocers apparently carried bulk bird seed by the late 1870s, but it must have been a nuisance to measure out and bag because the quantity of any single purchase was so small. Prepackaged seed solved that problem, and by around 1880, the Excelsior Bird Food Company was already advertising in the national grocer's trade paper. By the 1910s, alert companies such as the R. T. French Company, founded in 1880 to sell mustard and other condiments, recognized that entering the bird food business required little more than, well, seed money for attractive packaging and advertising in magazines. One member of the family, George J. French, was apparently a canary fancier in his leisure hours, and the company was able to take advantage of its established name and distribution to groceries to enter a new market. By 1929, French's Bird Seed and Biscuit was advertised in the same women's magazines that carried ads for the company's yellow mustard. By 1951, French's featured the mascot "Frenchy the Famous Canary Pirate," hearkening back to the origins of the little bird in the Canary Islands.[9]

Because there was so little difference among bird seeds, French's, Geisler's, and other companies not only relied on branding and advertising but also on books of advice with titles such as *Canaries for Pleasure and Profit*. These not only encouraged novices to take up bird keeping, but they taught brand loyalty. In its 1933 booklet on canaries, The Nature Friend, Inc., a New York

City company whose products were marketed to variety and grocery stores, offered its readers a seven-day feeding regime for the family canary. It required carefully scheduled meals of Magic Song Restorer, Magic Fruit and Egg, and Magic Private Stock Canary Seed, doses of Magic Bird Tonic and Vitamin Food, and constant access to Magic Bird Gravel with Charcoal for good digestion and Magic Jewel Bone (cuttlebone) for calcium (see fig. 6.3). The booklet closed with "An Imprisoned Bird's Daily Prayer": "Oh Captor, consider that I am your little prisoner, give

FIGURE 6.3. *The array of products for cage birds produced by The Nature Friend, Inc. From Joseph P. Leindorf [The Nature Friend],* How to Take Care of Your Canary, *New York, between 1933 and 1935. Author's collection. The company's most successful product, Magic Song Restorer, featured on its package a bedraggled canary inquiring in ethnic German dialect of another, healthy bird, "How come that you look so well?"*

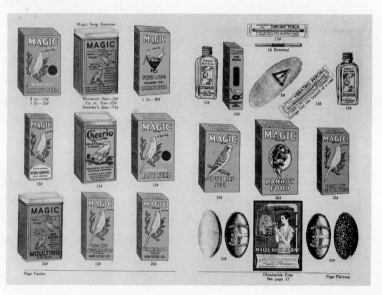

me my daily food, consisting of pure and wholesome rape and canary seed, and pray do not omit to give me a separate small dish
of MAGIC SONG RESTORER and GENERAL HEALTH FOOD. . . . Lead
me not into temptation by offering me some cheap imitation of
the so-called song restorers. If you deliver me from such evils I
will promise to sing my song of gratitude for the rest of my imprisoned life." How could a loving owner refuse?

As with caged birds, feeding pet fish in the early years required that owners be cooks, nutritionists, and even hunters.
While commercial fish foods, probably rice-flour cakes, were sold
as early as 1881, serious aquarists devoted time to securing and
preparing food for their fragile charges.[10] They frequented stag-
nant pools and open drainage ditches to collect *daphnia* ("ditch
fleas"), kept earthworms in boxes of dirt in their cellars, and gathered mosquito larvae in season. Books on fish keeping often included recipes for dry fish foods like this one:

> Quarter tumbler powdered cod
> Three quarters tumbler powdered shrimp
> Three tumblers flour
> One teaspoon Epsom salts
> Three teaspoons baking powder
> Three teaspoons powdered chalk.

After adding two raw eggs and some water, the fish food chef
was to spread the dough in a pan, bake it, dry thin slices, and grind
it in a coffee mill for use. William Innes, the aquarium expert who
provided this recipe, noted that finely ground, dry dog food also
made a good fish food and that fish dealers often used it as the
base for the preparations that they packaged and sold in their
stores. Thus fish food became a small sideline for the makers of

other pet foods; it was a way to extract profit from the crumbs. Well-known fish wholesalers such as Grassyfork Fish Farm, the largest wholesale goldfish-breeding operation in the United States, also packaged and sold food under their own names.

Provisioning Pets Becomes Profitable

The modern pet food industry dedicated to feeding dogs and cats originated in Victorian England, with Spratt's Patent, Limited, a firm that produced hard cakes of dog food intended primarily for conditioning field and show dogs. The 1895 catalog for the New York offices of Spratt's described the firm as the "greatest Dog and Poultry Food Concern in the world," and they were not exaggerating. Spratt's had begun producing Meat Dog Biscuits in England around 1860. Apparently James Spratt, an American businessman visiting England, had a proverbial "Eureka" moment after he saw stray dogs eating discarded hardtack on the London docks. Hardtack was the tough-as-nails biscuits baked for soldiers and sailors; it was a shipboard staple and field ration. Around the time of Spratt's insight, the British military establishment was engaged in experiments to create better battle rations for its troops in response to widespread malnutrition during the Crimean War. These trials included "meat biscuits."[11] Whether or not British soldiers ever enjoyed these toothsome treats is unclear, but Spratt made use of the same idea for a different end. The parallels between ideas about conditioning soldiers and conditioning hunting dogs are intriguing, however.

The company's decision to undertake manufacturing in the United States coincided with the appearance of the organized dog fancy in the early 1870s. Spratt's, the first commercial dog food in America, was also the first marketed and sold from coast to coast.

In fact, the marketing techniques of the company foreshadowed almost all the come-ons used by commercial dog food companies today. Recognizing that it had to create demand for a product that no dog owners felt they needed, Spratt's was a relentless advertiser. The company centered its efforts on dog shows, including the 1876 centennial, and provided free food to get exhibitors into the Spratt's habit. It bought the entire front cover of the very first issue of the official journal of the American Kennel Club (AKC) in January 1889 to trumpet its identity as "Contractor to the leading American and European Kennel Clubs" and its "Special Appointment" to that notorious dog lover Queen Victoria. Spratt's even provided free AKC pedigree registration forms; the flip side of the sheet was a full-page ad for its products.[12]

In 1881, the company took out an American patent for its most famous product, "Celebrated Patent Meat 'Fibrine' Dog Cakes," which included "Beetroot," the only vegetable "which retained its properties when made into a Biscuit."[13] Fibrine Dog Cakes were large, square biscuits intended to be broken up for feeding, although the company noted that forcing the animal to gnaw the unbroken biscuits would stimulate its digestive juices, just as health breads for people were intended to do. In fact, the company's explanation of the benefits of Fibrine Dog Cakes used vocabulary that echoed the preoccupations of the period's advocates of health food for humans: the biscuits were a "plain, wholesome diet" that would "obviate constipation, which is almost natural in the domestic dog, and the cause of more disease than anything else."[14] Old dogs with bad teeth should have their biscuits moistened, and dogs that traditionally enjoyed a diet of leftover people food might require coaxing by an initial moistening with "soup," although "an overweight, fat dog may be starved

three or four days without injury." Even so, the manual recommended that masters continue a weekly feeding that included a
mixture of the vegetables and starches that family dogs were
used to getting.

Like the bird food companies, Spratt's soon had a range of specialized offerings, including the basic Patent Meat "Fibrine" Vegetable Dog Cakes (with Beetroot) in quantities from 3 to 100
pounds, Patent Charcoal Dog Cakes for sour canine stomachs,
special Greyhound Cakes, Oatmeal and Plain Round Dog Cakes
(for use where "flesh" was part of the training diet of greyhounds
and hunting packs), Pet Dog Cakes ("especially valuable for pets
kept in the city"), and Patent Cod Liver Oil Old Dog Cakes (a
tonic food "invaluable for delicate or old dogs and those recovering from a sickness"). Puppies were served by Puppy Cakes,
Pepsinated Puppy Meal ("for weaning, for 'Bad doers,' and dogs
with weak digestions"), Bone Meal, and a powdered supplement
for a bitch who had no milk or for an orphaned litter. Later
Spratt's advertisements even echoed the era's concerns that purebred animals, like purebred (read "white") people, were less likely
to be able to reproduce successfully because of overrefinement;
the company's strengthening Malt and Cod Liver Oil Dog Cakes
were "excellent as a safeguard against sterility."[15] This claim
placed the company directly into the wider debate on purebred
dogs (see Chapter 1). Spratt's landed firmly on the side worried
about the effects of overbreeding, rather than the side that argued
for the superiority of the purebred over the mongrel. From the beginning, Spratt's also pushed brand recognition, ahead of many
manufacturers of foods for people. Every Fibrine Dog Cake was
stamped with the phrase "Spratt's Patent" and an "X." By the end
of the century, even Sears, Roebuck and Company experimented

with offering Spratt's in its catalog.[16] Spratt's seems to have been the first dog food company to take out display advertisements in national general interest magazines such as the *Saturday Evening Post* (fig. 6.4).

As a business, dog food manufacturing took several different paths. Spratt's began as a dog food company, but in America, most dog food companies had ties with other kinds of food production. By the 1890s, dry dog food had become a sideline of animal feed manufacture for regional companies throughout the northeastern United States. Commercial livestock feed was an outgrowth of both large-scale grain farming and the production and marketing of by-products in the growing meatpacking industry. "Feed tankage" (the slurry of odds and ends of commercial slaughter that was mixed with crackling and blood, dried, and pressed into "cheeses"), sold by packers for use in feed mixes for hogs and chickens, could just as easily be cooked up into feed for dogs.[17] The word "feed" was never used for dog food, however; feed was for livestock, while food was for the members of households. The most famous, although not the pioneering, example of this business model is the Ralston Purina Company. This livestock feed company, founded in 1894, first added dog food to its product line in 1926, although the product was sold only through licensed dealers of Purina livestock feed. The Purina Dog Chow that became America's most popular dry dog food was only added to the line in 1957, after six years of formulating and marketing experiments made with the intention of cracking an already established retail grocery market.[18]

Other companies developed dog food lines as a sideline to grain milling for human consumption or as an outgrowth of the expanding business of veterinary patent medicines. Old Grist

FIGURE 6.4. *Advertisement for Spratt's dog food,* Saturday Evening Post, *26 February 1927. Thomas Cooper Library, University of South Carolina.*

Mill Dog and Puppy Bread was introduced around 1905 by Potter and Wrightington, a Massachusetts company that specialized in "Hygenic Health Foods for family use." The makers mixed their special whole-grain flour with beef, bone meal, rice, and vegetables and baked them into "cakes" and a special "Boston Terrier Biscuit."[19] Around the same time, the A. C. Daniels Company of Boston began to offer "medicated dog bread" as an aid for convalescent or chronically ill pets.

Canned dog food, which first appeared in the 1910s, also developed as a regional business, with relatively low start-up costs.[20] Factory locations were determined by their proximity to sources of meat and meat by-products. Canning meat for human consumption actually began in the mid-1840s, but the economics of making metal cans prevented their use for animal food until the early 1900s. Because livestock lived in or near cities and towns all over the United States, slaughter took place in many communities as old, unproductive, or unwanted animals were converted into meat or the raw material for products from glue to soap. It was not difficult for either the slaughterhouses themselves or small contractors located near local stockyards to take meat and by-products people could not or would not eat, especially after the Pure Food and Drug Act of 1906, and can it for the delectation of dogs.

The packers of wet dog food always relied on multiple animal sources for the meat in their products. Horse meat became available in larger quantities as the American public turned from equine- to gasoline-powered vehicles in the 1910s and 1920s. The Hugo Strauss Packing Company of Brooklyn offered Purity dog food, composed of "Solid Cooked Horse Meat," and Laddie Boy Kennel Ration, a mixture of horse meat, cereals, and cod liver oil.

The Dr. Olding Food Products Corporation countered with Beef Ration, with a formula similar to that of Laddie Boy.[21] Other packers included lamb and mutton, pork, and even meat from wild game. The canned foods containing poultry that are so popular today were not developed until after World War II, when new, intensive animal-agricultural practices encouraged the consumption of chicken any day of the week, rather than just at Sunday dinner.

By 1940, canned dog food was a profitable business for regional packers all over the United States. It was now a sideline for the big Chicago packers, who went into the business in the 1920s and 1930s. Armour sold the Dash brand, while Swift's offered Pard (see fig. 6.5). When the Minnesota Department of Agriculture did an analysis of the composition of commercial dog foods in 1941, it tested 125 different canned and 75 different dry foods available for sale in that state alone.[22]

Selling dog food meant selling the very idea of packaged foods for household animals, and it required multiple approaches. Spratt's pioneered snob appeal, but it also promoted its product for canine health and even created the "life stages" approach used by companies today. By the 1920s, dog food companies were also appealing to owners' emotions and pocketbooks, to public interest in the developing science of nutrition, and to women's interest in easing the burden of housework. In the advertisement in figure 6.4, Spratt's used a blend of well-established ideas and images: the visual formula comparing pets and children by showing them at play together, the metaphor of the pet as friend, the claim that "meat-fed" dogs were less healthy, and an offer of a free booklet on dog care. Swift's advertised its "scientifically balanced" Pard dog foods by claiming that they prevented nervousness in purebred

FIGURE 6.5. *Advertisement for Pard, "Swift's Scientifically Balanced Dog Food,"*
American Home, *June 1939. Thomas Cooper Library, University of South Carolina.*

dogs. Figure 6.5 shows researchers in white coats, who lend cre-
dence to scientific claims, and a large picture of a chow, a popular dog of the 1930s that had (and has) a reputation for nerves and
testiness. Copywriters also suggested that dog food purchasers,
like the people who bought canned soup or boxed crackers, were
progressive consumers who understood that the time had come to
abandon old ways of caring for dogs. By the 1920s, dog food companies even used "reason why" approaches that reflected the era's
preoccupation with body odor and fat in people: "The time is past
when the dog is brought up entirely upon the scraps. . . . Most
dogs so fed are prone to obesity and some give off strong odors [a
polite way to describe canine flatulence] because of the highly
seasoned or too fat or perhaps too starchy foods."[23]

Commercial pet food, on the other hand, was the true canine health food. The Battle Creek Dog Food Company, located in the city known for its health resorts and commercial health cereals, advertised its Miller's Dog Food as "The Battle Creek Health Food for Dogs."[24] In 1935, Albers Brothers Milling Company, the makers of Friskies, published pictures of the laboratories where their food had been tested on "five generations of albino rats" to confirm the completeness of its nutrition.[25]

Marketing dog food also relied on promoting its convenience at a time when simplification of household routines was a new concern for American housewives, who were happy to be free of homemade "dog stews." While the first dog cakes had to be broken and soaked, kibbled or granulated food, an adaptation of granulated livestock feeds widely offered by the 1910s, had simply to be poured out. The front of the 1920s Spratt's dog food box contained the motto "No Trouble No Cooking No Mess," and mills increasingly used this idea in their pitches.[26] One company promoted its canned product as "Miller's Quick Lunch." In 1929, small ads in the *Ladies' Home Journal* for Ken-L-Ration, "The Dog Food Supreme," explained that the food was "packed in sterilized cans; ready to feed without muss or bother." Readily available, it was sold in "over 100,000 retail stores. . . . There is one in your neighborhood."

Finally, if none of these rational appeals worked, dog food companies could turn to celebrity endorsement, another approach to selling that swept the nation in the 1920s. Ken-L-Ration had to be good; after all, it was "Rin-tin-tin's FOOD."[27] In 1940, Gaines was able to promote its Gaines Meal and Gaines Krunchon as "the choice of the U.S. Antarctic Expedition."[28] At the end of World War II, Lassie, the collie star of movies and radio, became the celebrity spokes-animal for John Morrell and Company's Red Heart brand.

Still, dry dog "bread" of any brand was slow to be accepted by families who were used to sharing their victuals with canine family members. Domestic and popular veterinary advisors regarded dry dog food as inadequate for canine health into the 1930s. *Harper's Household Handbook* (1913) informed its readers, "Dog biscuit given day in and day out destroys appetite and thrift [here meaning the ability to thrive]."[29] As late as the 1930s, the *Sergeant's Dog Book,* a free pamphlet promoting Sergeant's line of pet products, recommended that a diet of the biscuits be varied with table scraps, "otherwise it will become distasteful."[30] For pet owners who did not like commercial dog food but needed the convenience of meat already cut up into usable portions, pet stores began to take advantage of improved refrigeration technology and offered their own meat departments, generally featuring fresh or frozen horse meat. Some even offered regular meat delivery to customers' homes, just as butchers still did for the family grocery order.

Dogs raised on the substantial diets of their middle-class owners also probably eyed their first Fibrine Dog Cake with suspicion. Companies worked hard to suggest that their foods were more appealing to dogs than those of their competitors. Old Grist Mill was "A Food Your Dog Will Like." Bresko Dog Food's makers explained that "dogs need not be coaxed to eat Bresko—they like it on the first taste."[31] Many companies encouraged shoppers to try their foods by offering free samples at stores or through the mails.

The acceptance of dog food was also slowed prior to World War I because it was an extra household expense at a time when a solidly middle-class lifestyle in most communities meant an annual family income between $1,000 and $2,000. In the 1890s, Spratt's various products cost between $7.50 and $8.00 per hundredweight, and considerably more per pound for smaller quantities. It was food for dogs from rich households. The widespread use of commercial dry foods probably received a boost from the meat shortage of World War I and was promoted anew by the U.S. government's restrictions on the use of cans in preparation for World War II, along with that war's subsequent meat rationing. Dog food, both wet and dry, gradually became part of the middle-class grocery list because of its convenience and availability, its gradually decreasing cost, changes in cooking practices, and changing beliefs about the needs of dogs. Even in the Depression, consumers spent $100 million on dog food. Not all of it was consumed by dogs, however. In 1936, Congress required that federal meat inspection regulations be extended to dog food because some poverty-stricken people were using canned meat intended for dogs as their source of animal protein.[32]

Given the generally unequal treatment received by "just plain cats" and the limited popularity of purebred cats, it is not surprising that cat food remained a relatively neglected part of the developing pet food market until after World War II. The 1895 Spratt's catalog had offered, but did not emphasize, an expensive Patent Cat Food available at five cents per packet. Potter and Wrighting- ton, makers of Old Grist Mill Dog Bread, followed with a similar product around 1910. A Johnson and Stokes catalog from around 1900 offered customers what seems to be the first wet cat food, associated like the early dog foods with show conditioning: "The *Walnut Cat Food* is carefully compounded by the Walnut Food. Co., from recipes used constantly by the Walnut Ridge Farms, the greatest breeding establishment of Angora cats in the world, to meet just this want. It keeps the cat in health, is an excellent laxative, tonic, preserves the health and condition, and promotes the growth of the fur. Price, 50c. per bottle."[33] Dr. A. C. Daniels Co., a maker of proprietary veterinary medicines since the mid-1880s, added Cat Crumbs to its list of products around 1910, although it discontinued the line to concentrate on medicines in the 1920s. Still, as with commercial dog food, no one assumed that cats should be fed on the commercial product alone. Boiled root vegetables in gravy, fresh raw meat and fish, bread soaked in milk, and "bits of meat from the kitchen stock pot" were required for a cat to stay healthy.[34]

By the 1930s, Spratt's offered five different dry cat foods, including Pepsinated Meal for "Delicate Kittens" and what seems to be the first modern kibble, a feline-sized version of the famous meat fibrine biscuits that contained fish meal and whole milk powder. It was still intended to be "softened" in milk.[35] From the 1930s to the 1950s, some producers of canned food advertised their products as suitable for both cats and dogs, a situation that gradually changed as more empirical studies on feline and canine nutrition were conducted by veterinary schools and pet food companies themselves (see fig. 6.6). In a development analogous to the appearance of hundreds of brands of canned meat for dogs, specialty canned cat food also appeared when commercial fisheries discovered the product was a way to dispose of fish parts such as the dark, oily parts of tuna that Americans would not eat.

By the 1950s, Puss-N-Boots cat food was advertised regularly in weekly magazines such as the *Saturday Evening Post* and *Life*. Cat food companies had difficulty finding celebrity animals to endorse their products, however, so they made them up. In 1969, the packers of Star-Kist tuna, owners of the 9-Lives brand, launched a campaign featuring Morris, a yellow tiger cat whose wisecracks about his people and his food preferences were intended to reflect what cat owners believed their own pets were thinking. (The first-person pet voice was now hip and ironic.) Morris was a tomcat rescued from a shelter by his handler, Bob Martwick. By 1975, Morris's popularity had spawned a full array of logo-enhanced products, from calendars and feeding dishes to books such as *The Morris Method: A Basic Book of Cat Care by Bob Martwick*. By then, the 9-Lives canned food line also contained eighteen "gourmet flavors," a trend in cat food manufacturing that continues today.

By 1958, the pet food business was large enough to spawn its own lobbying and public information arm, the Pet Food Institute, which now represents 97 percent of all manufacturers of dog and cat food. As part of the American food industry, the dog and cat food business has undergone the same kinds of historical

FIGURE 6.6. *Label for Super-meat Dog & Cat Food, 1940s. Author's collection. Canned food marketed for both dogs and cats was common into the 1950s. Note the absence of nutritional supplements.*

processes, including corporate consolidation and the elimination of many small, regional brands, that have shaped packaged foods for people. These days, the number of small companies promoting specialized "human grade" or health foods for pets also seems to be on the rise because of their ability to market through the Internet and the high-end "pet boutiques" appearing in some cities.

Foods for exotics and small animals followed a separate course. Special pelleted foods for rabbits appeared by the 1910s; before then, they received a mixture of raw vegetable scraps, grass, and hay. The popularity of pelleted feeds probably spread as hay suppliers became less common in cities with the gradual disappearance of the urban horse, and as millions of rodents were also raised for use as laboratory animals. In the 1950s, the Hartz Mountain Company became the powerhouse of small-animal food suppliers by establishing its own supermarket shelf space, where small quantities of pelleted feeds or seeds for rodent pets and other supplies were gathered for shopping convenience. Feed manufacture for Americans' other pet animals, including tropical fish, reptiles, and exotic birds, has continued to allow many niche producers, especially with web-based marketing opportunities.

Over-the-Counter Remedies

Sales of over-the-counter veterinary remedies helped keep small pet stores afloat and reflected the desires of owners to take good care of their pets. Distemper remedies, digestive aids, worming medicines, medicated soaps, and other aids developed from the compounds first created by veterinarians, druggists, and pet store "doctors" first became available in the 1870s. (After the Pure

Food and Drug Act of 1906, over-the-counter medicines, which had often been promoted as cures, all became remedies.) Sometimes lines of pet remedies grew out of initial success with commercial medicines for livestock. This was the case with the Dr. A. C. Daniels Company of Boston, which was founded in the 1880s and added products for dogs and cats in the early 1900s.[36] Some product lines were associated with companies known for their patent medicines for people. Philadelphia's Associated Fanciers and the Philadelphia Bird Food Company, makers of remedies for dogs, cats, and cage birds, were both attached to the Carl L. Jensen Company, makers of Jensen's Pepsin Tablets and Mexican Blood and Liver Purifier (the "Wonderful Medicine of the Aztec Priests").[37] Others, like H. Clay Glover, Inc., and the Polk Miller Drug Company, focused on dogs and occasionally on cats from the beginning. Based in New York City, Glover was a minor celebrity as the veterinarian for the Westminster Kennel Club show in New York and was one of the first veterinarians in the United State to specialize in dogs.[38]

The most colorful of these early entrepreneurs was Polk Miller, a druggist in Richmond, Virginia, and a sportsman whose line of products grew out of his efforts to doctor his own dogs. Miller's brand, Sergeant's, was named after a favorite dog that had "died a natural death at a good old age" thanks to his owner's expert care. While Miller's relatives and descendants, who took over the company in the 1890s, were careful to represent their founder as a man of dignity as well as compassion, the real Polk Miller was a more complex individual (see fig. 6.7). Miller abandoned his growing dog-remedy company so that he could embark on a much-longed-for career as a performer of "Negro dialect" stories and a banjo player specializing in what were called "plantation

REPRODUCTION FROM PAINTING OF POLK MILLER AND HIS DOG "SERGEANT"

POLK MILLER'S DOG BOOK

FIGURE 6.7. Cover, Polk Miller's Dog Book, 11th ed., 1926, Polk Miller Products Corp., Richmond, Virginia. Author's collection. Dr. Miller and Sergeant were both long gone by then, but the company used their portrait to personalize the product line, representing how its origins lay in the love of a man for a dog. The back cover featured Sergeant's Mange Medicine, which was guaranteed to grow hair for both dogs and people.

melodies." He traveled the United States with a group of African American musicians, the Old South Quartette.[39]

Like pet food manufacturers, makers of branded over-the-counter medicines for pet animals built their customer bases by using techniques that were popular with makers of other consumer goods. Free samples in paper envelopes, tins, and tiny bottles allowed customers to see results for themselves before buying.[40] Free booklets of instruction and advice, given out at the point of sale or available through the mail, taught readers to identify and interpret symptoms and how to treat pets with both nursing care and the products produced by the company. Like the makers of patent medicines for people, remedy makers also offered free medical advice at a time when people avoided visiting any kind of doctor except in emergencies. The Polk Miller Products Corporation took this last technique furthest. A $1.00 purchase of Sergeant's dog remedies included a coupon, signed by the druggist or "advertised dealer" who furnished the merchandise, that entitled the bearer to a year of free expert advice on "all subjects of *Diseases of Dogs, Sanitation, Feeding, Washing, etc.* . . . We bring the Veterinary to your very door at no additional cost whatever."[41] Into the 1940s, both the Dr. L. D. LeGear Company and Glover offered a Veterinary Welfare Department to handle inquiries by mail, and R. T. French had an advisor on canary health.[42]

Given all the advertising about improving the quality of the canine diet, it was inevitable that food supplements appeared in the 1920s and that they shared qualities with supplements intended for humans. Cod liver oil had been added to "medicated" foods for several decades when Ko-Vita Raw and Phosphated Norwegian Cod-liver Oil appeared as a pet tonic.[43] VITAKALK, a powdered supplement developed by German veterinarians and introduced to

American pet stores in 1928, was something new, however. It contained bone meal, brewer's yeast, and "dried vegetable substances" that were "partly treated by ultra violet rays" to provide vitamin D. Its maker, the Th. Goldschmidt Corporation, recognized "the problem of creating consumers' demand" when pet food itself was a relatively new phenomenon and freely shared its advertising strategy with the pet trade. It began with an "extensive mail advertising campaign" and a print ad campaign in professional publications for dog breeders and fur farmers, followed by advertising in magazines directed at sportsmen and the well-to-do, such as *Town and Country* and *Country Life*.[44]

Bird remedies generally remained a specialized sideline of veterinary patent medicine. The makers, who tended to be bird sellers, also marketed tonics and "medicated" foods to aid birds during molting or to treat loss of voice.[45] Patent remedies such as the Philadelphia Bird Food Company's Bird Bitters were available in drug stores and promoted in small advertisements in women's magazines by the 1890s; they were stocked by grocery stores and five-and-ten pet departments by the 1920s. Like patent medicine tonics generally, including the Lydia Pinkham elixirs that women relied on to relieve their "female troubles," Bird Bitters contained a considerable amount of alcohol, which may indeed have inspired a burst of song from the canary dosed with the remedy.

Bird owners were also the first pet owners to purchase therapeutic equipment for their pets, including baths that fit inside cage doors, sandpaper-covered perches that helped file down tiny toenails, and paper for cage floors covered with glued-on gravel to aid bird digestion. Aldon's Patent Spring Bird Perch was guaranteed to relieve the sore feet of the pet as well as provide exercise by means of its elasticity. This same belief in the restorative effects of "elastic" springs had guided the initial use of springs in upholstered seating furniture.[46] The Nature Friend, Inc., a company that sold its Magic bird foods and remedies through F. W. Woolworth and Kresge stores as well as groceries, offered a vibrating perch intended to mimic the movement of tree branches.[47]

Over-the-counter medicines, ointments, and vitamins remain an important part of the modern pet owner's stock of supplies, and they are often versions of similar medicines people can buy. Antibiotics are available without prescription for treating bacterial infections in birds, fish, reptiles, and small animals; topical ointments rely on the same low doses of steroids and antibacterials as first-aid treatments for people. Further, veterinarians sometimes recommend that owners adapt other common medications for pet use. I once administered small doses of a liquid antihistamine to a cat that had an allergic reaction to eating a butterfly; my mother gives her terrier with itchy skin the same antihistamines that I take for my hay fever. Cats and dogs are dosed with supplements purchased from health food stores as treatments for arthritis and other chronic health problems associated with advancing age. And as with so many other aspects of daily life, the Internet has created a new online community for do-it-yourself pet therapies.

Cages and Containers: Fashionable Housing

Cages and containers may reflect the ideas and values of pet owners better than any other artifacts, and many of the objects displayed in the photographs of Grider's Birdland, Lathrop's Pet Stock Shop, and the Supreme Brooklyn Pet Emporium were intended as housing for small animals. Their primary function was to restrain their inhabitants so that they could not escape and to provide conditions that permitted life; they held water, admitted air and light, and allowed the occupants a certain amount of movement. Working within these functional constraints, however, the designs of many of the cages and containers were decorative, even fanciful, until the mid-1960s, when utility and sanitation concerns largely trumped ornamentation. This remained the case until recently, as the use of molded high-impact plastics has permitted the development of fanciful modular cages for hamsters, and a few companies have brought back birdcages shaped like houses.

Decorative cages and containers have long been used as accents to interior decor, as a means of highlighting the aesthetic qualities of the animals within, and as settings for manipulating the behavior of animals for the delight of humans. Whether a bird was purchased from a city market or a bird store, it went home in a small transportation cage of woven rushes, cornstalks, or wood. These were too small to serve as permanent dwellings, so bird keepers had either to make or to purchase a cage. Few cages that can be firmly identified as being made in the 1700s survive, although a handful were preserved by antiquarians, at least partly because of their value as examples of artisanship. Some of these were almost certainly imported from the shops of English furniture makers or as part of the China trade (see fig. 6.8).[48]

Prior to the mid-nineteenth century, birdcages were usually boxy wooden frames with wire bars on three sides. Intended to hang against walls, they were used both inside and outside houses, near doorways, where birds were displayed and given fresh air. Wire was expensive, and almost all of it used in America was imported until the tools of English wire-drawing and the expertise of

FIGURE 6.8. *Birdcage, 1780–1800 (prob. English), mahogany with decorative stringing, brass wire, and glass. Courtesy, Winterthur Museum. Shaped to suggest a pagoda, this cage was made either to be hung or to stand on a tabletop. The practice of shaping birdcages like miniature transparent buildings continued into the twentieth century.*

immigrant craftsmen arrived in the 1830s.[49] Blacksmiths occasionally produced cages on demand; a large wrought-iron cage, probably intended to display a parrot or an unfortunate monkey, survives in the collection of the Winterthur Museum. Cage making was also a sideline for tinsmiths, who shaped and soldered together tin sheets and tubing to form milk pans, buckets, funnels, and other tools and containers. One battered, large cage, probably used for a parrot, surviving in the collection of Old Sturbridge Village, substitutes ⅜-inch tubing for wire.[50]

Advertisements for the bird stores of the mid-nineteenth century suggest that they were the innovators in the standard pet shop practice of selling the container with the animal. Concerned by the dearth of suitable housing for their imported canaries, the

Reiche brothers apparently convinced a fellow German immigrant, Gottlob Gunther, to produce all-wire "German style" cages beginning in 1848.[51] By the 1860s, bird stores and "fancy goods" stores, the gift shops of their day, ordered their cages from general wire-goods manufacturers, who appeared as wire itself became cheaper.

By the 1870s, a handful of specialist companies concentrated on cage making and shipped their goods to furniture, fancy goods, and general stores all over the United States. Occasionally they sold directly to shoppers in storefronts, as did M. Drew, "Wholesale & Retail Dealer in Birds and Cages, etc." on Fulton Street in Brooklyn.[52] By the turn of the century, the most successful cage making business in the United States was the Andrew B. Hendryx Company of New Haven, Connecticut. Established in 1874 in a region known for brass manufacturing, by 1911 the firm had 238 "skilled operatives" making "high grade brass bird cages," fishing tackle, and wire and stamped-brass household accessories.[53] Apart from his emphasis on style, company founder Andrew B. Hendryx and his son Nathan used modern business practices to give their products a competitive edge. Andrew Hendryx was an inventor who took out multiple patents relating to his cages as early as 1875. Unlike most other makers, the Hendryx Company always marked its cages and the glass feeders that accompanied them with its name. The company continually updated its cage designs to fit in with changing interior decor. By the 1920s, the company was using direct selling to consumers through national magazines.

The wide range of cages and the practice of frequent innovation in both methods of manufacture and designs reflect producer behavior in other kinds of consumer goods, from furniture to silverware, over the course of the nineteenth century.[54] Having patented cage features or designs called attention to a company's entrepreneurial spirit, technological advancement, and good taste. Beginning in the late 1860s, birdcages were the objects of vigorous patenting activity by a small group of competitors, mostly in the greater New York City area. Gottlob Gunther, George R. Osborn, Otto Lindemann, Andrew Hendryx, and others used patents, which were relatively easy and cheap to get in the United States, to call attention to their goods.

Many of their patents were intended to protect solutions to prosaic manufacturing problems associated with all-metal show cages. The specifics of individual patents probably mattered little to consumers; what counted was their cachet. The Osborn Manufacturing Company's 1876 wholesale catalog of cages took care to list sixteen patents taken out between 1863 and 1875 and promised potential buyers that "THE DEVICES for Feeding, Perching, Swinging, Attaching and Joining the different Parts, and for Hanging the Cage, are peculiarly [particularly] our own. They are the result of years of experience of skillful workmen, prompted by discriminating friends, people of taste and experience in the care of pet Birds and Animals, and to whom we owe many thanks for the interest which they have taken in our effort to elevate a neglected branch of industry and art."[55] Otto Lindemann and Company's 1888 wholesale catalog took pains to point out that its innovations, such as constructing cages without solder, were more healthful for the bird, who was apt to pick at loose bits of metal on a cage.[56]

Companies made cages in sizes and forms that accorded with the characteristics and requirements of their occupants as bird fanciers understood them. While typical canary cages of the time look pitifully small to our eyes, the cramped quarters reflected the popular belief that a canary would sing more if it had less room to fly.[57] Breeding cages, for example, had wooden backs and sides and were intended to be mounted against the wall, making the nesting female feel less vulnerable; they also had removable panels to separate bird families and contained wire or wire-cloth nesting pans. Cardinal and mockingbird cages were square, had sturdy wooden frames, and were relatively large. Many birdcages were constructed to be hung from a bracket in a warm kitchen or sunny window or from a special stand, which allowed them to swing a little, like a tree branch in a breeze.

Cages not only contained but framed their inhabitants in cultural attitudes. One characteristic way to celebrate the aesthetics of the bird was to present it as a natural object in a container that celebrated the artifice of the civilization that had captured and tamed it. The convention of using elaborate containers that were works of considerable artifice to display expensive, prized natural "objects" was well-established in Europe by the seventeenth century. At that time, well-to-do collectors created "wonder cabinets," where minerals, shells, and other natural objects were encased in elaborate cabinetry. Among the Dutch merchant class, beautiful birdcages and elaborate tulip-bulb containers displayed natural objects as symbols of trading wealth.[58] In 1856, *Godey's Lady's Book* praised cages offered by a local business in the shape of cottages, pagodas, and seashells and published one example shaped like a hot-air balloon. The pun in this particular cage design came partly from the earlier tradition in popular entertainment of sending animals up in the baskets of balloons. By the late nineteenth century, even cheap cages featured bars bent into complex lines, "cake stand" bottoms for tabletop display of birds, or "spangles" (bits of metal glitter) in the finish so that the cage would sparkle in sunlight. Novelty cages also were shaped as perfect spheres of wire, neoclassical urns, and, in the early twentieth century, even colonial- or mission-style lanterns.[59] By the 1920s companies such as the Art Cage Manufacturing Company produced modernistic cages designed on the "skyscraper set-back principle"; colored "Pompeian green," red, or ivory; or ornamented with tassels to match interior decoration.[60]

Many cages mimicked architecture. Playing with ideas about birds' domestic lives, architectural cages usually mimicked houses. By the 1880s, parlor canaries lived in wire and sheet-metal interpretations of Italianate villas, rustic Swiss cottages, and Second Empire mansions. Some writers disliked architectural cages, on the grounds of health or expense. But their artifice was what made them so attractive.[61] Birds were not the only residents of miniature architecture. Squirrels and white mice were also housed in tin cages that often looked like houses, barns, or old-fashioned, water-powered mill buildings (see fig. 6.9). The exercise wheels that were incorporated into the latter structures were the "waterwheels." Sometimes tinsmiths added moving parts on top of the cage that used the energy created by the running inmate to animate tableaux of little figures.

The most striking examples of the playful aesthetics of animal display, however, abandoned architecture for theatrical illusion. Well-to-do pet owners occasionally paid for novelty cages designed to manipulate the natural behavior of animals in amusing ways. The most ingenious example of this was a combination fish globe/birdcage that gave the illusion of the bird singing underwater when it occupied the highest perch, inside the double-walled globe. These illusion cages were in use in the United States as early as 1791, when one was mentioned in a Boston

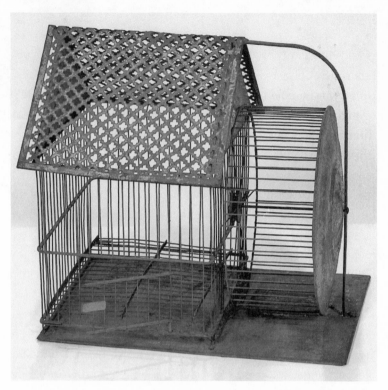

FIGURE 6.9. *Squirrel or rat cage, O. Lindemann and Company, New York, galvanized sheet iron, ca. 1890–1920. Author's collection. This model was intended to look like a Swiss chalet. The slide-out tray for cleaning the cage is missing; it probably rusted through.*

diary. They were still being sold in the early twentieth century—one is visible in the photograph of Lathrop's Pet Stock Shop (see fig. 6.1)—although their greatest popularity had passed by then.[62]

The 1950s saw experimentation with plastic as a cage material for the first time, when clear, high-impact plastics offered the possibility of a cage that was completely transparent and could be cast in only a few pieces. Plastic cages could look like anything. The Bernard Edward Company produced one that resembled a handbag complete with a handle on top; it also offered compatible accessories, including a detachable bathing pavilion (see fig. 6.10).

The 1970s saw the introduction of another new approach to small-animal cages, the modular cage with units that could be refigured to provide an environment that was intended to be more stimulating to the hamster or mouse inside and more entertaining for the human watchers outside. The ingenuity and humorous design of these cages reflect a new interest in creating miniature habitats for some caged animals. These cages are, however, still transparent; the animals inside cannot escape the gaze of onlookers unless they are provided with little sleeping pods. (In the 1960s, when hamsters still lived in boxy metal cages, I worried about this and provided homemade sleeping chambers and a modicum of privacy for my pet Sniffles in the form of cardboard toilet paper rolls and odds and ends of fabric that he could make into a nest.)

Like any dwelling, cages needed to be furnished to make them comfortable. In 1843, Bernard Duke's Seed and Horticultural Warehouse at 117 Chestnut Street in Philadelphia provided bird keepers with glass seed cups and water founts, ivory eggs to encourage laying and setting, breeding cages with shelves for nests

FIGURE 6.10. *Beco All-Plastic Bird Cage, model No. 45, with Bird Bath and Carrier Accessory, Bernard Edward Company, Chicago, styrene plastic, 1950s. Author's collection. The cage had received the Good Housekeeping Seal of Approval. The company literature pointed out that the cage could be "washed like any dish."*

and dividers to provide privacy for sitting hens, and "cow's and deer's hair, for making nests."[63] Over the next several decades the range of special cage furnishings available to middle-class bird keepers grew. Two lists of supplies from the 1870s show the considerable increase in inventory: "round earthen Mockingbird cups"; glass cage baths; perches and swings for inside cages; "nests of tin, wire, & willow"; packaged nesting materials that had been steamed to prevent transmission of vermin; cage awnings; and even "carpets" in the form of sanitary metal mats for the cage floor.[64] Some canary cages were provided with small brass bells for birds to strike. By the 1940s, the fad for parakeets, who were social, curious birds, had led to a new array of cage furnishings, including mirrors, ladders, roly-poly figures on wheels, and strings of bells.

The trend toward furnishing cages and containers was most marked in fishbowls and aquariums. In the mid-nineteenth century, most people kept the family goldfish in a simple glass globe that sometimes had a pedestal base to raise the container above a tabletop for easier viewing. However, the advent of the balanced aquarium introduced to households a different kind of container, one with a frame of metal that held four sheets of glass and a slate or metal bottom. The distortion of the handblown round vessel, which was considered part of the viewing fun with the parlor goldfish, and the limitations on its size were anathema to aquarists, who considered themselves natural scientists.[65] Well into the twentieth century, manuals on aquarium keeping assumed that serious amateurs would build their own aquariums, a delicate process that required sealing the floor and sides into the frame to prevent leaking.[66] Given the challenges of working with glass, most people either improvised with other kinds of containers or purchased their aquariums outright. By 1869, Philadelphia had two aquarium manufacturers listed in its business directory.[67] Commercial aquariums from the 1880s through the 1930s often featured decorative elements mimicking the furniture of the age, including gilt hairy paw feet.

The external form of most fish globes and aquariums may have been plain, but people soon found ways to make them ornamental. In 1854, *Godey's* published an illustration and instructions for a mat to be placed under a fish globe. The center was ringed with fully three-dimensional cherries and leaves, and an edging of raveled yarn was supposed to imitate the appearance of moss.[68] Aquarists also discovered that they could furnish their miniature worlds as elaborately as their own parlors, creating underwater landscapes with rockwork, seashells, and plants. Suggesting that a plain aquarium was indeed an apartment of sorts, Bishop the Bird Man's mail-order aquarium packages came either unfurnished or complete with suitable ornaments, shells, pebbles, and plants as well as the fish (see fig. 6.11). The top of the line was a vessel stuffed with gimcracks, a parlor within the parlor. By the 1890s, pet stores stocked an array of ceramic ornaments, including grottoes, ruins, and castles; floating miniature ducks and swans; and figurines of children holding fishing poles to balance on the edge of the vessel. By the 1920s, the selection was racier. A 1929 advertisement for imported aquarium novelties at "Astonishingly Low Prices" offered seductive mermaids and naked bathing beauties. Miniature shipwrecks, classical ruins that suggested Atlantis, deep-sea divers in helmets, sea monsters, and "gone fishing" signs soon followed, as did plastic plants that made aquarium housekeeping easier. By the 1950s, even utilitarian bubblers were also disguised as objects such as treasure chests or giant clams with hinged lids that opened and shut from air pressure.

Illustration of Bell-shaped Tanks with suitable Ornaments, the lowest illustration showing Bell Tank as it should appear, arranged complete.

BELL SHAPED GLASS TANKS

Popular Sizes.   Heavy.   Smooth Bottom.
Prices Exceptionally Low.

TWO-AND-A-HALF-GALLON BELL-SHAPED GLASS TANK.

Price, unfurnished, $1.25.

This Bell Tank, including 5 suitable Goldfish, 1 Silverfish, 1 Tadpole, Ornament, sufficient Plant, Pebbles, Shells, and a box of Imported Wafer Fish Food, also shipping can. **Price, complete, $2.25.**

THREE-GALLON BELL-SHAPED GLASS TANK.

Price, unfurnished, $1.50.

This Bell Tank, including 6 suitable Goldfish, 1 Silverfish, 2 Tadpoles, Ornament, sufficient Plant, Pebbles, Shells, and a box of Imported Wafer Fish Food, also shipping can. **Price, complete, $2.75.**

FOUR-GALLON BELL-SHAPED GLASS TANK.

Price, unfurnished, $1.75.

This Bell Tank, including 8 suitable Goldfish, 1 Silverfish, 2 Tadpoles, Ornament, sufficient Plant, Pebbles, Shells, and a box of Imported Wafer Fish Food, also shipping can. **Price, complete, $3.25.**

FIVE-GALLON BELL-SHAPED GLASS TANK.

Price, unfurnished, $2.25.

This Bell Tank, including 9 suitable Goldfish, 1 Silverfish, 2 Tadpoles, Ornament, sufficient Plant, Pebbles, Shells, and a box of Imported Wafer Fish Food, also shipping can. **Price, complete, $4.00.**

SIX-AND-A-HALF-GALLON BELL-SHAPED GLASS TANK.

Price, unfurnished, $2.75.

This Bell Tank, including 10 Suitable Goldfish, 1 Silverfish, 2 Tadpoles, Ornament, sufficient Plant, Pebbles, Shells, and a box of Imported Wafer Fish Food, also shipping can. **Price, complete, $4.75.**

EIGHT-GALLON BELL-SHAPED GLASS TANK.

Price, unfurnished, $3.50.

This Bell Tank, including 12 suitable Goldfish, 1 Silverfish, 2 Tadpoles, Ornament, sufficient Plant, Pebbles, Shells, and a box of Imported Wafer Fish Food, also shipping can. **Price, complete, $5.50.**

FIGURE 6.11. *Fish-globe packages sold by Henry Bishop (Bishop the Bird Man), in* Bishop the Bird Man's Treatise on Birds and Aquaria, *Baltimore, Maryland, 1911. Author's collection. The small goldfish offered as part of these packages had to swim through an overfurnished parlor in miniature.*

While some fish keepers try to re-create miniature natural settings in aquariums, many aquarists still enjoy whimsy in their underwater furniture as much as their Victorian predecessors did.

The Fashionable Pet

By the early 1900s, the supplies and equipment that occupied the most shelf space in pet stores, after inventory for birds and fish, were intended for the family dog. Lathrop's, Grider's, and the Supreme Brooklyn Pet Emporium all displayed an array of what catalogs called "dog furnishings." Many of the collars, harnesses, leashes, and other items were simple and practical, although not without ornament, but others were decorative, fashionable, and even whimsical. Whether or not dogs took any pleasure in their new possessions, purchasing constellations of things that belonged to their dogs was one way that some modern owners, participants in America's blossoming consumer society, expressed their feelings about their dogs, including their desire that dogs be as well dressed as their own fashionable selves. As with foods and patent medicines, cats were less likely than dogs to be the focus of expenditure, although collars, beds, and other objects intended for their use gradually became part of pet shop inventories.

The most common dog furnishing was the collar, a sign of ownership worn by most working and companion dogs, at least in towns and cities. Collars are probably the most ancient form of pet equipment; once dogs were established as hunting companions and guardians, humans soon realized that it was useful to restrain them and mark ownership. As early as the Roman Empire, wide collars studded with spikes were used as dog armor to protect the throats of valued animals from wild beasts and other dogs.

In colonial America, every respectable dog probably wore a collar, but common leather examples have not survived. Dog owners with money to spend dressed their dogs in a way that made small but fully intelligible statements about their prosperity. These collars were made of brass and were engraved with the dog owner's name and sometimes an inscription. Since all brass was imported from England, at least some of these collars were made there, although an example that seems to have been crafted in the United States survives in the collection of Historic Deerfield. It bears the inscription, "Jere Stebbin Esq's Dog W. Springfield / Who Dog Be You," perhaps an awkward paraphrase of poet Alexander Pope's famous epigram, "I am his Highness' dog at Kew / Prey tell me sir, whose dog are you?" (see fig. 6.12).[69] A dog's name is rarely found on such collars, since the animal was more ephemeral and probably less expensive than the metal band around its neck. Such collars were used over the lives of several dogs—unless they were stolen to be sold or melted down. In 1779, Jonathan Zane of Philadelphia advertised a reward of $3.00 for the return of a "Brass Collar, with a steel staple, and brass slide" to close it that had been "stolen off the neck of a small pyed [spotted] bitch." Zane was so incensed by the theft that he also offered the enormous sum of $40.00 for the arrest and conviction of the thief.[70]

Simple collar making was an obvious and easy sideline of the harness trade, where leather straps and metal buckles were already abundant and dog collars were one way to use up scraps. In the nineteenth century, making more expensive leather items for dogs also became a sideline of the fancy and sporting leather goods trade. Samuel Hipkiss of Boston manufactured "Fancy Leather Goods, Dog Collars and Furnishings, Base Ball, Tennis and Bicycle Belts and Furnishings, etc."[71] Better-quality collars were decorated with patterns of studs, a trace of their old function as a

FIGURE 6.12. *Dog collar, brass, eighteenth century (American), maker unknown. Courtesy of Historic Deerfield, Inc. Photography by Amando Merullo.*

way to protect a dog's throat from attack. Others were made of colored morocco, the fine leather that was also used for book bindings and purses. Collars were often lined with chamois or wool felt in a contrasting color, and owners sometimes embellished them with small bells. Even the metal collar of the late nineteenth century could be highly decorative. The collar shown in figure 6.13, worn by a medium-sized Philadelphia dog named Frank in the 1880s, featured decorative links stamped with a design of leaves and

FIGURE 6.13. *Dog collar, ca. 1880 (probably American), maker unknown, nickel plate over brass and steel, engraved "Frank / Jos. Wood 704 N. 3rd St. / Phila." Author's collection. This collar with links in the "aesthetic" style may have been worn by the dog of a Philadelphia hotel owner.*

flowers. It had no buckle but fastened shut with a slide and small padlock, another practice that hearkened back to the days when the collar was worth more than the dog—and that also reflected the continuing problem of the urban dog thief.

A wholesale catalog for the Medford Fancy Goods Company of New York City is a remarkable document of the arrival of dog collars into the realm of fashionable consumer goods (see fig. 6.14). Published in 1890, it advertised the company as "The Only Exclusive Manufacturers of Dog Collars and General Dog Furnishings." The text boasted that "we may justly be said to have created the trade in artistic goods of this character. . . . We began manufacturing when there was no such words as styles or fashions in these goods; all this has been created by the new designs constantly put forth each season."[72]

The Medford Fancy Goods Company offered a full line of traditional canine hunting gear—dog whips for guiding packs, plain leather leads and collars, and rigorous "choke" training collars with spikes—along with chain and spiked "Protection collars." Its specialty, however, was stylish collars for valued pets. Some collars were ornamented with rows of stamped metal dog heads or elaborate patterns of studs. Portly pugs and other pet dogs could be ornamented with lizard-skin collars, tooled and stamped leather harnesses in the Japanese taste, or belled collars and harnesses "intended more for display or show collar, to lead a dog by, than to chain him to any immoveable object." Anticipating contemporary novelty dog clothing, the firm offered a celluloid necktie and bell and a metal and leather collar in the style of a "French necktie" ornamented with a locket. Chain collars, generally sold in utilitarian nickel plate, could also be had in "Polished Brass, Plain Silver or Oxidized, Silver Plated, Solid Gold or Silver." The

FIGURE 6.14. *Cover,* Dog Collars and General Dog Furnishings, *Medford Fancy Goods Company, New York, New York, 1890. Courtesy, The Winterthur Library: Printed Book and Periodical Collection.*

product line even included fancy collars and harnesses named after celebrities and theatrical hits. The Roland Reed collar copied a style used by the comedian for his own dog; a pug harness was called the Mikado. A line of patent leather collars for cats was named after the Swedish Nightingale, Jenny Lind, perhaps as a pun on cats' singing voices.[73] Mailed to retailers in an effort to build a national market for Medford's goods, the catalog offered to help stores carrying its lines learn how to display them to best advantage, including providing nickel-plated show cases and polished brass collar stands for countertops.

By the late nineteenth century, stores selling dog furnishings had branched into other amenities that reflected the indoor lives of town dogs in particular. Leaders (leashes) of chain or leather, harnesses, tie chains, and muzzles reflected urban dog control laws and the interest of more dog owners in keeping their animals close to them as they walked in the city. Wicker dog beds, visible in the photograph of Lathrop's Pet Stock Shop (see fig. 6.1), gave small animals furniture of their own. By the 1920s, dog owners could purchase dog mattresses filled with cedar shavings, the forerunner of today's popular round dog beds, and small dog couches, miniature versions of the human beds that house dogs probably preferred. One Chicago seller promised that its dog couches had a "very smart finished appearance in complete harmony" with interior decor (see fig. 6.15). By the 1930s, small treadmills were available for city dogs that did not get enough exercise outdoors; the old "dog powers" once used to get more work out of dogs had now become exercise equipment.[74]

As more dogs lived indoors and as more Americans purchased as companions small breeds that had never lived in severe climates, the need for protective dog clothing became apparent.

FIGURE 6.15. *Page from Von Lengerke & Antoine,* Catalog of Sporting Goods, *Chicago, 1920s. Author's collection. This fashionable store offered five different styles of dog beds. Note also the worsted-wool dog sweaters and blanket coats, and the "scientific hitching post," which came with a "a package of specially prepared chemical compound that attracts the dog to the post and induces him to do his duty."*

Here the decorative impulse was irresistible from the very beginning. The May 1873 issue of *Godey's Lady's Book* offered what seems to be the first example of Victorian dog clothing, a crocheted jacket for an Italian greyhound made of light blue wool trimmed with black and red fringe and small bells as buttons (see fig. 6.16). The Medford Fancy Goods Company offered only a single corduroy "dog blanket," which looked like a miniature of the blankets used for horses but was trimmed with leather. By the 1920s, a Chicago store offered "coat style" dog sweaters made to order, woolen dog blankets, and even rubberized rain slickers. By then, city dogs' feet could be protected in bad weather with small

FIGURE 6.16. *An elaborate crocheted coat for an Italian greyhound,* Godey's Lady's Book, *May 1873. Courtesy, The Winterthur Library: Printed Book and Periodical Collection.*

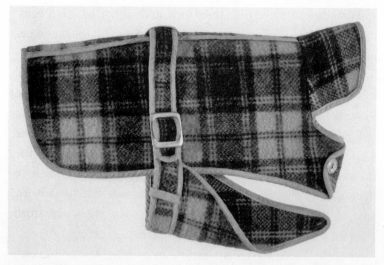

FIGURE 6.17. *Dog coat, plaid wool, maker unknown, 1930s–1950s (American). Author's collection. This coat is sized for a Scottish terrier or small bulldog.*

rubber boots. Dog coats tended to follow fashions in human outerwear; in the 1940s and 1950s red-and-black check "buffalo plaid" coats were popular for dogs, boys, and men (see fig. 6.17). Fashionable department stores also began to sell expensive dog equipment under their own labels, including stylish tweed garments with velvet collars. The accessory dog needed its own accessorizing.

Mail-order catalogs and a new kind of store, the urban dog boutique, now offer an array of both functional, status, and humorous clothing for dogs: protective gear such as life jackets and snow boots, jackets with logos from motorcycle companies or famous designers, and costumes for every major holiday. Prior to this recent development, the height of whimsical clothing for small dogs occurred in the 1950s and early 1960s, when a fad for tiny dogs, particularly miniature poodles and chihuahuas, brought its own tiny fashions. Woolen coats with fur collars, fake-fur coats, and small collars of colored leather decorated with glass gems paralleled the clothing of a certain kind of fashionable woman to a remarkable degree.

Even feeding dishes were eventually reshaped by fashion as much as by the requirements of function. American dogs and cats took their meals in tin pans, old plates, and other kitchen odds and ends. Kitchens and back porches, where they often dined, were functional spaces where heavy work was done. Apart from the occasional rocking chair and washstand with mirror, few were decorated as they are today, when kitchens are family gathering spaces. By the early 1900s, kenneled dogs had their own sturdy feeding dishes of heavy stoneware or metal, including special "anti-gulp" dishes for greedy eaters. In middle-class households, kitchen decor became more important in the 1930s, as less formal styles of living and the absence of household help pushed even prosperous families into kitchens for most of their meals. Brightly colored pet dishes, including special "spaniel bowls" with high sides and narrow openings to keep long ears from dragging in food, became part of this new kitchen decor.

Developments in pet toys also signaled changing ideas. Successful pet toys focus animals' natural behavior in ways that are harmless to both pet and owner and that allow pet owners to interact with their pets as gift givers, playmates, and "parents." The 1920s seem to have been the years when a wide variety of commercially produced pet toys became part of the usual inventory for pet stores. Some of these made life with pets indoors more convenient. Jazz Age house dogs could, for example, gnaw on boiled, cleaned bones that were easier on carpets than old soup bones with tidbits of fat and gristle left on them, and they could chase squeaky rubber cat heads and rats.[75] The natural scratching behavior of cats who lived indoors could be channeled toward scratching posts, for which a number of patents were taken out beginning in the 1930s. Pet food companies even began to offer toys such as rubber balls as premiums. By the 1950s, owners could buy rubber toys in the shape of gloves or shoes that were humorous comments about the destructiveness of pet dogs, toys shaped like miniature fire hydrants or mice that commented on cats' and dogs' natural behavior, and toys resembling pieces of meat, hot dogs, or hamburgers, which reflected their desires.

Even cage birds and exotic pets began to get increasing numbers of toys after World War II. By the 1940s, parakeets had plastic rolling toys and even life-sized plastic bird buddies that could be mounted onto perches. This development has recently become especially notable among parrot owners, who are increasingly interested in developing enriched environments for these birds as their social requirements are better understood. To some extent this desire to provide a richer life for birds reflected the relative prosperity of pet owners, but it also shows the popular impact of animal behavior studies, particularly the work of applied ethologists with both wild and zoo animals. The genealogy and spread of ideas about enriched environments needs further research, but in terms of the material culture of pet keeping, its impact is clear.

Buying for Pets Everywhere

Given their expanding place in the family, pets were inevitably recognized as participants in the great American festival of consumption, Christmas. At first, as the text on the postcard for Lathrop's Pet Stock Shop suggests, pets *were* the gifts, and their availability was tied to the species' natural cycles. The year's fresh crop of canaries was particularly popular for Christmas. By the early 1900s, shops like Edwards' Bird Store of Detroit, another business known for its aggressive advertising and willingness to ship animals across the United States, created holiday starter packages that put together bird, cage, food, and accessories.[76] Pet stores also promoted Christmas puppies and kittens, a practice that animal welfare groups across the United States still work to eliminate on the argument that it leads to too many relinquishments to shelters and rescue groups.

By the 1920s, enterprising pet dealers were suggesting that pets themselves receive Christmas presents. One Dallas, Texas, business owner reported that a good "method of securing additional business . . . is to keep a list of addresses to whom we have sold birds, and shortly before the holidays drop them a line suggesting they make a present to their pet of a new home (cage) or furniture (bird bath, shell cup, swing, etc.) It is surprising how many take kindly to this whimsical proposition, especially elderly people, whose birds mean as much to them as a dog does to his master."[77] Capitalizing on the traditions of special food for the holidays, in December 1932 Chappel Brothers, makers of Ken-L-Ration dog food, advertised a "Christmas gift package" of six cans in a special box printed with holiday decorations to be cut out by children. The ad featured a Scottish terrier sitting at a desk typing a letter to Santa.[78] The little dog was now the consumer, and it was a modern, demanding one who asked for a nationally marketed brand of food by name. By around 1950, Spratt's, the original dog food maker and promoter, and other pet product manufacturers began to offer Christmas stockings filled with foods and treats.

Pet stores may have been the settings most associated with specialized products and equipment, but by the 1920s, they faced serious competition from a number of other retail settings. "The drug store now sells dog foods, dog remedies, cat remedies, bird foods and bird seed," one writer for *Pet Dealer* warned. "The chain grocery store now sells dog food and bird seed. The house furnishing goods stores are selling birdcages and some of them birds. The sporting goods stores, hardware stores, trunk stores and others sell dog baskets, dog foods, dog remedies and dog furnishings. The five and ten cent stores sell goldfish and globes. A great many of the items sold by these stores are what are known as bread and butter items in the pet shop."[79] While going to the pet store was a shopping expedition into a tempting world of potential new friends, with a pet expert as the customer's guide, both housewives and working people wanted convenience in their shopping rounds. Some companies such as Hartz Mountain abandoned pet stores early, preferring to sell their entire lines through the new supermarkets that so changed the face of food shopping after World War II. This competition may have been unwelcome to pet store proprietors, but they were not really endangered—at least until the rise of the giant pet store chains a half-century later. The fact that pet supplies, and even some of the animals themselves, were now stocked in so many retail settings suggests just how widely pet keeping was infused into American society.

→ Epilogue ←

ONE VIEW ON PETS IN MODERN AMERICA

Writing a history of pet keeping in America has given me a unique perspective on life in my own household, and I hope that it has done the same for my readers. It is not easy to create a tidy ending to such a complex, ongoing story, so I find myself returning to the first-person voice of my introduction. The question is, What's new about owning pets in America today?

It is clear that Americans now share a broad, although far from uniform, consensus that pet keeping is a normal and enjoyable part of everyday life. Yet the emotional complexities of modern American pet keeping would not have developed without the patterns of popular thought that are the legacy of the nineteenth century's domestic ethic of kindness. By the 1870s, a large and culturally influential cohort agreed that pet animals were entitled to kind treatment and good care, although practical definitions of both behaviors depended on many factors ranging from the limits of family budgets to personal idiosyncrasy. The domestic ethic of kindness articulated new ways of feeling about household animals through new ways of speaking about them. The popular language of regard—pets as friends, family members, innocent dependents, or even children—became so widespread by the early twentieth century that it was thoroughly ordinary.

I see striking continuities between the talk and behavior of some dedicated pet lovers of 150 years ago and today. The old ideas about kindness, along with the metaphors and the ways of feeling these comparisons represent, are visible everywhere, from the corporate motto of Petsmart ("Where Pets Are Family") to the popular practice among local animal rescue groups of having a professional Santa Claus pose for photo portraits with prized pets as a holiday fundraiser. Institutional arrangements relating to pet animals lagged behind feelings; this is a constant in social history. Still, by the 1930s, the major organizational features of modern pet ownership were also finally in place, from sophisticated businesses dedicated to selling animals, supplies, and equipment to specialized services, including medical care and shelters run by municipalities and animal welfare groups for the adoption or disposal of unwanted or unowned cats and dogs.

The continuities are marked, yet pet keeping in twenty-first-century America is not the same as pet keeping in the 1870s or the 1930s. For one thing, it has been the subject of a tremendous burst of attention and interest in the last twenty years or so, and particularly in the last decade. Even if you do not own a pet, daily contact with mass media—innumerable articles on pets in magazines and newspapers, the numbers of books devoted to pets, the abundant advertising for pet products, and the presence of cable television channels dedicated largely to programming about pet animals—should suggest that public interest in pet animals, already substantial, continues on the rise.

No single social or cultural factor can account for this. Changing demographics are often cited as one reason. Especially in the past twenty or thirty years, Americans' living arrangements have changed dramatically; more of us live alone (around 25 percent) than ever before. This is one reason for the greater popularity of cats than ever before; they can tolerate irregular work schedules or even live completely indoors. But occupying a dwelling alone does not necessarily mean loneliness. It does not require the presence of pets, and many people who live alone do not have them. Nor does modern childhood explain the boom in pets, although pet keeping is, as it was in Victorian America, still associated with the idea of childhood. A stage of intensive pet keeping, especially of small animals such as hamsters, is often part of the life cycle of a family. Some pet keeping has a nostalgic tinge. For child-free baby boomers, pets were part of remembered childhoods of the postwar era, which may be another reason they have continued to embrace the practice with such gusto. Some argue that pets are child substitutes, and for certain owners this may be the case. In 2004, more than 60 percent of American households contained pet animals; 36 percent included children.[1] In some households, the better term would be "child alternatives," since people do not necessarily seek out pets because they cannot have children. Many would probably have pets if they did have children. Some people who use the term "furry children" in conversation about their pets seem to mean it ironically; they know that there is a difference, and to some extent they are deliberately, and humorously, evoking an old cultural stereotype that associates pet ownership with an absence of other meaningful relationships.

Prosperity in America leads us to spend more on the things we care about, such as keeping pets. It allows us to indulge in animals just as we indulge in restaurant meals or nice shoes. I once gave a talk about pet keeping to a church group, and during the question-and-answer session following my formal remarks, one listener attacked pet keeping as a by-product of Americans' wasteful lifestyles. I replied by suggesting that golf, on which Americans spent $66 billion for goods and services in 2000, was arguably more wasteful (and much more elitist) than keeping animals at home.[2] The American Pet Products Manufacturers Association (APPMA) reported that pet industry sales, exclusive of live animals, for 2004 totaled $34.4 billion. Cash sales of animals were the smallest part of the industry, totaling $1.6 billion, which, again, does not include all the informal trading, shelter adoptions, and picking up of strays that goes on. The dark side of pet keeping is less easy to find figures on, but one often-repeated statistic suggests the extent to which failed pet keeping has become every taxpayer's burden: the costs of animal control, sheltering, and killing and disposing of unwanted or unadoptable animals are estimated to be around $2 billion each year.[3]

A close look at that $34.4 billion suggests that, as a practice, pet keeping is relatively cheap. As a percentage of the entire American economy, with a $10.4 trillion gross domestic product in 2002, the pet industry is small. Using the APPMA's own figures, the estimated 64.2 million households that kept pets that year spent an average of slightly less than $500 per year on the practice, which seems a disproportionately small sum for an activity that is the subject of so much emotional investment and pleasure. Of course, expenditures on pets alone are not an adequate measure of public enthusiasm, but I cannot think of a way to factor in expenditures on pet-themed greeting cards, collectible plates, figurines, tote bags, costume jewelry, T-shirts, and other everyday objects.

The relatively small per-household average expenditure disguises the distribution of expenses. It is possible to spend an extraordinary amount for animals themselves or for food and equipment or especially for medical care. By the 1960s, pet product manufacturers recognized that prosperity and the love owners felt for their pets was a potent combination. They began to generate some bizarre products, such as the V.I.P. Electric Vibrating Pet Brush (fig. Epi.1). It was supposed to be soothing, but it buzzed like an angry hornet when it was switched on. In my own household, where four healthy, middle-aged cats and dogs reside at the time of this writing, we spent an estimated $1,100 on food and another $1,200 on vet bills, including heartworm and flea preventatives, in 2004. (I got off cheaply on the latter; no one had a serious emergency or needed dental work.) I probably spent

FIGURE EPI.1. *V.I.P. (Very Important Pet) electric vibrating pet brush, A. F. Dormeyer Mfg., Co., Chicago, ca. 1965. Author's collection.*

another $150 on dog and cat toys and new collars. If I spent al-
most $2,500 on my pets, someone else spent much less, but that
does not necessarily mean that they cared less for their pet
animals. Pets are part of the most modest American households
as well as the most prosperous. (Recently, I was struck by the
thought that, given the federal regulations on the complete nutritional contents of dry dog food, even dogs in poor households may
be getting more balanced diets than their owners, who rely on
cheap sugars, carbohydrates, and fats to keep them full.) A certain subset of pet owners, especially a small group of fashionable
urban dog owners, the audience for the magazine *Bark* and the
clientele for the dog boutiques popping up in chic neighborhoods
in large cities, does consist of really big spenders, but this group
probably attracts more attention than it deserves as a representation of pet keeping in America.

Feelings do shape expenditures, too. Ordinary Americans with
limited incomes will sometimes go to extraordinary lengths for
their animals, particularly when a much-loved cat or dog experiences a medical crisis. Modern small-animal veterinary medicine
is evolving at an extraordinary pace as medical advances for humans, developed in part through the use of animals for research,
are adapted as treatments for animal diseases and injuries. As our
pets live longer, thanks to vaccines and better general health, they
now suffer from the same chronic diseases of old age that afflict
us: heart problems, osteoarthritis, and cancer. Small-animal clini-
cians at the sophisticated clinics of veterinary schools are eager to
try their hands at kidney transplants and chemotherapy. I have
strong doubts about these therapeutic approaches, not on economic grounds—people are entitled to spend their incomes as
they choose—but on humane grounds, since the cats and dogs

subjected to these treatments suffer a great deal of fear and dis-comfort without understanding why. While a kidney transplant for a cat costs about $12,000, considerably less than one for a human being, only a tiny number of pet owners carry pet health insurance, which is now offered by several companies in the United States. When a pet animal needs expensive medical care, middle-class Americans pull out their credit cards.

So pet keeping today is shaped by our past history, by recent demographic changes, and by our ability as Americans to use our disposable income as we choose. But there are other factors in play, too, and one of the most important is, I believe, the contin-uing human desire for novelty; I use this word in a scientific sense. Like so many other pursuits, keeping pets reflects the cu-riosity of human beings, their desire not to be bored, and their wish to find pleasure in their daily lives. Some people find that engagement with animals offers a kind of stimulation that is not paralleled by any other kind of experience. This is different from fashion, the commercialized system that feeds and shapes our in-nate desires for novelty and newness. Fashion certainly creates fads for breeds of dogs. Rare breeds still serve as ambulatory sta-tus symbols just as they did 150 years ago. New interest in exotic animals, particularly wild-caught reptiles, is a modern fashion in pet keeping, not unlike the parrot craze of the early twentieth century, that is troubling for both animal welfare and environ-mental reasons.

For some pet owners today, life with animals seems to offer contact with a particular kind of goodness that cannot be found elsewhere. Like our nineteenth-century predecessors, we still view pets as a force for good. We have taken this belief to another level by incorporating pets into various therapeutic endeavors, including dog-training programs involving juvenile offenders and animal-assisted therapies. Evidence on the benefits of these efforts is still largely anecdotal, although they seem to be real in at least some instances.

Demographic change. Recent prosperity. Curiosity and boredom. Fashion. The desire to connect to goodness. All these factors and others, too, play their part in our decisions to keep pets and in our behaviors once an animal has entered the household, and their origins in our past are very clear. However, I think that something else is very different. Pet keeping in America today is marked by a deep, and I suggest unprecedented, tension between the apparent desire of American pet owners to experience animalness—the wholeness and otherness of animals—through contact with pets and an equally apparent trend toward increasing control of our pets' lives, including their behavior, their biology, and their routines, precisely because we want to bind them so closely to us.

Because so many pet owners seem to desire so much closeness, ambivalence about the animalness of our pets may be more acute today. Some pet owners work hard to celebrate the "animal." A careful perusal of pet store shelves makes apparent that some pet owners are adherents of "natural" approaches to their pets. Natural foods and natural training techniques channel the normal behaviors of animals, and enriched environments allow animals, particularly caged animals, to express a fuller range of behaviors, such as digging, chewing, hoarding, basking, catching live prey, and socializing with others of the same species. Simultaneously, pet owners engage in more aggressive interventions in their pets' lives than did their parents or grandparents. The dramatic surgical intervention of spaying and neutering is now normal science. I do not want to suggest for a moment that American pet owners return to keeping sexually intact cats and dogs, but I do think that once those of us who support spay/neuter programs made the practice routine, we accidentally opened the door to normalizing other medical interventions to control animal behavior, including declawing and debarking, the latter of which is, thankfully, much more rare. As we bring animals closer to us, their normal behaviors can seem intolerable.

These contrasting impulses, toward celebrating the natural animal and wanting life with a civilized pet, are augmented by our conviction that pet animals are distinctive individuals whose uniqueness should be celebrated. It is the idea of the pet, the unique individual creature whose presence is associated with our private hours of leisure and whose life is in our hands, that shapes the way many of us think about animals generally. That is, when we allow ourselves to think about animals. We still depend on animal bodies, but we do not witness that dependence, and we do not seem to have a good way to acknowledge and appreciate what our dependence actually means. Our ancestors knew that human life was obviously and constantly dependent on animals. With few exceptions, people believed that humans needed to be able to control animals—their work, their reproductive habits, and their bodies—in order to live. Even the most gentle stewardship prescribed by the domestic ethic of kindness did not suggest that human beings should not be in charge of animal lives.

Is thinking of animals as pets the only way to construct better lives for animals in the world? Must we reject the richness of other historical relationships with animals? Our history with animals, like American history generally, is a story rich with contradiction, complexity, violence, sorrow, cruelty, greed, gentleness, kindness, love, and joy. Perhaps this history with pets, with the animals we keep at home, offers one small path into thoughtful and historically grounded public consideration of what our relationships with animals should be like in the future. In relation to our lives with animals generally, however, there is much more history to be told.

✦ Acknowledgments ✦

When you work on a book manuscript for a long time, you wind up with a lot of debts that cannot really be discharged in acknowledgment pages. For one thing, you have been buttonholing innocent people at social events for years, compelled to share the latest tidbit of research that you uncovered. These are the unsung victims of scholarly preoccupation, and I salute them all.

More concretely, scholarly work is impossible without the precious commodities of time and money, and I have been fortunate to have a number of opportunities that advanced *Pets in America* with both. A National Endowment for the Humanities fellowship in 1989 gave me encouragement, along with a year to discover that the topic was far more complex than I first thought. A Fleming Fellowship at the Henry Francis du Pont Winterthur Museum, Gardens, and Library advanced my thinking on the material culture associated with pet keeping. An Eccles Fellowship from the Obert C. and Grace A. Tanner Humanities Center at the University of Utah supported early stages of writing, and a semester at the Shelby Cullom Davis Center at Princeton University took the writing a step further.

Then there are the librarians. Knowledgeable librarians advance the work of scholars in significant ways every day; their familiarity with and advocacy for their institutions' collections are essential to the work of telling the increasingly complex stories of American history. For assistance with research, I thank Eleanor Neville Thompson of the Winterthur Library and the rest of the library staff at that marvelous institution, Lorna Condon of Historic New England (the former Society for the Preservation of New England Antiquities), and the librarians at the Library Company of Philadelphia, the Hagley Museum and Library, the Archives Center of the National Museum of American History, the Library of Congress Division of Prints and Photographs, and the libraries of the University of Utah and the University of South Carolina. I offer special thanks to the late Maxine Lorang, researcher at Historic Cherry Hill in Albany, New York, who spent many hours locating documents and carefully checking quotations and notes against fragile original sources. Eventually her expertise on the "Bunnie Papers" far exceeded my own; coauthorship of the essay on the Bunnie States of America is a small tribute that I can make in her memory.

I thank my former colleagues in History at the University of Utah and the University of South Carolina for their kind interest in my work. I thank Keith McGraw and Phillip Sawyer from the Distance Education and Instructional Services at USC for their good-looking photographs. Over the years, as I have presented bits of the research to scholarly meetings, I have received helpful comments from fellow speakers and audience members; I thank them all. I thank senior editor Sian Hunter, project editor

Stephanie Wenzel, and the rest of the staff at the University of North Carolina Press for their fine work; the editorial board of the press for its enthusiasm about the project; and the anonymous manuscript reviewers for their thoughtful comments. I especially want to thank the following friends and colleagues: George Basalla; Susan Beck; Nancy Carlisle; Owen S. and Michale Connelly; Lowell Durham; Kathryn Edwards; Larry Gerlach; Karl and Pam Gerth; Larry Glickman; Beverly Gordon; Ray Gunn; Patricia Hanna; Eric Hinderaker; Mark Hirsch; Richard C. Hoffman; Rebecca Horn; Roger Horowitz; Paul E. Johnson; John and Joy Kasson; Kenyon and Gina Kennard; Thomas Lekan and Joseph Brunet; Paul Mackenzie; Patrick Maney; Ann, Carl, and Kate Martin; Katharine Martinez and Jim Coleman; Kelly Noor and the whole family; Miles Orvell; Karen Rader; Lynne Rasmussen; Lynn Robertson; Rodris Roth; Mary Rottman; Andrew A. Rowan; Michael Schlosser; Phillip Scranton; James A. Serpell; Laurie Spetsas; Nathan and Robin Stalvey; Susan Strasser; Liv Emma Thorsen; and Bernard O. Unti.

Chapter 5 grew out of an essay published as "Buying Your Friends: The Pet Business and American Consumer Culture," in *Commodifying Everything: Relationships of the Market* (2003), edited by Susan Strasser. Chapter 3 is based on a long essay titled "'The Eden of Home': Changing Understandings of Cruelty and Kindness to Animals in Middle-Class American Households, 1820–1900," in *Animals in Human Histories: The Mirror of Nature and Culture* (2002), edited by Mary Henninger-Voss. My discussion of animal metaphors in Chapter 3 was first sketched out in "Material Culture as Rhetoric: 'Animal Artifacts' as a Case Study," *American Material Culture: The Shape of the Field*, edited by Ann Smart Martin and J. Ritchie Garrison and published in

1997 by the H. F. du Pont Winterthur Museum and the University of Tennessee Press. Finally, a very early delineation of some of the themes in this book appeared in "Animal House: Pet Keeping in the Northeastern United States, 1850–1900," in *New England's Creatures, 1500–1900,* the proceedings of the 1993 Dublin Seminar for New England Folklife, edited by the seminar's founder, Peter Benes.

She is mentioned in the Introduction, but I do want to acknowledge the late and much lamented Margaret, a very tubby tabby cat, who sat on my work for almost eighteen years. What mattered a little hair on my keyboard and in my disk drive, compared with her purring company and the attention with which she listened as I read passages aloud?

My father was crazy about animals, and I am glad that he was able to read an almost complete draft of this manuscript before his death. I wish that he could see the completed book.

As always, I dedicate this project to my family, especially Paul. This time, however, my dedication includes all the four-footed members, too.

→ Notes ←

INTRODUCTION

1   Keith Thomas, *Man and the Natural World: A History of the Modern Sensibility* (New York: Pantheon, 1983), 112–15.

2   Olive Thorne Miller, *Our Home Pets: How to Keep Them Well and Happy* (New York: Harper and Brothers, 1894), 141.

3   A useful discussion of the challenges of collecting data, and of the strengths and weaknesses of various estimates for the cat and dog population in particular, is found in Elizabeth A. Clancy and Andrew N. Rowan, "Companion Animal Demographics in the United States: A Historical Perspective," in *The State of Animals in 2003,* ed. Deborah J. Salem and Andrew N. Rowan (Washington, D.C.: Humane Society Press, 2004), 9–11.

4   "New Survey Reports 77.7 Million Pet Cats, 65 Million Pet Dogs Owned in the U.S.," press release, 14 April 2003, American Pet Products Manufacturers Association, Inc., <http: www.appma.org> (accessed 18 February 2004).

5   See the analysis of owner-reported benefits and drawbacks of pet keeping in American Pet Products Manufacturers Association, Inc., *1999–2000 APPMA National Pet Owners Survey* (Greenwich, Conn.: by the association, 1999), 26–27, 94–95, 218, 270.

Chapter One

1   Mrs. R. Lee, *Anecdotes of the Habits and Instinct of Animals* (Philadelphia:
     Lindsay and Blackiston, 1853), preface. Lee's book seems to have been popu-
     lar; it was reprinted in other editions as late as 1890.

2   For a fascinating synthetic and comparative discussion of the complexities of
     dogs' relations to Native American groups, see Marion Schwartz, *A History of
     Dogs in the Early Americas* (New Haven: Yale University Press, 1997).

3   *Charleston City Gazette,* 18 July 1794.

4   Elizabeth F. Crane, ed., *The Diary of Elizabeth Drinker* (Boston: Northeastern
     University Press, 1991), 1:385, 386, 2:1245, 1586, 1833, 1175, 1007. On *Rey-
     nard the Fox,* see Joyce E. Salisbury, *The Beast Within: Animals in the Middle
     Ages* (New York: Routledge, 1994), 122–26.

5   For detailed accounts of these dogs, see James S. Rush, "The Dogs of Mount
     Vernon: A Study of Canine Activities on Washington's Plantation" (unpub-
     lished paper, Mount Vernon Ladies Association, undated [ca. 1996]); Mary V.
     Thompson, "George Washington's Dogs" (unpublished memorandum, 1996).

6   A useful account of the history of dog breeds can be found in Juliette Cun-
     liffe, *The Encyclopedia of Dog Breeds* (Bath, U.K.: Paragon, 1999), 170–85.

7   Excerpted diary of Deborah Norris Logan, age 70–77, Germantown, Pa., 1832–
     1839, in Penelope Franklin, ed., *Private Pages: Diaries of American Women,
     1830s–1970s* (New York: Ballantine, 1986), 475 (entry for 7 August 1837).

8   Wilma Sinclair LeVan Baker, *Father and His Town: A Story of Life at the Turn
     of the Century in a Small Ohio River Town* (Pittsburgh: Three Rivers Press,
     1961), 26–27; Alice Hughes Neupert, "In Those Days: Buffalo in the 1870s,"
     Niagara Frontier 24, no. 4 (Winter 1977): 88.

9   Peter E. Elmendorf to Harriet (Hattie) VR Elmendorf, 8 April 1855, box 48,
     file 1, Historic Cherry Hill, Albany, N.Y. (hereafter HCHC). Stories of the
     members of this extended family and their pets will appear in this book. Be-
     cause members of the family remained at the house from its construction in
     1787 until its establishment as a house museum in 1963, and because of the
     preservation of the family's extensive correspondence and related papers (they
     often read and enjoyed decades-old letters from one another), a detailed pic-
     ture of their lives, including their activities with pets, can be reconstructed.

10   Letter from Catherine (Kittie) B. Putnam Rankin to Edward Elmendorf
     Rankin, 31 July 1896, box 107, file 1, HCHC.

11   George Watson Little, D.V.M., *Dr. Little's Dog Book* (1924; rev. ed., New York:
     McBride, 1937), 14; advertisement for Barnum's American Museum, *Harper's*

Weekly, 25 April 1863, 272. The Great National Dog Show was held from 27 April to 2 May 1863.

12   "Exhibition of the New-York Poultry Society," *Harper's Weekly,* 10 April 1869, 229, 231.

13   Harriet Ritvo, *The Animal Estate: The English and Other Creatures in the Victorian Age* (Cambridge, Mass.: Harvard University Press, 1987), 82–121.

14   J. S. Ingram, *The Centennial Exposition, Described and Illustrated . . .* (Philadelphia: Hubbard Brothers, 1876), 675.

15   United States Centennial Commission, *Special Catalogue of Stated Displays of Livestock,* pt. 1, *Horses (September 1st to 14th),* and pt. 2, *Dogs (September 4th to 8th)* (Philadelphia: Sherman and Co., 1876).

16   The pug seems to have been introduced to Holland in the seventeenth century as a result of the China trade; from there it became popular in England in the eighteenth century. William Hogarth was so fond of his that he painted a widely reproduced portrait of Trump sitting before a framed likeness of his master. The image was also issued as a print in 1749. See David Bindman, *Hogarth and His Times: Serious Comedy* (Berkeley: University of California Press, 1997), 83 (catalog number 23).

17   On the history of the Boston terrier, see E. J. Rousuck, *The Boston Terrier* (New York: G. Howard Watt, 1926), 30–50, 141–53, and Henry J. Davis, ed., *The Modern Dog Encyclopedia* (Harrisburg, Pa.: Stackpole and Heck, 1949), 440–43. Rousuck avoids the issue of the Boston terrier's apparent origin as a fighting dog.

18   Gaston Fay, "Typical Dogs," *Century Magazine,* May 1885, 29.

19   Ritvo, *Animal Estate,* 87.

20   Thorstein Veblen, *The Theory of the Leisure Class,* introduction by Robert Lekachman (1899; repr., New York: Penguin, 1967), 142.

21   John W. Munson, "Typical Dogs: Pointers," *Century Magazine,* January 1886, 369. For a useful synopsis of the history and controversies surrounding American dog breeding, see Mark Derr, "The Politics of Dogs," *Atlantic Monthly,* March 1990, 49–72. Similar complaints made against breeders today are among the motivations for the creation of alternative registries such as the United Kennel Club.

22   "Save the Old-Fashioned Collie!," *Country Life in America,* 15 March 1912, 51–52.

23   George O. Shields, ed., *The American Book of the Dog* (Chicago: Rand, McNally, 1891), 622.

24   General interest magazines catering to upper middle-class audiences began to run articles illustrating and explaining the history and characteristics of pure-bred dog breeds by the late 1870s. See William M. Tileston, "Our Pets and Protectors," *Scribner's Magazine,* May 1878, 95–104. *Century Illustrated Monthly Magazine* ran a long series of essays on individual dog breeds under the title "Typical Dogs" between May 1885 and April 1886.

25   For discussion of the feist and other regional American dogs, see Mark Derr, *Dog's Best Friend: Annals of the Dog-Human Relationship* (New York: Henry Holt, 1997).

26   John Lynn Leonard, D.V.M., *The Care and Handling of Dogs* (Garden City, N.Y.: Garden City Publishing, 1928), 66–67.

27   For a statistical appendix of American Kennel Club registrations between 1878 and 1984, see Appendix G, Registrations, in Charles A. T. O'Neill et al., comps., *The American Kennel Club, 1884–1984: A Source Book* (New York: Howell Book House, 1985), 267–68.

28   Marlene Deahl Merrill, ed., *Growing Up in Boston's Gilded Age: The Journal of Alice Stone Blackwell, 1872–1874* (New Haven: Yale University Press, 1990), 71.

29   Claudia L. Bushman, ed., "Life along the Brandywine between 1880 and 1895 by Samuel Canby Rumford," pt. 1, *Delaware History* 23, no. 2 (Fall/Winter 1988): 137.

30   Journal of Gotham Bradbury, Farmington, Maine, 1881, entries for 26 January, 11 February, and 25 July, Downs Collection, Winterthur Museum and Library, Winterthur, Del.

31   A. Hyatt Verrill, *Pets for Pleasure and Profit* (New York: Charles Scribner's Sons, 1915), 120.

32   Edith E. W. Gregg, ed., *The Letters of Ellen Tucker Emerson* (Kent, Ohio: Kent State University Press, 1982), 1:175–76.

33   Calvin had originally been adopted as a stray by Harriet Beecher Stowe, who presented the Warners with him when she and her husband, Calvin (apparently the cat's namesake), left for a winter in Florida. Warner's essay on Calvin, originally printed in the *Hartford Courant* and collected in *My Summer in the Garden* (1871), is one of the richest and most perceptive descriptions of pet cat behavior ever published. I encountered it thanks to a reprint in Carl Van Vechten, ed., *Lords of the Housetops: Thirteen Cat Tales* (1921; repr., New York: Alfred A. Knopf, 1930), 226–38.

34   Charles Neider, ed., *The Autobiography of Mark Twain* (New York: Harper and Row, 1975), 29–30. In the same recollection of his childhood, Twain recalled

dosing one particularly sociable family cat named Peter with patent medicine forced on him by his mother as preventative for cholera in 1849 (38). This incident later found its way into *Tom Sawyer,* too.

35 Charles Neider, ed., *Papa: An Intimate Biography of Mark Twain by Susy Clemens, His Daughter, Thirteen, with a Foreword and Copious Commentary by Her Father* (Garden City, N.Y.: Doubleday, 1985), 99–100. "Mark Twain's Cats," taken by E. A. Van Eken of Elmira, N.Y., appeared in the April 1925 issue of the *Pictorial Review.*

36 Johnson and Stokes, *[Catalogue of] Poultry Supplies* (Philadelphia: by the company, [1899]), 41.

37 *[Catalogue of the] National Cat Show, Music Hall, Boston,* A. P. Peck, manager (Boston: Alfred Mudge and Son, 1878).

38 Margaret Harding Tileston Edsall, Diaries, 1878–1912, entry for 24 January 1878, courtesy Schlesinger Library, Radcliffe College, Cambridge, Mass.

39 *The Book of Household Pets, and How to Manage Them* (New York: Dick and Fitzgerald, 1866), 85; Jacob Biggle, *The Biggle Pet Book: A Collection of Information for Old and Young Whose Natural Instincts Teach Them to Be Kind to All Living Creatures* (Philadelphia: Wilmer Atkinson, 1900), 101; Verrill, *Pets for Pleasure and Profit,* 29.

40 Gregg, *Ellen Tucker Emerson,* 2:610.

41 Mitosi Tokuda, "An Eighteenth Century Japanese Guide-Book on Mouse-Breeding," *Journal of Heredity* 26 (1935): 481–84.

42 C. J. Davies, *Fancy Mice: Their Varieties and Management as Pets or for Show,* 5th ed., rev. (London: L. Upcott Gill, 1912), 2.

43 "My Visit to New York," Catherine B. Putnam, "Compositions, Kittie B. Putnam, [begun] September 24th, 1870," HCHC. On raising white rats and mice, see also Bushman, "Life along the Brandywine," pt. 1, 120, and *Book of Household Pets,* 84. The English enthusiasm for raising fancy mice may be a hitherto unrecognized outgrowth of the craze for chinoiserie generally, as the introduction of goldfish (reputedly in France in the mid-eighteenth century) also seems to have been. The first written guide to "the breeding of curious varieties of the mouse" was published in Japan in 1787. See Tokuda, "Eighteenth Century Japanese Guide-Book." While breeding fancy mice was an adult hobby in England as early as the 1830s, it seems never to have caught on in the United States. For the English fancy, see Davies, *Fancy Mice.* My thanks to Karen Rader for sharing these sources.

44 See, for example, the letter from Harry L. D. of East Boston, Mass., in "Our Post-Office Box," *Harper's Young People,* 2 November 1886, 15.

45 Dr. Herbert Richards, *The Playful Hamster* (Jersey City, N.J.: T.F.H. Publications, 1962), 7–8.

46 Letter from Helen M. C., Jefferson, N.Y., in "Our Post-Office Box," *Harper's Young People*, 30 November 1886, 78.

47 Letter from Fannie M. Jarvis (aged 9), in "The Letter-Box," *St. Nicholas: Scribner's Illustrated Magazine for Girls and Boys* (hereafter *SN*), September 1876, 742, described two pet squirrels given to her by her father's "hired men." See also letter from Effie W. Munson, Zanesville, Ohio, *SN*, November 1876, 60.

48 *Book of Household Pets*, 82.

49 Helen Kate Rogers Furness to her mother, Philadelphia, 23 August 1846, Historical Society of Pennsylvania, Philadelphia.

50 Betty Bright Low and Jacqueline Hinsley, *Sophie du Pont: A Young Lady in America. Sketches, Diaries, and Letters, 1823–1833* (New York: Harry N. Abrams, 1987), 90–91.

51 Windsor C. Robinson, ed., *The Diary of Aaron Greenwood*, vol. 1, *August 30, 1857 to July 6, 1859* (Gardner, Mass.: Gardner Historical Commission, 1963), 121 (entry for 19 July 1858); Abraham Ritter, *Philadelphia and Her Merchants, as Constituted Fifty and Seventy Years Ago, Illustrated by Diagrams of the Rover Front, and Portraits of Some of Its Prominent Occupants* (Philadelphia: by the author, 1860), 79. For other accounts of pet crows, see Mrs. S. B. C. Samuels, "Hoppers and Walkers," *SN*, July 1876, 597; Annabel Lee, "Jim Crow," *SN*, September 1874, 647–49. A number of wild animal pets, including a bear cub, kept by the author in the 1880s are mentioned in India Pearl Howes Russell, "The Story of My Life: Memories of Sweet Home," *Oregon Historical Quarterly* 101, no. 3 (Fall 2000): 356–57.

52 Bushman, "Life along the Brandywine," pt. 1, 120.

53 Neider, *Autobiography of Mark Twain*, 8–9.

54 Gregg, *Ellen Tucker Emerson*, 2:466.

55 William Lyon Phelps, *Autobiography with Letters* (New York: Oxford University Press, 1939), 108.

56 Lucy Larcom, *A New England Girlhood Outlined from Memory* (Boston: Houghton Mifflin, 1889), 95.

57 Mary V. Thompson, "Presidential Parrots," *Bird Talk*, July 1998, 68–71.

58 George Cugley, *Hints for Pets: A Short Treatise on Cage Birds, Dogs, Cats, Monkeys, Belgian Hares, Rabbits, Guinea Pigs, Squirrels, Rats and Mice, Ferrets, Pigeons and the Aquarium* (Philadelphia: Cugley and Mullen, 1900), 90–91.

59 Margaret Byington, *Homestead: The Households of a Mill Town* (1910; repr., Pittsburgh: University of Pittsburgh Press, 1974), 88.

60   Thomas Carlyle originally coined the phrase "little dewdrops of celestial melody" to praise the Scottish songs of poet Robert Burns; see Thomas Carlyle, *Past and Present* (1843), bk. 3, *The Modern Worker*, chap. 12, "Reward" (Project Gutenberg <http://www.gutenberg.org> [accessed 27 April 2005]). The term appeared on the frontispiece of George Holden, *Holden's Book on Birds* (Boston: by the author, 1880).

61   See, for example, Iowa farmwife Emily Hawley Gillespie's diary entry for 13 February 1885, written as she sat alone in her silent kitchen, her canary Birdy having retired for the night, in Judy Nolte Lensink, ed., *"A Secret to Be Burried": The Diary and Life of Emily Hawley Gillespie, 1858–1888* (Iowa City: University of Iowa Press, 1989), 294.

62   Gregg, *Ellen Tucker Emerson,* 1:8.

63   Neil Dana Glukin, "Pet Birds and Cages of the Eighteenth Century," *Early American Life* 8, no. 3 (June 1977): 38–41, 59.

64   Franklin, *Private Pages,* 483. Logan also kept a mockingbird, Mocky. Young Helen Kate Rogers also commented on the song of her mockingbird in a letter to her mother dated 2 February 1848, Collection Historical Society of Pennsylvania.

65   Ralph Waldo Emerson's daughter Ellen wrote to her sister Edith in 1853 that their cousin Charlie "has a little yellow bird that he keeps in a cage with a trap on top of it. The yellow bird sings and brings the other birds round and they hop into the trap and are caught. He and Haven [cousin Haven Emerson] have caught three this way, one escaped, they let one go, and are keeping the other to catch more" (Gregg, *Ellen Tucker Emerson,* 1:13).

66   For the typical cage bird stock of the early twentieth century, see Cugley and Mullen Co., *Catalog of the Bird Department* (Philadelphia: by the company, 1914), in Warshaw Collection of Business Americana, National Museum of American History, Smithsonian Institution, Washington, D.C.

67   Charles Reiche, *The Bird Fancier's Companion, or Natural History of Cage Birds, Their Food—Management—Habits—Treatment—Diseases, etc. etc.,* 3rd ed. (New York: Charles Reiche and Brother, 1867), 13.

68   Letter from Hattie Nourse, Athens, Ohio, *SN,* April 1878, 445.

69   Lensink, *"Secret to be Burried,"* 237, 241, 262; Ann Ellis, *The Life of an Ordinary Woman* (1929; repr., Boston: Houghton Mifflin, 1990), 60.

70   John Carter, *Solomon D. Butcher: Photographing the American Dream* (Lincoln: University of Nebraska Press, 1985), 4, 36, 45, 47.

71   Bayard Tuckerman, ed., *The Diary of Philip Hone, 1828–1851* (New York: Dodd, Mead, 1889), 2:27.

72   Catherine B. Putnam to Harriet Van Rensselaer Elmendorf, 11 May 1875, HCHC.

73   A photograph of one of these room-sized aviaries, in the Campbell House, Wilmington, Del., ca. 1890, can be found in the Decorative Arts Photography Collection, Winterthur Museum and Library.

74   Thomas M. Earl, *Pets of the Household: Their Care in Health and Disease* (Columbus, Ohio: A. W. Livingston's Sons, 1894), 101.

75   Gregg, *Ellen Tucker Emerson,* 1:132.

76   Emily W. Rankin, Inventory of Cherry Hill, July 1959, box 279, file 7, HCHC.

77   I. L. V. Lesley to Harriet (Hattie) Van Rensselaer Elmendorf, 11 January 1874, box 48, file 3, HCHC.

78   Harriet (Hattie) VR Elmendorf Gould to Harriet Maria Elmendorf, 6 April (no year). In a letter dated 16 March, apparently written early in the same visit, Hattie Gould had assured her mother that Polly was "no trouble at all," living in the kitchen with Minnie; see Harriet (Hattie) VR Elmendorf Gould to Harriet Maria Elmendorf, 16 March (no year), HCHC.

79   Letter from John W. Gould to Hattie Reed, 25 November 1895, Rankin box 8, HCHC.

80   Undated notebook page (ca. 1900) in the writing of one of the Rankin children discussing animal deaths, Bunnie Papers; Edmond W. Gould to Edward Elmendorf Rankin, 24 February 1899; Thomas? to Herbert Rankin, n.d., box 112, file 5, HCHC.

81   "Gold Fish," *Godey's Lady's Book,* February 1855, 119.

82   Lynn Barber, *The Heyday of Natural History, 1820–1870* (Garden City, N.Y.: Doubleday, 1980), chap. 8, "An Invention and Its Consequences," 111–24.

83   On the contents of simple aquariums, see letter from "J. L. D.," 1 June 1875, and reply, in "The Letter-Box," *SN,* August 1875, 649; Daniel C. Beard, "How to Stock and Keep a Fresh-Water Aquarium," *SN,* July 1881, 696–703.

84   Of course, what made Eddy Emerson's aquarium different from most others was that "Mr. Thoreau" had encouraged the boy to take it up; see Ellen Tucker Emerson to Haven Emerson, April 1859, in Gregg, *Ellen Tucker Emerson,* 1:184. Edward Emerson's aquarium apparently survived, if not thrived, for it reappeared in a letter of 1860, when "H. Mann [educator Horace Mann] brought for E's aquarium 4 great tadpoles, 2 Salamanders, Rowboats, Beetles, Bugs and Plants" (Ellen Tucker Emerson to Edith Emerson, 31 May 1860, in Gregg, *Ellen Tucker Emerson,* 1:214).

85   Kittie B. Putnam, composition book dated 1871, HCHC.

86   Nathaniel Hawthorne, *Twenty Days with Julian & Little Bunny by Papa,* intro-
      duction by Paul Auster (New York: New York Review Books, 2003), 4–5, 17,
      21–22.

                              CHAPTER TWO

1   Extracts from the diary of Deborah Norris Logan, 1833–1839, in Penelope
      Franklin, ed., *Private Pages: Diaries of American Women, 1830s–1970s* (New
      York: Ballantine, 1986), 458–59 (entry for 20 January 1833).

2   Harriet Beecher ("Hattie") Stowe (daughter) to Calvin Ellis Stowe, 1 Febru-
      ary 1852, Harriet Beecher Stowe Papers, Stowe-Day Foundation, Hartford,
      Conn.

3   Edward W. Rankin to Catherine (Kittie) Putnam Rankin, 9 December 1886,
      Historic Cherry Hill, Albany, N.Y. (hereafter HCHC).

4   Allan Nevins, ed., *The Diary of Philip Hone, 1828–1851* (1927; repr., New
      York: Kraus, 1969), 2:837 (entry for 25 January 1848).

5   Claudia L. Bushman, ed., "Life along the Brandywine between 1880 and
      1895 by Samuel Canby Rumford," pt. 1, *Delaware History* 23, no. 2 (Fall/Win-
      ter 1988): 117.

6   Thos. E. Hill, *Hill's Manual of Social and Business Forms* (Chicago: Hill's
      Standard Book Co., 1884), 156.

7   American Pet Products Manufacturers Association, Inc., *1999–2000 APPMA
      National Pet Owners Survey* (Greenwich, Conn.: by the association, 1999), 57.

8   Thomas M. Earl, *Pets of the Household: Their Care in Health and Disease*
      (Columbus, Ohio: A. W. Livingston's Sons, 1894), 148.

9   Samuel L. Clemens to Olivia L. Clemens, 26 April 1873, Hartford, Conn.,
      in Lin Salamo and Harriet Elinor Smith, eds., *Mark Twain's Letters,* vol. 5,
      1872–73 (Berkeley: University of California Press, 1997), 358. See also
      Clemens to William Dean Howells, 6–7 May 1880, Hartford, Conn., in
      Henry Nash Smith and William M. Gibson, eds., *Mark Twain–Howells Let-
      ters: The Correspondence of Samuel L. Clemens and William D. Howells,
      1872–1910* (Cambridge, Mass.: Belknap Press of Harvard University Press,
      1960), 305–6.

10   Alice Hughes Neupert, "In Those Days: Buffalo in the 1870s," *Niagara Fron-
      tier* 24, no. 4 (Winter 1977): 79.

11   Broadside, Bradley's Bird Swing, Washington, D.C., n.d. [ca. 1870], Warshaw
      Collection of Business Americana, National Museum of American History,
      Smithsonian Institution, Washington, D.C. (hereafter WCBA).

12   John Wilkinson, Sporting and Gymnasium Goods, *Special Price List* (Chicago, 1881).

13   Henry Bishop, *Bishop the Bird Man's Treatise on Birds and Aquaria* (Baltimore: Henry Bishop, 1912), 66.

14   A. Hyatt Verrill, *Pets for Pleasure and Profit* (New York: Charles Scribner's Sons, 1915), 103.

15   Letter from "Lilly T. R.," Platteville, Wisc., in "Our Post-Office Box," *Harper's Young People*, November 30, 1886, 78.

16   "Tom," *Oxford English Dictionary*.

17   According to the *Oxford English Dictionary*, the transformation of "puss" or "pussy" into coarse sexual slang for women's genitals took place more than two centuries after it appeared as a name for cats.

18   Advertisement for toy mouse, Smith & Egge, Bridgeport, Connecticut, *Harper's Weekly*, 22 April 1876, 335.

19   "Poulson 'Catnip Mice' Start a Circus with the Tabbies," *Novelty News*, June 1916, 56.

20   Brooks Brothers, *A Catalogue of Clothing and Many Other Things for Men and Boys* (New York City, 1915), 42; Sunrise Pet Supply Company, *Catalog of Dog Furnishings* (Hempstead, N.Y., n.d.), 4–5. See also Max Geisler Bird Co., *Illustrated Catalogue* (New York: by the company, [1928]), 50.

21   Letter from Lilly M. P., Wortendyke, N.J., in "Our Post-Office Box," *Harper's Young People*, 30 November 1886, 79.

22   Letter from Willie L. Brooks, Sacramento, Calif., about keeping the cat from bothering the canary, "The Letter-Box," *St. Nicholas: Scribner's Magazine for Girls and Boys* (hereafter SN), May 1876, 470; letter from Amalie about Jack the rooster, in "The Letter-Box," *SN*, August 1876, 678; letter from Mary Eichelberger, Bloomfield, Iowa, about her parrot, in "The Letter-Box," *SN*, May 1876, 470; letter about pet fox, *SN*, March 1882, 418; "Molly," age 16, in "My Aquariums," *Our Young Folks*, September 1872, 568; letter from Daisy Eaton, Plainfield, Conn., about death of St. Bernard puppy, *SN*, November 1878, 69–70.

23   Helen Kate Rogers Furness, letter to "Miss K. C. Brush" (the squirrel), 25 April 1850, Historical Society of Pennsylvania, Philadelphia.

24   Marlene Deahl Merrill, ed., *Growing Up in Boston's Gilded Age: The Journal of Alice Stone Blackwell, 1872–1874* (New Haven: Yale University Press, 1990), 37.

25   Letter from Frederick William Seward (1830–1915) to Frances Adeline Wor-

den, 15 November 1838, William Henry Seward Papers, Rush Rhees Library, University of Rochester, Rochester, N.Y.

26 "A Letter from a Big Dog," *SN*, December 1884, 155.

27 Grace Cogswell to Emily W. Rankin, 25 July 1901, box 117, file 2, HCHC.

28 Letter from Ella and Edwin R., in "The Letter-Box," *SN*, May 1878, 508.

29 Peter E. Elmendorf to Harriet (Hattie) Van Rensselaer Elmendorf, 27 September 1854, and Catherine (Kittie) Putnam to Peter E. Elmendorf and Harriet Maria VR Elmendorf, 13 February 1869, HCHC.

30 Emily Marshall Eliot, Diaries for 1869–1871, entry for 2 March 1869, courtesy Schlesinger Library, Radcliffe College, Cambridge, Mass.

31 Letter from Mamie E. K, Newburgh, N.Y., in "Our Post-Office Box," *Harper's Young People*, 30 November 1886, 79; letter from P. D. Noel, South Saint Louis, Mo., *SN*, August 1877, 701; Elizabeth Wood Coffin, *A Girl's Life in Germantown* (Boston: Sherman, French, 1916), 20.

32 Mary V. Thompson, "Presidential Parrots," *Bird Talk*, July 1998, 69.

33 "Birds desired to be tame" needed steady human contact and attention. C. F. Holden and G. H. Holden, *Holden's New Book on Birds* (Boston: by the company, 1881), 114, suggested placing their cages on a writing table and teaching them to light on a finger or shoulder and take food from the hand. See also Olive Thorne Miller, *Our Home Pets: How to Keep Them Well and Happy* (New York: Harper and Brothers, 1894), 112. This assumption underlies Jacob Biggle, *The Biggle Pet Book: A Collection of Information for Old and Young Whose Natural Instincts Teach Them to Be Kind to All Living Creatures* (Philadelphia: Wilmer Atkinson, 1900), 7, which argued that the character of the pet and the owner developed in tandem.

34 C. H. C. Williams, *Williams' New System of Handling and Educating the Horse; Together with Diseases and Their Treatment. Also a Treatise on Shoeing; Educating Cattle and Dogs, with Hints on Stable Management; with the Rules and Regulations for Trotting, Racing and Betting* (Claremont, N.H.: Claremont Manufacturing Co., 1878), 181.

35 Roy H. Spaulding, *Your Dog and Your Cat: How to Care for Them* (New York: D. Appleton, 1922), 115–16.

36 Samuel Canby Rumford and his brother had a pair of "fawn colored buck rabbits" who "learned to use a box of sand in one corner" of their playroom "in a most thoughtful manner" (Bushman, "Life along the Brandywine," pt. 1, 120).

37 Biggle, *Biggle Pet Book*, 10.

38 See, for example, George O. Shields, ed., *The American Book of the Dog*

(Chicago: Rand, McNally, 1891), 700, and James A. Watson, *The Dog Book: A Popular History of the Dog, with Practical Information as to Care and Management of House, Kennel, and Exhibition Dogs; and Descriptions of All the Important Breeds in Ten Parts* (New York: Doubleday, Page, 1905), for advice on house training in the "up-to-date flat," 35; George Watson Little, D.V.M., *Dr. Little's Dog Book* (New York: McBride, 1924), 119–20.

39   Harriet (Hattie) VR Gould to Harriet Maria Elmendorf, 1 June [1895], HCHC.

40   "Edward Loeb Dies at 75; a Hunch Led Him to Create Kitty Litter," *New York Times,* 6 October 1995; Harrison Weir, *Our Cats and All about Them* (Boston: Houghton Mifflin, 1889), 92; Eleanor Booth Simmons, *The Care and Feeding of Cats* (New York: Blue Ribbon Books, 1938), 22.

41   For a detailed discussion of how canary breeders trained their birds to sing through both exposure to older singers and the use of "bird organs," see Chas. N. Page, *Canary Breeding and Training* (Des Moines, Iowa: by the author, 1902), 51–59.

42   Chas. N. Page, *Parrots and Other Talking Birds* (Des Moines, Iowa: by the author, 1906). This small booklet of anecdotes about parrots and advice on their care received national distribution through O. Lindemann and Co., a manufacturer of bird and animal cages in New York City.

43   Biggle, *Biggle Pet Book,* 45–50. A letter from "Mamie E. K." of Newburgh, N.Y., reported on her "water-spaniel" Skip, who could "beg, speak, shake hands, and play hide-and-seek" ("Our Post-Office Box," *Harper's Young People,* 30 November 1886, 79).

44   See, for example, Harry J. Mooney, *How to Train Your Own Dogs* (Chicago: Sallfield, 1909). Mooney was "Trainer with Barnum and Bailey." The contents appeared originally as features in the *New York Evening Mail* in 1908.

45   For an example of this training literature and a discussion of early formal obedience trials, see Hans Tossutti, *Companion Dog Training: A Practical Manual on Systematic Obedience; Dog Training in Word and Picture* (New York: Orange Judd, 1942). The foreword claims that Tossutti was "the first organizer of dog training in classes, when he established the New England School for Dogs in 1928" and discusses the creation of American Kennel Club obedience-training competitions in 1936. Tossutti, who trained dogs for a variety of purposes, dedicated the book to his German shepherd and "the 3,000 pupils in my dog training classes in Boston, Massachusetts, from 1928 to 1940."

46   See Martha C. Armstrong, Susan Tomasello, and Christyna Hunter, "From Pets to Companion Animals," in *The State of Animals in 2001,* ed. Deborah J.

Salem and Andrew N. Rowan (Washington, D.C.: Humane Society Press, 2001), 78–79, 82–83. Annual shelter statistics compiled by the American Society for the Prevention of Cruelty to Animals show that 75 percent of "owned pets" (that is, pets not turned in to shelters) are spayed or neutered; see "Annual Shelter Statistics," National Shelter Outreach, ASPCA, <http://www.aspca.org/site/ PageServer?pagename+annualshelterinfo>.

47 "An Ordinance to prevent Dogs from running at large in the City of Philadelphia," in *Ordinances and Joint Resolutions of the Select and Common Councils of the Consolidated City of Philadelphia, as Passed by Them, and Approved by the Mayor, From January First to December Thirty-First, 1855* (Philadelphia: J. H. Jones, 1856), 213–14.

48 Harriet (Hattie) Elmendorf Gould to Catherine (Kittie) B. Putnam, 22 May, 2, 12 June, 7 July 1879, HCHC. Tom also knew which bedroom window to visit in the middle of the night to get back into the house.

49 Frederick T. G. Hobday, F.R.C.V.S., *Canine and Feline Surgery* (New York: William R. Jenkins, 1900), 127–29. This book is an American edition of an English text authored by the head of the Free Outpatients Clinique of the Royal Veterinary College, London.

50 The first book on small-animal surgical techniques, including spaying and neutering, widely available in the United States seems to have been the British text by Hobday, *Canine and Feline Surgery.* For the retraining of large-animal veterinarians, see Susan D. Jones, *Valuing Animals: Veterinarians and Their Patients in Modern America* (Baltimore: Johns Hopkins University Press, 2002), 123.

51 Johnson and Stokes, *[Catalogue of] Poultry Supplies* (Philadelphia, [1899]), 42.

52 John Lynn Leonard, D.V.M., *The Care and Handling of Dogs* (Garden City, N.Y.: Garden City Publishing, 1928), 355–56.

53 Spaulding, *Your Dog and Your Cat,* 159, 81.

54 Harriet Beecher Stowe to Mrs. Cannard, 18 June 1866, Stowe Papers.

55 Helen M. Winslow, *Concerning Cats: My Own and Some Others* (1900; repr., Ann Arbor, Mich.: Lowe and B. Hould, 1996), 12–13, 33–34.

56 Shields, *American Book of the Dog,* 623.

57 Bellamy Partridge, *Big Family* (New York: Whittlesey House, 1941), 271–72.

58 "Letter from a Big Dog."

59 American Humane Association, "The Dog: Suggestions on Its Care" (Albany, N.Y.: n.d. [ca. 1900–10]). For similar advice, see *BEST of EVERYTHING, by the Author of ENQUIRE WITHIN, Containing 1800 Useful Articles on How to Obtain "THE BEST OF EVERYTHING"* (London, 1874), 284–85.

60 Biggle, *Biggle Pet Book*, 12.

61 Letter from Lina Aldrich, SN, May 1881, 574.

62 Biggle, *Biggle Pet Book*, 54–56.

63 Trade card for Buchan's No. 11 Carbolic Disinfecting Soap (n.d. [ca. 1880]), and trade card for Morris Little and Son, Brooklyn, N.Y., and Lancaster, England (n.d. [ca. 1890]), author's collection.

64 Letter to Lever Brothers, Limited, New York City, from Walter Batts, proprietor of Woodside Boarding Kennels, Woodside, Long Island, N.Y., 6 February 1902, in WCBA (Animals 2/14–15).

65 Sterlingworth Chemical Company, *Big Book* (New York, 1914), unpaginated.

66 F. E. Vanderhoof, "Germicidal Animal Collar," U.S. Patent 2,219,569, received 29 October 1940 (filed 3 August 1938); Thomas A. Lamb Jr., "Flea-Guard Dog Collar," U.S. Patent 2,401,253, received 28 May 1946 (filed 5 April 1944).

67 Spratt's Patent (America), Limited, *Dog Diseases and How to Cure Them* (New York, n.d. [1890]), 8–9.

68 George Watson Little, D.V.M., *Dr. Little's Dog Book*, rev. ed. (New York: McBride, 1937), 17.

69 Interview with Anna Foster Grier, Pennington, New Jersey, 10 February 2001.

70 Jones, *Valuing Animals*, 132–33. See also O. H. V. Stalheim, *The Winning of Animal Health: 100 Years of Veterinary Medicine* (Ames: Iowa State University, 1994), 57–59.

71 William Findlay Brown and Ira Jewell Williams, comp., *A Digest of Laws and Ordinances Concerning Philadelphia with Notes of Decisions and City Solicitors' Opinions Relating Thereto, 1701–1904* (Philadelphia: J. L. H. Bayne, 1905), 910–11.

72 Jones, *Valuing Animals*, 130–32.

73 Elizabeth F. Crane, ed., *The Diary of Elizabeth Drinker* (Boston: Northeastern University Press, 1991), 2:944 (20 July 1797). This may have been transmitted from England, where thousands of cats were killed by an unknown epidemic; by August the disease had reached New York City. See ibid., n. 107.

74 For a detailed account of the rise of small-animal veterinary practice, see Jones, *Valuing Animals*, chap. 5, "Pricing the Priceless Pet," 115–40, and David M. Drenan, "The Growth and Development of Small-Animal Practice in the United States," *Journal of the American Veterinary Association* 169, no. 1 (July 1976): 42–49.

75 Walton called himself the "Oldest Dog Dealer in Boston . . . Established

1846," but he does not appear in the Boston city directories until the mid-1870s. According to the *Boston City Directory* (1884), his business was located at 111 Kingston Street.

76 Edward S. Schmid, *Illustrated Catalogue and Price List, Schmid's Bird and Pet Animal Emporium* (Washington, D.C.: by the author, 1903), 63–64.

77 In 1927, *Pet Dealer* reported on the "Royce C. Powell pet shop and dog hospital" in Cleveland, Ohio, praising Mr. Powell's provision of separate kennels for more than eighty dogs. The dog hospital operated without a licensed veterinarian. See *Pet Dealer*, April 1927, 10.

78 Veterinary Department, University of Pennsylvania, *Veterinary Record* 4 (1909): 15.

79 Sydney H. Coleman, *Humane Society Leaders in America, with a Sketch of the Early History of the Humane Movement in England* (Albany, N.Y.: American Humane Education Association, 1924), 110–11.

80 J. Elliott Crawford, "The Hospitalization of Small Animals," *AVMA Journal* (1928): 743–51.

81 Journal of John Codman (1814–1900), recording the voyage from New York City to Rio de Janeiro of the barque *Hollander* in 1847, Manuscript Collection of John Codman (1898–1989), box 4, folder 15, Historic New England, Boston, Mass.

82 Harriet (Hattie) VR Gould to Catherine (Kittie) Putnam Rankin, 30 July 1895, HCHC.

83 Little, *Dr. Little's Dog Book* (1924), 33, 208–14.

84 A. Emil Hiss, Ph.D., *The International Formulary*, 3rd ed., vol. 2, *Domestic and Veterinary Remedies* (Chicago: G. P. Engelhard, 1908, 1912), 184–85, 192.

85 Pepsin, the most important digestive enzyme in the stomach, had been isolated and, obtained from animal sources, was used medicinally by the late nineteenth century.

86 Price List for Dr. Marney's Dog and Cat Medicines (n.d. [1940s?]), Dr. Marney's Laboratories, Union Insurance Building, 1008 W. Sixth St., Los Angeles, Calif.

87 Harriet Beecher Stowe to Mrs. Cannard, 18 June 1866, Stowe Papers.

88 William Kampfmuller, *Our Pets; or, Book on Cage Birds; Their Home, Treatment, Breeding, Diseases, etc. etc. Also, an Appendix Containing the Treatment of Gold Fish and Aquaria* (Brooklyn: by the author, 1876; Boston: L. F. Adams, 1881), 90.

89   Jack Larkin, "The Faces of Change: Images of Self and Society in New En-
      gland, 1790–1850," in *Meet Your Neighbors: New England Portraits, Painters,
      and Society, 1790–1850*, ed. Jack Larkin et al. (Sturbridge, Mass.: Old Stur-
      bridge Village, 1992), 10.

90   Fuller and Negus family papers, Archives of American Art microfilm #611,
      citation received from Jessica F. Nicoll, curator, Old Sturbridge Village, Stur-
      bridge, Mass.

91   Martha Gandy Fales, "Hanna B. Skeele, Maine Artist," *Antiques*, April 1982,
      plate 4, *Joseph Dane's Italian Greyhound*, 1871–80.

92   For an overview of dog portraiture in England and the United States, along
      with a survey of high-society specialists in dog painting, see William Secord,
      Dog Painting, 1840–1940: A Social History of the Dog in Art (Woodbridge,
      Suffolk, U.K.: Antique Collectors' Club, 1992).

93   This postcard is in the author's collection.

94   Phila. A. 12 Apl. 1828 s2, p.l. 315 in Brown and Williams, *Digest of Laws and
      Ordinances*, 1243–44.

95   Dr. A. C. Daniels (Inc.), *Home Treatment for Cats and Kittens: Dr. A. C.
      Daniels' Veterinary Medicines and How to Use Them*, rev. ed. (Boston, 1917,
      1924), 7.

96   Crane, *Diary of Elizabeth Drinker*, vol. 3.

97   Betty Bright Low and Jacqueline Hinsley, *Sophie du Pont: A Young Lady in
      America. Sketches, Diaries, and Letters, 1823–1833* (New York: Harry N.
      Abrams, 1987), 95.

98   Harriet Beecher Stowe, "Aunt Esther's Rules," in *Stories and Sketches for the
      Young*, vol. 16 of *The Writings of Harriet Beecher Stowe*, Riverside ed. (1896;
      repr., New York: AMS Press, 1967), 111–12. She used a variation on the old
      gendered formula of cruelty and kindness (see Chapter 3) to illustrate her
      point: a little girl rescues a half-drowned kitten from some cruel boys who are
      throwing it repeatedly into the water; she holds it underwater until "all its
      earthly sorrows were over, and little kit was beyond the reach of dog or boy."

99   Children's literature was sometimes stunningly frank on the matter of killing
      unwanted animals, but the frankness of stories and poems such as "Both
      Sides," published in 1867 in *Our Young Folks*, probably made a difficult situ-
      ation even worse. The poem recounts a debate between a speaking cat and a
      woman over injustices done by both parties. The woman chastises the cat for
      the "cruel deed" of killing young robins; in reply, the cat points out that the
      woman had killed a chicken just last week and nests of "sweet young caterpil-

lars" without "even the plea of need." But the cat complains of the woman's worst offenses thus:

> I had four little kittens a month ago,—
> Black, and Malta, and white as snow;
> And not a very long while before
> I could have shown you three kittens more. . . .
> But what am I now? A cat bereft.
> Of all my kittens, but one is left.
> I make no charges, but this I ask,—
> What made such a splurge in the waste-water cask?
> You are quite tender-hearted. O, not a doubt!
> But only suppose old Black Pond could speak out.
> O bother! Don't mutter excuses to me:
> *Qui facit per alium facit per se* [He who acts through another acts himself].

100 Letter from Fred T., Dixon, Ill., in "Our Post-Office Box," *Harper's Young People,* 7 June 1887, 514.

101 Neupert, "In Those Days," 88.

102 Letter of Frederick William Seward (1830–1915) to William Henry Seward, Auburn, N.Y., 24 February 1837, Seward Papers.

103 Peter E. Elmendorf to Harriet (Hattie) VR Elmendorf, 12 March 1855, HCHC.

104 Mabel Colby ("age 14"), "Addie's Carlo," in *Our Young Folks,* March 1870, 181.

105 Luther Spaulding Bancroft commonplace book, Old Sturbridge Village.

106 This manuscript was found in a private collection of papers in Gorham, Maine. I purchased it from a rare book dealer in 1997.

107 H. H. Delong, *Boyhood Reminiscences: Dansville, N.Y., 1855–1865* (Dansville, N.Y.: F. A. Owen, 1913), 43.

108 Bushman, "Life along the Brandywine," pt. 1, 116–17. The Canby family pet graveyard was in use for decades and remained a local landmark until increasing urbanization led to the sale and demolition of the family homestead.

109 Interview with Nancy Carlisle, 20 June 1992, Historic New England.

110 Joan D. Hedrick, *Harriet Beecher Stowe: A Life* (New York: Oxford University Press, 1994), 76; Forrest Wilson, *Crusader in Crinoline: The Life of Harriet Beecher Stowe* (Philadelphia: Lippincott, 1941).

111 Undated notebook page (ca. 1900) in the writing of one of the Rankin children, discussing animal deaths, HCHC.

112   For published collections of posthumous photography, see Jay Ruby, *Secure the Shadow: Death and Photography in America* (Cambridge, Mass.: MIT Press, 1995); Stanley B. Burns, M.D., *Sleeping Beauty: Memorial Photography in America* (Santa Fe, N.M.: Twelvetrees Press, 1990).

THE BUNNIE STATES OF AMERICA

1   This account is drawn from a collection of the children's papers, titled the "Bunnie Papers" by their mother, in box 26, Historic Cherry Hill, Albany, N.Y. The collection includes a number of notebooks and a body of paper ephemera created by the Rankin children. Additional sources used for this essay include transcriptions of diaries of Herbert and Emily Rankin, a small group of photographs taken in the late 1890s, and selected other family papers. So many of these papers cross-reference one another that endnotes are used only in the case of unique bits of information.

2   [Edward Elmendorf Rankin and Herbert Rankin], "History of rabbits and establishment of the Bunnie States," box 326, f7, f16. The young historians opened their account this way: "We had wanted to make a history for a long time we had put the dates out in so many books that it was hard to find them and also dates differed from one another but every date that is stated in this book is known to be correct and has been carefully compared. We even got so far as to nearly finish one but it was all lost all but one page we finally made a great effort with the following result. The authors."

3   Will of Papaa Bunny, 9 September 1898, box 326, f17.

4   Declaration of Independence, 9 December 1898, box 326, f1; draft, ten article or laws by "National Consil," 28 November 1898; [Edward Rankin], "History of rabbits and establishment of Bunnie States, 21 August 1897 to 28 November 1898," box 326, f16.

5   *The Speaker,* May 1899, box 326, f2.

6   "EWR" (probably Edward Elmendorf Rankin), "The Whitey Children Case," December 1898(?).

7   Letter from EER to EWR's mother, 18 June 1899: "We now have three rabbits, one gold fish and twenty-six minnoes and three incubator chickens one is a bantam, which belongs to Emily one is a little smaller than usually which belongs to Herbert and mine is a game foul" (box 112, f6).

8   Receipt for purchase of garden by B. S. Supply Co., witnessed by Edward Elmendorf Rankin, 18 April 1899, box 326, f1.

9   *The Speaker,* May 1899; Herbert E. Rankin to Edward Elmendorf Rankin, 18 June 1899.

10   *The Speaker,* 28 June 1899.

11   List of reasons to have chicken house separate from Cherry Hill, box 326, f20.

12   Letter from Herbert W. Rankin to Edward Elmendorf Rankin, 27 June 1899, box 112, f6.

13   Letter from Kate M. Byington, Middlebury, Vt., to Emily Rankin, 18 July 1899, to console her on the death of her pet chicken, killed by a cat; letter from Herbert to Mr. Mathew Hale, Cambridge, Mass., November 1, 1899; letter from EER to father EWR, 24 July 1899: "we got a plymouth rock chicken from Mr. Hyman which turned out to be a rooster" (Miles Standish); letter from CBR to EWR, 28 July 1899: "The children are all well, and greatly enjoying two yellow hens that I was beguiled into getting for them"; letter from CBR to EWR, 23 August 1899. The children received two bantam chickens from a cousin (?) in the Van Rensselaer family.

14   Certificate from "Medical College," 25 October 1899: "Hereby H. E. Rankin has filled his course has pulled through the little brown hen, and is herby pronounced an able doctor this date the 25. of Oct. 1899. E. E. Rankin dr."

15   Herbert W. Rankin to Mathew Hale, Cambridge, Mass., 1 November 1899.

16   *The Company,* 7 December 1899, box 2, f2.

17   Emily W. Rankin (grandmother) to Emily W. Rankin, 15 January 1900, box 114, f1.

18   "B.S.F&G.Co. Egg Account, No. 1," May 1900, box 2, f10.

19   Constitution for B.S.F.&G.Co., n.d., box 2, f7.

20   Herbert E. Rankin, "Speaker. Advanced Littiurture," n.d. (July and December 1898), box 2, f2.

21   Emily W. Rankin, diary entry for 12 January 1901.

22   Ibid., 6, 8 April 1901.

23   Edward Elmendorf Rankin to Catharine Bonney Rankin, 28 June 1901; CBR to her sons, 30 June 1901.

24   Minute Book 3, Bunnie States.

CHAPTER THREE

1   Lydia H. Sigourney, *Letters to Mothers* (1838; 6th ed., New York: Harper and Brothers, 1846), 35–36.

2   For the most current full discussion of legislation prior to the Civil War, and the first efforts of organized animal welfare groups, see Bernard Oreste Unti, "The Quality of Mercy: Organized Animal Protection in the United States, 1866–1930" (Ph.D. diss., American University, 2002).

3   For a concise overview of the development of middle-class culture in the

nineteenth century, including a useful bibliography of the principal scholarship, see Mark C. Carnes, "The Rise and Consolidation of Bourgeois Culture," in *Encyclopedia of American Social History*, ed. Mary Kupiec Cayton, Elliot J. Gorn, and Peter W. Williams (New York: Charles Scribner's Sons, 1993), 1:605–20; Daniel Walker Howe, "Victorian Culture in America," in *Victorian America*, ed. Daniel Walker Howe (Philadelphia: University of Pennsylvania Press, 1976), 2–3.

4   Discussion of gentility in America is found in Richard L. Bushman, *The Refinement of America, 1750–1850* (New York: Norton, 1992).

5   Janet Todd, *Sensibility: An Introduction* (London: Methuen, 1986), 7–8. For the popular understanding of sensibility in eighteenth-century England, see also John Brewer, *The Pleasures of the Imagination: English Culture in the Eighteenth Century* (New York: Farrar, Straus and Giroux, 1997), 113–22. Keith Thomas points out that the concept of the man of feeling can be traced to latitudinarian religious thought during the Restoration, but by the late eighteenth century, sensibility was often separated from religiosity, most decisively by the rise of utilitarianism. See Thomas, *Man and the Natural World: A History of the Modern Sensibility* (New York: Pantheon, 1983), 175–76.

6   [William Wollaston], *The Religion of Nature* (1731), quoted in Thomas, *Man and the Natural World*, 75.

7   *A Manual of Politeness, Comprising the Principles of Etiquette, and Rules of Behaviour in Genteel Society* (Philadelphia: W. Marshall, 1837), 276, 7. For do-it-yourself gentility in American etiquette books, see Arthur M. Schlesinger, *Learning to Behave: A Historical Study of American Etiquette Books* (New York: Macmillan, 1946).

8   For the principal arguments of the new liberal Protestant theology and a discussion of its utility as an instrument of social control in one community, see Paul E. Johnson, *A Shopkeeper's Millennium: Society and Revivals in Rochester, New York, 1815–1837* (New York: Hill and Wang, 1978), chap. 5, "Pentecost," 95–115; Curtis D. Johnson, *Redeeming America: Evangelicals and the Road to the Civil War* (Chicago: University of Chicago Press, 1993).

9   Rev. Charles Grandison Finney, D.D., *Lectures on Systematic Theology*, edited by Rev. J. H. Fairchild (New York: George H. Doran, 1878), 154–56. These lectures, from Finney's course on systematic theology at Oberlin College, were first published in 1846.

10   The close relationship of animal welfare work to other forms of social activism is discussed in detail in Unti, "Quality of Mercy," 19–25.

11 The "Eden of Home," along with a score of other synonyms for "home," may be found in Rev. W. K. Tweedie, *Home; or, The Parents' Assistant and Children's Friend* (Norwich, Conn.: Henry Bill Publishing, 1873), 34–41.

12 Charlotte B. Tonna, *Kindness to Animals; or, The Sin of Cruelty Exposed and Rebuked*, Revised by the Committee of Publication of the American Sunday-School Union (Philadelphia: American Sunday-School Union, 1845), 8, 9, 12.

13 Harriet Beecher Stowe to Henry E. Burton, Esq., 20 December 1881, Stowe-Day Foundation, Hartford, Conn.

14 For the construction of domesticity, see Nancy F. Cott, *The Bonds of Womanhood: Women's "Sphere" in New England, 1780–1835* (New Haven: Yale University Press, 1977), chap. 2, "Domesticity," 63–100. For the antebellum conventions of domesticity, see Mary P. Ryan, *The Empire of the Mother: American Writing about Domesticity, 1830–1860* (New York: Haworth Press, 1982), esp. chap. 1, "From Patriarchal Household to Feminine Domesticity," 19–44. For the interplay of domesticity and liberal Protestant theology, see Barbara Leslie Epstein, *The Politics of Domesticity: Women, Evangelism, and Temperance in Nineteenth-Century America* (Middletown, Conn.: Wesleyan University Press, 1981), 45–87.

15 Reverend A. B. Muzzy, *The Fireside: An Aid to Parents* (Boston: Crosby, Nichols, 1854), 8. For changes in attitudes toward mothering, see Mary Lynn Stevens Heininger, "Children, Childhood, and Change in America, 1820–1920," in *A Century of Childhood, 1820–1920*, ed. Mary Lynn Stevens Heininger et al. (Rochester, N.Y.: Margaret Woodbury Strong Museum, 1984), 1–32; Nancy Shrom Dye and Daniel Blake Smith, "Mother Love and Infant Death, 1750–1820," *Journal of American History* 73, no. 2 (September 1986): 329–53; Ryan, *Empire of the Mother*, 45–55.

16 "Home Interests," *Youth's Penny Gazette*, 20 November 1850, 94, published by the American Sunday-School Union.

17 Catharine C. Beecher and Harriet Beecher Stowe, *The American Woman's Home, or Principles of Domestic Science* (1869; repr., Hartford, Conn.: Stowe-Day Foundation, 1987), 18; Muzzy, *Fireside*, 109.

18 Thomas, *Man and the Natural World*, 19, 24.

19 Francis Wayland, D.D., LL.D., *The Elements of Moral Science*, rev. ed. (1837; repr., Boston: Gould and Lincoln, 1865, 1871), 395.

20 John Bigland, *A Natural History of Animals* (Philadelphia: John Grigg, 1828), 187, 20.

21   A. L. Carroll, "An Apology for Dogs," *Harper's New Monthly Magazine,* June–November 1867, 192.

22   David Brion Davis, *The Problem of Slavery in Western Culture* (Ithaca, N.Y.: Cornell University Press, 1966), chap. 7, "The Legitimacy of Enslavement and the Ideal of the Christian Servant: The Failure of Christianization," 197–222.

23   For a discussion of the common-law tradition regarding animals as property, see Gary L. Francione, *Animals, Property, and the Law* (Philadelphia: Temple University Press, 1995), chap. 2, "The Dominion of Humans over Animals, the 'Defects' of Animals, and the Common Law," 33–49. Francione points out that, according to William Blackstone, stealing animals "kept for pleasure, curiosity, or whim" did not constitute a crime.

24   Harriet Beecher Stowe, "Dogs and Cats," in *Stories and Sketches for the Young,* vol. 14 of *The Writings of Harriet Beecher Stowe,* Riverside ed. (1896; repr., New York: AMS Press, 1967), 109.

25   Tonna, *Kindness to Animals,* 13. See also *The Dog, as an Example of Fidelity* (New York: General Protestant Episcopal Sunday-School Union, 1848), 83: A dog is "not to be regarded as mere property to be disposed of at the will of the owner." This argument was probably based on Psalm 50, verses 10 and 11: "For every beast of the forest *is* mine, *and* the cattle upon a thousand hills. / I know all the fowls of the mountains; and the wild beasts of the field *are* mine." This is one of a handful of biblical verses that advocates for kindness and that appeared repeatedly in nineteenth-century anticruelty literature.

26   John Locke, *Some Thoughts Concerning Education* (1693), section 217. Locke described the assumptions of his own education program for a "gentleman's son, whom, being then very little, I considered only as white paper, or wax, to be moulded and fashioned as one pleases." For a discussion of Locke's influence on progressive child-rearing practices in the United States, see Karin Calvert, *Children in the House: The Material Culture of Early Childhood, 1600–1900* (Boston: Northeastern University Press, 1992), 55–60.

27   Todd, *Sensibility,* 21–27.

28   Calvert, *Children in the House,* 105; quotation from "Childhood," *Godey's Lady's Book,* June 1832, 268. Influential minister Horace Bushnell argued that each child should be viewed as a "spiritually renewed" being, "seeming . . . to have loved what is good from his earliest years" (Horace Bushnell, *Views of Christian Nurture, and of Subjects Adjacent Thereto* [Hartford, Conn.: Edwin Hunt, 1847], 15, 6).

29   Bushnell, *Views of Christian Nurture*, 41, 14.

30   Jacob Abbott, *Agnes: A Franconia Story, by the Author of the Rollo Books* (New York: Harper and Brothers, 1853), v–vi.

31   Lydia Maria Child, *The Mother's Book, by Mrs. Child* (1831; repr., Cambridge, Mass.: Applewood Books, 1989), 6–8.

32   Dr. William A. Alcott, *Gift Book for Young Ladies; or Familiar Letters on Their Acquaintances, Male and Female, Employments, Friendships, &c* (Auburn, N.Y.: Orton and Mulligan, 1854), 271; Karen Halttunen, "Humanitarianism and the Pornography of Pain in Anglo-American Culture," *American Historical Review* 100, no. 2 (April 1995): 323–24. Antebellum arguments about juvenile delinquency similarly operated on the assumption that youthful disobedience led inexorably to future, more serious crime; see David J. Rothman, *The Discovery of the Asylum: Social Order and Disorder in the New Republic* (Boston: Little, Brown, 1971), 76.

33   Muzzy, *Fireside*, 74. See also "Be Kind to Animals," *Youth's Companion*, 2 June 1830, 6; "Cruelty," *Youth's Companion*, 25 July 1832, 6; "Kindness to Brutes," *Youth's Companion*, 21 September 1838, 74–75.

34   Lydia Maria Child, *The Boy's Reading-Book* (New York, 1846), 65, 33–34. For William Cowper as an inspiration to kindness, see "Stories about Cats," *Youth's Companion*, 30 October 1835, 95–96: "A very sweet poet, named Cowper, who loved animals and used to keep hares, a dog, and a cat in his room, and loved to see them sport about so merrily, said, 'he would not call that man his friend who would needlessly tread upon a worm.'" *Youth's Companion* often reprinted material from other periodicals with credit lines; this story was credited to the "Juvenile Miscellany." This passage was paraphrased from Cowper's "The Task" (1784), a 5,000-line work of blank verse that contained a lengthy discussion of cruelty to animals in Book 6, "The Winter Walk at Noon," ll. 560–67. See John D. Baird and Charles Ryskamp, eds., *The Poems of William Cowper*, vol. 2, *1782–1785* (Oxford: Clarendon Press, 1995), 251.

35   Aquinas also argued that cruelty to an animal was sanctioned if it damaged the "temporal" welfare of another person. See Thomas Aquinas, *Summa contra gentiles*, iii, 113. See also Thomas, *Man and the Natural World*, 151.

36   Halttunen, "Humanitarianism and the Pornography of Pain," 303.

37   James Turner, *Reckoning with the Beast: Animals, Pain, and Humanity in the Victorian Mind* (Baltimore: Johns Hopkins University Press, 1980), 9, 12. For a discussion of the circumstances surrounding the publication of these prints

(Hogarth later commented that he was proud of the series, since he believed that it had helped to relieve cruelty to animals) and a detailed visual analysis, see Ronald Paulson, *Hogarth*, vol. 3, *Art and Politics, 1750–1764* (New Brunswick, N.J.: Rutgers University Press, 1991), 17–36.

38   Mary Wollstonecraft, trans., *Elements of Morality for the Use of Children, with an Introductory Address to Parents. Translated From the German of the Rev. C. G. Salzmann*, 3rd American ed. (Wilmington, Del.: Joseph Johnson, 1796). The book was first published in English in 1790. See also *Pity's Gift: A Collection of Interesting Tales to Incite the Compassion of You for the Animal Creation* (London: T. N. Longman and Rees, 1801), a book that was in American hands soon after it was published.

39   "Cruelty and the Gallows," *Youth's Companion*, 22 April 1836, 195.

40   Arnold Arluke, Jack Levin, Carter Luke, and Frank Ascione, "The Relationship of Animal Abuse to Violence and Other Forms of Antisocial Behavior" (unpublished paper presented to the Eighth International Conference on Animal-Human Interactions, Prague, Czech Republic, 12 September 1998).

41   Sigourney, *Letters to Mothers*, 36–37.

42   Elizabeth B. Clark, "'The Sacred Rights of the Weak': Pain, Sympathy, and the Culture of Individual Rights in Antebellum America," *Journal of American History* 82, no. 3 (September 1995): 470, 476.

43   *Youth's Companion*, one of the most popular children's periodicals of the nineteenth century, continued publication until 1929. Nathaniel Willis and Asa Rand intended their publication to "warn against the ways of transgression, error, and ruin, and allure to those of virtue and piety" while it entertained children with a wide variety of stories clipped "from the various publications which we receive and peruse." See "The *Youth's Companion*," in *The History of American Magazines*, vol. 2, *1850–1865*, ed. Frank Luther Mott (Cambridge, Mass.: Harvard University Press, 1938), 262–74.

44   "The Puppy," *Youth's Companion*, 17 August 1838, 55; reprinted from *Youth's Penny Paper*.

45   "The Woodchuck," *Youth's Companion*, 18 December 1835, 123.

46   T. S. Arthur, "The Wounded Bird," *Youth's Companion*, 27 April 1848, 1.

47   Henry Ward Beecher, *Lectures to Young Men, on Various Important Subjects* (1844; 2nd ed., New York: Derby and Jackson, 1859), 147–48.

48   "Home Interests," *Youth's Penny Gazette*, 20 November 1850, 94.

49   Sigourney, *Letters to Mothers*, 37–38.

50   Mrs. Louisa Hoare, *Hints for the Improvement of Early Education and Nursery Discipline*, 3rd ed. (Dover: Samuel C. Stevens, 1826), 36–37.

51   *Master Henry's Rabbit* (Troy, N.Y.: n.p., n.d. [ca. 1840]), 10. *Master Henry's Rabbit* was first published in England. It was one volume in a series of didactic stories about Henry's moral progress. On the matter of thoughtlessness ("absence of mind") and cruelty to animals, see also "'Tenderness to Animals," *Youth's Companion*, 19 December 1834, 125.

52   This had not been true in earlier reformist discussions of child development. For example, in *Thoughts on the Education of Daughters: With Reflections on Female Conduct, in the More Important Duties of Life* (London: Joseph Johnson, 1787), Mary Wollstonecraft, perhaps drawing on Salzmann, included in her chapter "Benevolence" an anecdote about a girl who killed ants "for sport" (44).

53   "The Bird's Nest," *Youth's Companion*, 16 June 1833, 24; reprinted from the *Cincinnati Journal*. For a short story featuring the death of an "innocent" butterfly at the hands of a small girl, see "The Birth Day Present," *Youth's Companion*, 12 March 1829, 165.

54   The author was *Godey's Lady's Book* editor Sarah Josepha Hale, who published it in 1830 and included it in her *Poems for Our Children* and *The Juvenile Miscellany*, a Boston-based children's magazine. The popularity of the poem was guaranteed when it was set to music shortly thereafter by American composer Lowell Mason in an innovative songbook intended for use in elementary schools. By the 1840s, the poem had been incorporated into other children's songbooks and into the ubiquitous *McGuffey's First Reader* (with some textual alterations and without the author's byline). See Ruth E. Finley, *The Lady of Godey's: Sarah Josepha Hale* (Philadelphia: Lippincott, 1931), 279–83; Stanley W. Lindberg, *The Annotated McGuffey: Selections from the McGuffey Eclectic Readers, 1836–1920* (New York: Van Nostrand Reinhold, 1976), 14–15.

55   Jacob Abbott, *Friskie the Pony; or, Do No Harm to Harmless Animals* (1865).

56   [G. H. Hill], *Scenes from the Life of an Actor. By a Celebrated Comedian, Beautifully Illustrated* (1853; repr., New York: Benjamin Blom, 1969), 13.

57   "Against the Abuse of Cattle," *Youth's Companion*, 4 June 1829, 6.

58   Mrs. L. G. Abell, *Woman in Her Various Relations* (New York: R. T. Young, 1851), 53.

59   Dr. William A. Alcott worried that "whatever may be the apology, are not most of the animals around us, whether slain in one way or another—for food or for defence—are they not slain for sport? Where is the boy or young man to be found who hunts, entraps, fishes, &c., for any better reason . . . than because it is an amusement to him?" (Alcott, *Gift Book for Young Ladies*, 274).

60   "Nauticus Agricola" [pseud.], "The Murdered Robin," *Youth's Companion*, 23 June 1837, [illegible].

61   Alcott, *Gift Book for Young Ladies,* 273. Harriet Beecher Stowe, "Rights of
      Dumb Animals," *Hearth and Home,* January 1869, 24. See also "Be Kind to
      Animals," *Youth's Companion,* 2 June 1830, 6. For the continuing nineteenth-
      century debate about hunting, see Daniel Justin Herman, *Hunting and the
      American Imagination* (Washington, D.C.: Smithsonian Institution Press,
      2001).

62   William Lyon Phelps, *Autobiography with Letters* (New York: Oxford Univer-
      sity Press, 1939), 60–61.

63   H. H. Delong, *Boyhood Reminiscences: Dansville, N.Y., 1855–1865* (Dans-
      ville, N.Y.: F. A. Owen, 1913), 56; Claudia L. Bushman, ed., "Life along the
      Brandywine between 1880 and 1895 by Samuel Canby Rumford," pt. 2,
      Delaware History 23, no. 3 (Spring/Summer 1989): 168, 195; Henry Ward
      Beecher, "Country Stillness and Woodchucks," in *Eyes and Ears* (Boston:
      Ticknor and Fields, 1862), 139–41.

64   The metaphor of the hunt was still in common use throughout the 1800s to
      represent the economic activity of middle-class men. See Katherine C. Grier,
      "Material Culture as Rhetoric: Animal Artifacts as a Case Study," in *American
      Material Culture: The Shape of the Field,* ed. J. Ritchie Garrison and Ann
      Smart Martin (New York: Norton, 1997), 65–104.

65   For boys' taxidermy and amateur "cabinets" as an educational form of play, see
      Charley's Museum: A Story for Young People (Philadelphia: H. C. Peck and
      Theo. Bliss, 1857); Phelps, *Autobiography with Letters,* 54–55; Bellamy Par-
      tridge, *Big Family* (New York: Whittlesey House, 1941), 305.

66   See Clifton F. Hodge, Ph.D., *Nature Study and Life* (Boston: Ginn and Co.,
      1902), chap. 4, "Plan for Insect Study," 45–62.

67   Caroline Cowles Richards, *Village Life in America, 1852–1872* (Williams-
      town, Mass.: Corner House, 1972), 61–62.

68   Charles Neider, ed., *Papa: An Intimate Biography of Mark Twain By Susy
      Clemens, His Daughter, Thirteen, with a Foreword and Copious Commentary
      by Her Father* (Garden City, N.Y.: Doubleday, 1985), 155–56.

69   Claudia L. Bushman, ed., "Life along the Brandywine between 1880 and
      1895 by Samuel Canby Rumford," pt. 3, *Delaware History* 23, no. 4 (Fall/Win-
      ter 1989): 254–55; Bushman, "Life along the Brandywine," pt. 1, 138–39,
      and pt. 3, 248–51.

70   Lewis Henry Miller (1796–1882), the author of a large watercolor manuscript
      of everyday life in York County, Pennsylvania, illustrated a number of incidents
      along this line. "Wendel Reichel and the Cat, 1807" depicts a man strangling to

death a cat caught raiding his "meat tub." See Lewis Henry Miller, *Sketches and Chronicles: The Reflections of a Nineteenth Century Pennsylvania Folk Artist* (York, Pa.: Historical Society of York County, 1966), 58.

71 Elizabeth F. Crane, ed., *The Diary of Elizabeth Drinker* (Boston: Northeastern University Press, 1991), 1:556.

72 Samuel Clemens [Mark Twain, pseud.], *The Autobiography of Mark Twain,* ed. Charles Neider (New York: Harper and Rowe, 1966), 29–30.

73 Turner, *Reckoning with the Beast,* 45–46.

74 Lydia Maria Child, *Letters from New-York* (New York: Charles S. Francis, 1843), 10.

75 *Twelfth Annual Report of the Women's Branch of the Pennsylvania Society for the Prevention of Cruelty to Animals, for the Year Ending December 31, 1880* (Philadelphia: PSPCA, 1881), 10.

76 Beecher, *Lectures to Young Men,* 223.

77 See Peter W. Cook, "Cockfighting in North America and New England, 1680–1900," in *New England's Creatures, 1400–1900,* Dublin Seminar for New England Folklife Annual Proceedings, 1993, ed. Peter Benes and Jane Montague Benes (Boston: Boston University Press, 1995), 164–82. Lewis Miller's sketchbooks of everyday life in York County, Pennsylvania, illustrate a "Bear-Beat" and "Panther beat" on the common in the town of York drawing crowds of boys and men in the early nineteenth century. In retrospect, Miller called the bear bait a "barbarous custom" (Miller, *Sketches and Chronicles,* 29, 48, 62). Yankee Hill remembered gaining admission to a traveling menagerie set up on the Taunton, Massachusetts, town green as a boy by furnishing the tiger with "one cat, against whom I had a grudge." Her "monument [gravestone] was the 'tiger's maw'" ([Hill], *Scenes from the Life of an Actor,* 29).

78 Paul E. Johnson, "Strange Cargo: The *Michigan* Descent at Niagara" (unpublished paper read at the Conference on Festive Culture and Public Ritual, American Philosophical Society, 13 April 1996).

79 Richard B. Stott, ed., *William Otter: History of My Own Times* (Ithaca, N.Y.: Cornell University Press, 1995), 81–84, 146–49, 153, 167.

80 Michael Kaplan offers examples of the strategic, symbolic use of violence among working-class men in antebellum America in "New York City Tavern Violence and the Creation of a Working-Class Male Identity," *Journal of the Early Republic* 15 (Winter 1995): 591–617.

81 The early literature of the domestic ethic of kindness resolutely blurred class distinctions. See Turner, *Reckoning with the Beast,* 46–56. "Cruelty," *Youth's*

Companion, 25 July 1832, 39, makes explicit the connection between torturing insects as a boy and whipping a cart horse as a man.

82   Turner, *Reckoning with the Beast,* 79–82.

83   Utilitarian philosopher Jeremy Bentham's famous comment on animals and
      pain appeared as a speculative note: "The day *may* come, when the rest of the
      animal creation may acquire those rights which never could have been with-
      holden from them but by the hand of tyranny. . . . The question is not, Can
      they *reason?* nor Can they *talk?* but, Can they *suffer?*" (*An Introduction to the
      Principles of Morals and Legislation [1789],* chap. 17, sec. 1, <http://www.la
      .utexas.edu/ labyrinth/ipml/ipml.c17.s01.n02.html>).

      Reverend Dr. Humphrey Primatt, *A Dissertation on the Duty of Mercy and
      Sin of Cruelty to Brute Animals* (1776), was an "endeavor to plead the cause of
      the Dumb Creatures on the Principles of Natural Religion, Justice, Honour,
      and Humanity." Primatt argued that "pain is pain, whether it be inflicted on
      man or on beast; and the creature that suffers it, whether man or beast, being
      sensible of the misery of it while it lasts, suffers *Evil"* (Primatt, quoted in
      Turner, *Reckoning with the Beast,* 9–10).

84   While Keith Thomas has argued that the scholastic conception of the "beast-
      machine," an idea for which Descartes is best known, prevented recognition
      of animal pain, I argue that Descartes's model was never a popularly held idea
      but part of a separate discourse of academic science. Rather, people knew
      that animals and people felt pain. The question was whether pain was justi-
      fied or mattered, and whether the strong had the right to inflict pain on the
      weak. See Thomas, *Man and the Natural World,* 34–36.

85   Crane, *Diary of Elizabeth Drinker,* 2:1341.

86   Anne Hampton Brewster, diary, 1859–60, entry for 9 May 1859, Library
      Company of Philadelphia, Philadelphia, Pa.

87   Longfellow Diary, 11 September 1848, quoted in Dye and Smith, "Mother
      Love and Infant Death," 342.

88   Jack P. Greene, ed., *The Diary of Colonel Landon Carter of Sabine Hall,
      1752–1778,* 2 vols. (Charlottesville: University Press of Virginia for the Vir-
      ginia Historical Society, 1965), 1:216.

89   *Pennsylvania Packet (Claypoole's American Daily Advertiser),* 15 September
      1796.

90   *Pity's Gift,* 3rd ed., 69–71.

91   In its depiction of "service as an ideal sentimental community and the servant
      ties as filial and parental," the literature of the servant animal runs parallel to

literature that depicted the relations of kindly masters and loyal human servants in the mid- and late eighteenth century. See Todd, *Sensibility*, 13.

92 Wayland, *Elements of Moral Science*, 395. The most comprehensive account
of animal "crime and punishment" remains E. P. Evans, *The Criminal Prose-
cution and Capital Punishment of Animals* (1906; repr., London: Faber and
Faber, 1987). An example of this older strain of thinking about animals appears in the *Chronicles* of Lewis Henry Miller (1786–1882). A lifelong resident of York County, Pennsylvania, Miller produced an illustrated
remembrance of everyday life in his town. He told and illustrated the story of
"Mrs. Cath. Weiser frying a sausage, and A hound came and Stole it out of the
pan for his breakfast." Miller warned, "Woman Guard Your Kitchen. . . .
Teach a dog and put him in a way to fulfill his demands, and you make him a
Moral Agent" (Miller, *Sketches and Chronicles*, 82).

93 For a discussion of the tradition of drawing moral lessons from animals in pop-
ular natural histories, see Harriet Ritvo, *The Animal Estate: The English and
Other Creatures in the Victorian Age* (Cambridge, Mass.: Harvard University
Press, 1987), 15–30.

94 Sigourney, *Letters to Mothers*, 98. In *Pity's Gift*, a poem called "Epitaph on a
Lap-Dog" recited virtues of the animal and ended the verse with the lines,
"Such was the being underneath this shrine; / Study the character, and make
it *thine*" (76).

95 "Stories about Cats," *Youth's Companion*, 30 October 1835, 95–96.

96 "Thomas and His Chickens," *Youth's Companion*, 6 July 1827, 24. See also
"The Hen," *Youth's Companion*, 6 February 1835, 150 ("Extract from the 'IN-
TELLIGENT READER' recently published by Messrs. G. & C. MERRIAM,
Springfield").

97 For a more detailed discussion of metaphors and theories of metaphor in relation to material culture and attitudes toward animals, see Grier, "Material
Culture as Rhetoric."

98 Richard Tapper notes that animal stories can serve three purposes: "*through
non-human metaphor* they allow teachers and learners to avoid articulating difficult or embarrassing truths about humanities; they *create a distinction* between
human beings and other animals; and they can *reinforce morality* by giving it a
'natural' basis" (Richard Tapper, "Animality, Humanity, Morality, Society," in
What Is an Animal?, ed. Tim Ingold [London: Unwin Hyman, 1988], 51).

99 Child, *Boy's Reading-Book*, 37. See also "Canine Sagacity," *Youth's Companion*, 17 October 1828, 83; "Canine Affection," *Youth's Companion*, 3 October

1828, 75; "The Lives of Two Children Saved by a Dog," *Youth's Companion,* 16 September 1829, 68.

100   *The Dog, as an Example of Fidelity,* 10, 38. The copy I have examined was presented as a gift to a child: "George S. Payne / a token of affection from the Rector. / Grace Church, Christmas 1848."

101   "Animal Gratitude," *Youth's Companion,* 14 March 1827, 167, from "London paper"; "The Grateful Lioness," *Youth's Companion,* 19 May 1830, 207, from the *London Youth's Magazine;* "A Grateful Cow," *Youth's Companion,* 5 October 1831, 70, from the *Cheltenham Chronicle.*

102   "Anecdote of a Cat," *Youth's Companion,* 18 April 1828, 187; "Anecdote of a Cat" in *The Cabinet of Natural History and American Rural Sport* (Philadelphia: J. and T. Doughty, 1832), 2:246. In the latter source, the story is credited to *Good's Book of Nature.*

103   "Attachment of a Swallow," *Youth's Companion,* 2 September 1836, 62, reprinted from the *Greenfield Adv.; The Book of Household Pets, and How to Manage Them* (New York: Dick and Fitzgerald, 1866), 5. Keith Thomas notes that the family life of birds was occasionally the object of admiration in the seventeenth century. William Ramsay commented with pleasure on his pigeons' "mutual love, chastity, and constancy, obedience of the hen to the cock pigeon, care of the cock to the young," in *Man's Dignity* (1661). See Thomas, *Man and the Natural World,* 121.

104   *Picture Lessons, Illustrating Moral Truth.* For the Use of Infant Schools, Nurseries, Sunday-Schools, and Family Circles (Philadelphia: American Sunday-School Union, n.d.). The copy in the collection of the Winterthur Library is inscribed, "Zilpha Clarke / from LaFayette H.(?) S. School / Buffalo Apl 25, 1852."

105   "The Little Orphan Birds," *Youth's Companion,* 7 August 1835, 47. "The Robin," a poem included in *Boy's Reading-Book,* and Harriet Beecher Stowe's "The Nest in the Orchard" both used the formula of a destruction of a bird family. Each began with the death of the male at the hands of a hunter and chronicled the eventual death of the female and her brood from starvation, grief, or further hunting. See "The Robin," in Child, *Boy's Reading-Book,* 139–40; Harriet Beecher Stowe, "The Nest in the Orchard," in *Stories and Sketches for the Young,* vol. 16 of *The Writings of Harriet Beecher Stowe,* Riverside ed. (Boston, 1898), 334–38. Threats to other animal families also received occasional attention. See "The Cow and Her Calf," *Youth's Companion,* 21 September 1831, 72; "Barbarity of Whale Fishing," *Youth's Companion,* 4 July 1827, 23; "Remarkable Attachment of a Goat," *Youth's Companion,* 6 April 1831, 183.

This part of the domestic ethic of kindness to animals also doubled as a covert discussion about violence against families at a time of increasing interest in many kinds of social reforms. The temperance movement and the antislavery cause are the two most familiar today, but a public crusade against corporal punishment was also undertaken. See Myra C. Glenn, *Campaigns against Corporal Punishment: Prisoners, Sailors, Women, and Children in Antebellum America* (Albany: State University of New York Press, 1984), 30, 80.

106   Calvert, *Children in the House,* chap. 1, "The Upright Child: Swaddling Clothes and Walking Stools," 19–38.

107   Sigourney, *Letters to Mothers,* 39; Tonna, *Kindness to Animals,* 41.

108   Abell, *Woman in Her Various Relations,* 223; W. A. Wickham, *Practical Training of the Shepherd Dog* (Tipton, Iowa: by the author, 1891), 72, 80.

109   See also "Grace Greenwood" [Sarah J. Lippincott], *Heads and Tails: Studies and Stories of Pets* (New York: J. B. Ford, 1874).

110   Novels using dogs as plot devices included *A Dog's Mission* (Boston: Houghton Mifflin, 1881) and *We and Our Neighbors* (New York: J. B. Ford, 1875).

111   Harriet Beecher Stowe, "Our Dogs," in *Stories and Sketches for the Young,* vol. 16 of *The Writings of Harriet Beecher Stowe,* Riverside ed. (1896; repr., New York: AMS Press, 1967), 65–67, 71, 78, 79. Compare Stowe's descriptions of canine personalities with the following passage from the chapter "The Feelings of Living Property" in *Uncle Tom's Cabin,* wherein Mrs. Shelby objects to her husband's plan to sell Uncle Tom and describes the plantation's slaves: "O, Mr. Shelby, I have tried . . . to do my duty to these poor, simple, dependent creatures. . . . And how can I ever hold my head up again among them, if, for the sake of a little paltry gain, we sell such a faithful, excellent, confiding creature as poor Tom?" (Harriet Beecher Stowe, *Three Novels: Uncle Tom's Cabin or, Life Among the Lowly; The Minister's Wooing; Oldtown Folks* [New York: Library of America, 1982], 47).

112   Harriet Beecher Stowe, "Dogs and Cats," in *Stories and Sketches for the Young,* 103.

113   We commonly compare children to monkeys now, but in the nineteenth century the comparison of humans and primates almost always bore negative racial or class connotations. See Grier, "Material Culture as Rhetoric."

114   For an example of the use of the term "juveniles," see the reproductions of Currier and Ives advertising brochures in *Currier and Ives: A Catalogue Raisonné,* 2 vols. (Detroit: Gale Research, 1983), xli–xlii.

115   See also *The Two Pets,* colored lithograph, published by Nathaniel Currier,

New York, 1848; *Household Pets*, colored lithograph, published by Nathaniel Currier, New York, 1845.

116   For an explanation of the role of the trade card in the United States, including its important status as an early collectible, see Robert Jay, *The Trade Card in Nineteenth-Century America* (Columbia: University of Missouri Press, 1987).

117   The quilt featuring *Can't You Talk?* is in the collection of the National Museum of American History, Behring Center, Smithsonian Institution, Washington, D.C. The hooked rug is illustrated in Wendy Lavitt, *Animals in American Folk Art* (New York: Alfred A. Knopf, 1990), 51.

118   *Can't You Talk?* was already in circulation in several American versions when, in June 1878, *Our Dumb Animals*, the newspaper published by the Massachusetts Society for the Prevention of Cruelty to Animals, published it as a wood engraving by a Boston printer named Kilburn. The explanatory text imposed a one-directional interpretation on the image: "The intelligent four-footed playfellow understands all the child says, and does all the child requires, except answering his question! How kindly they look into each other's eyes, and how beautiful both are." The kitten is described as "a third witness" who demonstrates "the wide kinship of sympathy."

119   Sarah J. Eddy's compilation *Friends and Helpers* (Boston: Ginn and Co., 1899) included excerpts from the poetry of Shelley, Wordsworth, Emerson, Longfellow, and Dickinson, along with poems, stories, and essays urging kindness to animals that had been published explicitly for children during the nineteenth century by such authors as Lucy Larcom and Harriet Beecher Stowe. *Friends and Helpers* was extensively illustrated with reproductions of paintings by Rosa Bonheur, Sir Edwin Landseer, and others, along with photographs by Eddy.

120   Flora L. Carpenter, *Stories Pictures Tell*, bk. 1 (Chicago: Rand, McNally, 1918), 50. Anna M. Von Rydingsvärd, author of *Art Studies for Schools, or, Hints on the Use of High Art in the School Room* (1903), also discussed the merits and interpretation of the picture at some length.

121   Stowe, "Rights of Dumb Animals," 24.

122   The effects of these first-person accounts paralleled the impact of the antebellum slave narratives that have been credited with helping to expand the definition of cruelty to others by challenging "the 'right' to private violence against persons." First-person slave narratives "established their authors as fully sentient and ardent in their desires for freedom, love, family; this contrast made their brutalization the more horrific" (Clark, "'Sacred Rights of the Weak,'"

463–64, 470). See also Sydney H. Coleman, *Humane Society Leaders in America, with a Sketch of the Early History of the Humane Movement in England* (Albany, N.Y.: American Humane Association, 1924), 75–76.

123   Mark Twain, *A Dog's Tale* (1903; 1st American ed., New York: Harper and Brothers, 1905).

124   Locke, *Some Thoughts Concerning Education,* 113. We should note here that Locke did not use the term "pet" in his account (recall that, according to the *Oxford English Dictionary,* it was a relatively new word), although his phrase "use to be delighted with" and the list of animals suggests that the animals he mentioned were just that.

125   Muzzy, *Fireside,* 141–42. *Sweet Counsel: A Book for Girls* was a series of epistolary letters directed to an older girl named Mary. The "letter writer" advised, "If you wish your little brother and sister to have loving, fond little hearts, do your best to provide them with pets, as you have pets. They are almost, if not quite, as necessary to them as congenial companions. . . . If you would have children's hearts open, and their tenderness called forth betimes, get them pets, and let them be good to them, as far as their means allow" (Sarah Tyler [Henriette Keddie], *Sweet Counsel: A Book for Girls* [Boston: Roberts Bros., 1866], 154–56).

126   J. L. V. Lesley to Harriet Maria Elmendorf, 11 January 1874, Historic Cherry Hill, Albany, N.Y.

127   Beecher and Stowe, *American Woman's Home,* 394.

128   Sara Josepha Hale, *Manners; or, Happy Homes and Good Society All the Year Round* (1868; repr., New York: Arno Press, 1972), 244. On boyhood "tyranny," see also S. S. Messenger, "Edward and the Cat," *Youth's Companion,* 19 February 1829, 153–54: "You were unmerciful to the cat. . . . You were too proud to forgive a dumb beast for not obeying you; and like a little tyrant, would have had her put to death."

129   Adelaide F. Samuels, "How to Make and Stock an Aquarium," *St. Nicholas: Scribner's Illustrated Magazine for Girls and Boys,* February 1876, 254–57; Ernest Ingersoll, "A Talk about Canaries," ibid., February 1877, 247–54; Daniel C. Beard, "How to Stock and Keep a Fresh-Water Aquarium," ibid., July 1881, 696–703.

130   Olive Thorne Miller, *Our Home Pets: How to Keep Them Well and Happy* (New York: Harper and Brothers, 1894), 4. In 1905, George Angell, founder of both the Massachusetts Society for the Prevention of Cruelty to Animals and the American Humane Education Association, argued that "out of two

thousand criminals inquired of in American prisons, some years ago, it was found that only twelve had any pet during their childhood" (Unti, "Quality of Mercy," 496).

131   Jacob Biggle, *The Biggle Pet Book: A Collection of Information for Old and Young Whose Natural Instincts Teach Them to Be Kind to All Living Creatures* (Philadelphia: Wilmer Atkinson, 1900), 7–8.

132   Unti, "Quality of Mercy," 496–97.

133   Caroline S. Kirkland, "The Bee Tree," in *Western Clearings* (1845; repr., New York: Garrett Press, 1969), 76.

134   Beecher and Stowe, *American Woman's Home,* 394.

135   In an interesting allusion to what would now be called clinical depression, Miller also called for the "cheerful-thought cure," aided by pets (*Our Home Pets,* 195–96).

136   Chas. N. Page, *Parrots and Other Talking Birds* (Des Moines, Iowa: by the author, 1906), 4.

137   Medical Department, Equitable Life Assurance Society of the United States, *Pets: For Assurance of a Fuller Life* (New York, 1956), 48.

138   Gail F. Melson, "Fostering Inter-Connectedness with Animals and Nature: The Developmental Benefits for Children," in *People, Animals, Environment,* Fall 1990, 15–17, accessed through <http:/www.deltasociety.org>.

CHAPTER FOUR

1   Useful collections of this work include Roy Willis, ed., *Signifying Animals: Human Meaning in the Natural World* (London: Unwin Hyman, 1990); Tim Ingold, ed., *What Is an Animal?* (London: Unwin Hyman, 1988). An influential essay is Edmund R. Leach, "Anthropological Aspects of Language: Animal Categories and Verbal Abuse," in *New Directions in the Study of Language,* ed. Eric H. Lenneberg (Cambridge, Mass.: MIT Press, 1964), 23–63.

2   Betty Bright Low and Jacqueline Hinsley, *Sophie du Pont: A Young Lady in America. Sketches, Diaries, and Letters, 1823–1833* (New York: Harry N. Abrams, 1987), 94.

3   James Serpell, *In the Company of Animals,* chap. 4, "Pets in Tribal Societies," 48–58.

4   Susan D. Jones, *Valuing Animals: Veterinarians and Their Patients in Modern America* (Baltimore: Johns Hopkins University Press, 2002), 17–25, 40–47. In the poorer neighborhoods of Philadelphia, a handful of vendors continued to sell vegetables from horse-drawn carts until at least the 1960s.

5   Samuel Eliot Morrison, *One Boy's Boston, 1887–1901* (Boston: Houghton Mifflin, 1962), 22–25.

6   George A. Martin, *The Family Horse: Its Stabling, Care, and Feeding* (New York: Orange Judd, 1889), 5.

7   Jones, *Valuing Animals,* 47.

8   Martin V. Melosi, *Garbage in the Cities: Refuse, Reform, and the Environment, 1880–1980* (College Station: Texas A&M University Press, 1981), 27. See also Joel Tarr, "Urban Pollution—Many Long Years Ago," *American Heritage,* October 1971, 65–69, 106. The term "domestic animal economy" comes from Susan Dorothy Jones, D.V.M., "Animal Value, Veterinary Medicine, and the Domestic Animal Economy in the United States, 1890–1930" (Ph.D. diss., University of Pennsylvania, 1997), 5–7.

9   A detailed account of efforts on behalf of urban workhorses may be found in Bernard Oreste Unti, "The Quality of Mercy: Organized Animal Protection in the United States, 1866–1930" (Ph.D. diss., American University, 2002), chap. 11, "'Goodbye Old Man': The Passing of the Horse," 436–67.

10   Morrison, *One Boy's Boston,* 25–26. Morrison recalled that "a frequent sight in winter was that of a horse falling down in harness, through slipping or exhaustion."

11   J. F. Smithcors, *The American Veterinary Profession: Its Background and Development* (Ames: Iowa State University Press, 1963), 279–81. See also James P. McClure, "The Epizootic of 1872: Horses and Disease in a Nation in Motion," *New York History* 79 (January 1998): 4–22.

12   My rough figure is based on George Martin's estimates of horse numbers divided by the population of the United States in 1890 found in U.S. Census Bureau, *Historical Statistics of the United States, 1790–1970* (Washington, D.C.: GPO, 1976). For the purposes of comparison: in 1997 there were 208 million registered motor vehicles in the United States serving a population of around 270 million, almost one registered motor vehicle per person. See U.S. Census Bureau, "A Century of Change: America, 1900–1999," at <http://www.census.gov/Press-Release/www/1999/cb99-ff17.html>.

13   Billheads for Rainey and Glover, Metropolitan Sale and Exchange Stables, 6th Street, Washington, D.C., 18 February 1865; Monteith and Smith Livery Stables, Philadelphia, Pa., 1 May 1856, in Warshaw Collection of Business Americana, National Museum of American History, Smithsonian Institution, Washington, D.C. (hereafter WCBA).

14   Business card for Alfred H. Bates, Livery, Sale, and Boarding Stables, 17 Blanding Street, Utica, N.Y., ca. 1880, in WCBA.

15   Claudia L. Bushman, ed., "Life along the Brandywine between 1880 and
      1895 by Samuel Canby Rumford," pt. 2, *Delaware History* 23, no. 3 (Spring/
      Summer 1989): 178–79.

16   William Lyon Phelps, *Autobiography with Letters* (New York: Oxford Univer-
      sity Press, 1939), 9–10.

17   Ethel Spencer, *The Spencers of Amberson Avenue: A Turn-of-the-Century
      Memoir* (Pittsburgh: University of Pittsburgh Press, 1983), 8.

18   In his entry for 28 October 1857, mechanic Aaron Greenwood recorded rent-
      ing a horse and buggy for one dollar so he could attend a funeral in another
      town beyond walking distance. See Windsor C. Robinson, ed., *The Diary of
      Aaron Greenwood,* vol. 1, *August 30, 1857 to July 6, 1859* (Gardner, Mass.:
      Gardner Historical Commission, 1963), 79.

19   H. H. Delong, *Boyhood Reminiscences: Dansville, N.Y., 1855–1865* (Dans-
      ville, N.Y.: F. A. Owen, 1913), 25. Delong's father and Uncle Ed kept a "part-
      nership mare" named Kate in the 1850s; she lived in Uncle Ed's backyard.

20   Robert S. Lynd and Helen Merrell Lynd, *Middletown: A Study in American
      Culture* (New York: Harcourt, Brace, 1929), 251–52.

21   Jones, "Animal Value," 49, 50.

22   Martin, *Family Horse;* see also Professor Oscar R. Gleason, *Gleason's Horse
      Book* (Chicago: M. A. Donohue, 1892). On the title page, Gleason is de-
      scribed as "America's King of Horse Tamers."

23   Emily Holt, *Encyclopedia of Household Economy* (New York: McClure,
      Phillips, 1903), 133.

24   M. E. W. Sherwood, *Home Amusements* (New York: D. Appleton, 1881),
      144–45.

25   Ellen Tucker Emerson to Edward Emerson, from Concord, 25 March 1861, in
      The Letters of Ellen Tucker Emerson, ed. Edith E. W. Gregg (Kent, Ohio: Kent
      State University Press, 1982), 1:231–32.

26   F. H. Moore, "Horse or Automobile?," *Country Life,* March 1910, 564; John R.
      McMahon, *Success in the Suburbs: How to Locate, Buy, and Build; Garden
      and Grow Fruit; Keep Fowl and Animals* (New York: G. P. Putnam's Sons,
      1917), 273–74.

27   "Pony Contests Arouse Retail Trade Enthusiasm for Live Retail Stores," *Nov-
      elty News,* June 1916, 36.

28   Jones, *Valuing Animals,* 17–18.

29   Jones, "Animal Value," 6.

30   Bushman, "Life along the Brandywine," pt. 2, 169–70, 188.

31 Nan Hayden Agle, *My Animals and Me: An Autobiographical Story* (New York: Seabury Press, n.d.), 5.

32 Delong, *Boyhood Reminiscences*, 6.

33 On urban cows, see Jones, *Valuing Animals*, 21–22, 65–74.

34 Delong, *Boyhood Reminiscences*, 6.

35 Claudia L. Bushman, ed., "Life along the Brandywine between 1880 and 1895 by Samuel Canby Rumford," pt. 1, *Delaware History* 23, no. 2 (Fall/Winter 1988): 128.

36 Agle, *My Animals and Me*, 44–45. On sharing a cow, see also Robinson, *Diary of Aaron Greenwood*, 44. On being "flooded with milk" after the butcher took away the cow's calf, see Ellen Tucker Emerson, letter to Ralph Waldo Emerson, 3 August 1858, in Gregg, *Letters of Ellen Tucker Emerson*, 1:145.

37 Spencer, *Spencers of Amberson Avenue*, 4–5.

38 *Keeping One Cow; Being the Experience of a Number of Practical Writers, in a Clear and Condensed Form, upon the Management of a Single Milch Cow* (1888; rev. ed., New York: Orange Judd, 1906), vi, viii.

39 Henry E. Alvord, "The Village Cow in New England: Being the Journal of the Keeper," in *Keeping One Cow*, 35–50. Alvord described himself as owning "a comfortable little home in a village of a few thousand inhabitants . . . supporting my family by a moderate income earned from day to day." He was "fond" of work in his garden and "of domestic animals, all kinds of which were familiar to me as a boy" (35).

40 Christopher Shearer, "Jerusalem Artichokes as Cow-Feed," in *Keeping One Cow*, 71–72.

41 Meat was important and valued, but it was also the subject of some ambivalence in theories of health at the time. Recall the antebellum debate regarding "overstimulation," where the passions could become so aroused that they were difficult to control; some diet reformers believed that too much meat in the diet aroused the passions. See, for example, R. T. Thrall, M.D., *The New Hydropathic Cook-Book; with Recipes for Cooking on Hygienic Principles* (New York: Fowler and Wells, 1854), 5. This was a controversial point, but almost everyone agreed that too much meat in the diet could have an "overheating" effect. For the debate about meat, see Harvey Green, *Fit for America* (New York: Pantheon, 1986), xx.

42 "Marianne" [pseud.], *Right and Wrong; or Familiar Illustrations of the Moral Duties of Children* (Boston: William Peirce, 1834), 35.

43 Charles Neider, ed., *Papa: An Intimate Biography of Mark Twain by Suzy*

Clemens, His Daughter, Thirteen, with a Foreward and Copious Commentary by Her Father (Garden City, N.Y.: Doubleday, 1985), 152. The source for this appears to be Clemens's manuscript "A Record of the Small Foolishes of Susie & 'Bay' Clemens," kept intermittently between 1876 and 1885, entry for 7 June 1885 (typescript in possession of the Mark Twain House).

44   Clara Clemens, *My Father Mark Twain* (New York: Harper and Brothers, 1931), 28–29.

45   Emily W. Rankin, stories about Catherine B. Putnam's childhood, n.d. [1960s], box 250, file 14, Historic Cherry Hill Collections, Albany, N.Y.

46   Letter from Pearl Hobart, San Francisco, in "The Letter Box," *St. Nicholas: Scribner's Illustrated Magazine for Girls and Boys* (hereafter SN), July 1877, 636.

47   Mary Ellen Chase, with illustrations by Paul Kennedy, *Victoria: A Pig in a Pram* (New York: Norton, 1963).

48   The following account is drawn from the Margaret Harding Tileston Edsall Diaries, courtesy Schlesinger Library, Radcliffe College, Cambridge, Mass. (hereafter MHTED).

49   Entries for 16 February, 18, 30 March, 23 April, 1 May, 1 June 1878, MHTED.

50   "Animals," section titled "Anecdotes of Cattle," MHTED.

51   Entries for 15, 20 January, 21 May 1881, MHTED.

52   Entries for 4, 6 January 1881, MHTED.

53   Marlene Deahl Merrill, ed., *Growing Up in Boston's Gilded Age: The Journal of Alice Stone Blackwell, 1872–1874* (New Haven: Yale University Press, 1990), 53, 108, 129.

54   Poem by "Little Gobbler" from Brooklyn, N.Y., in "Our Post-Office Box," *Harper's Young People,* 30 November 1886, 79. I recall that, in the early 1960s, my elementary school music teacher's arsenal of seasonal songs included a Thanksgiving ditty in the voice of a turkey: "Thanksgiving Day is coming, gobble gobble gobble gobble, and I know I'll be eaten soon. . . . I would like to run away. . . . I don't like Thanksgiving Day."

55   Jacob Biggle, *The Biggle Pet Book: A Collection of Information for Old and Young Whose Natural Instincts Teach Them to Be Kind to All Living Creatures* (Philadelphia: Wilmer Atkinson, 1900), 84.

56   For a recent study on the aesthetics of "fancy" as they related to nineteenth-century decorative arts, see Sumpter Priddy, *American Fancy: Exuberance in the Arts, 1790–1840* (Milwaukee, Wisc.: Chipstone Foundation, 2004), esp. chap. 1, "A Brief History of Fancy," 1–16.

57   The first published account in English of fancy pigeons is found in John Ray, *The Ornithology of Francis Willoughby* (1678), where ten varieties were pictured. See also T. B. Coombe Williams, *A Bibliography of the Books Treating on Fancy Pigeons Contained in the Library of T. B. Coombe Williams* (1887; repr., Paoli, Pa.: John E. Norris, 1983), 16. The first English book devoted exclusively to pigeon breeding is John Moore, *Columbarium; or the Pigeonhouse, Being an Introduction to a Natural History of Tame Pigeons* (London: J. Wilford, 1735). This book was reprinted at least three times in the nineteenth century, and many authors cribbed from it. For Darwin's relationship to the pigeon fancy, see James A. Secord, "Nature's Fancy: Charles Darwin and the Breeding of Pigeons," *Isis,* June 1981, 162–86.

58   "Fancy Pigeons," *South Carolina Temperance Advocate and Register of Agriculture and General Literature,* 9 June 1842, 3.

59   The first exhibition of the Pennsylvania Poultry Society, held in November 1852, offered two-dollar prizes for the best pairs of Fantails, Croppers, "White Ruffs" (Jacobins?), and "Buff Carriers." The latter were not messenger pigeons but large birds with elaborate wattles around their beaks that took years to grow. See Pennsylvania Poultry Society, *Report of the Exhibition, Held at Philadelphia, November 24th, 25th and 26th, 1852* (Philadelphia: King and Baird, 1853), 11.

60   United States Centennial Commission, *Special Catalogue of the Display of Poultry* (Philadelphia: Sherman and Co., 1876).

61   William G. Barton, "Pigeons and the Pigeon Fancy," *Bulletin of the Essex Institute,* May–June 1884, 62–63.

62   Henry Wysham Lanier, "The Fun of Fancy Pigeons," *Country Life in America,* November 1914, 44–45.

63   W. B. Tegetmeier, F.Z.S., *Pigeons: Their Structure, Varieties, Habits, and Management* (London: George Routledge and Sons, 1868), 49.

64   "Some Pigeon Fanciers of Syracuse and their Collections," *Herald,* Syracuse, N.Y., 25 December 1898. An article in the June 1916 issue of *House and Garden* praised the pigeon fancy as a "cosmopolitan hobby" where "the prosperous businessman, the retired clergyman, and the school boy and the truck driver meet on a common level" (E. I. Farrington, "The Fun in Raising Fancy Pigeons," *House and Garden,* June 1916, 35).

65   "Choice Pets Free as Premiums," *Pet and Animals,* 1 September 1899, 15.

66   Examples of the literature promoting this kind of husbandry include F. Arthur Hazard, *Profitable Pigeon Breeding: A Practical Manual Explaining How to Breed Pigeons Successfully,—Whether as a Hobby or as an Exclusive Business*

(Washington, Mo.: American Pigeon Journal Co., 1922), and F. L. Washburn, *The Rabbit Book: A Practical Manual on the Care of Belgian Hares, Flemish Giants and other Meat and Fur Producing Rabbits* (Philadelphia: Lippincott, 1920).

67   The American Fur Fancier's Association, founded in 1906, pointed out that "scientific breeding" was one of the interests of its membership; in the early days of lab animal research, the pet stock fancy was an important source of both animals (mice, rats, and guinea pigs) and practical advice. For a discussion of the link between the mouse fancy and early scientific interest in establishing colonies of mice for laboratory research, see Karen A. Rader, *Making Mice: Standardizing Animals for American Biomedical Research, 1900–1955* (Princeton: Princeton University Press, 2004), 30–38.

68   The depredations of cattle, sheep, goats, and swine on gardens, orchards, public roads, and even graveyards, and of stray dogs on these animals in turn, led to early and repeatedly unsuccessful efforts to control beasts with fencing, ringing and yoking, impounding, and even destruction in the case of dogs. New Amsterdam, for example, had passed its first law prohibiting roaming hogs and goats in 1648, and its sheriff made the first request for a stray dog ordinance in 1660, apparently out of a desire to avoid being attacked during his nightly rounds. See John A. Duffy, *The History of Public Health in New York City, 1625–1866* (New York: Russell Sage Foundation, 1968), 11–12, 48. For an insightful discussion of animal control laws in Rhode Island, see Ruth Wallace Herndon, "'Breach' Sheep and Mad Dogs: Troublesome Animals in Rhode Island, 1750–1800," in *New England's Creatures, 1400–1900*, Dublin Seminar for New England Folklife Annual Proceedings, 1993, ed. Peter Benes and Jane Montague Benes (Boston: Boston University Press, 1995), 61–72.

69   New York City's decades-long struggle over pigs was atypical in that the city was the fastest-growing urban place in America, but it was indicative of battles going on in cities all over the country. After 150 years of tug-of-war between city fathers and pig owners, street cleaning in New York in the 1810s was still so ineffectual that poorer and more rural wards requested an exemption from the hog law. In 1825, when the Common Council decided to enforce the existing hog law in the city's Eighth Ward and sent in a cart to capture and remove pigs, a crowd attacked the cart, beat the driver and the accompanying marshals, and liberated the captured hogs. Hog cart riots occurred in 1826, 1830, and 1832, but the city did eventually control the

animals, at least in the most urban districts. See Paul A. Gilje, *The Road to Mobocracy: Popular Disorder in New York City, 1763–1834* (Chapel Hill: University of North Carolina Press for the Institute of Early American History, 1987), 228–32.

70   Charles Dickens, *American Notes* (1842; repr., New York: St. Martin's Press, 1985), 78–79.

71   *Ordinances and Joint Resolutions of the Select and Common Councils of the Consolidated City of Philadelphia, as Passed by Them, and Approved by the Mayor, from January First to December Thirty-First, 1855* (Philadelphia: J. H. Jones, 1856), 82–83; *Ordinances of the City of Philadelphia. From January 1 to December 31, 1912. And Opinions of the City Solicitor* (Philadelphia: Dunlap Printing, 1913), 138–39.

72   For a detailed discussion of municipal pound practices, see Unti, "Quality of Mercy," chap. 4, "'The Tender Sensibilities of Women': Caroline Earle White, the Women's Branch of PSPCA, and the Animal Shelter," 161–67, and chap. 12, "'Drawn from the Miserable Multitudes': Animal Control, the Humane Society, and the Companion Animal," 471–74.

73   William Findlay Brown and Ira Jewell Williams, comps., *A Digest of Laws and Ordinances Concerning Philadelphia with Notes of Decisions and City Solicitors' Opinions Relating Thereto, 1701–1904* (Philadelphia: J. L. H. Bayne, 1905), 910.

74   Olive Thorne Miller, *Our Home Pets: How to Keep Them Well and Happy* (New York: Harper and Brothers, 1894), 199–200.

75   Letter from John W. Gould to Harriet Mariah Elmendorf, 6 July 1895, box 104, file 8, Historic Cherry Hill Collections.

76   Unti, "Quality of Mercy," 477–78.

77   Edwin Tenney Brewster, "A City of Ten Million Cats," *McClure's*, May 1912, 62, 55.

78   Women's Branch, Pennsylvania Society for the Prevention of Cruelty to Animals, Minutes of 12 June 1869, quoted in Unti, "Quality of Mercy," 167–68.

79   Unti, "Quality of Mercy," 174–78.

80   Ibid., chap. 12, "'Drawn from the Miserable Multitudes': Animal Control, the Humane Society, and the Companion Animal," 468–510.

81   Elizabeth A. Clancy and Andrew W. Rowan, "Companion Animal Demographics in the United States: A Historical Perspective," in *The State of the Animals II: 2003*, ed. Deborah J. Salem and Andrew N. Rowan (Washington, D.C.: Humane Press, 2003), 13.

82   Information on their groups, explanations of their policies, and links to other related resources can be found at <http://www.alleycat.org> and <http://www.feralcat.com>.

83   The word "mascot" does not do the role of these animals justice; it means only "a thing, animal, or person supposed to bring good luck," and the term was not even in common use until the late nineteenth century.

84   The plaque is located on the brick building built in 1844 for the Vigilant Fire Company at 1066 Wisconsin Avenue NW. The structure was used as a firehouse until 1883.

85   For Old Abe's full biography, see Richard H. Zeitlin, *Old Abe the War Eagle* (Madison: University of Wisconsin Press, 1997).

86   John D. Lippy Jr., *The War Dog: A True Story* (Harrisburg, Pa.: by the author, 1962).

87   The details of Owney's life can be found in Charles A. Hugenin, "Owney, Canine Globetrotter," *New York History* 38 (January 1957): 29–50; James Bruns, comp., *Owney: Mascot of the Railway Mail Service* (Washington, D.C.: National Philatelic Collection, Smithsonian Institution, 1990). Owney has been in the collection of the Smithsonian Institution since 1911.

88   Katherine C. Grier, *Culture and Comfort: People, Parlors, and Upholstery, 1850–1930* (Rochester, N.Y.: Strong Museum, 1988), fig. 26, "Session Rooms, probably Active Hose Company, Rochester, New York, about 1873," p. 54.

89   Catharine Brody, "Dog Stars and Horse Heroes," *Saturday Evening Post*, 14 February 1925, 17.

90   Niall Kelly, *Presidential Pets* (New York: Abbeville Press, 1992).

91   C. C. Haskins, "For the Birds," *SN*, December 1873, 72–73. For a discussion of the widespread assault on bird life in nineteenth-century America, see Felton Gibbons and Deborah Strom, *Neighbors to the Birds: A History of Bird-watching in America* (New York: Norton, 1988), 107–25, 149–55.

92   C. C. Haskins, "The Army of Bird-Defenders. General Order, No. 1" *SN*, June 1875, 1.

93   Along with monthly lists of new members, the editors of *St. Nicholas* published special stories about birds to encourage the membership, along with "Grand Musters" of bird-defenders in June, July, and August 1875. Thousands of children's names appeared on the lists. By the time the third supplement of names appeared in October 1876, the ranks of the bird-defenders had begun to dwindle, however, and while letters from self-named bird-defenders appeared sporadically for another year or so, no more lists of members were published.

94   Other methods used by the adults who had proposed the organization—the
      emphasis on taking a pledge and publishing testimonial letters—echoed the
      tactics of prewar reform groups, particularly the temperance movement.
      The fact that the group's target membership was children was nothing new;
      missionary and Sunday school groups had already pioneered this approach.
      But the Bird-Defender call to direct action on the part of children was differ-
      ent because the organizers used a nationally distributed children's periodical
      to speak directly to individuals at home, bypassing other organizational struc-
      tures such as churches. See Ronald G. Walters, *American Reformers, 1815–
      1860* (New York: Hill and Wang, 1978), chap. 6, "Strong Drink," 123–44. No
      records of the Army of Bird-Defenders survive outside the pages of *St.
      Nicholas,* and no sources documenting the experience of a single child as a
      bird-defender have been located. The reasons for the decline of the club also
      remain unclear. Did children outgrow being bird-defenders? Was participa-
      tion in the club a fad? Perhaps the fact that the club was not attached to
      schools, where children could meet with adults who provided continuity, was
      its downfall. Still, the *St. Nicholas* Army of Bird-Defenders is noteworthy as
      an early effort at organized "humane education" on a national scale.

95   Letter re killing snakes, Richard B., *SN,* December 1874, 124; letter about
      hunting, John Lace Metcalfe, *SN,* April 1876, 405; letter about collecting
      eggs, Edward K. Titus, *SN,* June 1874, 517; letter about taking an empty bird's
      nest, Anita Hendrie, *SN,* October 1877, 829; editorial comment to E. S. and
      A. M. F. about cats, *SN,* October 1875, 779.

96   Gibbons and Strom, *Neighbors to the Birds,* esp. chaps. 6–8, 107–48.

97   Website for Wild Birds Unlimited, <http://wbu/com>, accessed 10 December
      2004.

98   Ernest Thompson Seton, *Lives of the Hunted, Containing a True Account of
      the Doings of Five Quadrupeds and Three Birds* (1905; repr., Berkeley, Calif.:
      Creative Arts Book Co., 1978), 9.

CHAPTER FIVE

1   "A Pet in Every Home," *Pet Dealer,* December 1928, 5.

2   Elizabeth F. Crane, ed., *The Diary of Elizabeth Drinker* (Boston: Northeastern
      University Press, 1991), 3:1124.

3   Diary of Deborah Norris Logan, 1833–1839, in Penelope Franklin, ed., *Pri-
      vate Pages: Diaries of American Women, 1830s–1970s* (New York: Ballantine,
      1986), 484.

4   George Bates, *A Biography of Deceased Butchers, And a Narrative of Facts, by*

    a Knight of the Cleaver, George Bates of Jenkintown, Montgomery County, Pa.
    (Philadelphia: Thos. E. Bagg, 1877), 33.

5   Henry B. Hirst, *The Book of Cage Birds,* 2nd ed. (Philadelphia: Bernard Duke,
     1843), 148, 151, 158.

6   *Rochester Daily Advertiser,* 1 December 1828.

7   Hirst, *Book of Cage Birds,* 280.

8   Trade cards for Campbell's Picture Frame and Bird Store, Manchester, N.H.,
     n.d., and McClunie Bros. Original Bird Store, Hartford, Conn., n.d., in War-
     shaw Collection of Business Americana, National Museum of American
     History, Smithsonian Institution, Washington, D.C. (hereafter WCBA). In-
     terestingly, several trade cards for their shop make a point of noting that "E.
     Reiche (late of Chas. Reiche & Bros) will always be found in attendance."

9   Henry Wadsworth Longfellow, from a letter of May 1867, education handout,
     n.d., Henry Wadsworth Longfellow National Historic Site, Cambridge, Mass.

10   "Facts about Dogs: A Visit to a Dog Fancier's Cellar—Value of Different Kind
     of Dogs," *New York Times,* 26 January 1874.

11   *Boston City Directory* (1868), 121. The Minute Book 1 of the Pennsylvania So-
     ciety for the Prevention of Cruelty to Animals records the arrest on 16 No-
     vember 1871 of a Philadelphia dog dealer named McQueen, of 1133 Coates
     Street, for cruelty to animals and drunkenness. See PSPCA Minute Book 1,
     Minutes of 16 November 1871, 114–15, Pennsylvania Society for the Preven-
     tion of Cruelty to Animals. My thanks to Bernard Unti for sharing this
     citation.

12   "At Home with a Rat Catcher and Animal Trainer," *Children's Museum: An Il-
     lustrated Monthly Magazine,* April 1881, 41–45.

13   *Boston City Directory* (1876), 77.

14   Advertisement for George Walton, Dog Doctor and Dealer in Choice Breeds
     of Dog, *Boston City Directory* (1884).

15   *Country Life in America* published the Kennel Directory every month; for one
     example of the directory, including the statement regarding breeders, see
     April 2004, 460.

16   Gwendoline Brook, "How Japanese Spaniels Paid on the Farm," *Country Life
     in America,* October 1907, 688, 704, 706.

17   Ernest Ingersoll, "A Talk about Canaries," *St. Nicholas: Scribner's Illustrated
     Magazine for Girls and Boys,* February 1877, 248. Isaac Costa, comp., *Gopsill's
     Philadelphia Business Directory for 1869* (Philadelphia: James Gopsill, 1869),
     143, published a list of thirteen bird dealers, including two women, who were

scattered about the city's residential neighborhoods, along with six cage makers and one individual who provided both birds and cages.

18 Complaint Book, Philadelphia Society for the Prevention of Cruelty to Animals, November 8, 1870, to May 31, 1872, no. 941, Atwater-Kent Museum, Philadelphia.

19 For a selection of anecdotes about the travel of American songbirds across the Atlantic, see Neil Dana Glukin, "Pet Birds and Cages of the Eighteenth Century," *Early American Life* 8, no. 3 (June 1977): 37–41, 59.

20 Charles Reiche, *The Bird Fancier's Companion, or Natural History of Cage Birds, Their Food—Management—Habits—Treatment—Diseases, etc. etc.,* 3rd ed. (New York: Charles Reiche and Brother, 1867), v; advertisement for Charles Reiche & Brother, 162 William Street, New York, in D. J. Browne, *The American Bird Fancier* (New York, 1850).

21 R. G. Dun and Company Collection, New York City, vol. 368, p. 500 S, courtesy Baker Library, Harvard Business School, Cambridge, Mass.

22 The church was built in 1840. The congregation may have been having financial trouble, which induced it to graft new one-story storefronts across its imposing facade around 1870. The building, long gone, ceased functioning as a church in 1885. See Edwin Monroe Bacon, *Bacon's Dictionary of Boston* (Boston: Houghton Mifflin, 1886), 65. For information on the shopping district, see Walter Muir Whitehall, *The Metamorphoses of Scollay and Bowdoin Squares: A Bostonian Society Picture Book* (Boston: Bostonian Society, 1973).

23 Charles Reiche, *The Bird Fancier's Companion,* 10th ed. (New York: by the author, 1871), 70. A single invoice from Charles Reiche and Bro. survives in WCBA. The receipt, dated 23 January 1878, acknowledges $65 prepaid from David L. Wilson of Washington, D.C., for a pair of "Chinese Silver Pheasants."

24 Cugley and Mullen Co., *Catalog of the Bird Department* (Philadelphia: by the company, 1914), 51, in WCBA. The owners offered to mount "any variety of large birds, dogs, cats, or wild animals. Prices begin at one dollar for canaries."

25 George H. Holden and his brother Charles F. Holden had become partners in the Reiches' Boston bird business in 1873. Charles died several years after the partnership began. See R. G. Dun MA, vol. 86, p. 340, courtesy Baker Library, Harvard Business School, Cambridge, Mass.

26 R. G. Dun and Company Reports, New York City, vol. 389, p. 2252, courtesy Baker Library, Harvard Business School, Cambridge, Mass.

27 George H. Holden, *Holden's Illustrated Catalogue of Birds, Cages and Seeds* (Boston: New York Bird Store, 1878), 27.

28   Benjamin Franklin Taylor, *The World on Wheels and Other Sketches,* 13th ed. (Chicago: S. C. Griggs, 1880), 255–57.

29   Henry Oldys, "Cage-Bird Traffic of the United States," *Yearbook of the United States Department of Agriculture, 1906* (Washington, D.C.: GPO, 1907), 165; Richard C. Banks, "Wildlife Importation into the United States, 1900–1972," *United States Department of Interior Fish and Wildlife Service Special Scientific Report—Wildlife, No. 22* (Washington, D.C.: GPO, 1973), 2–4.

30   George H. Holden, *Canaries and Cage Birds* (New York: by the author, 1883), 44.

31   Ibid., 278–89.

32   Ingersoll, "Talk about Canaries," 248; Oldys, "Cage-Bird Traffic," 170. Oldys estimated that the mortality rate during transport and in the store of "delicate" birds such as zebra finches was about 14 percent.

33   Reiche, *Bird Fancier's Companion* (1867), 70; C. F. Holden and G. H. Holden, *Holden's New Book on Birds* (Boston: George G. Holden, 1881), 122; Oldys, "Cage-Bird Traffic," 172; Cugley and Mullen Co., *Catalog of the Bird Department,* 4–5.

34   See the display advertisement, PARRAKEETS NOW READY FOR SHIPMENT, for J. C. Edwards ("Largest Breeders of Fancy Parrakeets in the United States" and "California's Oldest Expert Fancier"), Los Angeles, in *Pet Dealer,* February 1928, 9. Also see W. F. Flowers, "Tropical Bird Farm," *Pet Dealer,* April 1929, 28–29. This is an account of the development of a systematic breeding program for zebra finches undertaken in the mid-1920s. A display ad for the firm on p. 29 noted that 6,000 pairs of finches would be offered for sale that year and cautioned, "Do Not Confuse Our Birds with the Usual Sickly, Imported Specimens Offered Occasionally."

35   Lenny Burton, "Those Female Canaries," *Pet Dealer,* September 1927, 31.

36   Discussing the seasonal practice of trapping American wild birds, George Holden noted that "wily southern Negroes" earned their living that way; see Holden, *Canaries and Cage Birds,* 112, 164.

37   For a concise account of the Lacey Law and subsequent related measures, see Felton Gibbons and Deborah Strom, *Neighbors to the Birds: A History of Bird-watching in America* (New York: Norton, 1988), 154–60.

38   Ibid., 171.

39   Oldys, "Cage-Bird Traffic," 176; Max Geisler Bird Co., *Illustrated Catalogue and Price List* (St. Louis: by the company, [1910]), 11–12.

40   Cugley and Mullen Co., *Catalog of the Bird Department,* 21.

41 Chas. N. Page, *Parrots and Other Talking Birds* (Des Moines, Iowa: by the author, 1906), 32–34.

42 "First Annual Convention. Dinner at Hotel Manger Brilliant Climax—George Jenkins Makes Stirring Address Outlining Purposes and Accomplishments," *Pet Dealer,* December 1930, 6.

43 Hugo Mullert, *The Goldfish and Its Systematic Culture with a View to Profit,* 2nd ed. (Brooklyn, N.Y.: by the author, 1896), 5.

44 My parents have a farm pond in New Jersey that has become almost entirely populated by goldfish in the last ten years. The original colonization took place when small fish purchased each year for a patio fishpond were released each fall. The fish have bred so freely that their large numbers and easy visibility attract kingfishers and blue herons. The oldest fish have reached lengths estimated at ten to twelve inches. They live entirely on natural food in the pond. The overall color of the animals seems to be changing, reverting toward a greenish hue that makes the fish less visible to predators.

45 The Utica Bath and Garden, an elegant public bath and pleasure garden opened in that Erie Canal village in 1826, featured a goldfish pond among its "arbors, retreats, and places of refreshments." See Thomas L. McKenney, *Sketches of a Tour to the Lakes . . .* (Baltimore, 1827), 61, 62; "Utica Bath and Garden," *Utica (N.Y.) Sentinal and Gazette,* 13 June 26.

46 William Kampfmuller, *Our Pets; or, Book on Cage Birds; Their Home, Treatment, Breeding, Diseases, etc., etc. Also, an Appendix Containing the Treatment of Gold Fish and Aquaria* (Brooklyn: By the author, 1876; Boston: L. F. Adams, 1881), 104.

47 Mullert, *Goldfish,* 8.

48 A. E. Hodge and Arthur Derham, *Goldfish Culture for Amateurs* (New York: Frederick A. Stokes Co., n.d.), 4–5.

49 "A Growing Industry," *Pet Dealer,* February 1929, 19.

50 Advertisement for T. Mori and Co., *Pet Dealer,* May 1927, 8.

51 Thomas Quast, *Goldfish Industry,* Economic Circular No. 68 (Washington, D.C.: United States Department of Commerce, Bureau of Fisheries, 1929), 3, 10.

52 "Cruelties to Aquarium Fish," *Pet Stock World,* February 1915, 1.

53 "California Druggists Gave Away a Thousand Goldfish," *Novelty News,* March 1916, 46.

54 William T. Innes, *Goldfish Varieties and Tropical Aquarium Fishes: A Guide to Aquaria and Related Subjects,* 10th ed. (Philadelphia: Innes and Sons, 1928), 51.

55 Christopher Coates, *Tropical Fishes for a Private Aquarium* (New York: Liveright, 1933), 3–4.

56 "Will Introduce New Tropical Fish Types," *Pet Shop*, March 1928, 15.

57 K. H. Lansing, "Have a Fish Department," *Pet Dealer*, August 1927, 23.

58 F. L. Tappan, *Aquaria Fish: Management and Care of the Aquarium and Its Inhabitants* (Minneapolis: by the author, 1911).

59 Alfred Morgan, *Tropical Fish and Home Aquaria: A Practical Guide to a Fascinating Hobby* (New York: Halcyon House, 1936), 110.

60 By 1936, there were an estimated sixty clubs in the United States and Canada. See Edwin H. Perkins, *Tropical Fish: Their Breeding and Care* (New York: A. T. De La Mare, 1936), 147.

61 W. C. O'Brien, "Selling Tropical Fish," *Pet Dealer*, February 1928, 31, 32. The nomenclature for identifying tropical fish has been volatile, as has the range of species kept. See Innes, *Goldfish Varieties*, 264–84, and Coates, *Tropical Fishes for a Private Aquarium*, for lists of tropical fishes for home aquariums.

62 John W. Doscher, "Tropical Fish," *Pet Dealer*, September 1930, 14–15. On the creation of demand for new consumer goods between 1880 and 1920, see Susan Strasser, *Satisfaction Guaranteed* (1987; repr., Washington, D.C.: Smithsonian Institution Press, 1995).

63 William T. Innes, *The Complete Aquarium Book: The Care and Breeding of Goldfish and Tropical Fishes* (New York: Halcyon House, 1936), 235.

64 Ibid., 353–54.

65 A discussion of options for heating aquariums is found in Innes, *Goldfish Varieties*, 80, 111–14.

66 Advertisement for Hotpoint small appliances, *Ladies' Home Journal*, October 1919, 156; advertisement for William Tricker, Inc., *Pet Dealer*, October 1930, 11, and January 1932, 7.

67 Perkins, *Tropical Fish*, 24.

68 United States Centennial Commission, *Special Catalogue of the Display of Poultry* (Philadelphia: Sherman and Co., 1876); *J. C. Long & Co.'s Price List of Fowls and Pigeons, Birds and Pet Animals* (Philadelphia, [1874]), 17–25. Long noted that he was "Successor to J. M. Wade, No. 39, North Ninth Street."

69 George Cugley, *Hints for Pets: A Short Treatise on Cage Birds, Dogs, Cats, Monkeys, Belgian Hares, Rabbits, Guinea Pigs, Squirrels, Rats and Mice, Ferrets, Pigeons and the Aquarium* (Philadelphia: Cugley and Mullen, 1900).

70 Grosbeck Company, *Special Egg and Stock Bulletin* (Hartford, Conn.: by the company, 1910).

71   "Get Ready for the Baby Chick Season. Spring Is Almost Here." *Pet Dealer*, February 1928, 17.

72   Advertisement for National Pet Shops, *Pet Dealer*, May 1928, 7.

73   Catalog, N. P. Boyer & Co., Parkesburg, Chester County, Pa., n.d. [1870].

74   *J. C. Long Price List*, 1.

75   United States Centennial Commission, *Special Catalogue of Stated Displays of Livestock*, pt. 2, *Dogs (September 4th to 8th)* (Philadelphia: Sherman and Co., 1876), advertisement for Benson and Burpee.

76   Johnson and Stokes, *[Catalogue of] Poultry Supplies* (Philadelphia: by the company, [1899]), 41–42.

77   Henry Bishop, *Bishop the Bird Man's Treatise on Birds and Aquaria* (Baltimore: Henry Bishop, 1912), 70–72.

78   Spiegel Company, *Spiegel Home Shopping Book, Spring and Summer 1958* (Chicago: by the company, 1958), 491–93.

79   On the rise of national brands in the grocery business, see Strasser, *Satisfaction Guaranteed*.

80   Max Geisler Bird Co., *Catalogue* (1928), 9–10; advertisement for "Geisler's," *Pet Dealer*, September 1929, inside back cover; advertisement for Henry Bartels, *Pet Dealer*, October 1929, 30.

81   J. J. Sheeran, "He Built His Business on the Golden Rule," *Pet Shop*, March 1928, 18. Two catalogs for the business are known, one dated 1923–24 and a second undated (ca. 1930), where the firm had expanded its mail-order business to include tropical fish and rabbits.

82   J. Edward Tufft, "A Homelike Atmosphere Is Essentially a Part of the Success of Stores in Residential Sections and Must Be Emphasized," *Pet Dealer*, December 1928, 6; "Merchandise Well Displayed Is Half Sold," *Pet Dealer*, October 1929, 24–25.

83   Schmid's Bird and Pet Animal Emporium, *Illustrated Catalogue and Price List* (Washington, D.C.: by the company, 1901).

84   Cugley, *Hints for Pets*, 80–81; Cugley and Mullen Co., *Catalog of the Bird Department*, 3.

85   Mrs. Selma Bauerly, "Portland's Modern Pet Shop," *Pet Trade Journal*, June 1935, 6.

86   Innes, *Complete Aquarium Book*, 24.

87   *Pet Trade Journal* contained a humor column whose author and illustrator, Bert Holmes, often included stories about ignorant and inept pet owners and customers, under headings such as "Things That Get My 'Nanny' [Goat]"; see

Bert Holmes, "Logic & Laughter," *Pet Trade Journal*, April 1935, 14. See also "A Phonny 'Phone Phantasm," Bert Holmes, "Logic & Laughter," *Pet Trade Journal*, June 1935, 26; "Cages on the Street," *Philadelphia Times Sunday Edition*, 6 November 1892.

88 "Cages on the Street."

89 Arnold Arluke discusses the use of symbolic pets in a different context, the animal research laboratory, in "Sacrificial Symbolism in Animal Experimentation: Object or Pet?," *Anthrozoös* 2 (1988): 98–117. The shop pet shares some characteristics with the symbolic pet of labs, especially the animal who is named and "saved" from experimentation.

90 "Our Little Friend," *Saturday Evening Post*, 5 February 1927, 190; "Sunrise Song," ibid., 9 June 1928, 156; "Feathered Guest," ibid., 25 February 1928, 84. Hendryx also published samples of these advertisements in *Pet Dealer* to suggest to shop owners that they feature Hendryx cages in their windows during the weeks they ran; see *Pet Dealer*, October 1927, 11.

91 Untitled item, *Pet Dealer*, April 1927, 5.

92 W. B. Stoddard, "Department Store Pet Shops," *Pet Dealer*, December 1928, 3, 17.

93 Joseph B. Roberts Jr., *The Pet Shop Manual* (Fond du Lac, Wisc.: All-Pets Books, 1953), 40, 42–43.

94 Ibid. 93.

95 "Trends That Should Be Noted: Franchise Pet Shops in the Making," *Pet Industry*, June 1964, 6.

96 "Lending to Pet Shops," *Journal of Commercial Lending*, July 1992. Accessed through Infotrac, 30 October 2004.

97 *Special Report on Abuses in the Pet Industry* (Washington, D.C.: Humane Society of the United States, 1974), 1.

98 The literature on puppy mills is voluminous, and there are numerous websites devoted in part or totally to the debate. Important Humane Society of the United States exposés include "HSUS Raids Save Suffering Dogs: Kansas Puppy Mill & New York Kennel Shut Down," in *Close-Up Report* (Washington, D.C.: Humane Society of the United States, 1977); "Puppy Mills Exposed," in *Close-Up Report* (Washington, D.C.: Humane Society of the United States, 1991). A recent official response to the problem by the AKC is "High Volume Breeders Committee Report to the American Kennel Club Board of Directors," 12 November 2002, available on <http://www.akc.org> (accessed 20 February 2004).

CHAPTER SIX

1   Idella Grider Manisera, *Birds and Pets: Just What You Need to Know about Dietetics, Diseases, Treatments, Breeding, Correct Care* (Los Angeles: Gem Publishing, 1927), 108–9, 112; advertisement for Birdland, *All-Pets Magazine*, September 1950, 18.

2   Correspondence with Frederick Geisler, 25, 27 November, 2 December 2003.

3   *The Bird Keeper's Guide and Companion: Containing Plain Directions for Keeping and Breeding Canaries and all Other Song Birds* . . . (Boston: James Munroe, 1853), 51, 55.

4   Charles Reiche, *The Bird Fancier's Companion, or Natural History of Cage Birds, Their Food—Management—Habits—Treatment—Diseases, etc. etc.*, 3rd ed. (New York: Charles Reiche and Brother, 1867), 8.

5   Ibid., 71.

6   George H. Holden, *Holden's Illustrated Catalogue of Birds, Cages and Seeds* (Boston: New York Bird Store, 1878), 28, 33.

7   Philadelphia Bird Food Company, *No. 1 Fancier's Hand Books. The Practical Book of Birds. How to Breed the Different Varieties and Instructions for Keeping Them in Health and Constant Song* (Philadelphia, 1899, 1925), 11, 15.

8   Henry Bishop, *Bishop the Bird Man's Treatise on Birds and Aquaria* (Baltimore: Henry Bishop, 1912). Bishop's business was established in 1874. "Canary seed" and cuttlebone, "an article which all grocers should have in stock who keep bird food, etc., as it is a small and profitable item, and not liable to spoil," were carried by the wholesale grocer's trade by the 1880s, and probably earlier. See Artemas Ward, *The Grocer's Handbook* (Philadelphia: Philadelphia Grocer Publishing Co., 1882), 32–64.

9   Advertisement for French's Bird Seed, *Ladies' Home Journal*, July 1929, 117; advertisement for West's Quality Bird Foods, Magnesia Products Company, *Ladies' Home Journal*, October 1919, 198.

10   George Cugley, *Hints for Pets: A Short Treatise on Cage Birds, Dogs, Cats, Monkeys, Belgian Hares, Rabbits, Guinea Pigs, Squirrels, Rats and Mice, Ferrets, Pigeons and the Aquarium* (Philadelphia: Cugley and Mullen, 1900), 154. William Kampfmuller, *Our Pets; or, Book on Cage Birds; Their Home, Treatment, Breeding, Diseases, etc. etc. Also, an Appendix Containing the Treatment of Gold Fish and Aquaria* (Boston: L. F. Adams, 1881), 107, reported that fish food "could be had in every respectable bird and fish store." John C. Jewett and Sons, a Buffalo, New York, manufacturer of galvanized metal housewares,

offered in its wholesale catalog a selection of pet products associated with cage birds and aquariums, including "Genuine Prepared Fish Food" at $1.00 per dozen boxes. See John C. Jewett and Sons, *[Catalog]* (Buffalo, N.Y.: by the company, 1884), 52.

11   Mary Elizabeth Thurnston, *The Lost History of the Canine Race: Our 15,000-Year Love Affair with Dogs* (Kansas City: Andrews and McMeel, 1996), 235.

12   An advertisement in the May 1928 issue of *Pet Dealer* stated that the firm had been in business for seventy-five years. See advertisement for Spratt's Patent Limited, *Pet Dealer*, May 1928, 17; *American Kennel Gazette*, January 1889, cover. On its dominance of "benching and feeding," see James A. Watson, *The Dog Book: A Popular History of the Dog, with Practical Information as to Care and Management of House, Kennel, and Exhibition Dogs; and Descriptions of All the Important Breeds in Ten Parts* (New York: Doubleday, Page, 1905), 64.

13   Spratt's Patent Limited, *Catalogue and Short Treatise on Dog Diseases, Poultry Feeding, Etc.* (New York: Spratt's Patent Limited, 1895).

14   Ibid., 28, 33. For a discussion of this language in reference to the diet of Victorian humans, see Harvey Green, *Fit for America* (New York: Pantheon, 1986).

15   Advertisement for Spratt's Malt and Cod Liver Oil Dog Cakes, *American Kennel Gazette*, 30 September 1917, back cover.

16   Sears, Roebuck and Company, *Consumer's Guide, Catalogue No. 104* (1897; repr., New York: Chelsea House, 1976), unpaginated.

17   For a discussion of the by-products trade, see Rudolf A. Clemen, *By-Products in the Packing Industry* (Chicago: University of Chicago Press, 1927), 309–30. Tankage was originally used to create agricultural fertilizers, but by the 1920s, almost all of it went into the production of animal feeds.

18   For a time line and discussion of the history of Ralston-Purina, see <http://purina.com/company/profile/timeline>.

19   Potter and Wrightington, *Your Dog* (Charlestown, Mass.: by the company, n.d. [ca. 1910]), 3–5.

20   The Kennel Food Supply Company of Fairfield, Connecticut, may have been the first. It advertised its canned dog food in the *American Kennel Gazette* in 1916, promoting "Canned Meat" in two-and-a-half pound cans packed in cases of ten, twenty, and forty. See Advertisement for Kennel Food Supply Company, *American Kennel Gazette*, 30 June 1916, back cover.

21   Advertisement for Hugo Strauss Packing Company, *Pet Dealer*, November 1927, 25.

22 H. A. Halverson, H. J. Witteveen, and Ragna Bergman, *The Composition of Commercial Dog Foods* (Minneapolis: State of Minnesota Department of Agriculture and Dairy and Food, 1942).

23 "What Quantity to Feed," *Pet Dealer*, July 1928, 27.

24 Advertisement for Battle Creek Dog Food Company, *Pet Dealer*, June 1931, 11.

25 Albers Brothers Milling Company, *A New Day Dawns for the Dog: How to Train Your Dog, How to Keep Your Dog Healthy* (Seattle: by the company, 1935), 26.

26 Advertisement for Spratt's Dog Cakes, *Saturday Evening Post*, May 1928, 17.

27 Advertisement for Ken-L-Ration, *Ladies' Home Journal*, December 1930, 151.

28 A surviving piece of business correspondence between Gaines Food Company, Inc., and a feed dealer in Ticonderoga, New York, states that the "choice of these Foods by the U.S. Antarctic Service has struck the dog-owning public's fancy. They regard it as a real testimonial. Because of this, sales are easier—and bigger—than ever before" (Gaines Food Company, Inc., Sherburne, N.Y., to Hiram N. Floyd, Ticonderoga, N.Y., 2 May 1940, author's collection).

29 *Harper's Household Handbook: A Guide to Easy Ways of Doing Women's Work* (New York: Harper and Brothers, 1913), 181.

30 *Sergeant's Dog Book* (Richmond, Va.: Polk Miller Products Corp., 1932), 5.

31 *Sears, Roebuck and Co. Catalogue* (1927; repr., Bounty Books, 1970), 525.

32 Susan D. Jones, *Valuing Animals: Veterinarians and Their Patients in Modern America* (Baltimore: Johns Hopkins University Press, 2002), 119.

33 Johnson and Stokes, *[Catalogue of] Poultry Supplies* (Philadelphia, ca. 1900), 10.

34 *Cat Culture* (Newark, N.J.: Spratt's Patent [Am.] Ltd., n.d.), 36–38.

35 Spratt's Patent Limited, *Catalogue*, 32; *Cat Culture*, 61.

36 Michael Smith, D.V.M., "Spotlight: Dr. A. C. Daniels' The King of Veterinary Advertising," *Veterinary Collectibles Roundtable*, August 2001, 1–2, 5–8.

37 Associated Fanciers, *Our Friend the Dog: How to Care for Him in Health and Sickness* (Philadelphia: by the company, n.d. [ca. 1900]).

38 [B. T. Woodward, V.M.D.], *Diseases and Feeding of Your Dog* (New York: H. Clay Glover Co., 1928), 3.

39 Polk Miller, *Dogs: Their Ailments and How to Treat Them*, rev. ed. (Richmond, Va.: Polk Miller Drug Co., 1903). For Miller's subsequent career, see Doug Seroff, "Polk Miller and the Old South Quartette," *78 Quarterly* 1, no. 3 (1988): 27–40. My thanks to Mike Smith, D.V.M., for sharing this source.

40 On veterinary free samples, see Mike Smith, D.V.M., "Spotlight: Veterinary Free Samples," *Veterinary Collectibles Roundtable*, February 2001, 2, 8–11.

41   Polk Miller, *Diseases of Dogs and Their Treatment* (Richmond, Va.: by the author, 1908), 22, 23.

42   Dr. L. D. LeGear, V.S. [Veterinary Surgeon], *Dr. LeGear's Dog Book: The Proper Treatment of Dogs and Cats* (St. Louis: Dr. L. D. LeGear Co., 1942), 4; *Dogs* (New York: H. Clay Glover Co., 1940), 17; *The Canary: Its Care and Treatment by "Bird"* (Rochester, N.Y.: R. T. French, 1941), 71.

43   Advertisement for Ko-Vita Raw and Phosphagated Norwegian Cod-liver Oil, *Pet Dealer*, April 1927, 14.

44   "VITAKALK: The Story of a Pet Shop Seller," *Pet Dealer*, September 1928, 38.

45   Mike Smith, D.V.M., "Companion Bird Medicines," *Veterinary Collectibles Roundtable*, April 1997, 2.

46   Broadside for Aldon's Patent Spring Bird Perch (New York: Aldon and Brown, n.d. [1872]). For a discussion of the meaning of springs in upholstered furniture, see Katherine C. Grier, *Culture and Comfort: Parlor Making and Middle-Class Identity, 1850–1930* (Washington, D.C.: Smithsonian Institution Press, 1997).

47   *How to Take Care of Your Canary* (New York: Nature Friend, n.d. [ca. 1935]), 13.

48   Neil Dana Glukin, "Pet Birds and Cages of the Eighteenth Century," *Early American Life* 8, no. 3 (June 1977): 37.

49   Through the early nineteenth century, some cottage industry created short lengths of hand-drawn wire, especially for textile cards. According to an 1832 study commissioned by Congress, the United States consumed the relatively small amount of around twenty tons of imported brass wire each year, mainly for textile cards, brushes, birdcages, and use in machinery. Around this time, the small brass industry of Connecticut, which had hitherto focused on the production of cast buttons, began to produce brass wire with English equipment and immigrant workmen. See William Lathrop, *The Brass Industry of the United States: A Study of the Origin and Development of the Brass Industry in the Naugatuck Valley and Its Subsequent Extension over the Nation* (1926; repr., New York: Arno Press, 1972), 52.

50   In Louis Prang and Company's set of chromolithographs titled "Trades and Occupations," published in 1874 for classroom use, the "Tinsmith" image shows large birdcages as part of the assemblage of goods sold by the shop in front of the workroom. The prints can be found in the Library of Congress Division of Prints and Photographs.

51 George Holden, *Holden's Book on Birds* (Boston: by the author, 1880), 10, and advertisement for G. Gunther in the back of the book.

52 Billhead dated 15 May 1881, from M. Drew, Wholesale and Retail Dealer in Birds and Cages, etc., 171 Fulton Street, Brooklyn, in Warshaw Collection of Business Americana, National Museum of American History, Smithsonian Institution, Washington, D.C.

53 Entry for Nathan W. Hendryx, *Modern History of New Haven and Eastern New Haven County* (New York: S. J. Clarke, 1911), 2:318–19.

54 Philip Scranton, *Endless Novelty* (Princeton: Princeton University Press, 2000).

55 Osborn Manufacturing Company, 79 Bleecker St, New York, *Catalogue. Also Directions for the Care of Canary Birds* (New York: by the company, 1876), 4.

56 O. Lindemann & Co., *1888 Catalogue of Bird Cages Manufactured by O. Lindemann & Co.* (New York: by the company, 1888), 16.

57 Holden, *Holden's Book on Birds,* 119.

58 Sonia Roberts, *Bird-Keeping and Bird Cages: A History* (New York: Drake, 1973).

59 Cugley and Mullen Co., *Catalog of the Bird Department* (Philadelphia: by the company, 1914), 17, in Warshaw Collection of Business Americana, National Museum of American History, Smithsonian Institution, Washington, D.C.

60 "Annual Exhibition of Bird Cages," *Pet Dealer,* May 1928, 5.

61 Ernest Ingersoll, "A Talk about Canaries," *St. Nicholas: Scribner's Illustrated Magazine for Girls and Boys,* February 1877, 250.

62 Diary entry of the Reverend William Bentley (1759–1819), quoted in Nancy Carlisle, "Relics of Pets Past," *Antiques,* December 1994, 796–97. See also figure 1, p. 799, in the same article for a similar design offered by O. Lindemann and Company of New York, after 1912. "Another style [of cage] is a beautiful blend of the fish globe and the bird cage, in which the bird appears to be in the water with the fish" ("Articles for Domestic Use," *Godey's Lady's Book,* March 1856, 284).

63 Advertisement for Bernard Duke, 117 Chestnut Street, Philadelphia, in Henry B. Hirst, *The Book of Cage Birds,* 2nd ed. (Philadelphia: Bernard Duke, 1843), 280.

64 P. J. Murphy, Manufacturer, *Illustrated Catalogue and Price-List of Patent Japanned, Fancy Gilt, and Brass Bird Cages, etc.* (Buffalo, N.Y., n.d. [ca. 1880]).

65   Henry D. Butler, *The Family Aquarium; or Aqua Vivarium* (New York: Dick and Fitzgerald, 1858), 23.

66   The earliest books on aquarium making did not offer instructions that an amateur could follow comfortably. Henry Butler noted that the aquariums he had cared for at Barnum's Museum had been constructed by workmen from London, and apparently never having built one himself, he failed to provide a recipe for cement or even guidelines on size; see ibid., 30–36. R. Morris Copeland's *Country Life* also failed to provide information on the proper dimensions of an aquarium, although it did contain several recipes for cement; see R. Morris Copeland, *Country Life: A Handbook of Agriculture, Horticulture, and Landscape Gardening* (Boston: John P. Jewett, 1859), 253–54.

67   Thomas Perrins, 622 Arch Street; William Southworth, 17 North 6th Street, in *Gopsill's Philadelphia Business Directory for 1869*, comp. Isaac Costa (Philadelphia: James Gopsill, 1869), 134.

68   *Godey's Lady's Book*, November 1854, 454–55.

69   Alexander Pope (1688–1744) sent a puppy, progeny of his bitch Bounce, to the Prince of Wales at Kew, who had admired the dog. The couplet has its own title: "Engraved on the Collar of a Dog, Which I Gave to His Royal Highness."

70   "Jonathan Zane. Forty Dollars Reward. Dog's Collar stolen. Was stolen off the neck of a small pyed bitch, a Brass Collar, with a steel staple, and brass slide. Whoever will secure the thief, on conviction, shall receive the above reward, or for the Collar, only Three Dollars. Jonathan Zane" (*Pennsylvania Packet*, 25 November 1779).

71   *Boston Business Directory, 1894* (Boston: Littlefield Directory Pub. Co., 1894), 351.

72   Catalog, Medford Fancy Goods Company, New York, 1890, 3.

73   Ibid., 129, 71–72, 98, 128, 123.

74   "Mary Hamilton Behres Joins the Prettiest Models in the World," *Life*, 28 February 1938, 37–38. Mary Hamilton Behres was a wirehaired fox terrier who appeared in fashion photo shoots. In this feature, she was depicted walking on a treadmill sold by Abercrombie & Fitch for $19.95.

75   Sunrise Pet Supply Company, *Catalogue of Dog Furnishings* (Hempstead, N.Y.: by the company, n.d. [ca. 1930]), 5–6.

76   "For Christmas Gifts," circular for Edwards' Bird Store, 129 Michigan Avenue, Detroit, Mich., n.d. [ca. 1910].

77   William Bliss Stoddard, "Christmas Is Coming," *Pet Dealer*, October 1928, 3, 7–8; quotations pp. 3, 7.

78   Advertisement for Ken-L-Ration, *Ladies Home Journal,* December 1932, 190.

79   B. F. Lippold, "Problems of the Dealer," *Pet Dealer,* March 1928, 3, 24–25.

EPILOGUE

1   American Pet Products Manufacturing Association, "Fact Sheet: Industry Statistics and Trends," <http://www.appma.org/press_industrytrends.asp> (accessed 27 April 2005); The Annie E. Casey Foundation, "Kids Count Census Data Online: 2000 Census Date—Key Facts for the United States," <http://www.aecf.org/cgi-bin/aeccensus.cgi?action=data> (accessed 27 April 2005).

2   World Golf Foundation, *The Golf Economy Report* (St. Augustine, Fla.: WGF, 2002), 6, <2020_GER_F.pdf> (accessed 1 May 2005).

3   Elizabeth Forel, "Spay/Neuter Fact Sheet, March 1999," The Coalition for New York City Animals, Inc., <http://www.shelterreform.org/SpayFact.html> (accessed 1 May 2005).

→ Index ←